CAMBRIDGE GREEK AND LATIN CLASSICS

GENERAL EDITORS

PROFESSOR E. J. KENNEY
Peterhouse, Cambridge

AND

PROFESSOR P. E. EASTERLING
University College London

HOMER

ODYSSEY

BOOKS XIX AND XX

EDITED BY

R. B. RUTHERFORD

Tutor in Greek and Latin Literature,
Christ Church, Oxford

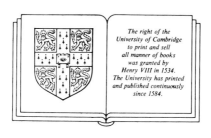

The right of the
University of Cambridge
to print and sell
all manner of books
was granted by
Henry VIII in 1534.
The University has printed
and published continuously
since 1584.

CAMBRIDGE UNIVERSITY PRESS

CAMBRIDGE

NEW YORK   PORT CHESTER

MELBOURNE   SYDNEY

Published by the Press Syndicate of the University of Cambridge
The Pitt Building, Trumpington Street, Cambridge CB2 1RP
40 West 20th Street, New York, NY 10011-4211, USA
10 Stamford Road, Oakleigh, Victoria 3166, Australia

© Cambridge University Press 1992

First published 1992

Printed in Great Britain at the University Press, Cambridge

*A cataloguing in publication record for this book is available
from the British Library*

Library of Congress cataloguing in publication data

Homer.
[Odyssey. Books 19–20]
Odyssey. Books XIX and XX / Homer ; edited by R. B. Rutherford.
p.   cm. – (Cambridge Greek and Latin classics)
English and Greek.
Includes bibliographical references and index.
ISBN 0 521 34517 0 (hard). – ISBN 0 521 34760 2 (pbk.)
1. Odysseus (Greek mythology) – Poetry. 1. Rutherford, R. B.
II. Title. III. Series.
PA4022.P19   1992
883′.01–dc20
91-3760
CIP

ISBN 0521 34517 0 hardback
ISBN 0521 34760 2 paperback

For Catherine

CONTENTS

PREFACE

Odyssean studies are booming. Apart from the steady flow of critical books and articles, the last decade has seen the publication of the first full commentary on the epic since 1948 – a six-volume work by six contributors of the highest scholarly distinction, first published in Italian and now reproduced in English, and in a more compact, three-volume format (without text and translation) by Oxford University Press. On a smaller and more modest scale, the interested reader, even if Greekless, may derive great benefit from Peter Jones's excellent *Companion* (Bristol Classical Press 1989), which is intended mainly for those reading Richmond Lattimore's translation. Readers will naturally ask where my book stands in relation to these works, and why books 19 and 20 are being singled out for further treatment.

This volume is not part of a larger project aimed at covering the whole of the *Odyssey*; but Alex Garvie's edition of books 6, 7 and 8 is scheduled to appear in this series, and in some ways the two volumes should complement one another, each providing detailed guidance on a particular part of the poem, and also, in our introductions, a broader perspective. Thus in my introduction (which can be read independently of the commentary), I try to place books 19 and 20 in the context of the *Odyssey* as a whole, and especially of its second half. The introduction also treats general issues concerning the composition and formulaic style of the poem, and the consequent critical problems; the examples of formulae and stylistic devices are not confined to books 19 and 20. The intention is therefore that the introduction should be of value to any reader of the *Odyssey*, whether or not he or she is especially concerned with these two books.

The commentary itself is of a 'literary' bent – that is, it pays more attention to the shaping of a scene, to the implications of a simile, or to techniques of anticipation, misdirection, and irony than to more 'realistic' concerns, such as the architecture and layout of Odysseus' house. This is in line with the general emphasis of the series, and I offer no apology, especially as the new Oxford *Odyssey*, mentioned above, is particularly helpful on such technical matters. My main aim has been to show the subtlety and consistency of the poet's art in these books, which often needs careful reading to appreciate: the assumption that

Homer is always simple and transparent, while it does express an important part-truth, is nevertheless damaging if it discourages readers from reading thoughtfully what the poet has evidently composed thoughtfully.

I hope that this book will be usable by readers of Homer at all levels. I have tried to make it as self-contained as possible, and to enable readers to use it with no other books on their desks apart from a Homeric dictionary such as Autenrieth's or Cunliffe's, or Liddell and Scott, and a text or some version of the rest of the *Odyssey*. Consequently, the introduction contains two sections on Homeric grammar and metre. These will seem jejune to the expert, but they are not intended for experts, who will naturally pursue more difficult questions elsewhere.

The choice of book 19 as the core of the book arose naturally from work I had been pursuing on recognition, irony and illusion in Homer. Few books illustrate so well the special qualities of the *Odyssey*, above all the poem's fascination with the gap between appearance and reality. The weary beggar is in fact the rightful king; Penelope's agony seems unbearable, her resistance to the suitors hopeless, but in fact salvation is at hand; the recognition of Odysseus by his wife seems inevitable, but is averted, and so forth. The psychological subtlety and the enjoyable ironies of the book are combined with superb pathos in the treatment of the queen; we also learn much about Odysseus' past (and about Homeric narrative technique) from the celebrated digression on the hero's scar. Book 19 is the longer and richer book, and the extent of the commentary reflects this; readers who have not the opportunity to read both are urged to read it rather than book 20. But the latter book is never dull, and has some splendid moments: the angry nightlong vigil of Odysseus, the crass arrogance and bullying of the suitors, oblivious of their impending doom, and above all the eerie vision of the prophet Theoclymenus, as sinister a scene as the biblical episode of Belshazzar's feast. At all points, however, I have tried to relate these episodes to the intricate and carefully shaped structure of the *Odyssey* as a whole.

I have tended to multiply references to ancient texts rather than to modern critics. Apart from the Oxford commentary and the *Companion* by Jones, I have found only three works consistently and lastingly valuable for my understanding of the *Odyssey*, namely the books by Stanford, Fenik and Austin; but of course there are many other books which are both useful and interesting, some of which I have listed in the bibliography. A growing impatience with the absurdities of scholarly polemic has impelled me to excise ruthlessly many citations of works which elaborate demonstrably wrong views or perpetuate arguments long ago decided, but no doubt this procedure might have been carried further.

I have been fortunate in my advisers and helpers. Stephen Halliwell, Emily Kearns, Robert Parker and Oliver Taplin read and commented on drafts at various stages, while Gregory Hutchinson, Robin Osborne, Peter Parsons, Nicholas Richardson and Christiane Sourvinou-Inwood lent me books and gave some more specific advice: I am grateful for all their suggestions. In 1987 I had the advantage of reading David Clark's unpublished Cambridge Ph.D. thesis on *Odyssey* 13–24, which I have found particularly instructive on book 20. The series editors offered a wealth of constructive and stimulating comment on the penultimate version, most of which I have gratefully incorporated; and the close and sensitive observations of the copy-editor, Susan Moore, did much to improve both form and substance of the final typescript. In working on Homer, and in this series, I am conscious again of the example set by Colin Macleod, *il miglior fabbro*, in his outstanding edition of *Iliad* xxiv. My pupils have often raised stimulating new questions or put old ones in a new way. The dedication acknowledges the most important debt of all.

R.B.R.

ABBREVIATIONS

This list excludes standard shortened versions of names of ancient authors and their works, and of modern periodicals.

Burkert, *GR* = W. Burkert, *Greek religion* (Eng. tr., Blackwell, Oxford 1985)

CAH = *Cambridge Ancient History*

Cunliffe = R. J. Cunliffe, *A lexicon of the Homeric dialect* (London, Glasgow and Bombay 1924)

Denniston, *GP* = J. D. Denniston, *The Greek particles*, 2nd edn (Oxford 1954)

FGrH = *Fragmente der griechischen Historiker* ed. F. Jacoby (Leiden 1923–)

Goodwin, *Greek grammar* = W. W. Goodwin, *A Greek grammar* (Macmillan, London 1879)

LSJ = H. G. Liddell, R. Scott, H. Stuart-Jones, *A Greek–English lexicon*, 9th edn (Oxford 1940), with Supplement (Oxford 1968)

MHV: see Parry

Monro, *Grammar* = D. B. Monro, *A grammar of the Homeric dialect* (Oxford 1882; 2nd edn, 1891)

OCD = N. G. L. Hammond and H. H. Scullard (edd.), *The Oxford Classical Dictionary*, 2nd edn (Oxford 1970)

Parry, *MHV* = Milman Parry, *The making of Homeric verse*, ed. Adam Parry (Oxford 1971)

PMG = D. L. Page (ed.), *Poetae melici graeci* (Oxford 1962)

P Oxy = *The Oxyrhynchus Papyri*, edd. B. P. Grenfell and others (London 1898–)

P.S.I. = *Papiri greci e latini* (Pubblicazioni della Società Italiana per la ricerca dei Papiri greci e latini in Egitto) edd. G. Vitelli and others (Florence 1912–)

RE = Pauly, Wissowa, Kroll (edd.), *Realencyclopädie der classischen Altertumswissenschaft* (Stuttgart 1893–)

Wace and Stubbings, *Companion* = *A companion to Homer*, edd. A. J. B. Wace and F. H. Stubbings (London 1962)

Weir Smyth, *Greek grammar* = H. Weir Smyth, *A Greek grammar*, revised by G. M. Messing (Harvard College 1956)

Shortened titles of books frequently cited (e.g. 'Fenik, *Studies*') may be elucidated from the Bibliography.

INTRODUCTION

1. THE POEM

(a) The Odyssey and the Iliad[1]

The *Odyssey* is commonly regarded as an inferior work to the *Iliad*, and even those who greatly admire the *Odyssey* frequently consider books 13–24 to be inferior to the first half of the poem. Both these conventional evaluations require attention before turning to the specific qualities of books 19 and 20.

The *Iliad* and the *Odyssey* are both the products of a tradition of heroic poetry, about which we can guess much but know little for certain. Many poems were known to ancient readers, as late as Aristotle and Callimachus, perhaps much later, which treated the war of Troy and its aftermath. Even in the Homeric poems we find many allusions to other mythological characters and tales, as when Diomedes is reminded of his father's exploits (*Il.* 4.370–400, 5.800–13), or Achilles of Meleager's (9.527–99). Moreover, the very themes of the two great epics – heroic wrath and the wanderer's return – can be seen to be traditional. Other wrathful heroes are referred to in the poems (notably Meleager, Aeneas, Ajax, Paris, and the quarrel between Achilles and Odysseus); and the *Odyssey* itself refers to and briefly recounts the homecomings of many other Greek warriors, in particular Agamemnon, Menelaus and Nestor. Adventures and events in the career of one hero may be adapted or transferred to another, as the poet chooses: thus in the lost poem called the *Aethiopis*, Eos obtained divine armour for her son Memnon, as Thetis does for Achilles in the *Iliad*. Many of Odysseus' adventures seem to be traditional tales, widespread in Greek and other mythologies.[2] Parallels have been drawn between the Cyclops-story

---

[1] In parts 1 and 2 of the Introduction I have deliberately limited citation of modern works, to which I naturally owe many points made here.

[2] For these and other examples, see D. L. Page, *The Homeric Odyssey* (Oxford 1955) ch. 1; *Folk-tales in Homer's Odyssey* (Ann Arbor 1973). See further the works cited by S. West in the Oxford *Odyssey* 1 56; also G. Crane, *Calypso* (Frankfurt am Main 1988); U. Hölscher, *Die Odyssee, Epos zwischen Märchen und Roman* (Munich 1988).

and similar tales in many languages; not only Odysseus but Heracles, Dionysus, Sisyphus, Orpheus, Theseus and Pirithous brave the terrors of the underworld (as does Gilgamesh in the far older Babylonian epic); and at 12.69–72 the *Odyssey*-poet himself seems to allude to his adaptation of an episode from the legend of Jason and the *Argo*, the adventure of the Clashing Rocks. In that passage Circe tells Odysseus that only one ship has ever passed through the Clashing Rocks successfully, 'the *Argo*, known to all men, sailing back from Aeetes' (70 Ἀργὼ πασιμέλουσα, παρ' Αἰήταο πλέουσα). There is reason to think that other characters and episodes in books 9–12 of the *Odyssey* may owe something to the Argonautic saga: Circe herself, daughter of the sun and sister of Aeetes, is a figure with strong links with that tradition.

Given the proliferation of such legends and the strong possibility of oral transmission, adaptation and reshaping of the different tales, it is obviously hard to determine the exact relation of *Iliad* and *Odyssey*. Which is likely to be the earlier, and does one show knowledge of the other? Could they be the work of the same author, as the ancients almost universally believed? Does similarity of language or parallelism of theme indicate direct imitation, or are such resemblances only the accidental product of the tradition, in which all bards may have shared a common stock of formulaic phrases and typical plots and episodes?

These complex questions will never be finally answered to the satisfaction of all readers. The view here adopted is that the *Iliad* and the *Odyssey* are by different poets, that the *Odyssey* is later, and that the *Odyssey*-poet knew the *Iliad* intimately, imitated and echoed it, and intended his poem to be a work on the same scale, dealing with many of the same characters and issues, but from a different perspective. But many of the comments made below are perfectly compatible with the view that the *Odyssey* is a later work by the same poet who composed the *Iliad*. What matters is that the *Iliad* should be the earlier work. The *Odyssey*, on this view, is, if not a response to the *Iliad*, at any rate a poem which reflects on and complements that poem. This is not, it should be repeated, something which can be 'proved'. Some of the considerations which seem to point towards this conclusion are set out below.

The *Iliad* and *Odyssey* are poems of comparable magnitude: the *Iliad* runs to 15,689 lines, the *Odyssey* to 12,110. The poems of the so-called Epic Cycle, apparently composed somewhat later than the extant epics, but drawing on earlier material, were notably shorter than the Homeric epics, as the surviving summaries indicate. The *Thebaid* had 7,000 lines, the *Oedipodeia* 6, 600. The *Sack of Ilium* contained only two books, the *Nostoi* ('Homecomings') five. Even if these were as long as the longest of Homer's books, about a thousand lines, we still have the impression of briefer, less ambitious lays.

More important than length is the design and conception of the poems. Aristotle contrasts the cyclic epics with Homer in quality and structure:

> [Homer] takes one part of the war and uses many others as epi-sodes, for example the catalogue of ships and the other episodes with which he breaks the uniformity of his poem. But the rest make a poem about one man or one period of time, like the poet of the *Cypria* and the *Little Iliad*. That is why the *Iliad* and *Odyssey* have material for only one tragedy or two, whereas there is matter for many in the *Cypria*.   (*Poetics*, ch. 23)

Aristotle also emphasises the importance of the spoken word in Homer:

> Homer especially deserves praise as the only epic poet to realise what the epic poet should do in his own person. In his own person the poet should say as little as possible ... other poets are playing a prominent role throughout, and only rarely use mimesis (i.e. direct speech by characters).   (*Poetics*, ch. 24)

It is indeed true that the fragments of the epic cycle include only the briefest of speeches (as is also the case with Hesiod, Homer's near-contemporary); events are narrated in a rapid and often disappoint-ingly flat manner, and speeches seem to be lacking even at moments of high tension or great significance, such as the cursing by Oedipus of his sons, or the killing of Astyanax.

The comparison of the surviving poems is naturally more suggestive than the reconstruction of lost works.[3] The two epics ascribed to Homer

---

[3] Of the vast bibliography on this subject I mention only a few works which seem to me especially helpful and persuasive: F. Jacoby, *Kleine philol. Schriften* I (Berlin 1961) 107–39; A. Heubeck, *Der Odyssee-dichter und die Ilias* (Erlangen 1954); W. Burkert, *Rh. M.* 103 (1960) 130–44; J. Griffin, *Homer: the Odyssey* (Cambridge 1987) 63–70. P. Pucci, *Odysseus Polytropos* (Ithaca 1987) also dis-cusses these issues, and raises some interesting questions, but his analyses often seem to me fanciful. See further my paper 'From the *Iliad* to the *Odyssey*', forth-coming in *B.I.C.S.* 38 (1991), and K. Usener, *Beobachtungen zum Verhältnis der Odyssee zur Ilias* (ScriptOralia 21, Tübingen 1990).

do indeed show profound similarities as well as important differences. The *Iliad* is a poem of war and tragedy, the *Odyssey* a poem of peace in the aftermath of war, of homecoming and reunion. Whereas the *Iliad* presents a grim picture of disintegration, with increasing savagery in battle and the threat of destruction hanging over a doomed city, the *Odyssey* is a poem of reintegration, in which the anarchic disruption of Ithacan society is ended by the return of the rightful king, while the unhappy tensions of the royal household are resolved by the homecoming of husband and father. Whereas the *Iliad* shows the cruelty and tragedy of war, in which compassion and humane feelings are precious but constantly endangered or abandoned, the *Odyssey* shows civilised values violated and neglected, but finally vindicated, particularly through its treatment of the institutions of hospitality and guestfriendship. Both poems are concerned with the social, political and emotional ties between human beings. Both deal, more specifically, with the intimate relationships of the family: father and son (Peleus and Achilles; Priam and Hector; Laertes, Odysseus and Telemachus), mother and son (Thetis and Achilles; Hecuba and Hector; Penelope and Telemachus), husband and wife (Hector and Andromache, contrasted in the *Iliad* with the unhappy and childless relationship between Paris and Helen; Odysseus and Penelope, contrasted in the *Odyssey* with the hapless Agamemnon and the adulterous Clytemnestra, and with the uneasily reunited Menelaus and Helen).

In both epics, the hero spends a great part of the time-span of the poem isolated from those closest to him; in both he makes a conscious and fundamental choice between an easier and more inglorious existence and the way of life which will enable him to fulfil his human and heroic potential. In both poems, the hero grows and matures in understanding through his experiences: both Achilles and Odysseus are more articulate and more reflective than their fellow heroes in either epic. Both poems reach their climaxes with the vengeance of the hero on his enemy or enemies. In neither, however, does the poet end his tale with bloodthirsty triumph; rather, he continues with scenes involving gentler emotions and more subtle, less straightforwardly 'heroic' actions.

The two epics both make extensive use of the supernatural, and in particular of the Olympian gods, immortal and magnificent beings who observe the actions of mankind with keen but often capricious interest, and who intervene to aid their favourites or to punish those who offend them. The *Odyssey* does not introduce the gods as readily as the *Iliad*: only Zeus, Poseidon and Athene are fundamental to the plot, though other gods such as Hermes figure from time to time. The *Odyssey* does, however, allow much more scope than the *Iliad* to magic, monsters and mysterious beings such as the enchantress Circe, the Sirens, and so forth.[4] This is particularly true of the wanderings (which are, however, narrated by the hero rather than the poet, and take place in a never-never land); but even in Ithaca Odysseus is magically transformed by Athene. This shifting and uncertain world, in which many things are not what they seem, provides a very suitable environment for the crafty and many-sided Odysseus.

It is clear that the happy ending of the *Odyssey*, which is brought about principally by Athene, but with Zeus's full approval, also satisfies the natural human desire to see justice done in the world and evildoers punished. There is an obvious contrast here with the *Iliad*, in which malevolent goddesses bring about the destruction of the pious and sympathetic Trojans to satisfy a grudge, and in which the human beings' hopes for divine justice are repeatedly disappointed. Some have seen this difference between the poems as reflecting a contemporary development in morality or theology,[5] and it is certainly true that both gods and men in the *Odyssey* condemn the wickedness of the suitors and of Aegisthus. But the difference in moral tone is closely related to the difference in the kind of story that is being told: since the *Iliad* is a tragic poem, it is natural that the characters should suffer beyond their desert, and that fate and the gods should seem cruel and unfair. Conversely, the tale of Odysseus' return against all odds satisfies our sense of what is right, and makes it more credible, at least for a time, that the universe is justly governed. It seems likely that the epic poets themselves contributed significantly to the Greek conception of divinity, and that there was a wide range of deities and other powers from which they chose and

---

[4] See further R. Carpenter, *Folk-tale, fiction and saga in the Homeric epics* (Berkeley and Los Angeles 1946); J. Griffin, *J.H.S.* 97 (1977) 39–53.

[5] See e.g. E. R. Dodds, *The Greeks and the irrational* (Berkeley and Los Angeles 1951) 28–37; *contra*, B. Fenik *Studies in the Odyssey* (Wiesbaden 1974) 208–30. For more recent accounts, with bibliography, see H. Erbse, *Untersuchungen zur Funktion der Götter im Homerischen Epos* (Berlin 1969) 237–41, W. Kullmann, *H.S.C.P.* 89 (1985) 1–23; R. Friedrich, *G.R.B.S.* 28 (1987) 375–400; an unorthodox but stimulating contribution by M. Winterbottom, *G.&R.* 26 (1989) 33–41.

adapted those which suited the needs of their particular tales.[6] Polytheism admits and encourages inconsistency. The gods of the *Iliad* are not wholly indifferent to human virtues and morality; nor are the gods of the *Odyssey* consistently and uniformly upholders of what is right. If they were, Odysseus' success would be too easy and the poem duller.

'The *Odyssey* is quite simply the epilogue of the *Iliad*', wrote the author of one of the finest works of ancient criticism, the essay 'On the sublime' (9.12) attributed to Longinus. The *Odyssey* does indeed have some of the qualities of a 'sequel' or follow-up to the other epic. The *Odyssey* seems to presuppose the *Iliad*: it never relates the actual tale which is narrated in the *Iliad*, but does do a most efficient job of filling in the story since *Iliad* 24. The death of Achilles, the dispute over the armour, the Wooden Horse, the sack of Troy, the recovery of Helen, the murder of Agamemnon, all find a place somewhere. Few characters are left unaccounted for, few questions unanswered. This would be a remarkable coincidence if the *Odyssey*-poet had never heard or encountered the *Iliad*.

More specifically, the reappearance of Achilles in book 11 of the *Odyssey* reproduces vividly much of the personality of the hero of the *Iliad*. We find the same sombre eloquence and bitter disillusionment, the same passionate concern for his far-off father that is typical of Achilles above all in *Iliad* 24. The contrast between the dashing, outspoken Achilles and the more subtle and canny Odysseus, present in essence in books 9 and 19 of the *Iliad*, is also revived and extended; both poems present these heroes as natural opposites.

These contrasts suggest that it is inappropriate to judge the *Iliad* and the *Odyssey* by the same standards, especially if that judgement is based in large part on the character of the hero of each. In Plato's *Hippias Minor*, Socrates refers to such a judgement: 'I have heard your father say that the *Iliad* is a finer poem than the *Odyssey* by as much as Achilles is a better man than Odysseus' (365b). The character of the hero influences the character of the poem: the *Iliad*, with its violent and passionate Achilles, is a poem of open warfare and heroic achievement, while the *Odyssey*, with its cautious and secretive hero, a schemer and wily rhetorician as much as a warrior, contains many more scenes of trickery

---

[6] See e.g. W. Burkert, *Greek religion* (Eng. tr., Oxford 1985) 119–25, 182–9, 246–50.

and deception. Instead of the heroic duel or the direct attack on a foe, the poet's attention is focused much more on the ironies of knowledge and ignorance, the gap between what is said or supposed and what is truly the case. Odysseus achieves his ends through the rhetoric of flattery and falsehood rather than through action. Even when he is at his most Iliadic, in the slaughter of the suitors, he has achieved his position of advantage by trickery and quickness of wit, and his revenge is exacted with that ambiguous and almost unheroic weapon, the bow.

Even the design of the poem seems affected by the indirect and deceptive methods of the hero. Its structure is more complex and intricate than that of the *Iliad*. Not only do we begin *in mediis rebus*, but much of the hero's experience is related in a retrospective narrative recounted by himself (books 9–12), and the poem contains many other tales within a tale, told by Odysseus and others. These tales supplement or resemble one another, in a kaleidoscopic pattern of stock elements and analogies. The poet also, like his hero, delays events, prolongs the suspense, and even defers the actual introduction of his hero for four books. Odysseus is not actually named in the proem to the first book (contrast the *Iliad*, which names its hero in line 1 of book 1), and he appears in person only at 5.149, by which time we have heard much about him from others. The poet also seems occasionally to deceive or misdirect his audience, leading them to expect a development which he then frustrates. This literary sophistication is paralleled in the self-consciousness of the poet concerning his own poetic creation and the deceptive power of poetry in general. Poets (Phemius and Demodocus) figure in the cast of characters, as they did not in the *Iliad*. Odysseus himself is more than once compared to a poet (19.203n.), particularly when he is telling his supremely persuasive lies, which regularly include substantial elements of truth. This self-awareness and these analogies between the poet and the hero find no parallel in the *Iliad*: while they do not necessarily provide an indication of separate authorship, they do illustrate some of the different concerns of the later poem.

(b) The second half of the Odyssey

The plot of the poem can be easily summarised. The island of Ithaca has been without its king for twenty years, and the royal household is dominated by local lords who are wooing the queen and threatening the inheritance and life of the young prince, Telemachus. Inspired by Athene, Telemachus seeks news of his father overseas, visiting Odysseus' comrades-in-arms Nestor and Menelaus (books 1–4). Meanwhile, the gods decree the release of Odysseus from his captivity on Calypso's island (book 5). After shipwreck at sea, he comes to the remote island of Scheria, dwelling-place of the Phaeacians, who entertain him though ignorant of his identity (books 6–8). There he reveals his name, narrates his many adventures (books 9–12), and is conveyed back to Ithaca on their ship (book 13). With the renewed guidance and aid of his patroness Athene, Odysseus infiltrates his household in disguise, deceiving servants and suitors, identifying himself to his son (book 16), but not otherwise revealing himself, even to his wife (see book 19). Enduring threats, assaults, and near-recognition, he finally participates in the archery-contest by which Penelope seeks to resolve her dilemma and to select, however reluctantly, a new husband (book 21). Securing the bow that no lesser man could draw, he shoots down the suitors and slays them all, aided by Telemachus and two loyal retainers (book 22). He then identifies himself and is accepted by his wife (book 23), visits his aged father, and sets the rest of his kingdom in order (book 24).

It is unlikely that the book-divisions in our texts of Homer go back to the poet's own time. In this tradition the 24 letters of the Ionic alphabet are used to identify the individual books, but it is uncertain whether any early alphabet familiar to Homer would necessarily have contained 24 letters. Early alphabets differed considerably, some not distinguishing between ε and η, ο and ω, others having several letters that later fell out of use. It is generally accepted that these divisions were made at a later date, by scholars and editors in Hellenistic Alexandria. Nevertheless, the difference between the first twelve books and the second is real enough, and the transition between them signalled with sufficient clarity, for the division into two 'halves' to be critically significant. Lines 88–92 in book 13 seem to echo lines 1–4 in book 1, and to indicate the end of a phase of Odysseus' experiences. With his return to Ithaca in book 13 we move from an unfamiliar, fairy-tale world to the more down-to-earth setting of a Greek community; we pass from predominantly sea-going adventures to land. Monsters and enchantresses give way to a more human, less supernatural drama. The goddess Athene rejoins the hero after long absence; this signals the return to land-bound adventures, and also the new prospects of success and restoration for the hero. Having been the ignorant, storm-tossed victim of the gods, Odysseus is now to be supported and guided by the gods; having suffered from and been frustrated by divine vengeance, he will now act as an instrument of divine punishment, testing the virtues and vices of the members of his household and visiting retribution upon the evil suitors. Having previously ignored or misinterpreted warnings,[7] he will now give them; having been kept in the dark and deceived by others, he will now be in control, deceiving, testing and playing games with his potential victims. In short, the first half of the *Odyssey* is primarily an account of the wanderings and sufferings of the passive Odysseus, whereas in the second half the hero takes a more active and aggressive role. In almost every scene he is the figure with most authority and most fully aware of the true situation.

The second half of the *Odyssey* has, however, been much criticised. These criticisms focus particularly on the alleged monotony and repetitiveness of books 14–21, the slowness of the action, the supposed inconsistencies of Penelope's characterisation, and the unsatisfactory nature of the poem's conclusion (the authenticity of which has been repeatedly questioned). Penelope's character and attitudes will be considered in §3 below; here something should be said in response to the other complaints.

The part of the *Odyssey* which most readers first encounter, whether in school-books, anthologies or elsewhere, is the first-person narrative of Odysseus, books 9–12. This has always been one of the most popular parts of the Homeric corpus. Judged by the standard of the Cyclops book or the visit to the Land of the Dead, the human experiences of Odysseus in Ithaca may well seem more everyday, less thrilling. The reader correctly discerns that this is a different kind of narrative; that does not mean that it is devoid of interest or psychological depth. Not only in the second half of the poem, but in the 'Telemachy' (books 1–4) and in the narrative of Odysseus' arrival in the land of the Phaeacians in books 6–8, the poet is fascinated by the theme of a mysterious stranger's appearance within a society or a household that does not recognise him. Thus Athene, disguised, arrives in Ithaca, Telemachus in Pylos and Sparta, Odysseus in Scheria. Each of these visitors is greeted with respect and hospitality; each eventually is recognised or makes him-

---

[7] See further Introd. 2 (*b*), pp. 21–2 below.

self or herself known. In the second half of the poem this pattern is modified, for Odysseus arrives not in a strange land, as he at first supposes, but in his own country; yet it is here that he is in danger, here that courtesy and hospitality will be most brutally denied, as the suitors abuse, mock and threaten to kill him, little knowing that this is the master of the house and their rightful king. In developing this situation, the poet repeatedly exploits his techniques of irony and ambiguity of meaning. Servants speak of Odysseus in his own presence,[8] the suitors jeer at his warnings and predictions (17.446–52, 478–80); omens foretell and pave the way for his triumphant revelation (15.160–81, 525–38, 17.541–7, 18.112–13, 117); Penelope and others sense the authority and sympathetic qualities of the stranger without realising the truth. It is this technique of delayed recognition and ironic resonance that is typical of the *Odyssey*, and especially of its second half, in which Odysseus is constantly among those whom he knows. This psychological drama of suspense and deception offers a more intellectual and perhaps more subtle aesthetic satisfaction than scenes of violence and unthinking action. Nor do these books lack emotional depth and poignancy: the ignorance and helplessness of Penelope are the source of much pathos, as in her misunderstanding and resentment of her son's attitude to her (§3(*a*) below), or in the scene in which she weeps uncontrollably for her husband as he sits, unrecognised, at her side (19.203–12).

It is a notable feature of Homeric narrative that similar scenes are often arranged in a deliberate and cumulative sequence, the parallelism contributing to the climactic effect.[9] Thus in the *Iliad* the scenes of supplication on the battlefield reach their climax when Lycaon vainly throws himself on Achilles' mercy; that scene itself is 'capped' in the supreme supplication of the poem, when Priam begs Achilles to relent and release the body of Hector. Many examples of this technique are to be found in the *Odyssey*. On a small scale, the pattern can be seen in the three episodes in which a suitor throws something at Odysseus (17.462–94, 18.387–411, 20.299–320). More significant is the treatment of delayed recognition: used on a small scale with Telemachus in Sparta, where the young man is not at first questioned and recog-

---

[8] 14.40, 61–8, 90; 19.363n.; 20.194n.
[9] See Fenik, *Studies* 102–4, 155–8, 181–7, etc.

nised, it is taken further in the case of Odysseus in Scheria, where the hero conceals his identity from king and court for at least twenty-four hours, and further still in Ithaca, where there are repeated deceptions and successive delayed revelations. In Sparta, the concealment is unintentional and incidental; in Scheria, Odysseus has been warned of the inhabitants' possible hostility to strangers (6.273–85, 7.14–17, 31–3), and himself needs time to recover confidence and win their trust. Only in Ithaca is the danger to the newly arrived stranger real and patent. There he needs to conceal his true name and test the loyalty and mettle of each retainer in turn. Consequently the theme of recognition is developed and varied; but the variations are not random or inconsequential. They form a deliberate and significant sequence.

The analogies between the Phaeacian episode and events in Ithaca go further than this: in numerous details, books 6–8 anticipate and foreshadow the events of the second half.[10] Thus in both places the hero finds himself on an unknown beach, bewails his fate, encounters a female figure whom he flatters and who offers him aid (Nausicaa and Athene); in both sections of the poem he approaches the centre of the community indirectly and gradually; in both, he conceals his identity and is tested and questioned by a quick-witted queen (Arete, Penelope). Both episodes culminate in self-revelation at a feast. In book 9, Odysseus reveals his name and narrates his adventures to the friendly Phaeacians, who are filled with awe and admire his poet-like art (11.333–4, 363–9). In book 22, Odysseus shocks and confounds the suitors by revealing himself through violent action, shooting down their ringleader with the great bow; and his movements as he tests and strings the weapon are compared with the action of a bard fingering the strings of a lyre (21.404–18). The ironic parallelism is unmistakable.

Books 13–24 are also criticised as repetitive, especially in the recurrent recognition-scenes. After the amusing encounter with Athene in book 13 (221–373), in which she tries unsuccessfully to make Odysseus reveal himself, the poet repeats or plays variations on this theme throughout – with Telemachus (16.1–221), the dog Argus (17.290–327), Eurycleia (19.335–507), Eumaeus and Philoetius together (21.188–244). Odysseus reveals himself to the suitors in book 22, and

---

[10] See *P.C.P.S.* 31 (1985) esp. 140–4. This will also be discussed by Alex Garvie in his commentary on books 6–8 in this series.

the theme reaches its culmination with the scene in which Penelope acknowledges him to be her husband (23.1–246).

As has already been said, these scenes are not arranged at random. In the first scene, Athene's knowledge is superior to Odysseus'. She knows who he is, but is herself disguised; moreover, she has concealed from him the fact that he is back in Ithaca, so that she may advise and disguise him, but also so that she may witness his delighted surprise when the truth is revealed. In this she is disappointed, for Odysseus' self-control is perfect. 'His words came back swiftly as he answered her, not telling the truth but keeping back what he might have said, and always guiding his thoughts, rich in guile, within his breast' (13.253–5). Although Athene herself remains unrecognised, she has not induced her protégé to lower his guard, and has to admit defeat at least in part. In subsequent scenes it is generally Odysseus who plays Athene's game and remains in control of the situation, choosing the proper moment for revelation, as with Telemachus in book 16 and the herdsmen in book 21. But the situation would lose its tension and drama if there were never any chance of Odysseus being identified accidentally: hence the unforeseen recognition by the dog Argus, which creates no danger because of the animal's weakened state, and thereafter, in book 19, the equally unforeseen and much more perilous recognition by the old nurse. This scene shows that the hero can slip up, but with Athene's aid he regains control of the situation and Penelope does not suspect.

Neither deliberate self-revelation nor accidental exposure puts another character in a position equal or superior to Odysseus' own. Even Athene in book 13, though she deceived Odysseus, was unable to make him give himself away. Only in book 23, in the second encounter with his wife, is the hero finally and incontrovertibly out-tested and out-witted. Here it is Penelope, in her uncertainty and doubt, who conceives a test to see whether Odysseus is truly her husband (23.107–10, 113–14). Once before, in book 19, she had attempted to do so (19.215 and n.), but Odysseus had sidestepped. In book 23 we see the tables turned, the biter bit, when Penelope asks the old nurse to bring out their marital bed for Odysseus to sleep in that night. 'Thus she spoke, testing her husband' (23.181). At the thought of anyone having tampered with the immovable bed, around which he had built the palace, Odysseus bursts out with open indignation: his famous caution and self-control vanish. The scene thus trumps all Odysseus' previous test-

ing and reverses Penelope's failure in book 19. Her success also sur-
passes even the wiles of Athene, the only other female who matches the
hero in cleverness and guile. Like other parallelisms between Odysseus
and Penelope, the scene in book 23 serves to show more vividly how
well matched husband and wife truly are: they perfectly exemplify the
ὁμοφροσύνη of the ideal marriage, of which Odysseus spoke in his ap-
peal to Nausicaa (6.183–5). It is also fitting and symbolic that the
crucial sign, the proof of Odysseus' identity, should be his knowledge of
the nature of their bed: it is deep-rooted, firmly and immovably set,
ἔμπεδος (a key-word in this scene: see 23.203, 206). Like their marriage
itself, it stands firm, unchanged by time.

Besides the central relationship between husband and wife, the *Odys-
sey* also highlights the uneasy growth to manhood of the fatherless Tele-
machus. In the first half of the poem two journeys are narrated at
length: that of Telemachus, leaving home to win renown and show
himself a man, his father's true son, and that of Odysseus, who is strug-
gling to return home and regain his kingdom and family. In the second
half these separate strands are woven together, with the reunion of man
and boy in book 16, and the loyal support that Telemachus gives to his
father in the action which follows. Particularly significant is the scene in
which Telemachus, like the suitors, makes trial of the bow (cf. 21.113–
17, in which he proposes to do so).

> Thrice as he tried to draw it, he made it tremble; thrice he rested
> from the effort, though his heart still hoped to string the bow and
> shoot through the iron. Then a fourth time he strained at it, and
> this time he would indeed have strung it, but Odysseus gave him a
> warning nod, and stopped him short, for all his eagerness.
>
> (21.125–9)

Again, this is typical of the poem's dramatic irony. Telemachus has at
long last proved himself – he *is* his father's son – but no-one in the hall
except the father and son themselves realises what has happened or
understands the significance of this moment.

Beyond the family circle lies the wider society of Ithaca itself, and the
reunion of the family also means the saving of Odysseus' royal line and
the security of the kingdom. The suitors are pursuing not only the
beautiful Penelope but royal or oligarchic power, a further aspect of the
plot which helps explain Telemachus' anxieties. Odysseus is not only

head of the household but the model of the good king under whom the
kingdom prospers. Such a ruler is 'gentle as a father to his people'
(2.234, cf. 47; 4.687–95, 5.7–12, 19.109–14, 365–8). The *Odyssey* pre-
sents Ithaca as a society out of joint. As we learn from book 2, there
have been no assemblies since the king left, an unrealistic but symboli-
cally effective departure from normal conditions. In book 2, Tele-
machus attempts to win support at an assembly, but the suitors have
things their way and the prince is humiliated. In book 4, Antinous and
the rest of the suitors browbeat the innocent Noemon, and plot violence
against Telemachus; in book 16, they hold an assembly among them-
selves, but deliberately exclude those outside their number, a sign of
incipient oligarchy (16.361–2). Conditions in Ithaca are unhappy
enough for the loyal herdsman Philoetius to be considering emigra-
tion (20.209–25). The households of Nestor and Menelaus, securely
governed, pious and hospitable, offer a contrast with the troubled state
of Ithaca. Likewise the ceremony and courtesy with which Telemachus
and his companions are greeted and sent off in Pylos and Sparta should
be contrasted with the non-reception offered to Athene in Ithaca,
where none of the suitors pays heed to the new arrival, and Telemachus
has to sit secretively with her in a corner of the hall in which he should
be presiding (1.113–25, 132–5).

This public dimension to the homecoming of Odysseus is acknowl-
edged by the hero himself when he overhears the unhappy slave-
woman cursing the suitors as she grinds corn for them (20.105–21), and
perhaps also as he spends his days conversing and sympathising with
the downtrodden Eumaeus (books 14, 15.301–495). These considera-
tions make it improbable that the *Odyssey* could ever have ended with
the retirement of Odysseus and Penelope to bed at 23.296, as many
modern critics have maintained on the doubtful basis of comments in
the ancient scholia.[11] The public themes of the poem also demand reso-
lution; more specifically, Odysseus himself anticipates possible trouble

[11] Schol. HMQ on 23.296: τοῦτο τέλος τῆς Ὀδυσσείας φησὶν Ἀρίσταρχος
καὶ Ἀριστοφάνης ('this is said by Aristarchus and Aristophanes to be the conclu-
sion [or 'climax'?] of the *Odyssey*'). Other scholia say much the same, using the
word πέρας ('limit') rather than τέλος. On the so-called Continuation see esp.
H. Erbse, *Beiträge zum Verständnis der Odyssee* (Berlin 1972) 166–250, who cites
earlier contributions extensively; C. Moulton, *G.R.B.S.* 15 (1974) 153–69 pro-
vides a good brief overview. S. West, *P.C.P.S.* 35 (1989) 113–43 is a very effec-
tive and balanced restatement of the case against authenticity.

from the suitors' kinsmen if he is successful in slaying his enemies (20.41–3, 23.137), and also seems to propose a journey to his estates (23.138), fulfilled in book 24 with his visit to Laertes. The Ithacan assembly-scene in book 24, whoever its author may have been, plainly echoes and brings to a conclusion the themes of the similar scene in book 2, just as the second underworld episode (24.1–204) echoes and 'caps' the earlier *Nekuia* (book 11). As in book 2, the prophet Halitherses harangues the Ithacans, and here he points out that his earlier warnings and those of Mentor have been justified (2.157–76, 224–41, 24.451–62). As in book 11, the poet stresses the contrast between Odysseus' successful return and, on the one hand, the death of Achilles at Troy in glorious battle, and on the other, the humiliating murder of Agamemnon by his wife and her lover. But whereas in book 11 Agamemnon had spoken bitterly of womankind in general, and had warned Odysseus not to be too open with Penelope, here he retracts his earlier suspicions, and gives Penelope her due tribute (11.440–56, 24.192–202). Odysseus' triumph is acknowledged and respected by his dead comrades, and here alone Odysseus is described as 'fortunate', in a unique variation on a stock formulaic line (24.192 ὄλβιε Λαέρταο πάϊ, πολυμήχαν' Ὀδυσσεῦ).

Although modern readers have found the final scenes of the *Odyssey* lacking in dignity and poetic quality by comparison with other parts of the epic, it can hardly be denied that the final book is *thematically* integrated. Odysseus' vigorous and Iliadic reassertion of authority over his subjects restores the kingdom from anarchy to order, but the divine favour which has been evident in the last few books averts serious bloodshed and ensures that this restoration will be peaceful and welcome. On the level of the family, numerous references have prepared us for an encounter between the hero and his aged father, a further instance of the poet's fascination with the parent–child theme. Three generations of the royal house are reunited and prepare for battle together, a moment of pride and renewed youth (520) for Laertes, who exultingly cries out:

τίς νύ μοι ἡμέρη ἥδε, θεοὶ φίλοι; ἦ μάλα χαίρω.
υἱός θ' υἱωνός τ'ἀρετῆς πέρι δῆριν ἔχουσι. (24.514–15)

'What a day this is for me, dear gods! How joyful I am! My son and my grandson are contending in valour together.'

As for the notorious scene in which Odysseus deceives his father with a characteristically glib lie (a further variation on the testing theme), this admittedly surprising and unnecessary delay in self-revelation should not be viewed as an incompetent interpolation or as the elaboration of an over-worked motif. The reader of the *Odyssey* has had ample evidence that Odysseus is not a straightforwardly honest or open-hearted hero; rather, through his many misfortunes he has become almost fanatically cautious and devious. His reluctance to reveal his identity immediately was seen before among the Phaeacians, as also in his dealings with Eumaeus, Telemachus and Penelope. In book 24, despite initial hesitation (235–40), this compulsive self-concealment continues even when there is no further need for caution; only when Laertes breaks down and weeps does Odysseus, filled with sudden dismay (318–19), realise how much he has hurt his father, and eagerly, almost incoherently, pour forth the truth (321–6). It is wittily apt that Laertes, the father of this man of cunning and caution, should himself demand proof (329), which Odysseus provides by revealing his scar and also recounting his patrimony, naming the gifts which his father had promised him as a boy, in the very orchard where they now stand. As with Eurycleia and Penelope, the medium of recognition is appropriate.

In short, the second half of the poem develops, with considerable variety, subtlety and suspense, the themes already introduced in books 1–12: the maturity and status of Telemachus; the providence of the gods; hospitality granted and denied; the individual parted from or unrecognised by the society in which he belongs; the uncertainties of human trust, and the gap between full knowledge of events and partial or total ignorance. Of these diverse themes the poet weaves an elaborate and intricate but not unduly extended narrative web.

2. ODYSSEUS

(a) Odysseus in the Iliad

In book 9 of the *Iliad*, Phoenix describes how he was sent to Troy as Achilles' mentor, 'to teach him all this, to be both a speaker of words and a doer of deeds' (9.442–3). After the death of Patroclus and the failure of all his hopes, Achilles admits that despite his pre-eminence in war 'others are better than I in council' (18.106). Amongst these others Odysseus is surely numbered. Less dashing and hungry for glory than Achilles, he is also more prudent and less impulsive. In the *Iliad*, it is he who is entrusted with the task of returning Chryseis to her father, and he who saves the day when Agamemnon's disastrous test of morale misfires in book 2; it is he who quells the rebellious Thersites, restores the army's spirits (2.243–335), and later rebukes Agamemnon for his hopeless determination to flee (14.82–102). Besides his good qualities in a crisis, he is renowned above all for his powers of oratory. The Trojan elder Antenor recalls his performance when the Greeks sent an embassy to Troy before the war began, in terms which stress both Odysseus' deceptively unimpressive appearance (cf. *Od.* 8.159–64) and his sublime eloquence.

> 'But when Odysseus of the many wiles rose swiftly to his feet, he kept standing there, looking downward, his eyes firmly fixed upon the ground, and did not move the staff forward or back but kept it motionless, looking like a man of no intellect. You would have called him a dullard and a fool. But when he sent forth his great voice from his chest, and his words fell like the winter snows, then could no man contend with Odysseus.'   (*Il.* 3.216–23)

That same eloquence is demonstrated in the *Iliad* itself, in books 9 and 19. In both episodes Odysseus is appealing to and opposing Achilles, first urging him to accept Agamemnon's offer of recompense, and later advising him to eat, and let the army breakfast too, before seeking vengeance on Hector. In both scenes, his reasoned and calculating advice is to be contrasted with the unrestrained passion of the younger Achilles (that Odysseus is the elder is made explicit at 19.219). In both scenes, Odysseus puts forward arguments that would appeal to himself, for in the *Odyssey* his readiness to acquire gifts from all sources and his hearty appetite are often emphasised. This practical and realistic outlook serves as a foil to the grief-stricken fasting of Achilles, the more romantic and histrionic of the two. The *Iliad* even hints at some antagonism between the two, especially in Achilles' reply to Odysseus in book 9 (309, 312–3):

χρὴ μὲν δὴ τὸν μῦθον ἀπηλεγέως ἀποειπεῖν . . .
ἐχθρὸς γάρ μοι κεῖνος ὁμῶς Ἀΐδαο πύλῃσιν
ὅς χ᾽ ἕτερον μὲν κεύθῃ ἐνὶ φρεσίν, ἄλλο δὲ εἴπῃ.

'I must speak my piece without respect of consequence ... for
hateful to me as are the gates of Hades is the man who hides one
thing in his heart and says another.'

This generalisation clearly hints at Odysseus' rhetorical insincerity.[12]

Achilles is not alone in the *Iliad* in his resentment of the cleverness of
Odysseus, 'the untypical hero', as Stanford has called him. In his re-
view of the troops, Agamemnon injudiciously hurls some angry abuse
at Odysseus which reveals his real opinions (4.339 'and you there,
versed in evil tricks, you crafty schemer'); and the despicable Thersites
is said to have made Achilles and Odysseus his chief targets for insults
(2.220). His failure to respond to Diomedes' cry to come and aid Nestor
(8.97) already worried ancient critics: did he not hear or was he turning
a deaf ear? It is also mentioned twice in the *Iliad* that Odysseus' beached
ships were stationed at the centre of the Greek lines (8.222–6 =
11.5–9): perhaps insignificant in itself, this reference becomes more
pointed when the poet adds that Achilles and Ajax were positioned at
the opposite extremities of the encampment, 'men who trusted in their
manhood and the might of their hands'. The prudence of Odysseus
is indirectly implied. Although these testimonies need to be weighed
against his close friendship with the noble Diomedes, the admiration
of Priam and Antenor, and his undoubted martial abilities, Odysseus
nevertheless emerges from the *Iliad* as a somewhat unusual figure. In
the funeral games, he is befriended in one contest by Athene, who
upsets the lesser Ajax's balance and sends him toppling into a heap of
dung (23.740–784, esp. 774, 782–3), and the vanquished hero ruefully
reflects that Athene is always protecting Odysseus, 'like a mother'. He
seems guilty of a foul in the wrestling match against the greater Ajax
(23.725–8), a struggle which is sometimes thought to foreshadow their
fateful competition for the armour of Achilles, which resulted in Ajax's
madness and suicide (*Od.* 11.543–67). It certainly seems likely that the
Iliad-poet knew much more about Odysseus than the poem tells. In
particular, in two passages he makes this hero describe himself with
some emotion as 'the father of Telemachus' (2.260, 4.354), a reversal
of the normal patronymic style (Peleiades, Laertiades, etc.) which is
not paralleled in the words of any other hero. Telemachus is wholly
irrelevant to the *Iliad*; it seems reasonable to deduce that other tales

---

[12] It is relevant that Odysseus has just suppressed the haughty conclusion of
Agamemnon's message to Achilles: compare *Il.* 9.157–61 with 299–306.

known to the poet had already recounted the stories of Odysseus'
family and the hero's homecoming.

The most Odyssean part of the *Iliad* is the dubious *Doloneia* (book
10),[13] the self-contained account of a night raid on the Trojan lines by
Odysseus and Diomedes. The arguments for supposing this book to be
an independent addition to the *Iliad* proper are strong.[14] Here alone are
unarmed men slaughtered while they sleep; here alone are guile and
deception prominent as opposed to open warfare. The crafty Odysseus
deceives and outwits the ineptly named Dolon, his inferior opposite
number. Also striking is the reference to Odysseus' maternal grand-
father the liar and oath-breaker Autolycus (10.267), a relation men-
tioned only here and at *Od.* 19.394–466 (see nn.). In *Iliad* 10, instead
of orthodox armour, Odysseus dons a boar's-tusk helmet of ingenious
design, formerly stolen rather than won or inherited by Autolycus from
another hero (10.261–71, almost a parody of passages describing the
transmission of heirlooms: cf. 2.100–8, 7.137–49, *Od.* 21.11–41, etc.).
These undertones of sub-heroic dishonesty and guile reveal Odysseus,
even at war amongst his peers, as a wilier and more devious hero than
the rest, though also more intelligent. It is not surprising that he is
already the favourite of Athene, the goddess closely associated with
wisdom and intelligence, nor that the two of them are said to have
conceived the device of the wooden horse, the ruse by which Troy
eventually falls (*Od.* 8.492–5) – a device to which the *Iliad*, with its
more heroic conception of war, never alludes.

Other poems in the epic tradition seem to have presented a more
villainous Odysseus, his guile being exaggerated into treachery and
malice. In the *Cypria*, Odysseus tried to avoid coming to Troy at all,
feigning madness (OCT Homer v, p. 103.25 = *Epic. Gr. Fragm.* ed.
Davies, p. 31.40–4; cf. *Od.* 24.118–19). When eventually exposed by
Palamedes, he took his revenge by murdering him (*Cypria* fr. 21 Allen =
20 Davies); the episode was later elaborated into a full-scale frame-up
and trial, a theme treated by all three of the fifth-century tragedians
and referred to by Virgil and Ovid. In a mysterious episode of the *Little*

---

[13] The 'Odyssean' character of this book is effectively argued on a linguistic
level by S. Laser, *Hermes* 86 (1958) 385–425 – see esp. his table of parallels on
p. 422; but his statements that a given line is later than a similar line in the other
poem often seem to make things too clear-cut.

[14] See further F. Klingner, *Hermes* 75 (1940) 337–68, reprinted in his *Studien
zur griechischen und römischen Literatur* (Zürich 1964) 7–39.

Iliad Odysseus even tried to kill Diomedes (fr. ix.2 Bethe = 9 Davies), something scarcely credible to the reader of the *Iliad* or even the *Doloneia*, where the two are bosom companions. In the *Odyssey* he dwells with Circe for a year and with Calypso for seven (though by the end of that time 'the nymph pleased him no longer', 5.153). Other versions, perhaps all later elaborations, associated him with other mortal women: the queen of Thesprotia ([Apollod.] *Epit.* 7.34–5), or the daughter of Thoas (ibid. 40). The author of the *Odyssey*, however, with his high regard for the bonds of marriage, makes clear that Odysseus has no choice but to sleep with the two goddesses, and that he finds no lasting satisfaction with Calypso, whom he finally rejects; and the possibility of a romantic entanglement with the susceptible Nausicaa is firmly avoided, to the disappointment of some modern readers.[15]

(b) Odysseus in the Odyssey

The hero of the *Odyssey*, then, is a complex personality who can be presented in very different guises: he has been seen as hero and anti-hero, philosophic sage and scheming crook, wise statesman and cynical opportunist, Everyman and Renaissance *uomo universale*.[16] Most readers of Homer will end up firmly preferring either Achilles or Odysseus as a character; it is perhaps a tribute to the powers of the poet or poets that few can be altogether neutral here. A full account of Odysseus' experiences and character would be out of place here, but two aspects not already discussed warrant fuller treatment: his development within the poem, and his career in comparison with that of Achilles.[17]

---

[15] W. J. Woodhouse, *The composition of Homer's Odyssey* (Oxford 1930) 64; contrast W. B. Stanford, *The Ulysses theme* (Oxford 1964) ch. 4, J. Griffin, *Homer on life and death* (Oxford 1980) 61–4.

[16] See esp. Stanford, *The Ulysses theme*, an absorbing and humane study. Also W. B. Stanford and J. V. Luce, *The quest for Ulysses* (London 1974); B. Rubens and O. Taplin, *An Odyssey round Odysseus* (London 1989), 'popular' but excellently illustrated.

[17] On the former topic I summarise here a view presented more fully in my paper in *J.H.S.* 106 (1986); see further K. Reinhardt, *Tradition und Geist* (Göttingen 1960) 47–124. On the latter see also A. Edwards, *Achilles in the Odyssey* (Meisenheim am Glan 1985); E. K. Borthwick, 'Odyssean elements in the *Iliad*' (inaugural lecture, Edinburgh 1983). G. Nagy, *The best of the Achaeans* (Baltimore 1979) discusses the contrast on a more general level.

As the one who devised the Wooden Horse, Odysseus is often styled 'the sacker of cities' (already at *Iliad* 2.278, 10.363; *Od.* 9.504 and seven other places in the poem). He departs from Troy apparently at the peak of his success, with glory and loot. But in his subsequent wanderings he loses treasure, ships, and in the end all his comrades in a series of disasters, some incidental or natural, some involving divine retribution. The poem is structured in such a way that Odysseus when he first appears is at the nadir of his fortunes, forgotten and isolated, imprisoned by Calypso on an island far from the known world. The poem charts his progress from this position of hopelessness and despondency, through further storm-tossed voyaging, through the restoring hospitality of the unheroic but admiring Phaeacians, to the point where, disguised as a beggar in his own land, he still appears helpless and impoverished but is in fact steadily regaining his rightful role of authority and strength. His apparent poverty and insignificance, mocked by the thoughtless suitors, in fact conceal terrible power and growing anger.

The tribulations of Odysseus are not inexplicable or meaningless hardships. Though perhaps originally independent episodes, his adventures have been arranged in an intelligible sequence and integrated in the moral and theological scheme of the poem. Throughout the *Odyssey* characters receive warnings from divine or authoritative sources: Aegisthus from Hermes, the suitors from Theoclymenus and Odysseus himself, and so forth; to forget or ignore such warnings is regularly disastrous. During the wanderings Odysseus or his men often ignore warnings or obey them only in part. In the ninth book, the encounter with the Cyclops, Odysseus fails to withdraw to safety before the giant appears, despite the urging of his companions; later, he insists on taunting the blinded monster, exulting in his victory and foolishly revealing his identity, which he had previously cloaked with the ingenious alias of 'No-man' (9.366–70, 502–5). His arrogance here is punished by the relentless persecution of Poseidon, the monster's father; not until he returns to Ithaca is Odysseus finally immune from his wrath. During his subsequent experiences Odysseus must learn to contain his heroic impulses, to suppress such spontaneous but ill-judged outspokenness, to observe the limits imposed by divine warnings. The change in his attitudes is movingly illustrated in Scheria, where he responds to the song recounting his exploits at Troy not with gratification but with grief –

sorrow for his own sufferings and those of his companions, perhaps also pity for those who suffered and died there on the Trojan side (8.521–31). Similarly in Ithaca, his pious cautioning of Eurycleia, after the slaughter is completed, should be contrasted with his unthinking mockery of the Cyclops in book 9. Eurycleia, about to utter a yell of triumph, is restrained by her master's sober words:

ἐν θυμῶι, γρηῦ, χαῖρε καὶ ἴσχεο μηδ' ὀλόλυζε.
οὐχ ὁσίη κταμένοισιν ἐπ' ἀνδράσιν εὐχετάασθαι.
τούσδε δὲ μοῖρ' ἐδάμασσε θεῶν καὶ σχέτλια ἔργα.
οὔ τινα γὰρ τίεσκον ἐπιχθονίων ἀνθρώπων,
οὐ κακὸν οὐδὲ μὲν ἐσθλόν, ὅτις σφέας εἰσαφίκοιτο.
τῶ καὶ ἀτασθαλίηισιν ἀεικέα πότμον ἐπέσπον.   (22.411–16)

'Old woman, let all rejoicing rest in your heart. Do not go too far, utter no cry of exultation. Vaunting over men slain is an impious thing. These men have perished thanks to the will of the gods and their own evil deeds, for they honoured no man, good or bad, who came their way. So by their own rash folly have they brought this end upon themselves.'

From the buccaneering hero of the earliest wanderings, there emerges a more sombre and authoritative figure. The man who was persecuted by the gods in the first half of the poem now exacts the punishment ordained by the gods from the offending suitors. His experiences have taught him the insecurity of human fortune – even that of the victors in the greatest war the Greek world had known. This theme runs through all his false tales in the second half of the poem; within the narrative proper, it is exemplified in the case of Eumaeus, a nobleman kidnapped as an infant and sold into slavery (15.390–484), as well as by the disasters that befall so many of Odysseus' fellow Greeks.

The insight Odysseus has gained is powerfully communicated in his speech of warning to the decent suitor Amphinomus (18.125–50), a speech which has echoes and resonances in other speeches by himself, Penelope and others in the later books (19.71–88, 328–34, with nn.). The ethos of these speeches, that man's mortality and uncertain hold upon the future should make one refrain from cruelty or arrogance, is an important part of the moral teaching of the *Odyssey*. Throughout, the poet recognises, and makes us realise, that human beings have certain needs and duties towards one another which they neglect at their peril. To abuse or use violence against an unprotected stranger, as the suitors bully Odysseus, is to lower oneself to the level of sub-human creatures such as the Cyclops or the Laestrygonians; and furthermore, even from a prudential point of view, those who abandon compassion and generosity can expect none in return. Hence the significance which attaches to the host–guest relationship in the poem, above all when the guest is unknown or defenceless: the obligations of guest-friendship are scrupulously and warmly observed by Nestor, Menelaus, the Phaeacians, Eumaeus (who despite his poverty generously entertains the beggar Odysseus) and Penelope, but they are callously ignored by the Cyclops, the Laestrygonians and of course the suitors. Nor is the hero himself, at first or ever, solely a moral paradigm: he himself has been punished for his savage treatment and heartless, perhaps blasphemous, abuse of the Cyclops, for whom the poet in the end even arouses our sympathy, in the touching scene with the ram (9.444–61).

These lessons are not so remote from the morality implicit in the last book of the *Iliad*. There too, the hero reaches a clearer insight into his own life and comes to recognise the limitations and destructiveness of his own selfish and self-absorbed anger. There too, the hero's mature reflections include the acknowledgement that he is not alone, that suffering and bereavement are part of the human lot, and that the conventional 'heroic' response, to strike out, win an immediate victory and seek revenge, is not the answer to everything. If we find Achilles' recognition of these truths more intensely tragic, that is partly because it is concentrated in a single scene and set of actions, his pity and magnanimity towards Priam; moreover, that scene is dominated by the imminent prospect of death for both men. In the *Odyssey*, the hero's development is more elusive, and its moral aspect can be discerned in several different parts of the poem, but the change is none the less real, and is paralleled by the way in which Odysseus from book 13 onward takes the initiative and controls the action.

The comparison between Odysseus and Achilles has further implications for this account of the hero of the *Odyssey*. The *Iliad* and the *Odyssey* can be seen as presenting two alternative heroic ideals: the greatness and the glory of the warrior doomed to an early death, and the endurance and wisdom of the successful strategist and schemer, who survives against all the odds and wins through in the end. In many passages of both epics Odysseus' form of heroism, which involves deceit, disguise and self-discipline, is contrasted with the behaviour of other heroes; and the outcome too is a contrast, for the *Odyssey* has a happy ending whereas by the end of the *Iliad* the outlook is bleak and tragic. By book 24 of the *Iliad* Achilles knows that he will not live to see the taking of Troy, that he will never return to Greece or see his aged father again. He imagines Peleus alone and persecuted by his neighbours, without the protection that he, Achilles, should be providing (*Il.* 16.15–16, 18.330–2, 19.321–5, and esp. 24.534–42).

In book 11 of the *Odyssey* Odysseus visits the land of the dead, encounters the ghosts of Agamemnon, Achilles and Ajax, and converses with them, the living man with the dead. The survivor, the man who has still a future, greets the men who have lost their future, who now spend their days absorbed in and eternally brooding on their past (cf. 24.23–98). In a number of ways these encounters shed light on Odysseus' own past and future. The exchange with Agamemnon, for example, in which the ghost of the king describes how he was tricked and murdered by Clytemnestra and her lover, includes many elements of contrast with Odysseus' career: the treacherous Clytemnestra is to be contrasted with the faithful Penelope, a motif which runs through the whole poem.[18]

Still more significant is the famous meeting with Achilles. The hero of the *Iliad* greets his old comrade with a certain wry humour, showing reluctant admiration of his ingenuity: 'you clever devil, what will you be up to next, now that you've even found your way down here?' (11.474–5, loosely paraphrased). Odysseus explains, not without a note of pessimistic self-pity, that he has still not come near Greece (in fact an exaggeration: see 10.29), and his next words combine flattery and envy of Achilles:

> 'But you, Achilles – no man has been more blessed than you in days past, or will be in days to come; for before you died we Greeks honoured you like a god, and now in this place you are a great lord among the dead. No, do not feel sorrow in your death, Achilles.'

[18] See S. West in the Oxford *Odyssey* 1 60; U. Hölscher, in *Festschrift R. Alewyn* (Cologne–Graz 1967) 1–16; A. F. Garvie's commentary on Aeschylus' *Choephori* (Oxford 1986) ix–xiii.

Thus I spoke, but at once he answered: 'Odysseus, do not gloss over death to me. I would rather be alive as a worker on the land, slaving as a poor serf for another, a man with no property and livelihood, than be king over all the lifeless dead. But tell me now all that you know of my princely son ... and tell me also what news you have of noble Peleus. Is he still honoured among the thronging Myrmidons, or do they despise him in Hellas and Phthia, because old age fetters his limbs? If only I might return to help him, return to the sunlight as I once was, when in the wide land of Troy I fought for the Argives and slew the bravest of the enemy host. If in that manner I might return, even for a brief moment, to my father's house, then I would make my strength and my unapproachable hands hateful to any man who does him violence or thrusts him from his proper place of honour.'

(Od. 11.482–503)

Here, as in the *Iliad*, the two heroes are contrasted, but the situation is very different. Odysseus is now the one who praises the heroic ideal, whereas Achilles, disillusioned by his short life and now by death, recognises the value of life on any terms, even a life without glory. Achilles grieves for his father and worries about him here, as in the *Iliad*; but he cannot help or defend him now. This is what Achilles wishes he could do, but it is also what Odysseus can and will do for his own father Laertes, and for his whole family. The men of violence, whom Achilles imagines dishonouring his father,[19] correspond to the suitors, who ravage Odysseus' lands and seek to steal his wife and throne. Achilles also feels sorrow at his separation from his son Neoptolemus; again, this recalls the *Iliad*, in which he thought of him as well as Peleus when he knew that he must die (19.326–37), and again there is a contrast with Odysseus, who will be reunited with his son as well as his father.

At the same time, however, we should not go too far and say that Achilles now wholly rejects the ideals of honour and heroic warfare that he valued in life. In *Odyssey* 11 as in the *Iliad*, there is a conflict of emotion in Achilles: on the one hand, the hero must seek renown, and glory is of supreme importance; yet on the other hand, what price

---

[19] Cf. Eur. *Troades* 1126–8 and the scholia *ad loc.*, for the legend that Peleus was driven into exile (perhaps based on this passage).

glory, if one is rewarded only with a short life, dying alone and sepa-
rated from one's home and family? It is this conflict that finds its fullest
expression in book 9 of the *Iliad* and its most disillusioned form in book
24. Nevertheless, Achilles will fight again after book 24, and will die in
battle and be buried in heroic style (cf. *Od.* 24.36–94); his disillusion-
ment does not lead him to abandon his way of life, even though he now
has doubts about its value. So too in the *Odyssey* he dismisses Odysseus'
praises as irrelevant, but still treasures the memory of his own prowess
and hopes that his son is as great as he once was. When Odysseus
assures him of Neoptolemus' successes at Troy, Achilles departs full of
pleasure and pride (*Od.* 11.540).[20]

Similarly, it is these same qualities of martial prowess and heroic
violence that make it possible for Odysseus to restore his kingdom to
order. It is a victory by force of arms, not a war won by diplomacy
(though peaceful counsels prevail in the closing lines of the poem). In
the *Odyssey* the heroic spirit of the *Iliad* is not dead or superseded, but it
is perhaps shown as less than all-important. War and glory are not ends
in themselves: the insights of the final book of the *Iliad* are further
explored and developed. Odysseus, like Achilles there, has reservations
about a glorious death – not that he would refuse it if it were necessary,
but he prefers to live, to survive, often by means which involve more
deception, self-abasement, even humiliation, than Achilles or Ajax
could ever have borne. He is often contrasted with them in this as in
other respects by later writers (e.g. Pind. *Nem.* 7.20–31, 8.23–8; Pl.
Hipp. Min. 363a–365c; Hor. *Odes* 4.6). As Horace remarked, one can
hardly imagine Achilles crouching inside the Wooden Horse.

It is not the case, then, that honour or renown have no value or have
changed their meaning in the *Odyssey*, but rather that the hero's eyes
are less firmly fixed upon them, his heart less inflexibly set on winning
glory for himself and the esteem of others. The ideals of peace, home,
domestic and civil harmony, which run through the *Odyssey* make it
not only a different, but almost an opposite kind of epic compared with
the *Iliad*. Achilles' great choice was a glorious death, Odysseus' is a
mortal life (when he refuses the offer of immortality from Calypso).
Achilles' story is that of a man increasingly isolated from his own soci-
ety, for even at the end of the wrath he still sits and dines apart from

---

[20] For further nuances in this scene see esp. Edwards, *Achilles* 47–69.

the rest of the host. The *Odyssey* tells of a man and wife reunited, a family and kingdom restored to peace and order. The heroic yields place to the domestic and civic, the warrior to the bringer of peace and prosperity. It is tempting to suppose that this confrontation of two opposite ways of life, of two different types of epic, is no accident: that, in short, the *Odyssey* is the first commentary on – and criticism of – the *Iliad*.

3. PENELOPE

(a) Penelope and Telemachus in earlier books

Homer's art of characterisation is not primitive or superficial, and his subtlety has sometimes been underestimated by those who deny that Penelope is a coherent and consistent personality. In the earlier books of the poem the main points are already made: she is devoted to Odysseus' memory and absorbed in her grief; she is clever and resourceful (as shown by the trick of the web), but her delaying tactics are exhausted; her relations with Telemachus are uneasy; and her role in the action, as for many books to come, is essentially passive, ordered around and dominated by others. In these earlier scenes, however, these points are made in a simpler way, whereas the presentation of the queen in later books is richer and in some ways more enigmatic.

Much has been written about the constitutional position in Ithaca.[21] It seems likely that, as with the question of Agamemnon's status in the *Iliad*,[22] the situation is deliberately left ill-defined. The suitors clearly hope and expect that the one who wins Penelope will also win the throne of Ithaca. Although in book 22, confronted by the vengeful Odysseus, Eurymachus attributes this design to Antinous alone (22.45–59), his motive of self-protection here is obvious, and his hypocrisy is familiar from earlier scenes (esp. 16.434–48). Telemachus is assured, however untruthfully, that no-one will try to usurp his place in his own household (1.402–4), but it seems plain that, even though he may be

---

[21] See e.g. M. I. Finley, *The world of Odysseus* (2nd edn, London 1978) 87–95. On the wider issues see A. M. Snodgrass, 'An historical Homeric society?', *J.H.S.* 94 (1974) 114–25; I. Morris, *Cl. Ant.* 5 (1986) 81–138.

[22] O. Taplin, in *Characterization and individuality in Greek literature*, ed. C. B. R. Pelling (Oxford 1990) 60–70.

the rightful heir, he cannot succeed to the throne without dispute unless he shows more authority and strength of character than he does in the assembly of book 2. The suitors themselves are described as βασιλῆες ('kings'), like Alcinous' elders; probably we are to assume that in the past Odysseus' line reigned without opposition, but that there is now a power vacuum. Penelope's crucial position as desirable consort is essential to the plot, and speculation about regency or vestiges of matriarchal rule is inappropriate.

Telemachus' pessimism in the earlier books of the poem is closely linked with his suspicion of his mother. He believes that she is unfaithful to Odysseus' memory and wishes to remarry; but he also feels that it would be wrong for him to expel her or force her to return to her father's house against her will (2.130–7). His distrust of her is strikingly revealed in his reply to Athene, who asks if he is indeed Odysseus' son: 'stranger, I shall tell you the truth. My mother certainly says I am his son, but for my part I really don't know. No man yet could ever tell of his parentage' (1.214–6). Penelope on her side is unhappily aware of his suspicion and uncertain how to respond. In book 1, when she descends to rebuke the minstrel, Telemachus replies sharply to her, and she is startled by his assertion of authority (1.328–64): here his speech is described by the poet as 'intelligent' (πεπνυμένον), but it is still meant to seem somewhat abrupt and high-handed. In book 2, he refrains from telling his mother of his journey overseas, for fear she may cry (373–6): again, shrewdness and sense may also be hurtful, as her eventual distress shows (4.703–5, 727–34). When we rejoin him in Sparta in book 15 he is sleeping uneasily, and Athene, in order to accelerate his return to Ithaca, sends him a deceptive warning to the effect that Penelope's relatives are urging her to marry the loathsome Eurymachus: 'you know what a woman's heart is like ... she no longer thinks of her children, or asks after her dear dead husband ...' (15.10–23). This is untrue and unfair, but it plays on Telemachus' own doubts (16.68–77, 126–7). This vision explains Telemachus' curtness and unfriendliness when he next meets his mother (17.36–60; 17.101–6 show that Penelope is hurt by his bluntness).

In book 19, in conversation with Odysseus, Penelope mentions her anxiety about Telemachus' hostility to her (157–61, 524–34), and much pathos and irony is made of their mutual misunderstanding. In book 21, Telemachus sends Penelope off to her room, so that the contest of the bow may proceed to its deadly conclusion (343–58). She departs astonished and distressed, to cry herself to sleep upstairs: again, his speech (which echoes that of book 1) is described as 'intelligent', but again his tone seems unduly assertive. Here, however, his intelligence is partly demonstrated by his ability to deceive. This episode plays yet another variation on the theme of misunderstanding, for Telemachus is concerned only to protect her and get her safely out of the way, but since Penelope does not know this, his action seems a pointless and offensive attempt on his part to exert his masculine authority. The theme reaches its conclusion in book 23, where Telemachus bursts out in indignation at his mother, reproaching her for her slowness in acknowledging Odysseus' identity: μῆτερ ἐμή, δύσμητερ ('Mother mine, no true mother', 23.97) – the furthest he has ever gone. Penelope and Odysseus in turn both gently reprove him and remind him that this encounter is for them to bring to its conclusion in their own way (23.104–16).

(b) Penelope in book 18

One passage not mentioned above calls for more extended treatment, namely the scene in book 18 in which Odysseus first sees Penelope after his arrival, though they do not yet converse. In that scene, Penelope, seized by a strange impulse in fact sent by Athene, descends to face Telemachus and the suitors, declares her intention to remarry, and reproaches her wooers for their failure to bring her gifts – a failure which, inflamed by passionate desire for her (212–3), they eagerly remedy. Few scenes have caused more critical controversy or confusion.[23] Discussion has centred particularly on Penelope's motives, on the apparent illogicality of her yielding at this point, and on Odysseus' reaction to her surrender (18.281–3):

ὣς φάτο, γήθησεν δὲ πολύτλας δῖος Ὀδυσσεύς,
οὕνεκα τῶν μὲν δῶρα παρέλκετο, θέλγε δὲ θυμὸν
μειλιχίοισ' ἐπέεσσι, νόος δέ οἱ ἄλλα μενοίνα.

[23] Page, Homeric Odyssey 124–5; more valuable, Fenik, Studies 116–20; U. Hölscher, Lebende Antike: Festschrift F. Sühnel, edd. H. Meller and H.-J. Zimmerman (1967) 27–33, and the later essay by the same author in Homer: tradition and invention, ed. B. Fenik (Leiden 1978) 51–67.

Thus she spoke, and the much-enduring noble Odysseus rejoiced, because she was winning gifts from them, and beguiling their minds with wheedling words, while her mind was set on other things.

It is important to be clear that at the beginning of this episode, the motives stated in lines 160–2 are those of Athene, not Penelope. The goddess inspires the queen to descend (previously her appearances had been voluntary and spontaneous), and to show herself to the suitors,

>   ... ὅπως πετάσειε μάλιστα
> θυμὸν μνηστήρων ἰδὲ τιμήεσσα γένοιτο
> μᾶλλον πρὸς πόσιός τε καὶ υἱέος ἢ πάρος ἦεν.   (18.160–2)

... so that she [Penelope] might particularly excite the hearts of the suitors and be honoured more than before by her husband and her son alike.

This is not what Penelope herself proposes to do; there is a gap, a discrepancy, between the divine will and the human instrument. Hence the 'pointless' (ἀχρεῖον) laugh that Penelope utters at line 163; hence also her own vagueness about her intentions. In 166 she says that she is going to warn Telemachus not to mingle with the suitors, whereas in 215–25 she reprimands him for permitting the fight between Odysseus and Irus. The contradiction shows her confusion. Further, Penelope refuses to adorn herself for the suitors' benefit, but Athene beautifies her, without her knowledge or consent, ἵνα μιν θησαίατ᾽ Ἀχαιοί ('so that the Achaeans would admire her', 191). This is clearly the same motive as in lines 160–2 (quoted above). Penelope, then, has no wish to seduce or dazzle the suitors with her beauty, but they nevertheless desire her all the more. Her own attitude to the suitors is unchanged: before she descends she prays that Artemis might slay her in her sleep (202–5), and even openly to the besotted suitors she makes plain the reluctance with which she confronts the prospect of marriage:

> νὺξ δ᾽ ἔσται, ὅτε δὴ στυγερὸς γάμος ἀντιβολήσει
> οὐλομένης ἐμέθεν, τῆς τε Ζεὺς ὄλβον ἀπήυρα.   (18.272–3)

'The night is drawing near, when hateful marriage will come upon a ruined woman, whose happiness Zeus has stolen from her.'

Why does Penelope choose to yield at this of all times, after years of faithful waiting, when Telemachus has told her that Odysseus is still alive (17.140–6), when hopeful signs and prophecies are arriving from all sides (esp. 17.155–61)? Again, in book 19, why does she, unprompted by Odysseus, propose the contest of the axes (19.570–81)? It would be a poor reply to say that the plot demands some such initiative to advance the action. The fuller poetic explanation emerges from the mood and speeches of Penelope and from what others have said of her. For twenty years she has waited, sinking steadily deeper into hopelessness and despair. Time and again she has been deceived by lying wanderers who bring alleged news of Odysseus. As Eumaeus told his disguised master:

> 'Old man, no roving traveller who comes here bearing news of my lord will be able to convince his wife and son. One vagrant after another comes here with his lies, just for the sake of bed and board, and with no desire to speak the truth. Yet when any such wanderer visits the land of Ithaca and sees my mistress and tells his deceptive tale, she receives him hospitably and kindly, questions him on every detail, indulging her grief until tears flow from her eyes [cf. 19.203–12, with n.] – such is a woman's way, when her husband has died in a far-off land.'   (14.122–30, cf. 361–89)

In book 19, as we shall see, Penelope's disillusionment and pessimism do not prevent her from listening to Odysseus, longing and praying, but they do prevent her from taking the final step, and believing his words, even when he swears an oath. Thus the characteristic pattern of omens ignored, assurances disregarded, is adapted to the special case of Penelope: her despair is greatest when she has most reason to hope.

Another factor which prompts her to yield is her concern about Telemachus. She is aware – cannot help being aware, after his recent expedition and shows of independence – that he is no longer a boy (18.175, 19.530), a fact that he himself is not slow to emphasise (18.229, 19.19n., 21.95).[24] She knows that the suitors have plotted to kill him, so far unsuccessfully (4.697–702, 16.409–33), and fears that they may try again (19.518–24, with n.). She believes that he resents her and wishes

---

[24] In general on the growth and maturing of Telemachus see H. W. Clarke, *A.J.P.* 84 (1963) 129–45.

the whole thing settled (19.159–61, 530–4). Her delaying tactics are now exhausted, with the trick of the web exposed. For the first time, she recounts an instruction that Odysseus had given her on his departure, in anticipation of his possible death overseas. If he failed to return before Telemachus' beard began to grow (that is, when his son came to manhood), she was to choose a new husband (18.257–71). This declaration, which is neither confirmed nor contradicted elsewhere in the poem, may be interpreted as a true account of Odysseus' parting, or a falsehood on Penelope's part (to save her own dignity?), or one inspired by Athene, or an *ad hoc* invention by the poet.[25] Within the world of the poem, it brings events to a head, reveals Penelope's anxiety about her son, and provides a further motive for the queen to yield at last despite her detestation of the suitors.

Odysseus, however, knows that Penelope's feelings are unchanged, and that her proposal to remarry is reluctantly made. He has received repeated assurance of her devotion from Athene (13.336–8, 379–81) and from Eumaeus (14.122–30, quoted above; cf. 17.554–5). The speech he has just heard his wife make, in bitter response to the suitors' odious flattery, has made her true feelings evident. Odysseus knows that she does not want the marriage of which she speaks, and is confident that he has returned in time to stop it; consequently he can take pleasure both in her fidelity and in the way that she extracts gifts from the suitors, so compensating for their depredations. Again Penelope's actions resemble her husband's, in acquiring gifts and wealth where she can. At the same time there is a dual irony, for Odysseus thinks that Penelope is craftily securing these gifts of her own accord, whereas in fact this is an added refinement of Athene's, and Penelope remains ignorant of her husband's presence and now has no hope of rescue from her wooers.[26] The provision of these gifts delights her husband but

[25] For such inventions cf. M. M. Willcock, *C.Q.* 24 (1964) 141–54, and *H.S.C.P.* 81 (1977) 41–53.

[26] The phrase νόος δέ οἱ ἄλλα μενοίνα ('her mind was set on other things') in 283 probably refers not to a particular plan Penelope has in mind (whatever Odysseus may think), but to the queen's passionate longing for Odysseus: that is, she is not reconciled to the marriage which she believes to be inevitable. Cf. Hölscher, in *Lebende Antike* (n. 23). The line echoes 13.381, in which Athene assured Odysseus of his wife's devotion. It also recalls 2.92, where Antinous complains of Penelope's postponement of her decision; but in book 2 it referred to Penelope's ingenuity (as with the web), whereas here it is Athene who orchestrates the deception, and Penelope's own devices are exhausted.

brings no true consolation to her. The scene also juxtaposes the self-control of Odysseus, seeing his wife at last after many years, with the oafish enthusiasm of the lustful suitors (18.212–13). The contrast between Penelope's miserable reluctance and her supreme desirability adds to the pitiful presentation of her ignorance.

(c) Penelope and Odysseus in book 19

Odysseus arrived at the palace at 17.260–347, disguised as a beggar by Athene's magical aid (on the extent of his transformation see 19.360, 380–1 nn.). Eumaeus sang his praises to Penelope, especially as a story-teller, and the queen, impressed by this account, summoned him to her presence, but Odysseus declined the interview at that point, out of caution and tact (17.507–90). In book 18 he witnessed her apparent surrender to the suitors without being seen or detected by his wife (see Section *b* above). In book 19, after Telemachus has retired, they converse together by the hearth, with only a few inattentive servants nearby (cf. 317, 601–2). The encounter between husband and wife has been long anticipated; we may well expect a recognition scene. But the poet frustrates our expectations, for the book ends with Penelope retiring to cry herself to sleep and with Odysseus still unrecognised by her; instead, the beggar has been detected by his old nurse, Eurycleia, during an interval in his conversation with Penelope.

The ironic art of the poet and the self-control of the hero are at their height here. Penelope, aware of the sympathy and sensitivity of her guest, becomes steadily more open with him. Having, as she supposes, tested and proved his honesty, she confides to him all her fears and doubts, asks his opinion of her mysterious dream (535–53), and requests his advice on whether or not to prepare the contest of the bow (571–81). Her intimacy with the beggar is further indicated by her mode of address: from ξεῖνε 'guest' (104, 124, 215, 253), she passes to ξεῖνε φίλε 'dear guest' (350), and after she has at first rejected his compliments to her (124–9), her praise of him grows more fulsome: 'if only this word of yours might find fulfilment …' (309); 'no man so wise has ever yet come to my house' (350–1); 'if only you were willing to sit in my halls and console me, sleep would never flow over my eyelids' (589–90). In the next book, she dreams that Odysseus has been with her, sleeping by her during the night (20.88–90, with n.).

Despite the sympathy which her guest offers, and the hopeful news he brings (300–7), despite even the obviously favourable dream, which hardly requires Odysseus' additional interpretation (555–8), Penelope still, as in book 18, can find no escape from her dilemma save in re-marriage. In book 18 she declared her intention to marry one of the suitors; here, she explains her method of choice. He who can string Odysseus' bow and perform the same feat that he could accomplish will be her husband. Instead of revealing himself to her or advising her to wait, Odysseus supports this plan, encouraging her to proceed, though adding that he is sure that Odysseus will come home before the suitors accomplish the test. Again, Penelope in her pessimism brushes this assurance aside (582–99).

Some modern interpreters of the *Odyssey* have found Penelope's be-haviour in this book so hard to comprehend that they have adopted the daring hypothesis that she does in some sense recognise her husband here, contrary to the surface meaning of the text.[27] Therefore, she pro-ceeds with the contest so as to offer Odysseus a chance to seize the bow (and, according to some, to 'win' her again). Critics differ on the ques-tion of how conscious this recognition is: according to some, she is fully aware of her husband's identity, and matches his cleverness with a sophisticated game of double-bluff; others see her intuition as vaguer, even subconscious; she suspects, but is not yet certain. A different ap-proach attributes the supposed illogicalities to the poet's imperfect ad-aptation of his sources: Homer, it is argued, knows a version in which Odysseus revealed himself to his wife in a scene very like this one, or in which she saw through his disguise and challenged him. In that hypothetical version, her surrender to the suitors was feigned, the result of a plot between her husband and herself. In other words, the oral poet has his different tales and variant versions, and in the complex process of large-scale composition he has blended various incompatible ele-ments, producing an uneasy hybrid.[28]

---

[27] P. W. Harsh, *A.J.P.* 71 (1950) 1–21 has been influential here; for varia-tions on this approach see A. Amory, in *Essays on the Odyssey*, ed. C. H. Taylor (Indiana 1963) 100–21; N. Austin, *Archery at the dark of the moon* (Berkeley, Los Angeles and London 1975) ch. 4, esp. 205–36; J. J. Winkler, *The constraints of desire* (New York and London 1990) 129–61.

[28] See Page, *Homeric Odyssey* esp. 124–5 for a fiercely analytical account along these lines. E. Schwartz, *Die Odyssee* (Munich 1924), cited in Fenik, *Studies* 164 n. 38, distinguished four different Penelopes, whom he assigned to his poets

The *Odyssey*, of course, must have had its sources (cf. 12.69–72; p. 2 above). It may indeed be true that in some earlier version of the tale Odysseus did reveal himself and conspire with his wife. The poet of the *Odyssey*, therefore, may be playing on the audience's expectations, their knowledge of such a tale, leading them to expect a recognition in this scene. But if Odysseus does not reveal himself to his wife in our *Odyssey*, this is a part of the poem's coherent design. We need no previous versions or layers, no subconscious recognitions, to make the scene between Odysseus and Penelope moving and significant.[29] The growth of Penelope's scepticism in the face of constant disappointment, her concern for her son's safety, her confusion in this period of strange signs and inexplicable impulses, have all been vividly set before us by the poet. On Odysseus' side, his ingrained reluctance to trust others, his compulsive preference to delay and bide his time, make it practically impossible for him to reveal his identity at this stage, even if he were sure that his wife could contain her joy and keep his secret. Husband and wife are alike in their suspicious and prudent natures: neither will completely trust and accept the other as yet. It remains true that there is a strong bond of affinity between them, of which Penelope is swiftly conscious. She speaks freely to the stranger, comments on his tact and understanding, thanks him for his advice. But always and consistently there is a final step, the step of recognition, which Penelope does not take; hence the intricate pathos and subtle ironies of their encounter, which other interpretations reduce to a forced and obscure guessing-game set by the poet to his audience. Nor will the critic who believes that Penelope does recognise Odysseus in this scene find it easy to explain away 20.61–82, the queen's grief-stricken prayer to Artemis, in which she longs for death, or 23.11–24, 59–68 (etc.), in which she greets with frank incredulity the news that her husband has returned.

It is a notorious fact that in book 24 of the *Odyssey* the ghost of the suitor Amphimedon, who recounts the events in Ithaca to the shade of Agamemnon, misrepresents the sequence of these events. He supposes

O, K, T and B, 'all different, and the later editions all bad' (Fenik, ibid.). For a more cautious and moderate position, but still allowing too much woolly-mindedness to the poet, see Griffin, *Homer: the Odyssey* 30–2.

[29]   In all essentials I am in agreement with C. Emlyn-Jones, *G.&R.* 31 (1984) 1–18. Good remarks also in H. Vester, *Gymn.* 75 (1968) 417–34; Fenik, *Studies* 39–47.

that Penelope did know her husband's identity, did conspire with him and plan the slaughter (24.127, 167–9). This apparent anomaly has been used in support of the theory that another version existed which presented this alternative sequence of events. This, however, is also what the suitors would expect a man to do. That Odysseus has not revealed himself to his wife after twenty years' absence is due to his supreme self-restraint: as Athene remarked (13.333–8), any *other* man would have been unable to keep himself from dashing off to see his wife right away. The suitors' brash and amorous reactions to Penelope's appearances have been previously contrasted with the sober self-discipline of the hero (18.212–13, 245–9; cf. 1.365–6, etc.). Amphimedon's misreading of the situation could, then, be a deliberate stroke of characterisation on the poet's part. Further, by alluding to a perhaps more familiar version, a hypothetical earlier *Odyssey*, the poet points to his own originality. Such a device is easily paralleled in later authors, notably Euripides (*Medea* 1301–5, *Phoenician Women* 748–52), but need not be regarded as impossible in 'oral' epic: the use and remoulding of the Meleager story in book 9 of the *Iliad* might provide a comparable example.[30]

In any case, it should be unnecessary to stress the poetic and dramatic advantages of the *Odyssey*'s presentation of events. In Euripides' plays of deception and recognition, the reunion between relations or lovers is commonly the high point, marked by lyric exultation and delight, and followed by a more down-to-earth discussion of what is to be done: a plotting scene in the *Electra*, a plan of escape in the *Iphigenia in Tauris* and the *Helen*. In the latter two dramas, there is no real difficulty in outwitting the naive barbarians, and the partners work cheerfully and successfully together to bring about a happy ending. In the *Odyssey*, Penelope plays only an unwitting and unhappy role in the deception, in conceiving the contest and producing the bow. Her continuing ignorance makes for multiple ironies, for we relish the blindness of the suitors even as we pity Penelope's. This also enables us to approve

[30] J. T. Kakridis, *Homeric researches* (Lund 1949) ch. 1 is the basic account; cf. M. M. Willcock, *Companion to the Iliad* (Chicago 1976) 106–10, for a summary; also J. March, *The creative poet* (*B.I.C.S.* Suppl. 49, 1987) 27–46. For later examples of such allusive reference see Pindar, *Ol.* 1.55 (retaining as an image the key detail from the tale rejected by Pindar); Virg. *Aen.* 4.421–3; *Ciris* 410 and 484–6, with Lyne's notes. For an interesting recent discussion of Amphimedon's misapprehension, see S. Goldhill, *Ramus* 17 (1988) 1–9.

and sympathise more warmly when she turns the tables on her crafty husband in book 23 (p. 12 above).

It is occasionally argued that Penelope rather enjoys the attentions of the suitors, and even that she would regret the return of her husband. Such interpretations usually lay heavy emphasis on Penelope's narration of her dream, in which she wept at the slaughter of her pet geese, who represent the suitors (19.541–3).[31] Despite the genuine difficulties of these lines, this interpretation should be vigorously rejected; it is a flagrant example of the critical tendency to assume that something more devious, ambiguous or disreputable must be more interesting and make better poetry than what is morally and poetically direct and simple. In no passage in which she addresses the suitors or speaks of them when they are absent does Penelope ever fail to use language that expresses hatred and contempt. In book 16, she confronts them to accuse them, correctly, of trying to murder her son, and is answered with the most odious hypocrisy and flattery. Throughout the poem, and not least in books 19 and 20, she remembers Odysseus with the deepest affection and loyalty; she weeps as she handles the bow, and whenever she thinks of him or what was his (21.55–6); when she faces the prospect of leaving his house, she knows that she will remember it always, even in her dreams (19.581 = 21.79). The warmth and depth of their mutual love is nowhere more wonderfully conveyed than in the two-ended simile which marks the moment when they embrace at last:

> Thus she spoke, and quickened in him the desire for tears. He wept as he held the true-hearted wife in whom his soul took delight. As land is welcome to shipwrecked sailors swimming, when out at sea Poseidon has struck their well-built vessel, as it was driven by wind and massed waves, and only a few have escaped to land from the grey sea by swimming, their bodies encrusted with thick brine – and gratefully they welcome their first step on the land, after escaping from misfortune – so welcome to her was the husband she kept her gaze upon, and her white arms around his neck even now would not let him go.   (23.231–40)[32]

---

[31] See n. on 19.535–58; also, e.g., J. Russo, *A.J.P.* 103 (1982) 9; A. H. Rankin, *Helikon* 2 (1962) 617–24.

[32] On the simile (which echoes Odysseus' experiences and complements an earlier simile at 5.394–9) see C. Moulton, *Similes in the Homeric poems* (Göttingen 1977) 128–9.

Those who would prefer to exchange this picture of simplicity and loving goodness for the cynical portrayal of Penelope in Horace's *Satires* (2.5.75–83) or in Nicolas Rowe's *Ulysses* may be left to spin whatever distorted images of Homer's greater and nobler poem they find most congenial.[33]

4. TRANSMISSION AND TECHNIQUE

(a) The poem's origins and transmission

In ancient times the *Iliad* and the *Odyssey* were both almost universally[34] considered the work of Homer, a poet of genius, often thought to have been blind, who was said to have lived in various parts of the Eastern Mediterranean, particularly on the island of Chios, at any time between the Fall of Troy (traditionally placed in what is for us the twelfth century B.C.) and the historical period of Greece (from about 700 B.C. onwards). But even the name 'Homer' is of late occurrence, and it is clear that no later Greek writer knew much, if anything, about the poet who bore this name, or about the circumstances and tradition in which the poems were composed. The investigation of the enigma of Homer is traditionally labelled 'The Homeric Question'.[35] Modern attempts to answer this question effectively began with F. A. Wolf's *Prolegomena ad Homerum* (1795),[36] and the debate has generated doubts and dilemmas unknown to ancient critics: not only the question of whether the same poet composed both epics, but questions concerning the relation between oral composition and literate transmission, between the continuum of oral tradition and an individual poet's originality .

There are good reasons, some of which will be discussed further be-

---

[33] On the former see N. Rudd's treatment in *The satires of Horace* (Cambridge 1966) 222–42; on the latter, Stanford, *Ulysses theme* 194.

[34] For the minority view of the separatists, see R. Pfeiffer, *History of Classical Scholarship* I (Oxford 1968) 230 n. 7.

[35] For surveys see J. A. Davison in Wace and Stubbings, *Companion* 234–65; Adam Parry in Milman Parry, *The Making of Homeric Verse* (Oxford 1971) introd.; H. W. Clarke, *Homer's readers* (London and Toronto 1981).

[36] Now available in translation with notes, by A. Grafton, G. W. Most, J. E. G. Zetzel (Princeton 1985; corrected reprint, 1988); see the review by M. D. Reeve, *J.H.S.* 108 (1988) 219–21.

low (Section *b*), for supposing that the poet or poets of *Iliad* and *Odyssey* drew upon the resources of a long oral tradition of hexameter poetry. Whether they themselves composed orally throughout their lives or made some use of writing to assist their performances or to preserve their poems is hotly disputed. The poets Phemius and Demodocus in the *Odyssey* are obviously oral bards, attached to or approved by royalty; but this does not necessarily tell us much about Homer or the conditions under which he worked: the portraits of these bards may be archaistic and idealistic, just as Alcinous and Odysseus represent ideal kings. It does seem probable on internal grounds that the *Iliad* at least was composed for aristocratic audiences: the concentration on the upper classes, the contemptuous treatment of the masses, and the satirical portrait of Thersites, all point in this direction. The *Odyssey* with its sympathetic picture of slaves and peasant life might be thought to have a more universal appeal. But we must beware of assuming what many more recent parallels show to be false, that poorer or lower-class audiences cannot enjoy or appreciate poetry dealing primarily with their superiors in rank and power. There is an ideological slant to the poems, in that they support aristocratic values and idealise royal rule: but this is as much a model for aristocrats to follow as propaganda in support of their rule. The Homeric poems may, then, be composed primarily for royalty and courts, but their audiences need not have been exclusively aristocratic.

The poems' place of composition is impossible to determine. Ionia or the islands (Chios included) have a strong claim, particularly in view of the dominance of Ionian dialect in the linguistic mixture of the text. But alternative hypotheses are possible,[37] and the poems were in any case soon famous throughout the Greek-speaking world. The date of composition is traditionally given as *c.* 750 B.C. for the *Iliad*, perhaps a little later (even 700?) for the *Odyssey*. Many of the arguments for these dates are indecisive. (1) There are similarities of language or subject-matter in poets firmly assigned to the seventh century (e.g. Archilochus, Tyrtaeus, Callinus, Mimnermus). This argument is weak because the poets in question may be drawing on epic poetry but not necessarily on Homer. Only with Alcman and Alcaeus in the late 600s do we seem to find imitations which beyond reasonable doubt draw on the Hom-

---

[37] Cf. the daring construction of M. L. West, *J.H.S.* 108 (1988) 151–72.

eric poems themselves.[38] (2) Similar arguments apply to the appearance of 'Homeric' episodes in artistic representations from around the mid-600s B.C., especially on pottery.[39] Nevertheless, the popularity of the Cyclops-episode in art from *c.* 670 may owe something to wider knowledge of the *Odyssey* as we have it. (3) It is argued that the ignorance of the Greeks of the classical period about Homer's date, origins and biography shows that he must have been a very remote figure, earlier than other archaic poets such as Hesiod (flor. between 730 and 680). But what we know about Hesiod, for one, comes almost entirely from his poems; the anonymity of the epic poet means that we have no access to Homer's biography through his works. Nevertheless, this argument may be allowed some weight, and no-one, presumably, would want to push Homer later than about 600.[40] (4) The poems appear to include references to artefacts and institutions (such as hoplite fighting tactics, introduced in their full form *c.* 675) which can be tentatively dated by archaeology or historical data. Here again caution is needed because of the changing views of archaeologists and the possibility of small-scale 'local' interpolation.[41] One element which seems more decisive than most is the *Odyssey*'s interest in Egypt: it is reasonable to

[38] Alcman, *PMG* 80 (cf. *Od.* 10) and 77 (cf. *Il.* 3.39, 13.769); Alcaeus fr. 44 L–P (cf. *Il.* 1.495–502). On the general point see J. A. Davison, *Eranos* 53 (1955) 125–40, reprinted in his *From Archilochus to Pindar* (London 1968).

[39] H. Friis Johansen, *The Iliad and early Greek art* (Copenhagen 1967); K. Schefold, *Myth and legend in early Greek art* (Eng. tr. London 1966). On the *Odyssey* in particular see F. Brommer, *Odysseus* (Darmstadt 1983), and O. Touchefeu-Meynier, *Thèmes odysséens dans l'art antique* (Paris 1968).

[40] Though see M. L. West, *Hesiod. Works and days* (Oxford 1978) 60–1.

[41] A very sceptical approach to such arguments is adopted by G. S. Kirk, *The Iliad: a commentary* I (Cambridge 1985) 7–10. See also his earlier paper 'Objective dating criteria in Homer', *Mus. Helv.* 17 (1960) 189–205 = Kirk (ed.), *The language and background of Homer* (Cambridge 1964) 174–90. The specific case of alleged hoplite tactics has been treated with considerable scepticism by J. Latacz, *Kampfparänese, Kampfdarstellung und Kampfwirklichkeit* (*Zetemata* 66, Munich 1977) 63–6, who is followed (so Dr Richardson informs me) by R. Janko in his forthcoming volume of the Cambridge *Iliad* Commentary. For two other recent contributions, both concerning Achilles' speech in *Iliad* 9, see W. Burkert, *W.S.* 10 (1978) 5–21 (who argues that the reference to the vast wealth of Egyptian Thebes in 9.381–4 dates the passage post-715 or even post-663 B.C., when the city was sacked); C. Morgan, *Athletes and oracles* (Cambridge 1990) 106ff. (on the reference to the wealth of Delphi at 9.404–5 – hardly before *c.* 700 B.C.?).

associate this with increased Greek contact with the country, especially in the reign of Psammetichus I (663–610).[42] This suggests that the traditional date for the *Odyssey* at any rate is too early; on the other side it might be pointed out that the *Odyssey*-poet's actual knowledge of Egypt is remarkably hazy.[43]

The earliest reference to 'Homer' appears to be from the seventh-century poet Callinus of Sparta, who is said by Pausanias to have attributed a *Thebaid* to Homer (Paus. 9.9.5 = Callinus fr. 6 West). Unfortunately we do not have the original words of Callinus and so cannot judge whether Pausanias' paraphrase is adequate.[44] After that it is hard to find firm ground for another century, until Theagenes of Rhegium (*c.* 525 B.C.) is said to have written an allegorical commentary on *Iliad* 21 (the battle of the Gods), and the Pre-Socratic thinkers Xenophanes (born *c.* 560?) and Heraclitus (flor. *c.* 500) criticised the Homeric myths.

More important and more controversial is the so-called Pisistratean recension. Unless all references to this are pure fiction (as has not uncommonly been maintained), the Athenian tyrant Pisistratus (died in 527), or his son Hipparchus (died 514), or both, instituted a formal procedure at the Athenian Panathenaic festival whereby the Homeric poems were recited by a series of rhapsodes, each taking up where the last had left off, presumably over a period of days.[45] If the fragmentary references to this innovation preserve a genuine tradition, then there must have been a written text of both poems available or compiled at Athens in the later sixth century. We need not suppose that all subsequent texts came to depend on this Athenian edition, but the period of Pisistratus and his sons marks the firm terminus before which the Homeric poems must have been composed and in which they were

[42] See generally A. B. Lloyd, *Herodotus Book II: introduction* (Leiden 1975) ch. 1, with further bibliography.

[43] Cf. S. West in the Oxford *Odyssey* 1 (Oxford 1988) 65.

[44] Similarly questionable is the alleged reference in Archil. 303 West; Stesich. *PMG* 192 need not have referred to Homer; Hes. fr. 357 M–W is surely spurious.

[45] The most important testimony is Plato [?], *Hipparchus* 228b; see also Isoc. *Panegyr.* 159, Lycurg. *Leocr.* 102, Cicero, *De oratore* 3.137. See J. A. Davison, *T.A.P.A.* 91 (1960) 23–47. For differing views on what this evidence shows, see R. Merkelbach, *Rh.M.* 95 (1952) 23–47; S. West, Oxford *Odyssey* 1 36–9; M. S. Jensen, *The Homeric question and the oral-formulaic theory* (Copenhagen 1980), who reprints the evidence in full on pp. 207–26.

committed to writing if they were not written down before. Thereafter the history of the transmission of the Homeric texts is more comparable to the normal patterns of corruption and divergence found in the history of (for instance) the text of Euripides. What makes the Homeric question so much more complex is our uncertainty about the period between the lifetime of the poet and the institutionalising of his work by the Pisistratid family. Depending on the date of 'Homer', and making allowances for the long reign of the Pisistratids (Pisistratus first having seized power *c.* 561), we are dealing with an intervening period of transmission which could be as long as two centuries or as short as 70 or 80 years. In that period did the Homeric poems grow or change, or merge into the monumental wholes they are today? Were they transmitted orally or in writing or both? Were they expanded, edited or adapted by successors or disciples of 'Homer', or were they recognised at once as masterpieces, and faithfully preserved? We simply do not know.

A watershed in the history of the Homeric question can be placed at about the middle of the twentieth century, with the emergence of the developed theory of Homer as oral poetry, propounded above all by Milman Parry.[46] Earlier discussion tended to assume the existence of a written text from the beginning. The debate begun by Wolf divided Homeric scholars into two camps: the 'analysts', those who broke each of the poems up (ἀναλύειν) into separate layers or sections by different poets (usually on the basis of logical or linguistic or stylistic inconsistencies); and the 'unitarians', who defended the consistency and unity of the works as they stood (and often also maintained they were both by the same poet).[47] The procedure of the analysts was not as wantonly destructive or negative as it might sound. By stripping away later and inferior passages, they sought to recover the earliest and noblest poem, the 'original' *Iliad* or *Odyssey* which had, they supposed, been elabo-

---

[46] Parry's articles are collected in *The making of Homeric verse* (Oxford 1971), edited with a superb introduction by his son. Parry's published papers range from 1928 to 1935, the year he died, but it took some time for his work to have its full impact.

[47] For a helpful account of these debates see E. R. Dodds, in *The language and background of Homer*, ed. G. S. Kirk (Cambridge 1964) 1–21 (=*Fifty years and twelve of classical scholarship*, ed. M. Platnauer (Oxford 1968) 1–17, 31–5). Also Clarke, *Homer's readers* 156–224.

rated or rehashed by the successors of 'Homer'. By contrast, the unitarians tended to over-react and to defend any part of the Homeric corpus at any cost. Both sides frequently exaggerated the certainty of their conclusions.

Perhaps the most important contribution of Parry and the oralists was to make clear that the Homeric poems did not simply originate with one poet or several at an identifiable time in (say) the second half of the eighth century: they had their roots in several centuries of poetic composition, and used stories, characters and formulae which had been used by generations of poets before them. The proof of this was above all linguistic: by analysis of the language of Homer, Parry and others have shown that it is a poetic language, incorporating elements from different dialects and different periods (just as the social and cultural setting of the poems includes elements from different stages of Mediterranean society); and by analysis of the repeated formulae in particular, Parry established that the poetic language of the epics could not have been devised by a single poet or a single generation: it formed a medium which must have been refined and developed by many hands. Homer, of whom Alexander Pope had written that he 'is universally allow'd to have had the greatest invention of any writer whatever', was shown to be a profoundly traditional artist. Rather than being the first and greatest of all poets, he was seen to be composing with a long line of poets behind him; perhaps he was at the mid-point of the great tradition of oral poetry, or perhaps the *Iliad* and *Odyssey* represent its final flowering. At any rate, the problem of reading Homer was radically redefined: the challenge is to gauge Homer's use of the tradition, and to divine the nature of his superiority to his predecessors.

It is sometimes suggested that Parry's work has made the analytic-unitarian arguments obsolete. This is surely not so. We now have a clearer and more precise conception of oral tradition, but however much he may have drawn on earlier poems, there must have been a poet who conceived the overall form and plot of the *Odyssey* and composed a work which bore some relation to the text we have; if that *Odyssey* were immediately written down, we would call that the authentic *Odyssey* and regard any later additions or omissions as corruptions of the authentic text. What complicates the picture is our uncertainty of when the poem was committed to writing and by whom. Another factor that must be considered is the possibility that the poet himself repeatedly and throughout his career performed and modified his poem, changing or compressing or expanding it according to his own inclination or the tastes of the audience.[48] It is easy to see that the stories narrated in the Homeric poems could be told in a shorter, more straightforward way: in essence, all that the tale of Odysseus really demands is the homecoming and the slaughter[49] (though we must beware of equating 'simpler' or 'shorter' with 'earlier' or 'more authentic'). In that case we may hope that what has been preserved is the record of one of his best versions, even his greatest performance, but of course this cannot be guaranteed.

Milman Parry did not *prove* that the poets of the *Iliad* and *Odyssey* were oral bards themselves in the sense that they had no knowledge of writing and made no use of it.[50] The Greek alphabet was adapted from the Phoenician in the course of the eighth century,[51] but the chronology of this revolutionary change, like the dating of the Homeric poems themselves, is too uncertain for us to determine whether the availability of writing and of writing materials was itself a factor which influenced the creation of the poems.[52] To many scholars, perhaps over-impressed by the modern oral traditions studied by Parry and his followers, it has

[48] S. West, Oxford *Odyssey* I 43 points to the possibility (which has some textual basis) of a version involving a visit by Telemachus to Idomeneus in Crete; and P. Jones in his *Homer's Odyssey: a companion* (Bristol 1989) discusses a number of 'alternative routes' for which he finds (often persuasively) evidence in our surviving version.

[49] Cf. Dodds, in *Language and background* 2–5, on the 'concertina' form of the *Iliad*, in which, most obviously, the battle narratives could be quite severely reduced (especially those of books 12–15 and 17). He remarks, however, that the *Odyssey* 'has a much greater structural unity and lends itself less easily to a theory of gradual accretion round a nucleus' (p. 7). This is in response to analytic criticism, but is not irrelevant to discussion of the poem as the creation of an oral poet.

[50] See A. Parry's introd. to *MHV*, p. lxi n. 1, an important footnote which corrects Dodds and others on this point.

[51] See esp. L. H. Jeffery, *CAH* (2nd edn) III 1 (1982) 819ff.

[52] In the Homeric poems themselves there is only one reference to writing, and that is cryptic and deliberately sinister, concerning a message of the 'kill the bearer' variety (*Il.* 6.169–70 with 178). Elsewhere the heroes seem to be illiterate (as *Il.* 7.175–89 probably implies). In any case, the absence of books and letters from the heroic world is a natural archaism, and tells us nothing about the poet's own society.

seemed unlikely that the Homeric poet or poets themselves knew an alphabet or wrote down any part of their works, but these possibilities cannot be ruled out. Indeed, the very magnitude of the poems as they now stand would seem to argue against their being created in this form for performance alone. Neither poem could be recited (let alone sung) by a single poet or by a series of performers in less than two or three days. It is possible to hypothesise a festival occasion (like the later Panathenaea) at which the poems were ceremonially performed (though it seems more likely that the occasion would be adapted to such colossal poems rather than that poems of such inconvenient length should be created for serial performance). We should further admit that the modern audience's average tolerance of public entertainment is no adequate guide to what the ancient enthusiast for epic song would sit through with enjoyment: the fifth-century Athenians might watch sixteen plays in four days at the City Dionysia, and we may recall the devotion of modern audiences at Bayreuth. It is certainly possible to identify possible intervals, points at which the song might be suspended.[53] The difficulty is that there is so much which unifies the structure of both epics, which bridges possible breaks. What happened if an aristocrat could manage the first two days but missed the third? The analogy from fifth-century tragedy does not work here, as each tetralogy was performed in a single day. If, then, both poems are substantially the work of a single oral poet of the late eighth or early seventh century, I incline to agree with those who hold that the advent of writing offered him the opportunity of large-scale composition, on a scale beyond that of his predecessors or contemporaries or the poets within his own work (Demodocus, it will be recalled, sings three short songs in a single day). If, as I believe, the *Iliad* is by a different poet from the author of the *Odyssey*, we may suppose that the glorious example of the former inspired emulation, and that another bard accordingly made use of the new art of letters to preserve his own master work.

We have to accept that we shall never know the precise mechanism by which this was done. Did one poet (or two) become literate and

---

[53] Thus Oliver Taplin (in a forthcoming book entitled *Homeric soundings*, to be published by Oxford University Press) sees the *Iliad* as being performed in three days, with the breaks coming at the end of book 9 (the *Doloneia* being excised) and at 18.353. The *Odyssey* is simpler, with a strong break between the two halves, at 13.93.

make use of writing himself? Did he have the aid of a scribe or slave? Did a son or a disciple or loyal friend recognise the genius of the man who brought the tale of Achilles to perfection, and decide to memorise and record the great poem for himself and posterity? We cannot tell. One possible route of preservation which merits at least passing consideration is the 'guild' of poets known as the Homeridai or 'Sons of Homer', who claimed descent from the great poet and were based on Chios in classical times.[54] They are known to have existed by at least the late sixth century, and their prestige as interpreters of the poems does seem to imply that they were older than that. Here at least we have a possible channel by which the Homeric poems might have been studied and recorded even before the Pisistratids.

Nothing that has been said so far would rule out the possibility of interpolation, omission or corruption even after the poem was committed to writing. Hence analytical arguments are still advanced, although they need to be couched more cautiously and with a realisation of the special problems of oral poetry. Thus if inconsistent linguistic forms occur in different parts of the poem, it may be argued that this is not due to multiple authorship in the analytic sense, but results from the traditional diction of the poet, which includes elements from different dialects and periods. Similarly on the level of plot, there are passages which present contradictions or inconsistencies, 'problem' passages which used to be explained as interpolations, but in which we may prefer to see the oral poet combining motifs and collating different versions.[55] It would be very optimistic to suppose that in every respect the *Iliad* and the *Odyssey* are untouched by later additions on both a large and a small scale. But in many cases the arguments for later intrusion of material are weak, in others the counter-arguments are at least finely balanced. Each case must be assessed on its merits, but the

---

[54] See Pindar, *Nemean* 2.1–5 and scholia; Acusilaus, *FGrH* 2 F 2, Hellanicus 4 F 20; Pl. *Ion* 530d, *Rep.* 10 599e, Isoc. *Helen* 65. Modern discussion in T. W. Allen, *Homer: origins and transmission* (Oxford 1924) 42–50 (receptive to the ancient testimonies); D. Fehling, *Rh.M.* 122 (1979) 193–210 (radically sceptical).

[55] This approach is adopted with particular enthusiasm by P. Jones, *Homer's Odyssey: a companion* (Bristol 1989). But at times it may be too easy an explanation: inconcinnity and disturbing elements may occasionally be used deliberately, to surprise, misdirect or otherwise intrigue the reader. Cf. above, Section 3(*b*) on the complex scene in book 18. In general on 'false preparation' see O. Taplin, *The stagecraft of Aeschylus* (Oxford 1977) 94–6.

critic has a duty to bring to the debate not only detailed knowledge of the poem and its language, but also an appreciation of the poet's literary and thematic concerns. If, as has been suggested above, the possibility exists that the *Odyssey* is essentially as the master poet wished it to be, then our first task is to try to explain and appreciate it as it is; only later should we turn to the possibility of divergent sources or contradictory traditions prior to the poet and fuelling his imagination; and last of all to the analytical explanation, that difficulties are caused by later additions and re-editing. Such an approach may be criticised as unhistorical, but as we have seen, the 'historical' testimony for the genesis of the poems is too slender for us to base a critical method on external evidence or principles. The method recommended here is, I firmly believe, more faithful to the poetry.

(b) Formulae and the oral style

Any reader of Homer knows that the poet repeats himself. There are many lines and half-lines which recur in similar situations throughout both poems. Sometimes blocks of lines, even quite lengthy passages, may be repeated. The standard line for daybreak, ἦμος δ᾽ ἠριγένεια φάνη ῥοδοδάκτυλος Ἠώς ('once early-born rosy-fingered dawn appeared'), occurs twice in the *Iliad* and twenty times in the *Odyssey*. The standard greeting to Odysseus, Διογενὲς Λαερτιάδη, πολυμήχαν᾽ Ὀδυσσεῦ, appears seven times in the *Iliad* and fifteen times in the *Odyssey*. The stock line introducing a speech by Odysseus, τὸν [τὴν] δ᾽ ἀπαμειβόμενος προσέφη πολύμητις Ὀδυσσεύς ('in answer to him/her the cunning Odyssseus replied') appears five times in the *Iliad* and forty-five times in the *Odyssey*, and the first part of it is used with a different name–epithet combination as subject a further forty-four times in the two poems.

On a larger scale, the story of Penelope's deception with the web, a narrative of almost twenty lines, is repeated twice after its first airing, with small variations (see 19.124–63,154 nn.); the catalogue of Agamemnon's gifts is recounted first by the king in council and then by Odysseus to Achilles, with tiny changes (*Il.* 9.122–57, 264–99, a passage of over thirty lines); Tiresias' prophecy to Odysseus in book 11 of the *Odyssey* is repeated almost verbatim by Odysseus to Penelope in book 23. Messengers regularly convey their messages using the same

words as their masters; innumerable warriors die in the formulaic style
in the *Iliad*; feasts are consumed, sacrifices are conducted, and ships
are launched in recurrent language in both epics. Above all, there are
the so-called 'stock' epithets ('much-enduring Odysseus', 'swift-footed
Achilles', 'Zeus gatherer of the clouds'), the standard descriptions of
heroes, gods, cities, peoples, artefacts ('well-benched ships') and natural
objects ('the wine-dark sea') – epithets which are used so regularly that
they must become conventional, almost a part of the name or noun
itself. They are employed, it seems, automatically, even when the epi-
thet is not particularly appropriate, and in a very few cases where it
actually conflicts with the context.[56]

It was from the noun–epithet combinations that Milman Parry's
researches began. By a close and precise analysis of Homeric usage he
established what had only been approximately or inadequately stated
before, that Homeric poetry employs repeated metrical formulae to
assist the composition and memorising of long tales. The recurrent
phrases most commonly consist either of whole hexameter lines, or of
half-lines beginning or ending with the caesura. It has been said that
Homer composes in set phrases as other poets compose in individual
words, but this formulation, while suggestive, is exaggerated, as will
be argued below. Nevertheless, the systems of formulaic phrases which
Parry discovered were so numerous, and showed such economy (in
the sense that superfluous or duplicated phrases were kept to a mini-
mum[57]), that it was impossible to suppose them the creation of a single
poet, or even a generation of poets. The argument from the diversity
of linguistic forms and the mixture of dialects reinforced this conclu-
sion: the Homeric poems were composed in a traditional language
which had been developed, extended and refined by generations of
bards – a language rich in set phrases or formulae which were adapted
to the composition of hexameter epic verse. Certainly these phrases
must be stately or poetic, suited to the grandeur of heroic song, but it
was their metrical usefulness that was primarily responsible for their
recurrence and preservation. Parry also argued that the constant repe-
tition of the stock epithets and stock lines dulled the hearer's reactions:

[56] See Parry, *MHV* 146–72, esp. 120–9, 134–8, 150–2. An example is *Od.*
16.4–5 'the loud-barking dogs fawned upon Telemachus, and *did not bark* at his
approach'.

[57] But see D. Shive, *Naming Achilles* (Oxford 1988).

they should not be given special weight in any given context, and this was adequate explanation of the anomalous or inappropriate uses mentioned above.

Despite his untimely death, Parry's work has had enormous influence and has changed the face of Homeric scholarship, above all in the English-speaking world. But his findings have left readers of Homer with many problems. Two pre-eminent issues have dominated recent discussion and criticism of Parry's theories and those of his followers: (1) Is Homer wholly traditional, or is there room for innovation, creativity, originality? (2) Given Parry's emphasis on the oral, traditional style of the Homeric poems, can literary criticism in the usual senses be anything but anachronistic? Do we, in fact, need a new approach, an 'oral poetics'? Both these questions require fairly detailed discussion.

(1) It is not uncommon for general works and even for scholarly articles to include assertions that the Homeric poems are composed wholly in formulae, and therefore that both the form and the subject matter of the poems are entirely traditional. This claim is unprovable, and usually rests either on an over-enthusiastic acceptance of Parry's conclusions, or on a questionable extension of the meaning of 'formula'. In terms of actual repetitions of lines or phrases only about a third of the Homeric corpus is formulaic; that is, about two-thirds of the lines in the poems are not repeated in whole or in part elsewhere. It may well be that if more epic poetry survived we would find more repetitions and could conclude from them that some lines which occur only once in our texts are in fact formulaic and traditional. But it is as likely that we would find further unique lines and unduplicated expressions. Parry's fascination with the inherited language and the idea of traditional epic led him to lay much more emphasis on the tradition than on any individual bard's contribution to that tradition. His conception of Homer's 'originality' was strictly limited, and indeed finds expression only in the occasional *aperçu*.[58] But innovation and expansion of the tradition there must have been, both on the level of content and on that of verbal expression, or else we are presented with an absurd infinite regress, with every predecessor of 'Homer' telling the story of Achilles or Odysseus in an identical form and style. Although because of the loss of

---

[58] Cf. esp. *MHV* 324, with A. Parry's remarks on this passage in his introd., pp. lii–liii.

earlier poetry we can never prove that a particular expression, simile or incident must be Homer's own invention, common sense tells us that such invention must have occurred, and that audiences welcome novelty (as Telemachus remarks in the *Odyssey* itself (1.351–2)), even if this is novelty within a traditional context.

Some points can be made with some degree of probability despite the absence of evidence. (a) It seems *a priori* plausible that in poems such as the *Iliad* and *Odyssey* some episodes are likely to be more 'traditional' than others. Any martial epic could make use of the language and formulae employed in the Iliadic battle-scenes, with variations only in the cast of characters. Heroic duels, festive celebrations, exhortations by commanders to their troops, burials and lamentations, might reasonably be seen as falling into set patterns; similarly, scholars have analysed the 'typical scenes' which recur (though often with significant variations) in both epics: the welcoming and entertainment of guests, sacrifices, arming-scenes, catalogues, and so forth.[59] Some of the most frequent classes of similes (such as the comparisons of warriors to lions) are probably also typical and traditional.[60] It is notable, however, that these are all narrative categories (except for the stock speeches of commanders in battle). The longer speeches of the poems, which include many of the most memorable passages in Homer, seem much more tied to their context and less readily transferred *en bloc* to another song or another singer's repertoire. The parting of Hector and Andromache contains too much that is associated with Troy and with their families to be usable in another war-epic about another city. Nor is it easy to suppose that the response of Achilles to the Embassy, or Priam's appeal to Achilles in *Iliad* 24 (in which he himself stresses the uniqueness of his situation), are simply part of the tradition of epic poetry, whether concerned with Achilles or with others. Exceptional situations call forth unusual language and vocabulary.[61]

---

[59] See esp. W. Arend, *Die typischen Scenen bei Homer* (Berlin 1933); Parry, *MHV* 404–7; J. B. Hainsworth, *Homer* (*G.&R.* New Surveys 3, 1969) 25–6. For a good general discussion see Fenik, *Studies* 153–70.

[60] Cf. Section 4(d) below; also M. Mueller, *The Iliad* (London 1984) 112–16, on simile-families.

[61] J. Griffin, *J.H.S.* 106 (1986) 36–57 has demonstrated that the speeches in Homer embrace a different range of vocabulary from the narrative, and that the vocabulary of Achilles' speeches is very different from that of Agamemnon's. The oral style is not monolithic.

(b) Even if much more of the Homeric poems is traditional than we are accepting here, it remains true that the individual poet must decide how to shape and use that traditional material. It is he who chooses and arranges his scenes and speeches, and who plans the structure of the poem as a whole; for even if he simply accepts a sequence of scenes which a predecessor has devised, that too is his own choice, and he must relate such scenes to the larger structure of his own song. To take an example from the *Odyssey*, it is very likely that the tales of the Greeks' homecomings, as narrated by Nestor and Menelaus in books 3 and 4, are not 'original' creations by the *Odyssey*-poet. These stories had no doubt been told before, and the poet may well be retelling them in some of the same words as his predecessors. But that does not exhaust their meaning in and relevance to the *Odyssey*. These stories gain added significance when told to Telemachus, and when they preface the homecoming of Odysseus, who surpasses each of his peers in the end, although he is the last to come home. Further, the adventures of Menelaus and the death of Agamemnon provide both similarities to and pointed contrasts with the homecoming of Odysseus: these analogies are not inherent in the stories themselves, but are drawn out and illuminated by the poet (not least by the parallel use of formulae). Similarly in the *Iliad*, the tale of Meleager told by Phoenix, though almost certainly pre-existing in large part, is given new life and meaning by its inclusion in *Phoenix's* speech, addressed to *Achilles*, on *this* occasion. To say that something is traditional does not exclude its being put in an unexpected context and adapted to new uses.

(c) Similar considerations arise on the verbal level of individual formulae. Some formulae are more memorable and more striking in some contexts than in others. Parry himself admitted this with reference to a line in the *Iliad* (1.33 = 24.571), ὣς ἔφατ'· ἔδδεισεν ὁ γέρων καὶ ἐπείθετο μύθωι ('thus he spoke; the old man was afraid, and heeded his word'), which, he remarks, seems hardly notable in the context, 'but, when it appears again, in the scene between Priam and Achilles, it becomes one of the very pathetic verses in Homer'.[62] Another example is the moving phrase εἴ ποτ' ἔην γε ('if it/he was ever really so', see 19.315n.), which occurs four times in the two epics, with quite different effects in each passage. It is obvious that the same words and formulations can have a different tone, even a different sense, in different contexts.

[62] *MHV* 306.

(d) Parry's analyses concentrated on the mechanical, metrical con-
venience of formulaic composition, the assistance which it gave to a
poet whom he saw as essentially an improvisor (on the inadequacy of
this conception see below). As a result, although he was far from deny-
ing the beauty and dignity of the style of Homer – indeed, he praised
it eloquently and often, in general terms[63] – he gave less attention to
the literary advantages which the formulaic language offers. Recent
critics have done much to expand the conception of what the tradi-
tional poet can do within the tradition, using a style which is his
proper medium, not a straitjacket. In particular, it has been shown
that Homer often (not always) adapts his formulae or modifies the
conventional phrase because of context: where the stock formula would
be clumsy, less pointed, or superfluous, he is able to change or adjust
it.[64]

(i) In the *Odyssey*, the hero is constantly addressed with the line
διογενὲς Λαερτιάδη, πολυμήχαν' Ὀδυσσεῦ, but in 24.192, and only
there, a variation is admitted, as Agamemnon, who has just heard the
news of Odysseus' slaughter of the suitors, exclaims ὄλβιε Λαέρταο πάϊ,
πολυμήχαν' Ὀδυσσεῦ ('blessed son of Laertes, Odysseus of the many
wiles!'); only now is Odysseus in a situation where that epithet could
be used without absurdity.

(ii) The standard line to a new arrival, τίς πόθεν εἰς ἀνδρῶν; πόθι
τοι πόλις ἠδὲ τοκῆες; ... ('who are you, and whence do you come?
Where is your city, and where do your parents dwell?') occurs six times
in the *Odyssey*; but in 7.238, when the silent Arete begins to question
the hero, the line is modified, its second half becoming τίς τοι τάδε
εἵματ' ἔδωκεν; ('who was it who gave you these clothes?'), startling
Odysseus and forcing him to explain his encounter with Nausicaa, from
whom he received them.

(iii) It is normal for a Homeric character praying to a god to men-
tion the past claims he or she has on the deity, and previous occasions
when the god has given aid (e.g. *Iliad* 1.453, 16.236; cf. Sappho 1.5–7
L–P). Instead in *Od*. 6.325 Odysseus prays to Athene with the words
'hear me now at any rate, since you never heard me before, when I was

---

[63] See e.g. *MHV* lii, 374 ('incantation of the heroic'), 418.
[64] See already Parry, *MHV* 156–61; and esp. Macleod, *Iliad XXIV* 40–2,
46–7. Further, M. W. Edwards, *H.S.C.P.* 84 (1980) 1–28.

being shipwrecked …': the forms of piety are modified to become a reproach to his neglectful patroness.

(iv) The phrase ἰσόθεος φώς ('godlike man') is used twice in the poem, at 1.324 and 20.124, in both places of Telemachus. (It is much more frequent in the *Iliad*). In the first scene it has a special aptness in context, as Athene has just given the young man strength and confidence, and he has realised with wonder that she must be a goddess (320–4); with this secret knowledge he now confronts the suitors and answers them back. In the later scene, in book 20, the use is less pointed, but still suits the young prince getting up on the day which will see him achieving his manhood and fighting alongside his father.[65]

(e) Formulae are redeployed in a different way in 17.326, the line which describes the demise of the aged dog Argus: Ἄργον δ' αὖ κατὰ μοῖρ' ἔλαβεν μέλανος θανάτοιο ('and then the doom of black death seized Argus'). Elsewhere in the epic poems this phrase is used only to describe the deaths of men. Is this a merely casual extension, or is it an attempt to bring out the special status of the loyal hound, a friend and companion in the past, still acute enough to recognise his master now – almost human?

(2) Even before the 'oral' revolution, it was commonplace to refer to the contrast between 'primary' epic (Homer, and e.g. *Beowulf*) and 'secondary' or 'literary' epic (Virgil, Lucan, Milton, Ariosto, etc.).[66] This distinction had a number of undesirable implications: on the one hand, the earlier epics might be regarded as unliterary and primitive,[67] while on the other, Virgil and other imitators of the form might be dismissed as derivative and inauthentic. The researches of Parry and his followers led in some quarters to a further separation of 'oral' and 'literary' epic, based not on evaluation but on the conviction that Homer, being a traditional oral poet, could not be judged by the same criteria as a pen-poet such as Virgil, composing painstakingly in his study, creating a highly self-conscious literary work for learned readers.

[65] On the use of 'stock' epithets in the *Odyssey* see further Austin, *Archery at the dark of the moon* ch. 1.
[66] E.g. C. M. Bowra, *From Virgil to Milton* (London 1945) ch. 1; C. S. Lewis, *Preface to Paradise Lost* (Oxford 1942) chh. 3–7.
[67] As in the implications of the title of Brooks Otis's influential book, *Virgil: a study in civilised poetry* (Oxford 1964).

It has indeed been claimed that literary criticism of a conventional kind has no place in the study of Homer: a new 'oral poetics' is required.[68]

These claims are probably overstated. It must again be emphasised that the Parryists have not proved that Homeric poetry is oral poetry, only that it is composed in what appears to be a traditional style which was probably created by oral poets. But even if the *Iliad* and the *Odyssey* were composed originally without the aid of writing, that does not mean that they are crude, unsophisticated, ill-constructed works. Oral composition and oral performance would indeed rule out some forms of artistry which we acknowledge in literary epic: in particular, the densely packed richness of each line of Virgil's poetry, in which so much is suggested rather than stated, and in which every word is chosen and placed with the utmost care. But oral poetry of the quality of Homer could not be composed impromptu, by an improvisor making it up as he goes along. Oral composition is compatible with extended premeditation, rehearsal, repeated improvement and enrichment at successive performances. As for the audience, it is not obvious that those who listened to Greek epic poetry demanded or expected fundamentally different things from most readers of heroic narrative. They surely wanted excitement, suspense, surprises, human interest, memorable personalities, variation of scene and tone, passion and pathos, dramatic events which could be dramatically delivered by a gifted bard. All of these the Homeric poems provide.

Advocates of a new 'oral poetics' often attach great importance to the principle of parataxis ('setting alongside'), which in this context refers to the supposed looseness of structure in Homeric epic. Scenes (it is said) are juxtaposed without much relation between them; the poet dwells on the immediate matter in hand, developing a particular episode for its own sake, without regard to a larger whole.[69] This curious analysis (like the demonstrably false assertion that the Homeric

---

[68] For such arguments see e.g. J. A. Notopoulos, *T.A.P.A.* 80 (1949) 1–23, F. M. Combellack, *Comparative literature* 11 (1959) 193–208, A. B. Lord, *H.S.C.P.* 72 (1968) 46; the counter-arguments are well put, in general terms, by G. S. Kirk, *Homer and the oral tradition* (Cambridge 1978) 69–73.

[69] On this school of thought see A. Parry's remarks in *MHV* xlvii–xlviii, lv–lvi.

poems do not include cross-references and foreshadowing[70]) ignores the elaborate architecture of both poems. Explicit and implicit preparation for subsequent events and retrospective reflections on events past occur constantly;[71] comparable scenes are placed in a significant sequence (for example, the recognition-scenes in the second half of the *Odyssey*: Introd. 1 (*b*) above); and the audience or reader, having been led to anticipate important events such as the reunion of Odysseus and his wife, is satisfied and delighted by the firm control which the epic poet has over his tale. On the level of large-scale structure and dramatic effects, 'literary' criticism has much scope, and much of value to say about the *Iliad* and the *Odyssey*.

On the smaller scale, in dealing with the individual episode or speech, the situation is somewhat less clear. In a suggestive paper published in 1970 Hainsworth drew a distinction between the dramatic or 'literary' architecture of the poems, and the 'oral' technique of the episodes: 'both of [the poems] combine brief and strong dramatic plots with broad expanses of paratactic narrative ... we find ourselves applying organic criteria to the essential plot and paratactic criteria to the episodes'.[72] This seems to draw the boundary-line too precisely. Some episodes, notably the debates and dialogues, recognitions and test-scenes, or the most important (and less conventional) battle-scenes, are constructed with as much attention to detail and dramatic effect as any 'literary' poet might hope to achieve: metre and dialect apart, the arguments in *Iliad* 9, or the delicate and subtle scene in which Calypso and Odysseus part in *Odyssey* 5, would not seem out of place in Sophocles. Elsewhere, in scenes which perhaps owe more to the tradition, we may detect more carelessness and paratactic construction of the kind which the oralists have sought to explain. Here again, however,

---

[70] Page, *Homeric Odyssey* 141–2 is particularly blatant (esp. 142 'Delicate and subtle preparations now for what will follow in five hundred lines' time ... such artifice lies beyond his power, even supposing that it lay within the bounds of his imagination'). Even Adam Parry is too tentative (*MHV* lvii n. 1).

[71] Cf. G. E. Duckworth's old but still valid account, *Foreshadowing and suspense in the epics of Homer, Apollonius and Vergil* (Princeton 1933). N. J. Richardson, *C.Q.* 30 (1980) 269 assembles material on this topic from the exegetical scholia to the *Iliad*.

[72] J. B. Hainsworth, *J.H.S.* 90 (1970) 90–8, at p. 95.

the critic has a duty to consider the text fairly and sympathetically, rather than ascribing to the poet the limitations ordained by modern theorising.

The study of formulaic usage and analysis of the larger dramatic structure may be combined in one area of growing importance in Homeric research: the examination of significant repetitions.[73] Again this represents a rebellion against Parry's limited conception of the oral bard's poetic resources, and a return to a more literary critical approach.[74] That repetition can be poetically significant would hardly be questioned: the difficulty is to ascertain what repetitions are in fact meaningful, and what their significance is.[75] Some cases seem certain: it cannot be accidental that, amidst other parallels, Patroclus' death and Hector's are described in the same trio of lines, used nowhere else in the Homeric poems (*Il.* 16.855–7 = 22.361–3). The resemblances highlight the common tragedy of Greek and Trojan, both brought low at their prime, both doomed because of unkind gods. Repetitions of this kind can be plausibly seen as significant when (as here) the lines in question are not commonplace, and when other connections reinforce the verbal similarity. Examples in the *Odyssey* include (a) 19.250 = 23.206 (of Penelope) σήματ' ἀναγνούσηι, τά οἱ ἔμπεδα πέφραδ' Ὀδυσσεύς: in the earlier passage, Penelope is mistaken in thinking that the beggar has given her true evidence that he has met her husband (cf. n. *ad loc.*), whereas in the later scene she is correct, has recognised that this is indeed 'Odysseus', and has outsmarted or out-tested her husband. The similarity of phrasing points up the differences: Penelope bewildered and deceived versus Penelope overjoyed and successful in

[73] Cf. Macleod, *Iliad XXIV* 43–5; Rutherford, *P.C.Ph.S.* 31 (1985) 133–50.

[74] See e.g. *MHV* 407, reviewing Arend: 'the healthy result of this reading of early poems shows itself in his not finding falsely subtle meanings in the repetitions, as meant to recall an earlier scene where the same words are used . . .'

[75] Cf. the interesting study by W. Moskalew, *Formulaic language and poetic design in the Aeneid* (*Mnemos.* Suppl. 73 (1982)). There is nothing so systematic on Homer, but W. Schadewaldt in his *Iliasstudien* (Leipzig 1938) did much of the fundamental work. See also G. M. Calhoun, 'Homeric repetitions', *Univ. of Calif. Publ. in Cl. Phil.* 12 (1933) 1–25; H. Bannert, *Formen des Wiederholens bei Homer* (*Wien. Stud.* Beiheft 13, Vienna 1988); and O. Taplin's forthcoming *Homeric soundings* (n. 53 above).

her own deceptive test. (b) Another example is 6.230–5 = 23.157–62, passages in which Odysseus is bathed and beautified by Athene. In both a simile is used (one of the very rare cases in which similes are repeated verbatim). In the earlier scene, Nausicaa admires the handsome appearance of the stranger, and hints to her maids that she is attracted to him; in the later, the bathing precedes the final recognition by Penelope, and after so long an absence we might expect the queen to be overwhelmed by her husband's renewed good looks (23.115–16 and 166–70 suggest that Odysseus expected this process of ablution to be decisive). Nausicaa's impressionable *naïveté* is contrasted with Penelope's maturer caution, but also with her deeper love. (c) In two passages Odysseus weeps at the song of Demodocus, and Alcinous notices his distress (8.93–6 = 532–5); in the first scene he tactfully suggests a change of scene and concludes the singing, but in the later passage, where Odysseus' grief is more intense, he asks him to explain and identify himself. The earlier passage paves the way for the later, whetting the listener's anticipation and also showing Alcinous' consideration and restraint. (d) Verbal similarities and repetitions heighten our awareness of the analogies between Odysseus' homecoming and that of Agamemnon; in particular, the slaughter of the suitors, in which the returning king prevails by guile over the would-be usurpers, is a reversal of Agamemnon's downfall, and the scene is described in similar terms: see 11.420 ∼ 22.309, 381–9.

See also 4.538–40 ∼ 481–3 (more intense grief at more serious news; Menelaus' earlier distress becomes trivial in the light of his brother's death); 4.45–6 ∼ 7.84–5; 8.100–3 ∼ 250–3; 9.539–42 ∼ 482–90 (real escape contrasted with near-disaster). See further commentary on 19.104, 105, 154, 170, 209; for less plausible cases, see 19.439–43, 20.346 nn.

Obviously, there is room for disagreement over some or all of these examples, and even in Virgilian studies, or in criticism of Greek tragedy, readers do not always agree about the significance of an echo, an allusion, a 'mirroring-scene' or the like; but it would be bad method to assume that a feature so prominent in epic poetry cannot under any circumstances offer any advantage to the poet other than compositional convenience.

(c) Rhetoric[76]

(i). *Introductory*. Rhetoric, in the sense of the codified technique of composing speeches, is usually said to have originated in the mid-fifth century B.C., with the written textbooks of sophists such as the Sicilian Gorgias. But statesmen and generals had spoken effectively, in life and in literature, long before Gorgias; and the rhetorical treatises themselves frequently drew on poetry for their examples. Homer's heroes admire and value effective oratory: Phoenix was sent to Troy with Achilles to make him 'a doer of deeds and a speaker of words' (*Il.* 9.443), and Antenor describes the different styles of Menelaus and Odysseus with the enthusiasm of a connoisseur (3.203–24).[77] Aristotle praised Homer for saying as little as possible in his own person (see p. 3 above), and indeed we find that some 55 per cent of the Homeric corpus consists of direct speech. It is interesting to note that the proportion is somewhat higher for the *Odyssey* than for the *Iliad*: discounting the special case of the narrative portions of books 9–12, in which the hero himself recounts his adventures, I calculate 6,835 lines of direct speech out of a total of 12,103. The corresponding figures for the *Iliad* are 7,018 out of 15,690. It would be absurd to argue from this relatively small difference that the *Iliad* is a poem of action, the *Odyssey* more concerned with words – one has only to think of the dialogue in the *Iliad* between Hector and Andromache, or of the debate-scenes on Olympus and on earth; but it would perhaps be fair to say that dialogue and conversation, including reminiscences, for their own sake (as opposed to deliberative discussion which leads to a decision about necessary action), are more prevalent in the *Odyssey*.

There is in fact a broader sense of rhetoric, that of employing the proper words to create an effect on one's audience, which is as applica-

---

[76] D. Lohmann, *Die Composition der Reden in der Ilias* (Berlin 1970) and I. de Jong, *Narrators and focalizers* (Amsterdam 1987) are two very different but valuable studies, both primarily concerned with the *Iliad*. For a briefer account see M. W. Edwards, *Homer, the poet of the Iliad* (Johns Hopkins 1987) 88-97. There is a survey of work on the speeches by J. Latacz, *Gräzer Beiträge* 2 (1974) 395–422. On the *Odyssey* C. J. Larrain, *Struktur der Reden in der Odyssee 1–8* (*Spudasmata* 41, Hildesheim 1987) should also be mentioned, though his approach may be found excessively formalistic.

[77] Cf. further *Od.* 8.171–3; *Il.* 1.248–9; Hes. *Th.* 81–97.

ble to the poet himself as to any of his characters. For all the distinctions that must be drawn between narrative and character-speech, the poet's own style of story-telling is eloquent and varied, as many examples in the commentary show (we need only remember the similes: see Introd. 4(d) below). But one particular aspect of the interrelation of narrative and speeches is important: the author may have a different understanding of the situation from the character, and so the speech may have a different meaning and purpose from its ostensible or superficial content. In other words, the speeches by or addressed to the ignorant characters (in these two books especially Penelope and the suitors) may be used to create irony.[78] Such irony may be conscious and intentional (as when Odysseus uses language with a double meaning for himself, also appreciated by the poet's audience),[79] or it may be unconscious, as when Eumaeus expresses to Odysseus his conviction that Odysseus will never return, or when the suitors scoff at or sarcastically compliment the beggar Odysseus.[80] Ironic effects are also achieved when a speech is spoken formally to one person but has added significance for another, or is deliberately aimed by the speaker at another person present. Thus Odysseus' rebuke of Melantho in 19.71–88 is partly aimed at awakening Penelope to the maid's wrongdoing (see esp. 83); in so doing, it aligns the beggar on the queen's side and provides a suitable opening cue for their conversation.

(ii) *Formal speeches.* When modern scholars deny the presence of rhetoric in Homer, they are usually referring to the formal speech-structures and the elaborate range of figures of speech and thought later systematised by rhetorical theorists. But while it is of course true that Homeric characters do not follow schoolbook rules, it is still possible to identify certain categories of speeches, and as with the typical scenes, the patterns followed are worth attention because of the possibility of

---

[78] See further A. F. Dekker, *Ironie in de Odyssee* (Leiden 1965); Hölscher, *Untersuchungen* (a landmark work, but many of his best points are developed further and in English by Fenik). See also on double meanings W. B. Stanford, *Ambiguity in Greek literature* (Oxford 1939) esp. ch. 7.

[79] E.g. 14.53–4, 151–2, 16.106, 17.419 ~ 19.75, 19.109ff.

[80] E.g. 14.362–8, 18.37, 112–3, 122–3; 19.363ff. (Eurycleia's speech), esp. 370–4; 20.194, with n.; 21.91–2, 397–400, 402–3. Also noteworthy is the unconscious relevance of Demodocus' songs to the unrecognised Odysseus in book 8.

interesting divergences. Amongst those which have been studied are
the leader's exhortations to his men on the battlefield or before entering
battle; prayers to the gods; the monologues of an isolated hero in diffi-
culties; supplications; laments for the dead; consolatory speeches to the
surviving mourner; taunts voiced by attacking or victorious warriors,
and similar speeches of denunciation and abuse.[81] The formal speeches
in the Greek and Trojan assemblies perhaps come closest to later delib-
erative oratory of the kind familiar from the classical period: see esp.
Il. 2.110–41, 284–332, 337–68; *Od.* 2.40–256. These speeches, though
sometimes presented in sequence, tend to be self-contained; much more
fast-moving and polemical are the cut-and-thrust exchanges of the
quarrel in *Iliad* 1 (or the abortive quarrel between Menelaus and
Antilochus in 23.543–611). We should also recall that two of the most
important aims of later forensic oratory, the arousal of indignation and
the appeal to pity, are anticipated in Homeric practice. Thus in *Od.* 2,
Telemachus tries to arouse the Ithacan people to anger against the
suitors, but cuts a poor figure and succeeds only in exciting their pity
for himself (2.81). In the *Iliad*, Odysseus and Phoenix appeal to Achilles
to pity the Greeks; Lycaon's appeal to the same hero, for all its elo-
quence, fails to save his own life; and Priam through his courage and
self-abasement moves Achilles at last to pity him and to acknowledge
the common sorrow of the human condition.

   Moreover, Homer and his speakers have an intuitive grasp of form
and figurative language, so that many argumentative moves and ver-
bal or rhetorical devices which were only later given formal titles are
already used effectively and indeed sublimely in the *Iliad* and the *Odys-
sey*. Thus in *Il.* 9.96–102, Nestor's opening address to Agamemnon
('with you shall I begin, with you will be my ending') is appropriately
courtly rhetoric for addressing a proud king (cf. the encomiastic lines
in Theoc. 17.1–4, Virg. *Ecl.* 8.11, Hor. *Ep.* 1.1.1, addressing their
patrons), and serves to temper the rebuke which his subsequent speech
contains. Odysseus when introducing the tale of his wanderings (9.1ff.)
anticipates many of the techniques of the proem, building up his audi-
ence's expectation, securing their goodwill and magnifying the signifi-

---

[81] J. Latacz, *Kampfparänese* (n. 41 above); B. Fenik in *Homer: tradition and
invention*, ed. Fenik (Leiden 1978) 68–90; M. Alexiou, *The ritual lament in Greek
tradition* (Cambridge 1974), etc.; see also the studies reviewed in Latacz's survey
(n. 76 above).

cance of what he has to say, rounding off with the elegant rhetorical question τί πρῶτον τοι ἔπειτα, τί δ' ὑστάτιον καταλέξω; ('what then am I to recount first, what last?').[82] Again, in the embassy episode of the *Iliad*, Odysseus' speech to Achilles is an elaborate and polished argumentative assault, of which a rhetorician might be proud. We should contrast with this Achilles' responding speech, which is far more powerful, far more memorable, but which achieves its effects less by calculated argumentation, more by the sustained emotional intensity which piles one idea on another, with little thought of the most effective order and no thought at all of how to flatter or reassure his audience. The highly naturalistic qualities of this speech are brought out all the more clearly by the juxtaposition with Odysseus' more sober, controlled performance. Yet this is not a contrast between a skilled orator and an angry man without such skill; rather, Achilles makes use of the devices of formal rhetoric only to transcend them or put them to daring and startling new uses: for instance, in his magnificent use of rhetorical questions (9.337–41). Other devices which might be noted in that speech are the epigrammatic lines at 318–20, which generalise and make more irrefutable Achilles' own position; the enumeration of his achievements (325–32); the jeering references in 348–50 to all that Agamemnon has managed to do without Achilles (Demetrius, *On style* 55 remarked on the effect of the repeated particle δή here); the pounding repetition of negatives in the climactic passage at 379–91 (οὐδ' εἰ ... οὐδ' ... again and again) and further at 401, 404; and the repeated polarisations that are central to Homer's art as to Demosthenes': between the speaker and his opponent; between thankless drudgery at Troy and a life of peace and prosperity at home; between Hector in the past and Hector now; and finally, near the end of the speech, between the two fates of Achilles, mentioned here for the first time, and reserved for the finale as his most sombre and ominous argument against the ambassadors (410–16; in particular, 414–16 ∼ 412–13).[83] Achilles is by far the most eloquent and memorable orator in the *Iliad*, just as Odysseus is in the *Odyssey*;[84] but his eloquence is of a different kind.

---

[82] Cf. Pease on Virg. *Aen.* 4.371; Tarrant on Sen. *Ag.* 649.

[83] See further Lohmann, *Die Composition* 231–76, for a detailed account of these speeches.

[84] Cf. J. Griffin, *J.H.S.* 106 (1986) 36–57.

(iii) *Responsion*. Speeches do not stand alone; one character often takes up and reacts to key-words or particular points in an interlocutor's speech. This technique, which artistically reproduces or heightens something natural in ordinary dialogue, is especially common in scenes of conflict or polemic.[85] Thus in *Od.* 21, when Antinous has complained that the suitors will be disgraced if they cannot even string the bow of Odysseus (329), Penelope responds that the suitors cannot hope for any kind of noble reputation in view of what they are doing; 'so why do you count this as disgraceful?' (333 τί δ' ἐλέγχεα ταῦτα τίθεσθε;). An amusing instance of the same device is 8.164–6: the Phaeacian prince Euryalus concludes his speech to Odysseus, who has just declined to compete in their games, with the words 'you don't look to me like an athlete', to which Odysseus indignantly reacts: 'stranger, you have not spoken well. You look to me like a fool!' (166) Again, in 24.24–34 Achilles, meeting Agamemnon in the underworld, draws a contrast between the great and glorious career Agamemnon had in life and his inglorious death; here he compliments and sympathises with Agamemnon ('if only you had died in the war at Troy, the united Achaean forces would have built you a tomb and you would have won great glory for your son hereafter'). Agamemnon responds with compliments to Achilles and a detailed account of Achilles' own funeral and the glory that will for ever be his (esp. 94 ~ 33). Neither hero is content; both their deaths are to be contrasted with the glorious success of Odysseus, of which they are promptly told by the suitors' ghosts (note 192 ~ 36; 196 κλέος again, here applied to Penelope's endurance). A striking instance of balanced responses is to be found in the scene preceding Odysseus' recognition by Penelope, where the two of them, each uncertain of the other, are fencing and seeking an opening. In 23.174–80 Penelope replies to her husband in a speech which answers his own, is identical in length, and begins with δαιμόνιε, answering his δαιμονίη; both give instructions to the old nurse; and Penelope certainly and Odysseus probably gives these orders in the hope that the other will give way or give himself away. The subtlety of this exchange shows how well matched Penelope and Odysseus are.

(iv) *Tact and understatement*, the delicate and sensitive courtesies which

---

[85] Cf. Macleod, *Iliad XXIV* 52.

the Greeks associated with the word ἦθος ('character'), are also promi-
nent in the *Odyssey*: in 1.197–8, where Athene–Mentes refrains from
telling Telemachus of Calypso's role as Odysseus' captor, instead refer-
ring to 'cruel hard men' who hold him captive; in 7.303–7, where
Odysseus tells a white lie to save Nausicaa from her father's displeasure,
and the audience is meant to notice; or in book 14, where he draws out
Eumaeus and sympathetically encourages him to tell of his misfortunes,
partly by giving a fictitious version of his own (see below). In Scheria,
despite his urgent desire to return home, he tells Alcinous he would
gladly stay a year if he so wished, provided he in the end received a trip
home and 'glorious gifts', a double hint to which the king generously
responds (11.355–61). In the rather awkward encounter with Ajax in
book 11, he tries unsuccessfully to make peace, complimenting the dead
hero by equating him with Achilles (557 ἶσον Ἀχιλλῆος . . . ἀχνύμεθα);
normally, and in the preceding scene, Ajax is seen as strictly second-
best to Achilles (550–1, cf. 470; *Il.* 2.768–9; *PMG* 898). For further
examples of tact see 4.116–82 (where Menelaus, Helen and Pisistratus
converse together, avoiding questioning the weeping Telemachus; he
does not speak again until 290, by which time Helen has given the
company her calming drug); 8.400–15 (after his earlier boorishness
Euryalus makes peace with Odysseus with a gift); 8.457–68 (the grace-
ful farewell between Odysseus and Nausicaa); 15.195–216 (Telemachus
and Pisistratus consider how the former, who is in haste, can avoid
Nestor's hospitality without offending him).

Compliments and flattery are part of Odysseus' stock-in-trade. He
needs all his charm and politesse with Calypso in book 5, who has been
summarily told by Hermes that she must set Odysseus free, though she
chooses to let him think it was her own idea (5.160–70 and esp. 190–1;
cf. 7.261–3, where we learn that Odysseus has half-guessed the truth).
He uses flattery to Penelope in book 19, where he praises her as being
like a just and benevolent king (106–14, with 111n.) – like himself,
indeed. He compliments Nausicaa in book 6 and Athene in book 13 by
comparing them to goddesses (6.148–52 and 13.230–1; in the latter
case, of course, he is double-bluffed and the poet achieves an ironic
effect, since she really is one!).

(v) *Examples.* Another principle of oratory which has received much
attention from modern scholars is the use of the paradigm or example
from the past (in Homer, usually from other myths, occasionally in-

vented or embroidered).[86] A simple version of this style of argument is
to be found in Nestor's first speech in the *Iliad* (1.254–84): having
expressed his dismay at the dispute between Achilles and Agamemnon,
he argues: 'you should heed my advice; I used to be the companion of
better men than you, and they heeded my advice, as follows ... they
were better than you, and they listened to me; so you should listen
to me'. This combines an *a fortiori* argument with an orderly ring-
composition structure; on the level of characterisation, it is an assertion
by Nestor of the authority which his age brings, but one which also
illustrates his typical garrulousness; it may also be seen as providing a
less emotional gap, during which the quarrelling pair may be expected
to cool down (though they do not). More elaborate paradigms are em-
ployed by Phoenix in *Iliad* 9 (the tale of Meleager, which corresponds
to that of Achilles in a complex web of analogies and contrasts), and by
Nestor again in *Iliad* 11 (a tale addressed to Patroclus but with a mes-
sage aimed at Achilles through him: note esp. 656–8, 664–5, 762–
3, 792–803).[87] In the *Odyssey*, paradigms are employed extensively,
though they are often introduced less obviously and more as stories,
whether told by Odysseus himself or by others (cf. below on the lies).[88]
The story of Orestes, who slew Aegisthus and avenged his father, is
regularly employed by Athene and others as a stirring example for the
inert Telemachus.[89] A further, relatively simple example is voiced by
Antinous to the hero at 21.288–306. Declaring that the stranger must
be drunk to ask for a chance at stringing the bow, he briefly narrates

[86] N. Austin, *G.R.B.S.* 7 (1966) 295–312; B. K. Braswell, *C.Q.* 11 (1971)
16–26; M. M. Willcock, *C.Q.* 14 (1974) 141–54. See further R. Oehler, *Mytho-
logische Exempla in der älteren griechischen Dichtung* (diss. Basel, Aarau 1925);
Lohmann, index s.v. 'Paradeigma'.

[87] In the *Iliad* note also the complementary tales told by Glaucus and Dio-
medes (6.129–41 and 152–205), on which see J. Gaisser, *T.A.P.A.* 100 (1969)
165–76; Macleod, *Iliad XXIV* 11–13; de Jong, *Narrators and focalizers* 162–72.

[88] There is also the αἶνος told by Odysseus at 14.462–506 (the word is used by
Eumaeus at 508) in the hope of securing a cloak for the night. Perhaps the *ainos*
is a lower form of paradigm, as suits Odysseus' beggar role? Cf. Hes. *WD* 202–
12, with West's notes. (But *Il.* 23.652 points the other way.)

[89] The *Odyssey* generally underplays the matricidal aspect of Orestes' tri-
umph: see Garvie, *Aeschylus: Choephori* (n. 18) x–xi. Only in 3.310 is her death
mentioned, and even there it is not made explicit that Orestes killed her, though
we can hardly doubt that the poet knew this story.

what happened to the Centaur who got drunk and was punished and mutilated by the Lapiths, and warns Odysseus that he will suffer a similar fate. In fact this paradigm rebounds on the suitors themselves: like the Centaur, they are abusing hospitality and through their excessive revelry calling down a horrible end upon themselves.

More subtle and suggestive is the intriguing episode of Menelaus' and Helen's story-telling in Sparta (4.233–89). Here the paradigmatic aspect is not explicit, but both stories carry interest and implicit encouragement for Telemachus, while also having thematic links with later parts of the poem. They give him a clearer and larger idea of his father's ingenuity and ability, so contributing to the general educative process enacted in the Telemachy. Helen's tale describes Odysseus' powers of deception and disguise and presents herself as a clever woman, who spotted his identity while bathing and washing his feet. This foreshadows Eurycleia's identification of the hero in book 19; in Helen's case, it is used to present her as a loyal friend who did not betray Odysseus but protected him and regretted her desertion of Menelaus (261–4, where she attributes her wrongdoing to the influence of ἄτη, divinely-sent delusion, and finishes with a graceful compliment to Menelaus). Her husband's tale singles out Odysseus' self-discipline within the Wooden Horse, even though the men within were tempted to reveal themselves by Helen herself, who came mimicking their wives' voices: 'some divine power must have bade you do so, one who wished to grant glory to the Trojans' (274–5). This story stands in contrast with Helen's own: hers was a tale of self-exculpation, Menelaus' conveys an implicit rebuke, a sign of the continuing shadow of the past which mars their happiness together.[90] Both stories glorify Odysseus, and Menelaus' too anticipates important aspects of the hero's future career (on Odysseus' self-control see 17.238, 284, 18.90–4, 19.211–12, 20.9–22).[91]

---

[90] Also conveyed by the opening of the book, where it is made clear that Menelaus has no legitimate heir, and his son by a slave-woman bears the significant name Megapenthes ('great sorrow'). These grievances can be aired in this scene without animosity because the drug has placated the participants (a point I owe to Dr Alison Adams).

[91] For further paradigms see 20.66–78, with 61–82n. The digression on Odysseus' scar, while not formally a paradigm, has some things in common with the form: see 19.390–1 n.

(vi) *Conversation*. Formal speeches and elaborate persuasive struc-
tures do not exhaust the art of the poet of the *Odyssey*. Less obvious and
yet central to the success of the poem is the skill with which he handles
more informal dialogue, sustained conversation which appears natural
and straightforward while often carrying additional ironies, or intro-
ducing ingenious echoes or motifs important to the poet's design. Al-
though the Eumaeus-episode in book 14, or book 19 itself (with its
sequel in the recognition-scene in book 23), would illustrate this amply,
perhaps the supreme example is Odysseus' encounter with Athene in
book 13. From the beginning here we have irony of situation: Odysseus
is back in Ithaca without knowing it, he is talking to Athene without
knowing it. The ironies are heightened through the speeches, in which
each tries to deceive the other, Odysseus for self-protection, Athene for
her own amusement. Each successive speech advances the situation
while also adding a fresh tone or tint to the rich characterisation of the
hero and his patroness. In 228–35 Odysseus adopts his pose as a strang-
er and compliments the disguised Athene; in 237–49 Athene patronises
him ('you are foolish, stranger, or from a very long way off ...') and
mischievously holds up until the end of her speech the revelation that
he is in Ithaca; in 256–86, despite his joy that he is home, Odysseus is
cool and collected and immediately launches upon one of his lies ('ah
yes, Ithaca; I've heard of that place even far away at my home in Crete
...' and so on); in 287–310 Athene has to admit defeat, and reveals
herself, caressing her protégé and lovingly mocking his perpetual cau-
tion, in one of the loveliest scenes in Homer. In that speech she teases
him for not recognising her, draws attention to the fact (previously
unsuspected by him) that she has helped him all through his wan-
derings, and promises help to come: her language introduces themes
which will be important for the whole of the second half (esp. 307 σὺ δὲ
τετλάμεναι καὶ ἀνάγκηι; 310; and later 336 πειρήσεαι 'you shall test'; on
this theme see 19.215n.). Odysseus' response to her openness is typical:
suspicion and questioning ('where were you all this time? ... I don't
believe I really am in Ithaca'), though combined with polite apprecia-
tion (314–15). In each case the poet continues to surprise us: instead of
openly expressing joy and gratitude, Odysseus is still cautious and pet-
ulant; instead of resenting his doubts, Athene delights in his suspicious
and cunning nature (330–2). There are few more sophisticated and
enjoyable scenes in ancient literature.

(vii) *Author/character ambiguity*. For the most part a firm distinction has been drawn above between the authorial voice and the character's speech. Something should be said about the interesting cases in which this boundary-line is unclear, an area brilliantly explored for the *Iliad* by de Jong, from the standpoint of modern 'narratology'. In essence, her point is that this is not an adequate description of the options available to the poet: apart from the obvious borderline case of indirect speech, Homer often makes use of what she calls 'embedded focalisation', which means that we cannot simply say that the narrator is objective: the authorial voice often empathises with characters and reproduces some of their feelings and attitudes. A simple example is *Il.* 24.3–8 (de Jong, 111): 'but Achilles continued weeping remembering his dear companion, ... yearning for the manliness and brave strength of Patroclus, and all the actions he had followed through and the hardships he had suffered with him, experiencing wars with men, and the baleful waves'. Here the narrator 'enters into' Achilles' thoughts and elaborates the description, conveying some of Achilles' emotions through the expressions (e.g. 'the baleful waves') which arise out of the character's vivid memories. In other cases there are unresolved ambiguities, often intended to tease or surprise the audience. The latter practice is prominent in *Odyssey* 23. At line 86, when Penelope has descended, 'she pondered long in her heart, wondering whether to question her dear husband ...' It seems to us here that Penelope has acknowledged the beggar's identity, but a few lines later we realise that this was the narrator's knowledge intruding on the character's thoughts. Similarly at 181 'thus she spoke, testing her husband' may reflect Penelope's hopes, but not her knowledge. Cf. 19.209, with n.

Ambiguities of this kind are less frequent in book 19, partly because so much of the book is composed of speeches. But at 19.53–4, when Penelope descends 'looking like Artemis or golden Aphrodite', the description has additional point if it is seen as 'focalised' – that is, if it conveys Odysseus' thoughts and feelings when he sees her. Line 250 is a clearer case: there the signs described as 'certain', 'firm' (ἔμπεδα) are in fact not so, but only seem like proof to Penelope (cf. 218n.). At 392, there is another case rather like those in book 23: the nurse 'coming closer, proceeded to wash her master; and at once she recognised the scar': the words 'her master' are added at the last possible moment before the nurse gains the knowledge here provided by the narrator. In book 20 there are a number of uncertain cases: at 12 and 29 the epithets for the suitors could be Odysseus' or the narrator's, being appropriate to both (cf. 386);[92] at 259, when Telemachus offers his father 'a base couch and a small table', the epithets seem more pointed if they convey Telemachus' perception of the situation ('*this* is the best I can do for my father!') than if they are merely 'objective' description; while at 269 the phrase in the second half of the line is probably the suitors' perception (cf. 274). By far the most interesting and most difficult case in these books, however, is Theoclymenus' vision: his own speech (351–7) is preceded by lines which definitely do not describe 'objective' reality, nor what the suitors and the others in the hall see: esp. 347–8 οἱ δ' ἤδη γναθμοῖσι γελώων ἀλλοτρίοισιν, | αἱμοφόρυκτα δὲ δὴ κρέα ἤσθιον ('now they laughed with others' mouths, and devoured meat that was stained with blood'). What Theoclymenus sees is introduced as though it were reality, without any introductory 'he thought he saw', or any other hint that this is a hallucination. The effect is intensely powerful: it shocks us into the realisation that in some sense this is already the reality: the suitors' bloody doom is something far more certain and imminent than any hallucination.

(viii) *Silence*. We may also note the occasions when speech is avoided; significant silences are another feature which Greek tragedy derived from Homeric epic.[93] The most memorable silence of the *Odyssey* is Ajax's majestic disdain for Odysseus' overtures in the underworld (11.563), imitated by Virgil in his presentation of Dido (*Aeneid* 6.467–71). Less solemn, but more pathetic, is the scene in book 16, where Telemachus and Eumaeus greet one another after the former's absence overseas. On Eumaeus' side it is an emotional reunion, on Telemachus' a friendly and reassuring greeting, but the key figure of the scene is Odysseus, the boy's unrecognised father, seeing his son for the first time after 20 years, and remaining silent and deferential in the background, in his beggar garb.[94] See also 23.85–96, where Odysseus and Penelope

---

[92] De Jong, *Narrators and focalizers* 275 n. 106 also cites 20.121, where 'the sinners' (i.e. the suitors) seems likely to be Odysseus' focalisation.

[93] On silences in tragedy, see O. Taplin, *H.S.C.P.* 76 (1972) 57–97. For comments in the Homeric scholia, see N. J. Richardson, *C.Q.* 30 (1980) 281.

[94] For further passages illustrating the importance of the unspoken or implicit in the Odyssey, see S. Besslich, *Schweigen – Verschweigen – Übergehen* (Heidelberg 1966).

silently watch one another, each uncertain; it is the brasher and impatient Telemachus who breaks the silence.

(ix) *Odysseus' lies*. Rhetoric is traditionally associated with lying and deception. In the *Odyssey*, some of Odysseus' most impressive rhetorical performances are false tales or half-truths. In books 19 and 20, the most prominent example is the account he gives of himself to Penelope at 19.172–202 and 269–307 (the second passage introduced by a protestation of his truthfulness, 269). The poet emphasises the skill of Odysseus at composing plausible tales in a famous line, 19.203: ἴσκε ψεύδεα πολλὰ λέγων ἐτύμοισιν ὁμοῖα ('as he uttered many a lie he made them look like the truth': see n.). The lies of Odysseus are a sufficiently important part of his character and of the poem to justify a continuous account, more detailed than would be appropriate in the Commentary.[95]

This is the fourth of Odysseus' large-scale lies. The full list is as follows. (a) 13.256–86, told to Athene, who of course knows his true identity and laughs at his cleverness; (b) 14.192–359, the longest of the lies, told to Eumaeus; (c) 17.415–44, told to Antinous: this is an abridged version of (b), but with a slightly different ending (despite Eumaeus' presence!); (d) the passage in book 19, already cited; (e) 24.259–79, 303–14, told to Laertes. All of these except the first are believed for the most part. In all but the last Odysseus poses as a Cretan: partly because of the fame and wealth of the island, partly because it is conveniently remote, and partly because it was well known for trade and travel. (For Cretan traders cf. *Homeric hymn to Apollo* 393–9.) It is tempting to think also of the saying 'all Cretans are liars' (first found in Epimenides 3 в 1 D–K), though it is also possible that the saying may have had part of its origin in Odysseus' tales. (In the *Homeric hymn to Demeter*, the goddess pretends to have come from Crete (123), per-

---

[95] The longest tale, to Eumaeus, is well analysed by Fenik, *Studies* 67–71. For further discussion see W. J. Woodhouse, *Composition of Homer's Odyssey* chh. 17–18, though his account is marred by his obsession with recovering the 'real' adventures of the 'historical' Odysseus, which he sees as enshrined in what for Homer rank as the 'lies' (cf. Fenik 171 n. 69). Other studies contributing useful points include C. R. Tranham, *Phoenix* 6 (1952) 31–43, P. Walcot, *Anc. Soc.* 8 (1977) 1–19 and S. Goldhill, *The poet's voice* (Cambridge 1991) 36–48. I have not seen G. Bluemlein, *Die Trugreden des Odysseus* (diss. Frankfurt 1971). On the broader topic of the legacy of the lies to later literature (e.g. the ancient novel) see Hölscher, *Die Odyssee* 210–34.

haps because this is suitable to a lying tale. That poem seems to be
influenced by the *Odyssey*: see Richardson's comm., pp. 32–3.)

Lies (b), (c) and (d) are closely akin in content. In both (b) and (d)
the listener is convinced by the falsehoods, but refuses to believe the one
true element, that Odysseus will soon be back in Ithaca. In (e), as in
(d), the result of the tale is to cause terrible grief for the auditor: in book
24, Laertes, believing that the tale means his son is dead, is overcome,
and Odysseus is dismayed at what he has done.[96] Thus (e) mirrors (a):
in both book 24 and book 13, the results of Odysseus' lie take him
wholly by surprise, whereas in the intermediate scenes he is in control of
the situation.

The longest of the lies, (b), told to Eumaeus, has many similarities
with the true life story of Eumaeus himself, which he narrates to his
guest in 15.351–484. This is obviously deliberate: the two stories are
similar in length (167 lines vs 133, longer than any of the others listed
above), and they are told in parallel scenes, with a number of detailed
correspondences. Compare especially Odysseus' reaction to Eumaeus'
tale (15.486–92), in which he compares Eumaeus' fate with his own,
and Eumaeus' response to Odysseus' lie (14.361–2). It is not made
clear whether Odysseus actually knew Eumaeus' life story already, and
so suited his tale to the hearer, but this would be in accordance with his
normal rhetorical tactics (cf. *Od.* 6.180–5, where he shrewdly guesses at
Nausicaa's preoccupation with finding a husband).[97] Besides the paral-
lel tale of Eumaeus, we should also note the lying tale which an un-
named Aetolian told to Eumaeus in the past (14.378–85).

In the first half of the poem we find no such large-scale lies as these,
but Odysseus' appeal to Nausicaa (6.149–85), his self-presentation to
Alcinous and Arete (7.241–97, with Fenik 16–17), and his plea to
the Cyclops (9.259–71) all attest his rhetorical skill and talent for dis-
simulation. It is of course in Ithaca that he has most need of self-
concealment. As for the variety of his tales, he himself remarks at the
end of his narrative to the Phaeacians that he hates to go over the same
ground twice (12.450–3)!

---

[96] Cf. *J.H.S.* 106 (1986) 161–2 on this scene.
[97] For a different view see D. J. Stewart, *The disguised guest* (1976) 90–1.
Stewart thinks that this is the first time Odysseus has ever heard Eumaeus' tale,
and that the parallels are therefore 'coincidental', the work of the poet; hearing
this tale brings home to Odysseus how fragile human fortunes are. This is an
attractive idea, but cannot be established from the text.

The 'lies' are not composed out of pure imagination. They include details relevant to the addressee, they present from a different slant important themes of the poem (especially hospitality, the aftermath of the Trojan war, the fragility of human fortune, the exotic world that lies beyond the familiar Greek mainland), and they echo or reflect various adventures experienced by Odysseus or his fellow heroes. In particular, the Egyptian adventures narrated by Odysseus in book 14 are closer to Menelaus' travels than to anything he has been through himself; and this must be the poet's own doing (if we may draw this distinction for the sake of convenience), for in the plot of the *Odyssey* the hero has had no opportunity to learn the story of Menelaus' homecoming (4.351–586). More broadly, these stories give a more 'realistic' perspective on Mediterranean life in the Greek colonising period of the eighth and seventh centuries. The adventures described in book 14 could easily have happened to a Greek soldier of fortune, a mercenary enlisted by the kings of Egypt.[98] The lies provide a foil to the more fantastic and magical adventures which Odysseus has 'really' undergone, as described in books 9–12. The images of history are not, however, unambiguous: we also seem to be dealing, not least in book 19, with remote recollections of an age long past, the empire of Minoan Crete, which had entered its decline at least 500 years before Homer's day.

A number of common elements link the various lies. (a) The narrator calls himself a Cretan (13.256, 14.199, 19.172). In the lie told in book 17 he is not explicit, but the resemblance to the fuller version in 14 justifies the assumption. Crete is also where the lying Aetolian came from (14.382). According to the lie told in book 19, the speaker met Odysseus when the latter was blown to Crete by ill winds, and this was also the Aetolian's story (19.185–7, 14.382–5). A passage in the Telemachy provides a model in the real experiences of the heroes: at 3.291 Nestor describes how on the initial journey home storms swept some of the Greek fleet to Crete. On the significance of Crete see above, and 19.172–8n.

(b) Phoenicians brought Odysseus to Ithaca according to the lie told to Athene (13.272–86). They play a more villainous role in the story he tells Eumaeus, in which a Phoenician τρώκτης (lit. 'gnawer',

[98] Cf. R. Meiggs and D. Lewis, *Greek historical inscriptions* (Oxford 1969) no. 7; L. H. Jeffery, *Archaic Greece* (London 1976) esp. 50–1, 56; O. Murray, *Early Greece* (Fontana, Glasgow 1980) 215–23.

i.e. crook) lures the narrator away from Egypt to sell him as a slave
(14.287–98; compare the deceitful Thesprotians in 14.339–47). This
matches the sad tale of Eumaeus' abduction as a child, again by
Phoenicians (15.415–84, esp. 416 τρῶκται).[99]

(c) The third common element is Idomeneus, a major figure of the
second rank in the *Iliad*, prominent especially in book 13. In *Odyssey*
13 Odysseus claims to have fled from Crete after killing Idomeneus'
son (259); in book 14, he and Idomeneus set out to Troy together (237);
in book 19, he himself is Idomeneus' younger brother! Thus Odysseus
progressively builds up his Cretan status, so that in book 19, con-
fronting a queen, he is himself of royal blood. The Aetolian who had
previously deceived Eumaeus also told of Odysseus having stayed with
Idomeneus. Rather than hunting for allegedly authentic versions un-
derlying these resemblances (as does Woodhouse), we should relish the
kaleidoscopic variations which both Odysseus and the poet delight in
playing on a varied yet limited set of biographical and geographical
motifs.

(d) A fourth common element, Thesprotia (part of Epirus, in NW
Greece beyond Ithaca), has also been discussed in efforts to recover the
'original' wanderings. In 14.314–30 Odysseus describes his (fictional)
visit to the king of the Thesprotians, and claims to have heard that
Odysseus had recently been there, but had left in order to consult the
oracle at Dodona (327–8), to learn whether he should return to Ithaca
openly or in secret. In 19.269–307 he elaborates this tale for Penelope,
including some elements of his real experiences (esp. 275–6, the cattle
of the Sun; 279, Phaeacians). Again we see that the encounter with
Eumaeus in book 14 is a lesser anticipation of the meeting with Pene-
lope here. Some have conjectured that in an earlier version the real
Odysseus genuinely consulted the oracle of Dodona.[100] Further, Thes-
protia is associated with the later wanderings of Odysseus, as narrated
in the lost Cyclic poem known as the *Telegoneia*, a work of uncertain

---

[99] On the Phoenicians in general see Murray, *Early Greece* 70–2, 91–4;
D. Harden, *The Phoenicians* (Penguin 1971); J. D. Muhly, *Berytus* 19 (1970) 19–64.

[100] For reconstructions of this putative version see Woodhouse, *Composition*
144ff.; C. G. Hardie in *Evolution of consciousness: studies ... for O. Barfield*, ed. S.
Sugerman (Middletown, Conn., 1976) 136ff.; S. West, in her introd. to the
Italian *Odyssey* 1 lxxxiii–xc (not reproduced in the English edition; but see
L.C.M. 6 (1981) 169–75).

date. In that poem Odysseus married Callidice, queen of the Thesprotians, and only years later returned to Ithaca: again, the motif of detention overseas by other women, and belated homecoming (see the summary of the poem by Proclus, p. 109.13–20 Allen = p. 72.10–18 Davies). But in the *Odyssey* the story of Odysseus' visit to the oracle is surely just a tamer and more conventional reflection of the awesome encounter with Tiresias.

(d) Similes[101]

The extended simile is a distinctive feature of Homeric style, inherited by later epic writers in the western tradition, such as Virgil and Milton, but apparently not shared by other primary epic. It consists of a comparison which is developed in detail, usually for two or three lines, and which regularly introduces elements which at first sight bear no relation to the narrative events which prompted the simile. Shorter comparisons do occur in Homer (e.g. *Iliad* 24.572, Achilles leapt up λέων ὥς, 'like a lion'), but the extended simile is the norm. In books 19 and 20 of the *Odyssey* they occur at the following places: 19.109–14, 205–12 (the latter passage includes two complementary comparisons), 518–24 (a mythological parallel: cf. 20.66–78, which is introduced in a rather similar way, but goes well beyond the limits of a simile, becoming a mythological paradigm or illustrative example[102]); 20.13–16, 25–30. For more detailed comments on these see the Commentary.

Similes are much more numerous in the *Iliad* than in the *Odyssey*: the proportion is approximately three to one. This is usually explained by

[101] See in general the studies by H. Fränkel, *Die homerischen Gleichnisse* (Göttingen 1921), C. Moulton, *Similes in the Homeric poems* (Göttingen 1977); M. Coffey, *A.J.P.* 78 (1957) 113–32; short accounts by C. M. Bowra, *Tradition and design in the Iliad* (Oxford 1930) ch. 6, and M. W. Edwards, *Homer, the poet of the Iliad* (Johns Hopkins 1987) ch. 12; see also Macleod, *Iliad XXIV*, 48–50. There are lists of the similes in both epics in the books by W. C. Scott, *The oral nature of the Homeric simile* (*Mnem.* Suppl. 28, Leiden 1974) and D. J. N. Lee, *The similes of the Iliad and the Odyssey compared* (Melbourne 1964) (a book otherwise of little value). R. Friedrich, *A.J.P.* 102 (1981) 120–37 discusses the relation of the *Odyssey*'s similes to the poem's themes; on this aspect see also Moulton, *Similes* 126–34, 141–53.

[102] Cf. Edwards, *Homer, the poet* ch. 11, with bibliography, and the works cited in n. 86 above.

the 'monotony' of the battle books of the *Iliad*, which required diversifi-
cation; or, more acceptably, it is argued that the setting of the *Iliad* is
unchanging, at least as far as the human characters are concerned,
and therefore the similes introduce variety and remind us of the world
beyond the Trojan plain, of the world of normality and peacetime,
whereas the *Odyssey*, with its changes of scene and its much-travelled
hero, has less need of the additional diversity provided by the similes.
There is certainly some truth in this, but the similes have many other
functions besides offering variety and colour. The following list of func-
tions, and the examples given, are not exhaustive.

(i) Similes may serve to make an action more vivid or more easily
imaginable to the audience: this applies particularly to the movements
and actions of supernatural beings.[103] Similarly psychological states can
be made more comprehensible by a physical comparison (*Od.* 20.25–
30, with n.).

(ii) They may characterise individuals or types, or capture the es-
sence of a relationship: thus attacking warriors are like lions or wolves,
retreating armies are like panicky deer; Hector's resolution is like a
woodcutter's tireless axe (*Il.* 3.60–3), while the carefree Paris is like a
proud stallion who has broken free of his tether and runs towards the
pastures where he will find the mares (6.506–11). Ajax's resistance to
the Trojan onslaught is like the brutish stubbornness of an ass at which
boys are throwing sticks (*Il.* 11.558–65), and so forth. More subtly, the
simile may suggest something about the relationship or situation which
is not obvious and which is not the primary motivation for the simile.
Achilles mocks the weeping Patroclus: 'why are you crying, like a foolish
girl who runs along by her mother pleading to be picked up, clutching
at her clothes, and holds her up when she is in a hurry? ...' (*Il.* 16.7–
10).[104] On the surface this is insulting: Patroclus' grief is womanish. But
it also suggests the intimacy of their relationship, and recalls the pity
which Achilles, here cast in the mother's role, inwardly feels for Patro-
clus (16.5 ὤικτιρε). In the *Odyssey*, a notable simile describes Eumaeus'
joy at the homecoming of Telemachus (*Od.* 16.14–21): he is compared
with a father greeting a long-lost son, who has been in danger overseas

---

[103] See e.g. *Il.* 5.864–7, 15.80–3, 24.80–2.
[104] It is sometimes said or implied that similes do not appear in speeches, only
in the narrative, but this is quite untrue: see Moulton, *Similes* 100, 118.

for ten years. Telemachus has indeed been in danger, and he does treat the swineherd as almost a father figure (witness the affectionate address ἄττα, 'dada', in 31), but the simile has added point because the real father, Odysseus, is also present, unrecognised. Two favourite themes of the *Odyssey*, appearance vs reality, and open emotion contrasted with suppressed emotion, are given a fresh airing through the ironically apt simile.[105]

(iii) The simile may add weight and significance to an occasion: this is especially the case when similes are accumulated, above all when the Achaean forces set out to war in book 2 of the *Iliad*: their advance is described in no fewer than four similes, and others follow describing the chieftains and Agamemnon. But a single simile also can reinforce the significance of a key moment, and heighten the tension: for example, the comparison of Odysseus with a bard as he strings the bow before the slaughter (*Od.* 21.404–9), or the comparison of Penelope's joy on recognising Odysseus with the happiness of a shipwrecked sailor making land (23.233–40, quoted above, p. 37).

(iv) Similes are usually (though not invariably[106]) drawn from the familiar world of everyday life. (It goes with this that the similes are sometimes anachronistic: that is, they may include ideas or customs alien to the heroic world.[107]) They describe practices or events which would be commonplace for Homer's audience: farming, hunting, dancing, craftsmanship (e.g. *Od.* 9.384–8, 391–4) and the like (though we may allow that even these practices are stylised). This not only makes the events narrated more accessible to the audience (see (i) above), but also creates a powerful tension between the normal or everyday experiences described in the simile, and the extraordinary or shocking experiences of the hero.[108] The juxtaposition heightens our sense of the

[105] The simile is 'capped' or recalled at 216–19. On linked similes of this kind see esp. Moulton, *Similes* ch. 1 and pp. 133–9.

[106] For notable exceptions see *Il.* 2.781–5 (though notice 783 φασί), 3.6, 7.208–10, 13.242–3, 298–300.

[107] See Bowra, *Tradition and design* 121. An example of an idea anachronistically or inappropriately introduced in a simile is the justice of Zeus, described in a famous simile in *Il.* 16.384–93. The idea that the gods constantly watch for and punish mortal wrongdoers is undoubtedly current – it figures in speeches in the *Iliad*, as well as in the *Odyssey* and in Hesiod – but the main narrative of the *Iliad* presents the gods as capricious and little concerned with justice.

[108] Cf. Macleod on *Il.* 24.48off.

achievements or the ordeals of heroic man. In the same way, similes which portray beauty and order and peace are often introduced to illustrate horror and chaos, whether in war or in some other kind of suffering.[109] The bloody wound of Menelaus, which may mean death for him and humiliation for the Greeks, is compared with a beautiful work of human artistry, an ivory cheek-piece for a horse, dyed by a woman of Maionia or Caria (*Il.* 4.141–7). The point of contact is the spreading red colour on both the artefact and the human body; but the power of the simile stems from the contrast between the perfect tranquillity of the woman's meticulous work and the shocking violence of the hero's sudden agony. In the *Odyssey*, the monstrous Scylla scoops up six of Odysseus' men like a fisherman pulling in his catch (12.251–5); here there is reversal of the norm, as is fitting in the monstrous and unnatural world of the wanderings, as the human beings are fished for by the sea-creature rather than the other way round. A similar effect is gained by juxtaposing 'low' or unheroic similes with heroic or dignified action in the narrative (e.g. *Il.* 12.433–5, *Od.* 9.383–8 and 391–4, 20.25–30).

(v) The similes normally have one explicit point of contact with the narrative (the so-called *tertium comparationis*). But they may also contain other elements which are relevant to the narrative or its major themes, or which suggest further connections (cf. (ii) above). Thus in *Il.* 23.222–5, Achilles' grief for Patroclus is compared with that of a father who has lost his son; this comparison reminds us of Priam, whose son Hector has been slain by Achilles, and of Peleus, Achilles' father, who will soon lose his heroic son. The simile thus paves the way for the all-important scene in book 24 where Achilles and Priam meet, and where the father–son relationship is the basis of Priam's appeal to Achilles' pity (24.486–506). Similes may also occasionally foreshadow subsequent events more specifically. Patroclus is compared with a wounded lion, whose own strength has destroyed him, at the very height of his aristeia (*Il.* 16.751–4): his downfall is near, and has been predicted and anticipated in other ways. See also 18.207–14, 219–21, 22.410–11, all anticipating the fall of Troy.

A particularly rich and complex thematic simile in the *Odyssey* occurs at 8.521–31, where Odysseus weeps at Demodocus' song describing his

<hr />

[109] D. H. Porter, *C.J.* 68 (1972) 11–21; O. Taplin, *G.&R.* 27 (1980) 14–16.

own exploits at the sacking of Troy.[110] Here he is compared with a woman whose husband has fallen in battle defending his city, and who sobs over his corpse while the victorious soldiers beat her and drag her away to a life of slavery. Thus the hero Odysseus, the 'sacker of cities', is compared with a helpless woman, a victim like the Trojan women; the implication is surely that he grieves not only for his own side but for what he himself has done in the past as a warrior and a conqueror. The glory of the sack of Troy is tinged with a sense of loss and sorrow, as throughout the *Odyssey*.

In an earlier context we have seen that critics often contrast 'primary epic' with 'secondary' or 'literary' epic, Homer with (for example) Virgil, and that these contrasts often underestimate the sophistication and richness of the earlier form. So also with the similes, there has been a tendency to exaggerate the contrast between Homer's and Virgil's: Homer's, it is said, are elaborated without reference to the context, while Virgil's are carefully integrated and correspond point by point with the narrative.[111] Fränkel's book already showed that this contrast is overdrawn, and recent work has happily adopted a more positive attitude and emphasised the richness and variety of Homer's use of similes. There is a danger of over-reaction: it should be admitted that some similes are casually and even inappropriately introduced,[112] and that details are often included purely for their pictorial effect, for their own sake. But it is clear that in both *Iliad* and *Odyssey* similes may be functional as well as ornamental: Homer may employ them as subtly as Virgil to illuminate the personalities of his characters or the themes of the poems.

---

[110] See further *J.H.S.* 106 (1986) 155–6.

[111] See e.g. D. West's studies of 'multiple-correspondence similes', e.g. *J.R.S.* 59 (1969) 40–49. It is in any case questionable whether such tidy-mindedness should be considered solely as a virtue: cf. C. A. Martindale, *Comparative criticism* 33 (1981) 224–38.

[112] A classic example is the simile which compares the Myrmidons entering battle with wolves sated by feasting upon a deer, and seeking water from a fountain (*Il.* 16.156ff.). Ingenuity can defend this juxtaposition of opposites, but it is probably better to admit a false note here (so e.g. Bowra, *Tradition and design* 116).

5. METRE, GRAMMAR AND TEXT

(a) Metre[113]

The metre of Homeric epic, as of all Greek epic thereafter (and of its
Latin imitators), is the dactylic hexameter ('six-measure line'). It is
traditionally divided into six 'feet' which are potentially of equal length
(though the last foot of each line is a special case). Its scheme is as
follows:

$$\overset{\text{1}}{-\cup\cup} \Big| \overset{\text{2}}{-\cup\cup} \Big| \overset{\text{3}}{-\cup\cup} \Big| \overset{\text{4}}{-\cup\cup} \Big| \overset{\text{5}}{-\cup\cup} \Big| \overset{\text{6}}{-\times}$$

In this notation – is a long or 'heavy' syllable, ∪ a short or 'light' one.
Two long syllables form a *spondee* ($--$), while one long and two short
($-\cup\cup$) form a *dactyl*. Thus all but the last foot can be either a dactyl or
a spondee. The last foot is $-\times$, where × indicates that the syllable can
be either long or short; but it is always two syllables only. A syllable
normally contains only a single vowel or diphthong (a diphthong is a
combination of vowels pronounced as one, e.g. ευ in Ἀχιλλεύς).

In Greek, the vowels ε and ο are naturally short, η and ω are natu-
rally long. The other vowels, α, ι and υ, may be either long or short. All
diphthongs (e.g. αι οι ει) are long (but see below on Correption). But it
is necessary to distinguish between the length of a *vowel* and the metri-
cal quantity of a *syllable*: though the distinction is often blurred in
ancient treatments and modem handbooks, these are different things.
A syllable containing a long vowel or diphthong is 'heavy', and both
syllable and vowel may then be described as long. But a syllable con-
taining a short vowel may be either 'light' or 'heavy' according to what
consonants follow: there is no question of the vowel itself becoming
long. What matters is whether the syllable ends with a consonant: if it
does so, or if it contains a long vowel or diphthong, the syllable is long.

---

[113] For fuller accounts see M. L. West, *Greek metre* (Oxford 1982) and the
simplified version, *An introduction to Greek metre* (Oxford 1987), though even the
latter is quite hard for the complete beginner; D. S. Raven, *Greek metre* (London
1962) 17, 21–6, 43–5; C. M. Bowra, in *Companion to Homer*, ed. Wace and Stub-
bings, 19–25. See also M. Howatson's entry on 'Metre' in the revised *Oxford
companion to classical literature* (Oxford 1989).

Thus in the first word of the *Odyssey*, ἄνδρα, the first α is short but the syllable is 'heavy' and therefore long.[114]

Where two consonants are found together, they are normally divided between syllables: e.g. in καρδίη the first syllable is καρ (long syllable) the second δι (short). The aspirate or 'rough' breathing does not count as a consonant. ζ ξ ψ count as double consonants (σδ, κς, πς). However, a short syllable is permitted (though not often) before certain combinations of consonants: a 'mute' or 'plosive' (π β φ τ δ θ κ γ χ) followed by a 'liquid' or 'nasal' (λ ρ μ ν). For example, in 20.92, which begins τῆς δ' ἄρα κλαιούσης, the second syllable of ἄρα must be short, despite the fact that the two consonants κλ follow. Some of these combinations are rare; and in all cases where this shortening is found it is a special licence, usually in order to fit into the hexameter words which otherwise would not scan.

Diphthongs, as explained above, are normally pronounced as one syllable. When this is not so, modern texts print a double dot above the second letter concerned. This indicates that the vowels are to be pronounced and scanned separately; again this allows greater metrical flexibility. There are examples on virtually every page of Homer: see e.g. 19.4 and 9 in the example below: also 19.20 ἀϋτμή, 30 κλήϊσεν, 31, 72, 82, 101, etc. The double dot (also known as a diaeresis) must never be ignored in scansion.

When vowels meet at the end of one word and the beginning of another within the line, there may be *elision*, which is always indicated in modern texts (though not in the earliest manuscripts surviving from antiquity). Effectively this means that the first vowel is dropped or ignored in pronunciation. Examples are frequent: at 20.136 ὄφρα ἔθελε αὐτός becomes ὄφρ' ἔθελ' αὐτός and is scanned accordingly; in 20.137 σίτου δὲ οὐκέτι becomes σίτου δ' οὐκέτι; in 20.140 γε ὡς becomes γ' ὡς, and so on. As the last example shows, the aspirate or rough breathing does not prevent elision. In Homer elision never occurs between one line and another (as occasionally happens in later Greek and Latin poetry), but it may occur at the caesura: see e.g. 19.4 and 7 in the example below.

However, it often suits the poet to follow other procedures when vowels meet at word-end.

---

[114] See further West, *Greek metre* 8–9; W. S. Allen, *Vox graeca* (3rd edn, Cambridge 1987) 104–10.

(a) Crasis ('mixing', 'blending'). This means that two or more vowels are slurred together and produce one long syllable: e.g. *Od.* 3.255 καὶ αὐτός becomes καὐτός. This is also known as 'synecphonesis' ('joint pronunciation') or 'synizesis' ('sitting together'): the fine distinctions between these terms need not trouble the beginner. But this phenomenon is distinct from elision. It is most common when the first word concerned is monosyllabic (e.g. καί δή μή ὦ).

Crasis is also quite common within words, especially when the first vowel is ε. Examples are *Il.* 23.834 χρεώμενος, where the vowels εώ are pronounced as one sound; *Il.* 4.308 ἐπόρθεον (often printed as ἐπόρθουν); *Il.* 2.811 πόλιος.

(b) Hiatus ('gap', 'opening'). This means that both vowels simply retain their normal pronunciation: e.g. 19.314 ἐπεὶ οὐ, 460 εὖ ἰησάμενοι. This is especially common when the second word originally began with a digamma (Ϝ, the Greek letter which is pronounced as 'w', lost at an early date from some dialects, including Attic and Ionic, and not represented in their alphabets).[115] Examples of phrases in which the presence of the digamma causes hiatus are 19.309 ξεῖνε   ἔπος, 313 ἔτι   οἶκον.

(c) Correption (from the Latin *corripere*, 'to tighten up'). This means the shortening of a vowel which is naturally long, or a diphthong, before another vowel (which is almost always long). This also happens in mid-word, though very rarely: 20.379 ἔμπαιον (with αι short) is an example from these books. It is one of the many ways in which the epic poet makes his verses more flexible and fits recalcitrant words into the hexameter.

The hexameter line is not easily pronounced in one breath in recitation, and the poet would naturally not wish each line to be a single self-contained unit. All Homeric verses have at least one strong break, the caesura (the Latin equivalent for the Greek τομή, 'cut' or 'severance'). This term is conventionally applied to the one main break in the line, though it is more loosely applicable to any division between words which does not coincide with the end of a foot. All Homeric verses have a caesura, in this more restricted sense. This may fall at one of three

---

[115] Cf. Monro, *Grammar* §§388–406; L. R. Palmer, in Wace and Stubbings, *Companion* 100–1. The old edition of Homer by van Leeuwen and da Costa reinstates digammas (first attempted by Payne Knight in his editions of 1808, 1820).

places: (a) after the first syllable of the third foot (the so-called 'masculine caesura') e.g. *Od.* 19.204:

$$- \quad \cup \quad \cup \quad - \qquad \cup\cup \; - \quad \cup\cup \quad - \cup \cup \; - \qquad -$$
τῆς δ' ἄρ' ἀκουούσης   ῥέε δάκρυα, τήκετο δὲ χρώς

(the broad gap in mid-line indicates the place where the caesura falls);
(b) after the first *short* syllable of a dactylic third foot (the 'feminine caesura'), e.g. 19.210:

$$- \quad - \quad - \quad \cup\cup- \quad \cup \qquad \cup- \; \cup \; \cup - \cup \quad \cup \quad - \; \cup$$
θυμῶι μὲν γοόωσαν   ἑὴν ἐλέαιρε γυναῖκα

or (c) after the first syllable of the fourth foot, e.g. 5.203 (etc.):

$$-\cup \; \cup \; - \quad - - \quad \cup\cup - \qquad \cup \; \cup - \; \cup \qquad \cup \; - \quad -$$
διογενὲς Λαερτιάδη,   πολυμήχαν' Ὀδυσσεῦ

Of these (b) is the commonest type, (c) the least common by far (in the *Odyssey* in only about nine lines per thousand).

Most of the notable features of Homeric metre can be illustrated by the scansion of a fairly short passage. Here is the opening of book 19 of the *Odyssey*, with metrical annotation:

$$- \; \cup \; \cup|- \quad \cup \; \cup| \; - \quad \cup \; \cup| \; - \; \cup \; \cup| \; - \cup \; \cup| \; - \quad -$$
αὐτὰρ ὁ ἐν μεγάρωι   ὑπελείπετο δῖος Ὀδυσσεύς,

$$- \quad -|- \; \cup \; \cup| - \qquad \cup \quad \cup| \; - \; -|- \quad -|- \; -$$
μνηστήρεσσι φόνον   σὺν Ἀθήνηι μερμηρίζων·

$$- \; \cup \; \cup| - \; \cup \; \cup \; - \qquad \cup \; \cup|- \quad \cup \; \cup|- \; \cup \quad \cup| \; - \; -$$
αἶψα δὲ Τηλέμαχον   ἔπεα πτερόεντα προσηύδα·

$$- \; \cup \; \cup| \; - \quad -|- \; \cup \qquad \cup| \; -\cup\cup| - \quad \cup \; \cup| - \; -$$
Τηλέμαχε, χρὴ τεύχε'   ἀρήϊα κατθέμεν εἴσω

$$- \quad \cup \; \cup| \; - \quad -|- \qquad - \quad -|- \qquad \cup \; \cup| \; - \; \cup \; \cup|- \; \times$$
πάντα μάλ', αὐτὰρ μνηστῆρας   μαλακοῖς ἐπέεσσι   5

$$- \quad -| \; - \; \cup \; \cup| - \quad \cup \qquad \cup| \; - \quad -| \; - \quad \cup \; \cup| - \; \times$$
παρφάσθαι, ὅτε κέν σε   μεταλλῶσιν ποθέοντες·

$$- \quad - \; | \; - \; \cup \; \cup|- \qquad \cup \quad \cup| \; - \; \cup \; \cup| - \; \cup \; \cup|- \; \times$$
ἐκ καπνοῦ κατέθηκ',   ἐπεὶ οὐκέτι τοῖσιν ἐώικει,

$$-\cup \quad \cup| \; - \; -|- \quad \cup \qquad \cup|- \quad \cup \; \cup| \; - \quad \cup \; \cup| \; - \; -$$
οἷά ποτε Τροίηνδε   κιὼν κατέλειπεν Ὀδυσσεύς,

$$- \quad \cup \; \cup| \; - \quad -| \; - \qquad - \; |- \quad \cup \; \cup|- \; \cup \quad \cup|- \; -$$
ἀλλὰ κατήικισται,   ὅσσον πυρὸς ἵκετ' ἀϋτμή.

$$- \quad \cup \; \cup| - \quad \cup \; \cup| \; - \; \cup \qquad \cup|- \quad \cup \; \cup|- \; \cup \quad \cup| \; - \; -$$
πρὸς δ' ἔτι καὶ τόδε μεῖζον   ἐνὶ φρεσὶν ἔμβαλε δαίμων,   10

$$- \quad -| \; - \; -| \; - \; \cup \qquad \cup| \; - \qquad - \; |- \; \cup \; \cup| \; - \; -$$
μή πως οἰνωθέντες,   ἔριν στήσαντες ἐν ὑμῖν,

$$- \quad - \; |- \qquad -| \; - \; \cup \qquad \cup| \; - \qquad -|- \; \cup \; \cup| \; - \; \times$$
ἀλλήλους τρώσητε   καταισχύνητέ τε δαῖτα

$$- \quad -| \; - \; - \; -|- \qquad \cup \qquad \cup|- \; \cup \quad \cup| \; - \; \cup \quad \cup| \; - \; \times$$
καὶ μνηστύν· αὐτὸς γὰρ   ἐφέλκεται ἄνδρα σίδηρος.

In the above passage, the vertical lines mark the end of feet, the large gap half-way along the line marks the caesura. Other notable features are as follows:

1. Lines 1, 3 and 10 have 5 dactyls, the maximum number possible.
2. Line 2 has a spondaic fifth foot, which in Homer is a relative rarity (about 5 per cent of his hexameters contain such a foot).
3. There are elisions in lines 4, 5, 7, 9 and 10; elision occurs at the caesura in lines 4 and 7.
4. Correption occurs in 7 ἐπεὶ οὐκέτι, where the second syllable of ἐπεὶ would normally be long; and at 13 ἐφέλκεται ἄνδρα, where the last syllable of ἐφέλκεται would also normally be long.
5. There is hiatus at 1 ὁ ἐν and μεγάρωι ὑπ., at 6 παρφάσθαι, ὅτε and at 9 -ισται, ὅσσον.
6. In line 4 ἀρήϊα the combination ηι could be a diphthong, but is in fact scanned as two separate syllables: editors indicate this by the double dot above the second vowel concerned. Thus ἀρήϊα has four syllables, not three. Similarly in line 9 ἀϋτμή the α and the υ are pronounced separately .
7. Some common short words are associated closely (a) with the word before, e.g. 'enclitics'[116] such as μοι, particles such as μέν, δέ, γάρ, κε(ν) or (b) with the word which follows: e.g. the definite article, and some particles, notably καί, ἀλλά. The caesura may not interrupt one of these combinations. Thus in line 6 ὅτε κέν σε forms a unit, and the caesura falls after σε, not after κέν. Similarly in line 13 the caesura must follow, not precede γάρ. For fuller details see West, *Greek metre* 25–6, and his glossary s.v. 'appositives'.

Aesthetic evaluation of metrical features is a perilously subjective area, in which critics must generally steer an uneasy course between the self-evident and the entirely speculative. In particular, too much is often read into the number of long and short syllables in a line, and large deductions are made about the poet's intention to make sound mirror sense. The archaeologist Schliemann is said to have fallen in love with the beauty of Homer's verse on hearing it read aloud, before

[116] For this term see Goodwin, *Greek grammar* §§140–6: basically it means a word which loses its accent and is pronounced as if part of or closely linked to the preceding word.

he knew a word of the language; but it could hardly be supposed that he actually understood, however intuitively, the subject matter of the verses he heard. There are undoubtedly some passages in which a deliberate metrical effect is being cultivated for a discernible end: the most famous example, much discussed by ancient critics, is the scene in book 11 of the *Odyssey* in which Sisyphus painfully thrusts his boulder up to the top of the hill, his efforts being described in slow-moving lines, and then the stone rolls down to the foot of the hill again in a rapid, entirely dactylic line (11.593–8; cf. Dion. Hal. *On the composition of words* 20).[117] There are also some onomatopoeic words in Homeric Greek, and in lines including these, or lines which seem to contain a preponderance of harsh letters such as kappa, we may legitimately speak of sound echoing sense;[118] but on the whole it is more prudent to think of the sound and metre of a line as being adapted or well suited to the sense: it cannot normally convey the meaning of the line independently of the hearer's linguistic understanding.

In fact, it is unprofitable to separate metre from the poet's other stylistic resources, such as repetition, rhetorical figures, the shaping of long and short sentences, or devices which emphasise or isolate particular words or phrases (of which the most familiar is probably 'enjambment', the running over of the last word(s) of a clause or a sentence into the next line). For examples of enjambment which seem deliberately emphatic, see 19.87 (Τηλέμαχος), 118, 271 ἀγχοῦ, 272 ζωοῦ, 393, 20.6, 40.

One prominent stylistic device which the regular stichic metre emphasises is the repetition of a key-word at the opening of successive lines: e.g. *Il.* 2.671–3, *Od.* 16.118–20, 301–3; Hes. *WD* 317–19, 578–80; cf. Fehling, *Wiederholungsfiguren* 324–5. Even lines which do not involve repetition may achieve a comparable effect: e.g. 19.210–11 (θυμῶι μὲν ... | ὀφθαλμοὶ δ' ...).

---

[117] Cf. Pope, *Essay on criticism* (1711):

> When Ajax strives some rock's vast weight to throw,
> The line too labours, and the words move slow;
> Not so when swift Camilla scours the plain,
> Flies o'er th' unbending corn, and skims along the main.

[118] E.g. *Il.* 1.49 κλαγγή, 4.125 λίγξε βιός, *Od.* 9.394 σίζ' ὀφθαλμός, 20.13, 15 ὑλάκτει ... ὑλάει. In general see W. B. Stanford, *The sound of Greek* (Berkeley and Los Angeles 1969); N. J. Richardson, *C.Q.* 20 (1980) 283–7.

Another device of emphasis may be seen in lines which elaborate on a word or thought in the preceding line, e.g. 19.579–80:

νοσφισσαμένη τόδε δῶμα
κουρίδιον, μάλα καλόν, ἐνίπλειον βιότοιο . . . (see n. ad loc.)

Cf.19.246, 266, or 19.131 (Penelope lists the neighbouring islands rather than simply referring to them by the general word 'islands' in 130); 175–7. Again, lines which elaborate on a character's name and status, rather than referring to the person in question in the briefest possible way, obviously add importance to that character's role, or show the speaker's respect: thus for Eurycleia at 19.375 her mistress is not just 'Penelope', but κούρη 'Ικαρίοιο, περίφρων Πηνελόπεια. In his solemn oath to Penelope Odysseus does not just swear by Zeus, but devotes the whole line to the supreme god: ἴστω νῦν Ζεὺς πρῶτα, θεῶν ὕπατος καὶ ἄριστος (19.303). See also 20.148 (with n.), 283, 388. The honorific lines which often open speeches have a similar effect: see 19.165 = 262, 336, 583; 19.546, 20.112.

There is a tendency for the caesura to provide a sense-pause as well as a metrical division: often a new clause will begin at this point, and sometimes the two halves of the line will be in contrast, or opposed in sense: e.g. 19.445, 449, 548, 20.102, 247, 384. The caesura can be exploited for very different effects according to context: in 19.468–70 the six self-contained half-lines each mark a stage in the seemingly inevitable exposure of Odysseus now that the nurse has recognised him, and the effect is highly dramatic; by contrast, in Eurycleia's speech at 20.149–56 the frequent sense-breaks in mid-line mark the stages at which she thinks of another point to make to her subordinates, or turns to some of them with fresh instructions, and the mood is one of comic bustling and bossiness.

Successive lines may present opposed or antithetical points, so clarifying the structure of an argument. Similarly, there is a tendency for gnomic pronouncements, generalising about a particular case, to be self-contained lines; e.g. 15.74. Sometimes these are the conclusion of a speech: e.g. 19.163, 360 (cf. the many proverbial one-liners in Hesiod, esp. in the *Works and Days*).

Not the least of the hexameter's effect, however, is subliminal. The regularity and stately movement of the metre reinforces the listener's consciousness of the heroic age as a time of dignity and splendour: in this respect, as on the more technical level, the hexameter and the artificial epic dialect work together, creating a world which is more beautiful and more glorious than the everyday world in which the audience normally exists.

(b) Grammar[119]

The form of the Greek language which beginners normally encounter first at school and university, and which is given pride of place in all standard grammars, is Attic Greek, the formal prose of Athenian literature of the fifth and fourth centuries, the Greek written by (most notably) Thucydides, Plato and the orators. Even in the work of its clearest and simplest exponents, such as Xenophon and Lysias, it is a more formal and sophisticated language than the Greek commonly spoken by the ordinary Athenian of the period. But the gulf between fifth-century Attic prose and the language of Homeric epic is very much greater. First, the Homeric epics are poetry, of a very elevated and dignified kind; secondly, they were composed at least 250 years before the earliest surviving Attic writers were active, and draw on earlier poetry going back much further; thirdly, they are composed in a rich and artificial poetic style which is a composite of different dialects: primarily Ionic and Aeolic, with an additional element of Arcado-Cypriot. An Attic element may have been imposed later, perhaps as a result of regular performance in Attica from the time of Pisistratus onwards (p. 41 above), but for the most part the language of Homer seems remote and often opaque, just as the language of Chaucer or Langland is difficult even for the well-read modern reader (though ancient Greek readers were much more intimately familiar with Homer than the ordinary modern reader is with these early writers). A very large number of authoritative books have been written describing and analysing the

---

[119] See further P. Chantraine, *Grammaire homérique* I (3rd edn, Paris 1958) and II (2nd edn, Paris 1963); D. B. Monro, *A grammar of the Homeric dialect* (2nd edn, Oxford 1891). More briefly, W. B. Stanford, in the introd. to both volumes of his Macmillan edition of the *Odyssey*. Briefer still is the sketch of 'the chief peculiarities of the Homeric dialect' in Autenrieth's *Homeric dictionary* xvii–xxi. For the historical dimension see L. R. Palmer, *The Greek language* (London and Boston 1980) 83–101 or J. B. Hainsworth, *CAH* (2nd edn) III 1 (1982) 850–65.

Homeric language. What follows cannot replace or précis such works, but may at least prove useful for quick reference before turning elsewhere. Most of the examples are drawn from books 19 and 20.

1. Vocabulary

The vocabulary of the Homeric poems is very large, and includes many words which are never or rarely employed in later Greek writers: some of those which are employed only rarely are used by writers who are consciously imitating a particular Homeric phrase or passage. Moreover, there is a surprisingly large number of words which occur only once in Homer: the so-called *hapax legomena*. Many words used by Homer are incomprehensible to modern readers; from ancient commentaries and lexica we know that scholars in Hellenistic times were also often baffled; and it is plausible that a limited number of words (mostly embedded in formulae) carried no clear meaning even for the epic poets who used them: e.g. 19.145 τανηλεγέος. Usually a conventional 'poetic' translation has developed in English for even the terms which perplex experts; the lexicon by Liddell and Scott, and still more the works of Cunliffe and Autenrieth, offer suggested renderings for even the most obscure words and titles. For more advanced analysis of etymology and meaning see H. Ebeling, *Lexicon Homericum* (Leipzig 1880–5; in Latin), P. Chantraine, *Dictionnaire étymologique de la langue grecque* (Paris 1968), and the massive *Lexicon des frühgriechischen Epos* (Göttingen 1955–), which as of early 1990 has reached kappa.

2. Morphology

This is probably the area in which beginners find most difficulty. The greatest obstacles lie in the forms of verbs: by comparison nouns and adjectives are much more straightforward.

Metrical convenience, dialect mixture and linguistic development all create variations and irregularities in form. The first in particular gives rise to a number of artificially lengthened, shortened or modified forms of words, for example:

(i)   ε appears as ει: e.g. κεινός ('empty'), χρύσειος, σπεῖος, θείω.
(ii)   ο appears as ου: e.g. πουλύς, μοῦνος.
(iii) ο appears as ω: e.g. Διώνυσος.

(iv) η may be shortened to ε, as in many forms of the subjunctive: e.g. εἴδετε for εἴδητε.

(v) ω may be shortened to ο: again this should be noted esp. with reference to misleading forms of the subjunctive, e.g. 8.292 τραπείομεν.

(a) Verbs

1. The augment in past tenses is often omitted, usually for metrical reasons.

2. Verbs in όω άω έω which in Attic would contract are often given in their uncontracted form, e.g. φιλέω: φιλέων (19.195), φιλεόντων (24.485), etc.

3. Reduplication of the initial syllables of a verb in the second aorist active and middle is common, and this reduplication can also affect future tenses. For example, φείδομαι yields πεφιδοίμην (9.277) as 1 sing. aor. optative, φράζω produces πεφραδέειν (19.477) and πεφραδέμεν (7.49) as aor. active infinitives, χολόω has κεχολώσομαι as its future middle (e.g. *Il.* 23.543), κεχολωμένος as aor. middle participle (*Od.* 8.276, 19.324, etc.).

As in many languages, the verbs 'to be' and 'to go' include many variant forms and irregularities.

(i) εἰμί '*I am*'

Present

	Indicative	*Imperative*	*Subjunctive*	*Optative*
1 sing.	εἰμί		ἔω	εἴην
2 sing.	εἶς, ἐσσί	ἴσθι	ἔῃς	εἴης, ἔοις
3 sing.	ἔστι	ἔστω	ἔῃ, ἔῃσι, εἴῃ	εἴη, ἔοι
2 and 3 dual	ἐστόν	ἐστόν	ἦτον	εἴητον, εἴτον
1 plur.	εἰμέν		ὦμεν	εἴημεν, εἶμεν
2 plur.	ἐστέ	ἔστε	ἦτε	εἴητε, εἶτε
3 plur.	εἰσί, ἔασι	ἔστων	ὦσι, ἔωσι	εἴησαν, εἶεν

Present participle
ἐών ἐοῦσα ἐόν
Present infinitive
ἔμμεναι, ἔμεναι, ἔμμεν, ἔμεν, εἶναι *are all possible*

Imperfect indicative

1 sing.	ἦα, ἔα, ἦν, ἔην	*3 dual*	ἤστην
2 sing.	ἦσθα, ἔησθα	*1 plur.*	ἦμεν
3 sing.	ἦεν, ἦν, ἔην	*2 plur.*	ἦτε
2 dual	ἤστον	*3 plur.*	ἦσαν, ἔσαν

Future indicative ('I shall be'; in this tense the variation between one and two sigmas is frequent)

1 sing.	ἔσσομαι	*1 plur.*	ἐσσόμεθα
2 sing.	ἔσσεαι, ἔσεαι, ἔσηι	*2 plur.*	ἔσσεσθε
3 sing.	ἐσσεῖται, ἔσεται, ἔσται	*3 plur.*	ἔσσονται
2 and 3 dual	ἔσεσθον		

Fut. participle
ἐσ(σ)όμενος -η -ον
Fut. infinitive
ἔσ(σ)εσθαι

Past iterative ('I used to be')

1 sing.	ἔσκον
3 sing.	ἔσκε

The other parts of this tense are not found.

(ii) εἶμι '*I (shall) go*'

Present

	Indicative	Imperative	Subjunctive	Optative
1 sing.	εἶμι		ἴω	ἴοιμι, ἰοίην
2 sing.	εἶ	ἴθι	ἴηισθα, ἴηις	ἴοις
3 sing.	εἶσι	ἴτω	ἴηι	ἰείη, ἴοι
2 dual	ἴτον	ἴτον	ἴητον	ἴοιτον
3 dual	ἴτον	ἴτων	ἴητον	ἰοίτην
1 plur.	ἴμεν		ἴωμεν	ἴοιμεν
2 plur.	ἴτε	ἴτε	ἴητε	ἴοιτε
3 plur.	ἴασι	ἰόντων	ἴωσι	ἴοιεν

Imperfect indicative ('I was going')

1 sing.	ἤϊα	*3 dual*	ἴτην
2 sing.	ἤιεισθα	*1 plur.*	ἤιομεν
3 sing.	ἤϊε, ἴε, ηἴει	*2 plur.*	ἤιτε
2 dual	ἤιτον	*3 plur.*	ἤισαν, ἴσαν, ἤϊσαν, ἤϊον

(b) Nouns and adjectives

1. Homer often uses η as the ending for feminine nouns of the first declension (e.g. Τροίη, Ἀθήνη, πυρή), where Attic uses long α.
2. The genitive singular of second declension nouns and adjectives ends in -οιο as well as -ου: e.g. θανάτοιο, αἰθομένοιο.
3. Dative plural of nouns and adjectives often ends with an additional iota: -οισι, -αισι. A nu is usually added to this ending before a vowel.

Special suffixes may be added to nouns and proper names (esp. place-names) in addition to the regular cases:

-θε(ν)   'from x' e.g. 19.28 τηλόθεν 'from far away', 19.99 ἐμέθεν 'from me', 20.31 οὐρανόθεν 'from heaven'.

-φι(ν)   equivalent to genitive or dative singular or (less frequently) plural: e.g. βιήφι 'by force', θεόφιν 'by/from the gods'.

-θι   'at' or 'in x', e.g. οἴκοθι 'at home', ἄλλοθι 'elsewhere', ὑψόθι 'on high', 'high up'.

-δε -ζε -σε   indicating direction towards, 'to x', e.g. Ἰθάκηνδε 'to Ithaca'; 19.186 Κρήτηνδε 'to Crete'; 187 Τροίηνδε 'to Troy'; οἴκονδε or οἴκαδε (19.282) 'homeward'; ἄστυδε 'to the town' (19.190); χάμαζε 'to the ground' (not found in books 19 and 20, but cf. the similar χαμάδις at 19.63, 599).

(c) Pronouns

(i) The main (personal) pronouns

'I'	*Singular*	*Plural*
Nominative	ἐγώ(ν)	ἄμμες
Accusative	με, ἐμέ	ἧμας, ἡμέας
Genitive	ἐμεῖο, ἐμέο, ἐμεῦ, μευ, ἐμέθεν	ἡμέων, ἡμείων
Dative	μοι, ἐμοί	ἄμμι(ν)

'*You*'	*Singular*	*Plural*
Nominative	τυ, συ, τύνη	ὔμμες
Accusative	σε	ὔμμε, ὑμέας
Genitive	σεῖο, σέο, σέθεν, τεοῖο	ὑμέων, ὑμείων
Dative	τοι, τεῖν	ὔμμι

'*He*', '*she*', '*it*'	*Singular*	*Plural*
Nominative	[*not found; Homer usually employs* ἐκεῖνος, ὅδε *or* οὗτος]	
Accusative	ἑέ, ἕ, μιν, αὐτόν	σφε, σφέας, σφας
Genitive	εἷο, ἕο, εὗ, ἕθεν	σφείων, σφέων
Dative	ἑοῖ, οἱ	σφι(ν), αὐτοῖς

(ii) The definite article

ὁ ἡ τό is regularly used as a pronoun ('he', 'she', 'it') in Homer. See e.g. *Od.* 19.46 ἡ δέ ... εἰρήσεται 'she will ask me ...'; 19.61, 70, 100, 106, etc. In this use it regularly introduces a new clause.

The Attic forms of the definite article are as follows: Homeric variations are given after the familiar forms.

Nom. sing.	ὁ	ἡ	τό
Acc. sing.	τόν	τήν	τό
Gen. sing.	τοῦ	τῆς	τοῦ (*Hom.* τοῖο)
Dat. sing.	τῶι	τῆι	τῶι
Nom. acc. dual	τώ	τώ	τώ
Gen. dat. dual	τοῖν	τοῖν	τοῖν (*Hom.* τοῖιν)
Nom. pl.	οἱ	αἱ	τά (*Hom. masc. and fem.* τοί ταί)
Acc. pl.	τούς	τάς	τά
Gen. pl.	τῶν	τῶν	τῶν (*Hom. fem.* τάων)
Dat. pl.	τοῖς	ταῖς	τοῖς (*Hom.* τοῖσι τῆισι/τῆις/ταῖσι)

(iii) The relative pronoun

Besides ὅς (ἥ ὅν), ὅ (ἥ τό) is often used for the relative 'who'.

(iv) Possessive adjectives and pronouns

τεός = σός	'your'
ἑός = ὅς	'his/her'
ἁμός = ἡμέτερος	'our'
ὑμός = ὑμέτερος	'your'
σφός = σφέτερος	'their'

(d) Particles

The following common particles should be noted; in some cases their meaning differs from that normally found in Attic.

ἄρα (= ἄρ, ῥά)   'so', 'next'
δή 'indeed'
εἰ or αἴ (as in εἰ δ' ἄγε) exclamatory: 'come on', 'come now'
ἦ 'surely'
οὖν 'in fact'
περ 'just', 'even'
τε 'and'; but notice also the use of τε to indicate a general or gnomic statement, e.g. *Il.* 20.198 ῥεχθὲν δέ τε νήπιος ἔγνω: 'a fool understands something when it is done' (note here also the 'gnomic' aorist, often used in such generalisations)
τοι 'I tell you' (assertion); but the word may also be equivalent to σοι, dative singular of the second person pronoun: 'to you'

(e) Prepositions: some variant forms

ἄν, ἄνα, ἄμ
εἰς, ἐς
ἐν, εἰν, ἐνί, εἰνί
κατά, καταί, κάτ, κάμ
παρά, παραί, πάρ
πρός, προτί, ποτί
σύν, ξύν
ὑπό, ὑπαί

3. Syntax: a few hints

(a) Compound verbs are often broken up (*tmesis*, 'cutting' or 'severing'): e.g. 19.15 ἐκ δὲ καλεσσάμενος, 90 ἐκ ... ὀνόμαζε, 531 κατά ... λιποῦσαν; 20.260. This in fact reflects an earlier stage in the development of Greek, in which these prefixes were still separate adverbs. In later Greek it becomes a mark of poetic style.

(b) Prepositions very frequently follow the noun which they govern (as is found in a lesser degree in classical Greek, e.g. with ἕνεκα (cf. Latin *causa, gratia*)). See e.g. 19.55, 20.16 τοῦ ἔνδον.

(c) The accusative of respect and double accusative are very frequent. See e.g. for the former 19.122 βεβαρηότα με φρένας οἴνωι ('that I am weighed down *in* my wits by wine', i.e. that my wits are befuddled with wine), 20.19 μένος ἄσχετος; for the latter 19.90, 104, 115 τῷ ἐμε νῦν τὰ μὲν ἄλλα μετάλλα.

(d) Homeric style has a strong tendency to 'parataxis' (setting alongside). This means that a self-contained clause is used, and then the sentence is continued with another clause added, the two being connected merely by a word for 'and' (καί, δέ) whereas in later Greek we might expect one to be subordinate to the other. See e.g. 19.418–23, 449–58. The importance of this principle has often been exaggerated, however. There are many more complex and periodic sentences in Homer, not least in speeches (e.g. 19.141–7, 20.61–5, 314–19).

(e) The particle κέ or κέν is normally preferred to ἄν in sentences involving some degree of uncertainty, hypothesis about the future, or conditions: e.g. 19.6, 17, 25, 27, 45.

(f) The subjunctive often conveys a simple future intention; the optative indicates a wish or potential action, less immediate than the subjunctive.

(g) A phrase worth noting is βῆ ἰέναι or ἴμεν, etc., βᾶν ἰέναι, etc.: 'he/they made their way' (lit. 'he/they went to go'). See e.g. 19.429, 20.146.

(c) Note on the text[120]

The sources for the text of the *Odyssey* are as follows. (a) The medieval manuscripts, of which a large number survive, but not nearly so many as for the *Iliad*. Attempts to classify them in 'families' have been unsuccessful. The earliest was transcribed in the tenth or eleventh century. (b) The quotations in other ancient authors and lexicographers, some of the most interesting of which I have cited.[121] It should be noted that ancient authors often quoted from memory, so that variations in these

---

[120] See further G. Pasquali, *Storia della tradizione e critica del testo* (2nd edn., Florence 1952) 201–47; J. A. Davison, in Wace and Stubbings, *Companion* 215–33. S. West's excellent account in the Oxford *Odyssey* I 33–48 covers only the ancient period of the transmission.

[121] For books 19 and 20 these are listed in La Roche's edition of the *Odyssey* (Leipzig 1867) 331–6.

sources are not necessarily significant: this applies especially to missing lines. (c) The fragmentary papyri from Ptolemaic and Roman Egypt which preserve portions of texts much older than any of our complete manuscripts; the oldest papyri including parts of books 19 and 20 go back to the third century B.C.[122] (d) The textual comments and quotations in the 'scholia', that is, the marginal comments in many of our manuscripts, which draw on the work of earlier scholars as far back as Alexandrian times. The scholia on the *Odyssey*, however, are much less ambitious and less well-informed than those on the *Iliad* (another sign of the greater popularity of the latter); moreover, they tail off and become much more cursory for the later part of the *Odyssey*.[123] In Dindorf's edition the scholia on *Odyssey* 19 and 20 occupy only twenty-five pages, whereas those on book 1 alone occupy sixty-five! Possibly this suggests that parts at least of the second half were read less in ancient times, e.g. in schools; more probably, it reflects the increased weariness of a series of scribes copying and abbreviating the earlier versions of the scholia. For a larger-scale commentary on book 20 see M. W. Haslam, *P Oxy* LIII, no. 3710 (second century B.C.).

The problems which confront an editor of Homer do not, then, arise from lack of evidence: throughout antiquity no author is better known, more widely quoted and read. The difficulties are rather (a) the nature of the Homeric language (in large part an artificial poetic creation which can be reconstructed systematically only from its use in the poems, and which is only partly obedient to external philological rules), and (b) the uncertainties of the transmission, as outlined in Introd. 4(a) above, which may mean that the 'text' was oral, or orally revised, or at any rate fluid, in the earliest stages. The early papyri and quotations often show considerable divergence from our standard text: in particular, they include additional lines and omit some which are in all or most of our manuscripts. It seems likely that the text was regularised, and perhaps therefore stabilised, only in Hellenistic times. Ancient and modern scholars have also suggested, with or without manuscript support, the deletion or transposition of many passages. Some of these

---

[122] For those of the Ptolemaic period see S. West, *The Ptolemaic papyri of Homer* (Cologne 1967); see further R. Pack, *The Greek and Latin literary texts from Greco-Roman Egypt* (2nd edn, Ann Arbor 1965; 3rd edn imminent).

[123] See G. Dindorf, *Scholia Graeca in Homeri Odysseam* (Oxford 1855).

proposals, especially many of those intended to eliminate repetition, are rendered implausible by the obvious repetitiveness of Homeric style in general. Others still deserve consideration, and are usually discussed in the Commentary. There are of course many lines in both the *Iliad* and the *Odyssey* which are 'superfluous' in the sense that the poem reads intelligibly without them, but no-one would propose the deletion of every single line of this kind. In view of this, inclusiveness seems the best policy, and I have advocated the deletion of only a very few lines which distinctly jar or which introduce contradictions or difficulties in the immediate context.

On the level of orthography and dialect, we must again acknowledge that it is impossible to recover the 'original' text with certainty: the poet himself, if he wrote down the poem himself at all, may not have spelt words consistently or as modern linguists would wish, and it is generally accepted that an Attic edition has introduced some different dialect forms. When all is said and done, this makes little difference to a modern reader. More important is the not infrequent occurrence of alternative words and phrases in our texts. Sometimes one alternative is clearly preferable on contextual or aesthetic grounds, but at other times the choice may seem less clear, and I have mentioned quite a large number of these alternatives in the apparatus, to remind the reader of the degree of small-scale variation in the sources for the Homeric text.

The text presented in this volume is my own, but it is not based on any fresh examination of the manuscripts: any such attempt would naturally have to concern itself with the *Odyssey* as a whole. I have mainly relied on the collations of T. W. Allen (Oxford, 2nd edn 1913), P. Von der Mühll (Basel 1946), and J. Russo (in vol. v of the Italian edition published by the Fondazione Lorenzo Valla, Rome 1985). But my apparatus is greatly simplified, partly for the benefit of students, partly because it is not in this area that I feel I have any novel suggestions to make. I have not reported obvious scribal errors, variations of spelling, or the use of slightly different words with the same meaning. Nor have I given full details of which manuscripts contain a given reading: for this the reader should consult the above editions. I present manuscript evidence in the form

20 ἵξετ᾽: ἵκετ᾽

This indicates that both readings are found in the manuscript tradition; the reading preferred here is given first. When a reading is found also or only in a papyrus I signal this by the symbol 'p'; when it is an ancient or modern editor's suggestion, I say so explicitly.

HOMER
ODYSSEY
BOOKS XIX AND XX

ΟΜΗΡΟΥ ΟΔΥΣΣΕΙΑΣ Τ

Αὐτὰρ ὁ ἐν μεγάρωι ὑπελείπετο δῖος Ὀδυσσεύς,
μνηστήρεσσι φόνον σὺν Ἀθήνηι μερμηρίζων·
αἶψα δὲ Τηλέμαχον ἔπεα πτερόεντα προσηύδα·
"Τηλέμαχε, χρὴ τεύχε' ἀρήϊα κατθέμεν εἴσω
πάντα μάλ', αὐτὰρ μνηστῆρας μαλακοῖς ἐπέεσσι   5
παρφάσθαι, ὅτε κέν σε μεταλλῶσιν ποθέοντες·
'ἐκ καπνοῦ κατέθηκ', ἐπεὶ οὐκέτι τοῖσιν ἐώικει,
οἷά ποτε Τροίηνδε κιὼν κατέλειπεν Ὀδυσσεύς,
ἀλλὰ κατήικισται, ὅσσον πυρὸς ἵκετ' ἀϋτμή.
πρὸς δ' ἔτι καὶ τόδε μεῖζον ἐνὶ φρεσὶν ἔμβαλε δαίμων,   10
μή πως οἰνωθέντες, ἔριν στήσαντες ἐν ὑμῖν,
ἀλλήλους τρώσητε καταισχύνητέ τε δαῖτα
καὶ μνηστύν· αὐτὸς γὰρ ἐφέλκεται ἄνδρα σίδηρος'."
    "Ὣς φάτο, Τηλέμαχος δὲ φίλωι ἐπεπείθετο πατρί,
ἐκ δὲ καλεσσάμενος προσέφη τροφὸν Εὐρύκλειαν·   15
"μαῖ', ἄγε δή μοι ἔρυξον ἐνὶ μεγάροισι γυναῖκας,
ὄφρα κεν ἐς θάλαμον καταθείομαι ἔντεα πατρὸς
καλά, τά μοι κατὰ οἶκον ἀκηδέα καπνὸς ἀμέρδει
πατρὸς ἀποιχομένοιο· ἐγὼ δ' ἔτι νήπιος ἦα.
νῦν δ' ἐθέλω καταθέσθαι, ἵν' οὐ πυρὸς ἵξετ' ἀϋτμή."   20
    Τὸν δ' αὖτε προσέειπε φίλη τροφὸς Εὐρύκλεια·
"αἲ γὰρ δή ποτε, τέκνον, ἐπιφροσύνας ἀνέλοιο
οἴκου κήδεσθαι καὶ κτήματα πάντα φυλάσσειν.
ἀλλ' ἄγε, τίς τοι ἔπειτα μετοιχομένη φάος οἴσει;
δμωιὰς δ' οὐκ εἴας προβλωσκέμεν, αἵ κεν ἔφαινον."   25
    Τὴν δ' αὖ Τηλέμαχος πεπνυμένος ἀντίον ηὔδα·
"ξεῖνος ὅδ'· οὐ γὰρ ἀεργὸν ἀνέξομαι ὅς κεν ἐμῆς γε
χοίνικος ἅπτηται, καὶ τηλόθεν εἰληλουθώς."
    "Ὣς ἄρ' ἐφώνησεν, τῆι δ' ἄπτερος ἔπλετο μῦθος.

4–12 (= 16.291–8) marked in two MSS with an asterisk: see Comm.   10
δ' ἔτι : δέ τι   17 καταθείομαι : καταθείομεν   20 ἵξετ' : ἵκετ'

κλήϊσεν δὲ θύρας μεγάρων εὖ ναιεταόντων.   30
τὼ δ᾽ ἄρ᾽ ἀναΐξαντ᾽ Ὀδυσεὺς καὶ φαίδιμος υἱὸς
ἐσφόρεον κόρυθάς τε καὶ ἀσπίδας ὀμφαλοέσσας
ἔγχεά τ᾽ ὀξυόεντα· πάροιθε δὲ Παλλὰς Ἀθήνη,
χρύσεον λύχνον ἔχουσα, φάος περικαλλὲς ἐποίει.
δὴ τότε Τηλέμαχος προσεφώνεεν ὃν πατέρ᾽ αἶψα·   35
"ὦ πάτερ, ἦ μέγα θαῦμα τόδ᾽ ὀφθαλμοῖσιν ὁρῶμαι.
ἔμπης μοι τοῖχοι μεγάρων καλαί τε μεσόδμαι
εἰλάτιναί τε δοκοὶ καὶ κίονες ὑψόσ᾽ ἔχοντες
φαίνοντ᾽ ὀφθαλμοῖς ὡς εἰ πυρὸς αἰθομένοιο.
ἦ μάλα τις θεὸς ἔνδον, οἳ οὐρανὸν εὐρὺν ἔχουσι."   40
    Τὸν δ᾽ ἀπαμειβόμενος προσέφη πολύμητις Ὀδυσσεύς·
"σίγα καὶ κατὰ σὸν νόον ἴσχανε μηδ᾽ ἐρέεινε·
αὕτη τοι δίκη ἐστὶ θεῶν, οἳ Ὄλυμπον ἔχουσιν.
ἀλλὰ σὺ μὲν κατάλεξαι, ἐγὼ δ᾽ ὑπολείψομαι αὐτοῦ,
ὄφρα κ᾽ ἔτι δμωιὰς καὶ μητέρα σὴν ἐρεθίζω·   45
ἡ δέ μ᾽ ὀδυρομένη εἰρήσεται ἀμφὶ ἕκαστα."
    Ὣς φάτο, Τηλέμαχος δὲ διὲκ μεγάροιο βεβήκει
κείων ἐς θάλαμον, δαΐδων ὕπο λαμπομενάων,
ἔνθα πάρος κοιμᾶθ᾽, ὅτε μιν γλυκὺς ὕπνος ἱκάνοι·
ἔνθ᾽ ἄρα καὶ τότ᾽ ἔλεκτο καὶ Ἠῶ δῖαν ἔμιμνεν.   50
αὐτὰρ ὁ ἐν μεγάρωι ὑπελείπετο δῖος Ὀδυσσεύς,
μνηστήρεσσι φόνον σὺν Ἀθήνηι μερμηρίζων.
    Ἡ δ᾽ ἴεν ἐκ θαλάμοιο περίφρων Πηνελόπεια,
Ἀρτέμιδι ἰκέλη ἠὲ χρυσέηι Ἀφροδίτηι.
τῆι παρὰ μὲν κλισίην πυρὶ κάτθεσαν, ἔνθ᾽ ἄρ᾽ ἐφῖζε,   55
δινωτὴν ἐλέφαντι καὶ ἀργύρωι· ἥν ποτε τέκτων
ποίησ᾽ Ἰκμάλιος, καὶ ὑπὸ θρῆνυν ποσὶν ἧκε
προσφυέ᾽ ἐξ αὐτῆς, ὅθ᾽ ἐπὶ μέγα βάλλετο κῶας.
ἔνθα καθέζετ᾽ ἔπειτα περίφρων Πηνελόπεια.
ἦλθον δὲ δμωιαὶ λευκώλενοι ἐκ μεγάροιο.   60
αἱ δ᾽ ἀπὸ μὲν σῖτον πολὺν ᾕρεον ἠδὲ τραπέζας

30 μεγάρων : θαλάμων   31 ἀναΐξαντ᾽ Ὀδυσεὺς καὶ : ἀναΐξαντε πατὴρ καὶ
34 φάος: φόως (already known to schol.)   40 θεὸς : θεῶν (some MSS, Plut. ap.
Stob.)   46 ἀμφὶ Bekker (ἀμφὶς MSS)   60 placed after 54 by Bothe

καὶ δέπα, ἔνθεν ἄρ' ἄνδρες ὑπερμενέοντες ἔπινον·
πῦρ δ' ἀπὸ λαμπτήρων χαμάδις βάλον, ἄλλα δ' ἐπ' αὐτῶν
νήησαν ξύλα πολλά, φόως ἔμεν ἠδὲ θέρεσθαι.
ἡ δ' Ὀδυσῆ' ἐνένιπε Μελανθὼ δεύτερον αὖτις·   65
''ξεῖν', ἔτι καὶ νῦν ἐνθάδ' ἀνιήσεις διὰ νύκτα
δινεύων κατὰ οἶκον, ὀπιπεύσεις δὲ γυναῖκας;
ἀλλ' ἔξελθε θύραζε, τάλαν, καὶ δαιτὸς ὄνησο·
ἢ τάχα καὶ δαλῷ βεβλημένος εἶσθα θύραζε.''

    Τὴν δ' ἄρ' ὑπόδρα ἰδὼν προσέφη πολύμητις Ὀδυσσεύς·   70
''δαιμονίη, τί μοι ὧδ' ἐπέχεις κεκοτηότι θυμῷ;
ἦ ὅτι δὴ ῥυπόω, κακὰ δὲ χροῒ εἵματα εἷμαι,
πτωχεύω δ' ἀνὰ δῆμον; ἀναγκαίη γὰρ ἐπείγει.
τοιοῦτοι πτωχοὶ καὶ ἀλήμονες ἄνδρες ἔασι.
καὶ γὰρ ἐγώ ποτε οἶκον ἐν ἀνθρώποισιν ἔναιον   75
ὄλβιος ἀφνειὸν καὶ πολλάκι δόσκον ἀλήτῃ
τοίωι, ὁποῖος ἔοι καὶ ὅτευ κεχρημένος ἔλθοι·
ἦσαν δὲ δμῶες μάλα μυρίοι, ἄλλα τε πολλὰ
οἷσίν τ' εὖ ζώουσι καὶ ἀφνειοὶ καλέονται.
ἀλλὰ Ζεὺς ἀλάπαξε Κρονίων· ἤθελε γάρ που·   80
τῶι νῦν μή ποτε καὶ σύ, γύναι, ἀπὸ πᾶσαν ὀλέσσῃς
ἀγλαΐην, τῇ νῦν γε μετὰ δμωῇσι κέκασσαι,
ἤν πώς τοι δέσποινα κοτεσσαμένη χαλεπήνῃ,
ἢ Ὀδυσεὺς ἔλθῃ· ἔτι γὰρ καὶ ἐλπίδος αἶσα.
εἰ δ' ὁ μὲν ὣς ἀπόλωλε καὶ οὐκέτι νόστιμός ἐστιν,   85
ἀλλ' ἤδη παῖς τοῖος Ἀπόλλωνός γε ἕκητι,
Τηλέμαχος· τὸν δ' οὔ τις ἐνὶ μεγάροισι γυναικῶν
λήθει ἀτασθάλλουσ', ἐπεὶ οὐκέτι τηλίκος ἐστίν.''

    Ὣς φάτο, τοῦ δ' ἤκουσε περίφρων Πηνελόπεια,
ἀμφίπολον δ' ἐνένιπεν ἔπος τ' ἔφατ' ἔκ τ' ὀνόμαζε·   90
''πάντως, θαρσαλέη, κύον ἀδεές, οὔ τί με λήθεις
ἔρδουσα μέγα ἔργον, ὃ σῇ κεφαλῇ ἀναμάξεις·
πάντα γὰρ εὖ ᾔδησθ', ἐπεὶ ἐξ ἐμεῦ ἔκλυες αὐτῆς,

72 δὴ ῥυπόω: οὐ λιπόω (variant cited in schol.)   73 ἐπείγει : ἱκάνει   76–
7 omitted in p   77 (= 17.421) omitted in some MSS; deleted by Knight
83 ἤν πώς (mentioned and preferred by schol.) : μή πώς

ὡς τὸν ξεῖνον ἔμελλον ἐνὶ μεγάροισιν ἐμοῖσιν
ἀμφὶ πόσει εἴρεσθαι, ἐπεὶ πυκινῶς ἀκάχημαι."   95
῏Η ῥα καὶ Εὐρυνόμην ταμίην πρὸς μῦθον ἔειπεν·
"Εὐρυνόμη, φέρε δὴ δίφρον καὶ κῶας ἐπ' αὐτοῦ,
ὄφρα καθεζόμενος εἴπηι ἔπος ἠδ' ἐπακούσηι
ὁ ξεῖνος ἐμέθεν· ἐθέλω δέ μιν ἐξερέεσθαι."
῝Ως ἔφαθ', ἡ δὲ μάλ' ὀτραλέως κατέθηκε φέρουσα   100
δίφρον ἔϋξεστον καὶ ἐπ' αὐτῶι κῶας ἔβαλλεν·
ἔνθα καθέζετ' ἔπειτα πολύτλας δῖος Ὀδυσσεύς.
τοῖσι δὲ μύθων ἄρχε περίφρων Πηνελόπεια·
"ξεῖνε, τὸ μέν σε πρῶτον ἐγὼν εἰρήσομαι αὐτή·
τίς πόθεν εἰς ἀνδρῶν; πόθι τοι πόλις ἠδὲ τοκῆες;"   105
Τὴν δ' ἀπαμειβόμενος προσέφη πολύμητις Ὀδυσσεύς·
"ὦ γύναι, οὐκ ἄν τίς σε βροτῶν ἐπ' ἀπείρονα γαῖαν
νεικέοι· ἦ γάρ σευ κλέος οὐρανὸν εὐρὺν ἱκάνει,
ὥς τέ τευ ἦ βασιλῆος ἀμύμονος, ὅς τε θεουδὴς
ἀνδράσιν ἐν πολλοῖσι καὶ ἰφθίμοισιν ἀνάσσων   110
εὐδικίας ἀνέχηισι, φέρηισι δὲ γαῖα μέλαινα
πυροὺς καὶ κριθάς, βρίθηισι δὲ δένδρεα καρπῶι,
τίκτηι δ' ἔμπεδα μῆλα, θάλασσα δὲ παρέχηι ἰχθῦς
ἐξ εὐηγεσίης, ἀρετῶσι δὲ λαοὶ ὑπ' αὐτοῦ.
τῶ ἐμὲ νῦν τὰ μὲν ἄλλα μετάλλα σῶι ἐνὶ οἴκωι,   115
μηδ' ἐμὸν ἐξερέεινε γένος καὶ πατρίδα γαῖαν,
μή μοι μᾶλλον θυμὸν ἐνιπλήσηις ὀδυνάων
μνησαμένωι· μάλα δ' εἰμὶ πολύστονος· οὐδέ τί με χρὴ
οἴκωι ἐν ἀλλοτρίωι γοόωντά τε μυρόμενόν τε
ἧσθαι, ἐπεὶ κάκιον πενθήμεναι ἄκριτον αἰεί·   120
μή τίς μοι δμωιῶν νεμεσήσεται, ἠὲ σύ γ' αὐτή,
φῆι δὲ δακρυπλώειν βεβαρηότα με φρένας οἴνωι."
Τὸν δ' ἠμείβετ' ἔπειτα περίφρων Πηνελόπεια·
"ξεῖν', ἦ τοι μὲν ἐμὴν ἀρετὴν εἶδός τε δέμας τε
ὤλεσαν ἀθάνατοι, ὅτε ῎Ιλιον εἰσανέβαινον   125

109 ἤ Bekker : ἢ   110 omitted by Plato, Philodemus, Plutarch, Themistius
114 omitted in one MS   122 omitted by some MSS; partially quoted in
different form by Aristotle

Ἀργεῖοι, μετὰ τοῖσι δ' ἐμὸς πόσις ᾖεν Ὀδυσσεύς.
εἰ κεῖνός γ' ἐλθὼν τὸν ἐμὸν βίον ἀμφιπολεύοι,
μεῖζόν κε κλέος εἴη ἐμὸν καὶ κάλλιον οὕτω.
νῦν δ' ἄχομαι· τόσα γάρ μοι ἐπέσσευεν κακὰ δαίμων.
ὅσσοι γὰρ νήσοισιν ἐπικρατέουσιν ἄριστοι,   130
Δουλιχίωι τε Σάμηι τε καὶ ὑλήεντι Ζακύνθωι,
οἵ τ' αὐτὴν Ἰθάκην εὐδείελον ἀμφινέμονται,
οἵ μ' ἀεκαζομένην μνῶνται, τρύχουσι δὲ οἶκον.
τῶι οὔτε ξείνων ἐμπάζομαι οὔθ' ἱκετάων
οὔτε τι κηρύκων, οἳ δημιοεργοὶ ἔασιν·   135
ἀλλ' Ὀδυσῆ ποθέουσα φίλον κατατήκομαι ἦτορ.
οἱ δὲ γάμον σπεύδουσιν· ἐγὼ δὲ δόλους τολυπεύω.
φᾶρος μέν μοι πρῶτον ἐνέπνευσε φρεσὶ δαίμων
στησαμένηι μέγαν ἱστὸν ἐνὶ μεγάροισιν ὑφαίνειν,
λεπτὸν καὶ περίμετρον· ἄφαρ δ' αὐτοῖς μετέειπον·   140
'κοῦροι, ἐμοὶ μνηστῆρες, ἐπεὶ θάνε δῖος Ὀδυσσεύς,
μίμνετ' ἐπειγόμενοι τὸν ἐμὸν γάμον, εἰς ὅ κε φᾶρος
ἐκτελέσω, μή μοι μεταμώνια νήματ' ὄληται,
Λαέρτηι ἥρωϊ ταφήϊον, εἰς ὅτε κέν μιν
μοῖρ' ὀλοὴ καθέληισι τανηλεγέος θανάτοιο·   145
μή τίς μοι κατὰ δῆμον Ἀχαιϊάδων νεμεσήσηι,
αἵ κεν ἄτερ σπείρου κῆται πολλὰ κτεατίσσας.'
ὣς ἐφάμην, τοῖσιν δ' ἐπεπείθετο θυμὸς ἀγήνωρ.
ἔνθα καὶ ἡματίη μὲν ὑφαίνεσκον μέγαν ἱστόν,
νύκτας δ' ἀλλύεσκον, ἐπεὶ δαΐδας παραθείμην.   150
ὣς τρίετες μὲν ἔληθον ἐγὼ καὶ ἔπειθον Ἀχαιούς·
ἀλλ' ὅτε τέτρατον ἦλθεν ἔτος καὶ ἐπήλυθον ὧραι,
μηνῶν φθινόντων, περὶ δ' ἤματα πόλλ' ἐτελέσθη,
καὶ τότε δή με διὰ δμωιάς, κύνας οὐκ ἀλεγούσας,
εἷλον ἐπελθόντες καὶ ὁμόκλησαν ἐπέεσσιν.   155
ὣς τὸ μὲν ἐξετέλεσσα, καὶ οὐκ ἐθέλουσ', ὑπ' ἀνάγκης·

129 ἐπέσσευεν : ἐπέ(γ)χευε, ἐπέκλωσεν. Cf. 18.256 (same variants)   130–
61 deleted by Roemer   130–3 omitted by ancient edd., following Aris-
tarchus? See schol.   135 deleted by Knight   138 φρεσὶ : μέγα   153
(= 10.470, 24.143) omitted by some MSS

νῦν δ' οὔτ' ἐκφυγέειν δύναμαι γάμον οὔτε τιν' ἄλλην
μῆτιν ἔθ' εὑρίσκω· μάλα δ' ὀτρύνουσι τοκῆες
γήμασθ', ἀσχαλάαι δὲ πάϊς βίοτον κατεδόντων,
γιγνώσκων· ἤδη γὰρ ἀνὴρ οἷός τε μάλιστα   160
οἴκου κήδεσθαι, τῶι τε Ζεὺς κῦδος ὀπάζει.
ἀλλὰ καὶ ὥς μοι εἰπὲ τεὸν γένος, ὁππόθεν ἐσσί·
οὐ γὰρ ἀπὸ δρυός ἐσσι παλαιφάτου οὐδ' ἀπὸ πέτρης.''
    Τὴν δ' ἀπαμειβόμενος προσέφη πολύμητις Ὀδυσσεύς·
''ὦ γύναι αἰδοίη Λαερτιάδεω Ὀδυσῆος,   165
οὐκέτ' ἀπολλήξεις τὸν ἐμὸν γόνον ἐξερέουσα;
ἀλλ' ἔκ τοι ἐρέω· ἦ μέν μ' ἀχέεσσί γε δώσεις
πλείοσιν ἢ ἔχομαι· ἡ γὰρ δίκη, ὁππότε πάτρης
ἧς ἀπέηισιν ἀνὴρ τόσσον χρόνον ὅσσον ἐγὼ νῦν,
πολλὰ βροτῶν ἐπὶ ἄστε' ἀλώμενος, ἄλγεα πάσχων.   170
ἀλλὰ καὶ ὣς ἐρέω ὅ μ' ἀνείρεαι ἠδὲ μεταλλᾶις.
Κρήτη τις γαῖ' ἔστι, μέσωι ἐνὶ οἴνοπι πόντωι,
καλὴ καὶ πίειρα, περίρρυτος· ἐν δ' ἄνθρωποι
πολλοί, ἀπειρέσιοι, καὶ ἐννήκοντα πόληες·
ἄλλη δ' ἄλλων γλῶσσα μεμιγμένη· ἐν μὲν Ἀχαιοί,   175
ἐν δ' Ἐτεόκρητες μεγαλήτορες, ἐν δὲ Κύδωνες,
Δωριέες τε τριχάϊκες δῖοί τε Πελασγοί·
τῆισι δ' ἐνὶ Κνωσός, μεγάλη πόλις, ἔνθα τε Μίνως
ἐννέωρος βασίλευε Διὸς μεγάλου ὀαριστής,
πατρὸς ἐμοῖο πατήρ, μεγαθύμου Δευκαλίωνος.   180
Δευκαλίων δ' ἐμὲ τίκτε καὶ Ἰδομενῆα ἄνακτα·
ἀλλ' ὁ μὲν ἐν νήεσσι κορωνίσιν Ἴλιον εἴσω
οἴχεθ' ἅμ' Ἀτρεΐδηισιν, ἐμοὶ δ' ὄνομα κλυτὸν Αἴθων,
ὁπλότερος γενεῆι· ὁ δ' ἄρα πρότερος καὶ ἀρείων.
ἔνθ' Ὀδυσῆα ἐγὼν ἰδόμην καὶ ξείνια δῶκα.   185
καὶ γὰρ τὸν Κρήτηνδε κατήγαγεν ἲς ἀνέμοιο,
ἱέμενον Τροίηνδε παραπλάγξασα Μαλειῶν·

161 κῦδος : ὄλβον   163a quotations in Clement and Sextus add ἀλλ' ἀνδρῶν
γένος εἰσί (obviously an explanatory gloss)   170–1 omitted in some MSS
175–7 omitted by Plato; deleted by many edd.   176 ἐν δ' Ἐτεόκρητες : ἐν δέ
τε καὶ Κρῆτες   178 τῆισι : τοῖσι (already an ancient variant)

στῆσε δ' ἐν Ἀμνισῶι, ὅθι τε σπέος Εἰλειθυίης,
ἐν λιμέσιν χαλεποῖσι, μόγις δ' ὑπάλυξεν ἀέλλας.
αὐτίκα δ' Ἰδομενῆα μετάλλα ἄστυδ' ἀνελθών·   190
ξεῖνον γάρ οἱ ἔφασκε φίλον τ' ἔμεν αἰδοῖόν τε.
τῶι δ' ἤδη δεκάτη ἢ ἑνδεκάτη πέλεν ἠώς
οἰχομένωι σὺν νηυσὶ κορωνίσιν Ἴλιον εἴσω.
τὸν μὲν ἐγὼ πρὸς δώματ' ἄγων ἐῢ ἐξείνισσα,
ἐνδυκέως φιλέων, πολλῶν κατὰ οἶκον ἐόντων·   195
καί οἱ τοῖς ἄλλοις ἑτάροις, οἳ ἅμ' αὐτῶι ἕποντο,
δημόθεν ἄλφιτα δῶκα καὶ αἴθοπα οἶνον ἀγείρας
καὶ βοῦς ἱρεύσασθαι, ἵνα πλησαίατο θυμόν.
ἔνθα δυώδεκα μὲν μένον ἤματα δῖοι Ἀχαιοί·
εἴλει γὰρ Βορέης ἄνεμος μέγας οὐδ' ἐπὶ γαίηι   200
εἴα ἵστασθαι, χαλεπὸς δέ τις ὤρορε δαίμων·
τῆι τρισκαιδεκάτηι δ' ἄνεμος πέσε, τοὶ δ' ἀνάγοντο.''
   Ἴσκε ψεύδεα πολλὰ λέγων ἐτύμοισιν ὁμοῖα·
τῆς δ' ἄρ' ἀκουούσης ῥέε δάκρυα, τήκετο δὲ χρώς.
ὡς δὲ χιὼν κατατήκετ' ἐν ἀκροπόλοισιν ὄρεσσιν,   205
ἥν τ' Εὖρος κατέτηξεν, ἐπὴν Ζέφυρος καταχεύηι·
τηκομένης δ' ἄρα τῆς ποταμοὶ πλήθουσι ῥέοντες·
ὣς τῆς τήκετο καλὰ παρήϊα δάκρυ χεούσης,
κλαιούσης ἑὸν ἄνδρα παρήμενον. αὐτὰρ Ὀδυσσεὺς
θυμῶι μὲν γοόωσαν ἑὴν ἐλέαιρε γυναῖκα,   210
ὀφθαλμοὶ δ' ὡς εἰ κέρα ἕστασαν ἠὲ σίδηρος
ἀτρέμας ἐν βλεφάροισι· δόλωι δ' ὅ γε δάκρυα κεῦθεν.
ἡ δ' ἐπεὶ οὖν τάρφθη πολυδακρύτοιο γόοιο,
ἐξαῦτίς μιν ἔπεσσιν ἀμειβομένη προσέειπε·
''νῦν μὲν δή σευ, ξεῖνε, ὀΐω πειρήσεσθαι,   215
εἰ ἐτεὸν δὴ κεῖθι σὺν ἀντιθέοις ἑτάροισι
ξείνισας ἐν μεγάροισιν ἐμὸν πόσιν, ὡς ἀγορεύεις.
εἰπέ μοι ὁπποῖ' ἄσσα περὶ χροῒ εἵματα ἔστο,
αὐτός θ' οἷος ἔην, καὶ ἑταίρους, οἵ οἱ ἕποντο.''

205 ὄρεσσι : ὄρεσφιν   216 εἰ ἐτεὸν δὴ κεῖθι MSS : εἰ δὴ κεῖθι πλέοντα p
219 omitted in one MS

Τὴν δ' ἀπαμειβόμενος προσέφη πολύμητις Ὀδυσσεύς·   220
"ὦ γύναι, ἀργαλέον τόσσον χρόνον ἀμφὶς ἐόντα
εἰπέμεν· ἤδη γάρ οἱ ἐεικοστὸν ἔτος ἐστὶν
ἐξ οὗ κεῖθεν ἔβη καὶ ἐμῆς ἀπελήλυθε πάτρης·
αὐτάρ τοι ἐρέω ὥς μοι ἰνδάλλεται ἦτορ.
χλαῖναν πορφυρέην οὔλην ἔχε δῖος Ὀδυσσεύς,   225
διπλῆν· αὐτάρ οἱ περόνη χρυσοῖο τέτυκτο
αὐλοῖσιν διδύμοισι· πάροιθε δὲ δαίδαλον ἦεν·
ἐν προτέροισι πόδεσσι κύων ἔχε ποικίλον ἐλλόν,
ἀσπαίροντα λάων· τὸ δὲ θαυμάζεσκον ἅπαντες,
ὡς οἱ χρύσεοι ἐόντες ὁ μὲν λάε νεβρὸν ἀπάγχων,   230
αὐτάρ ὁ ἐκφυγέειν μεμαὼς ἄσπαιρε πόδεσσι.
τὸν δὲ χιτῶν' ἐνόησα περὶ χροῒ σιγαλόεντα,
οἷόν τε κρομύοιο λοπὸν κάτα ἰσχαλέοιο·
τὼς μὲν ἔην μαλακός, λαμπρὸς δ' ἦν ἠέλιος ὥς·
ἦ μὲν πολλαί γ' αὐτὸν ἐθηήσαντο γυναῖκες.   235
ἄλλο δέ τοι ἐρέω, σὺ δ' ἐνὶ φρεσὶ βάλλεο σῇσιν·
οὐκ οἶδ' ἢ τάδε ἕστο περὶ χροῒ οἴκοθ' Ὀδυσσεύς,
ἦ τις ἑταίρων δῶκε θοῆς ἐπὶ νηὸς ἰόντι,
ἤ τίς που καὶ ξεῖνος, ἐπεὶ πολλοῖσιν Ὀδυσσεὺς
ἔσκε φίλος· παῦροι γὰρ Ἀχαιῶν ἦσαν ὁμοῖοι.   240
καί οἱ ἐγὼ χάλκειον ἄορ καὶ δίπλακα δῶκα
καλὴν πορφυρέην καὶ τερμιόεντα χιτῶνα,
αἰδοίως δ' ἀπέπεμπον ἐϋσσέλμου ἐπὶ νηός.
καὶ μέν οἱ κῆρυξ ὀλίγον προγενέστερος αὐτοῦ
εἵπετο· καὶ τόν τοι μυθήσομαι, οἷος ἔην περ.   245
γυρὸς ἐν ὤμοισιν, μελανόχροος, οὐλοκάρηνος,
Εὐρυβάτης δ' ὄνομ' ἔσκε· τίεν δέ μιν ἔξοχον ἄλλων
ὧν ἑτάρων Ὀδυσσεύς, ὅτι οἱ φρεσὶν ἄρτια ᾔδη."
Ὣς φάτο, τῇ δ' ἔτι μᾶλλον ὑφ' ἵμερον ὦρσε γόοιο,
σήματ' ἀναγνούσῃ τά οἱ ἔμπεδα πέφραδ' Ὀδυσσεύς.   250
ἡ δ' ἐπεὶ οὖν τάρφθη πολυδακρύτοιο γόοιο,

---

220 τὴν δ' ἀπαμείβετ' ἔπειτα πολύτλας δῖος Ὀδυσσεύς p   224 μοι ἰνδάλλεται
ἦτορ : φρεσὶν εἴδεται εἶναι   227 δαίδαλον : δαίδαλα   233 λοπὸν MSS :
λέπος Galen   246 ἔην ὤμοισι μελάγχροος Galen, Herodian and others
250–1 omitted in some MSS

καὶ τότε μιν μύθοισιν ἀμειβομένη προσέειπε·
"νῦν μὲν δή μοι, ξεῖνε, πάρος περ ἐὼν ἐλεεινός,
ἐν μεγάροισιν ἐμοῖσι φίλος τ' ἔσηι αἰδοῖός τε·
αὐτὴ γὰρ τάδε εἵματ' ἐγὼ πόρον, οἷ' ἀγορεύεις,   255
πτύξασ' ἐκ θαλάμου, περόνην τ' ἐπέθηκα φαεινὴν
κείνωι ἄγαλμ' ἔμεναι· τὸν δ' οὐχ ὑποδέξομαι αὖτις
οἴκαδε νοστήσαντα φίλην ἐς πατρίδα γαῖαν.
τῶι ῥα κακῆι αἴσηι κοίλης ἐπὶ νηὸς Ὀδυσσεὺς
ὤιχετ' ἐποψόμενος Κακοΐλιον οὐκ ὀνομαστήν."   260
    Τὴν δ' ἀπαμειβόμενος προσέφη πολύμητις Ὀδυσσεύς·
"ὦ γύναι αἰδοίη Λαερτιάδεω Ὀδυσῆος,
μηκέτι νῦν χρόα καλὸν ἐναίρεο μηδέ τι θυμὸν
τῆκε πόσιν γοόωσα· νεμεσσῶμαί γε μὲν οὐδέν·
καὶ γάρ τίς τ' ἀλλοῖον ὀδύρεται ἄνδρ' ὀλέσασα   265
κουρίδιον, τῶι τέκνα τέκηι φιλότητι μιγεῖσα,
ἢ Ὀδυσῆ', ὅν φασι θεοῖς ἐναλίγκιον εἶναι.
ἀλλὰ γόου μὲν παῦσαι, ἐμεῖο δὲ σύνθεο μῦθον·
νημερτέως γάρ τοι μυθήσομαι οὐδ' ἐπικεύσω
ὡς ἤδη Ὀδυσῆος ἐγὼ περὶ νόστου ἄκουσα   270
ἀγχοῦ, Θεσπρωτῶν ἀνδρῶν ἐν πίονι δήμωι,
ζωοῦ· αὐτὰρ ἄγει κειμήλια πολλὰ καὶ ἐσθλὰ
αἰτίζων ἀνὰ δῆμον· ἀτὰρ ἐρίηρας ἑταίρους
ὤλεσε καὶ νῆα γλαφυρὴν ἐνὶ οἴνοπι πόντωι,
Θρινακίης ἄπο νήσου ἰών· ὀδύσαντο γὰρ αὐτῶι   275
Ζεύς τε καὶ Ἤλιος· τοῦ γὰρ βόας ἔκταν ἑταῖροι.
οἱ μὲν πάντες ὄλοντο πολυκλύστωι ἐνὶ πόντωι·
τὸν δ' ἄρ' ἐπὶ τρόπιος νεὸς ἔκβαλε κῦμ' ἐπὶ χέρσου,
Φαιήκων ἐς γαῖαν, οἳ ἀγχίθεοι γεγάασιν,
οἳ δή μιν περὶ κῆρι θεὸν ὣς τιμήσαντο   280
καί οἱ πολλὰ δόσαν πέμπειν τέ μιν ἤθελον αὐτοὶ
οἴκαδ' ἀπήμαντον. καί κεν πάλαι ἐνθάδ' Ὀδυσσεὺς
ἦην· ἀλλ' ἄρα οἱ τό γε κέρδιον εἴσατο θυμῶι,
χρήματ' ἀγυρτάζειν πολλὴν ἐπὶ γαῖαν ἰόντι·
ὣς περὶ κέρδεα πολλὰ καταθνητῶν ἀνθρώπων   285

275–7 omitted in a few MSS

οἶδ' Ὀδυσεύς, οὐδ' ἄν τις ἐρίσσειε βροτὸς ἄλλος.
ὥς μοι Θεσπρωτῶν βασιλεὺς μυθήσατο Φείδων·
ὤμνυε δὲ πρὸς ἔμ' αὐτόν, ἀποσπένδων ἐνὶ οἴκωι,
νῆα κατειρύσθαι καὶ ἐπαρτέας ἔμμεν ἑταίρους,
οἳ δή μιν πέμψουσι φίλην ἐς πατρίδα γαῖαν.   290
ἀλλ' ἐμὲ πρὶν ἀπέπεμψε· τύχησε γὰρ ἐρχομένη νηῦς
ἀνδρῶν Θεσπρωτῶν ἐς Δουλίχιον πολύπυρον.
καί μοι κτήματ' ἔδειξεν, ὅσα ξυναγείρατ' Ὀδυσσεύς·
καί νύ κεν ἐς δεκάτην γενεὴν ἕτερόν γ' ἔτι βόσκοι,
ὅσσα οἱ ἐν μεγάροις κειμήλια κεῖτο ἄνακτος.   295
τὸν δ' ἐς Δωδώνην φάτο βήμεναι, ὄφρα θεοῖο
ἐκ δρυὸς ὑψικόμοιο Διὸς βουλὴν ἐπακούσαι,
ὅππως νοστήσειε φίλην ἐς πατρίδα γαῖαν
ἤδη δὴν ἀπεών, ἢ ἀμφαδὸν ἦε κρυφηδόν.
ὡς ὁ μὲν οὕτως ἐστὶ σόος καὶ ἐλεύσεται ἤδη   300
ἄγχι μάλ', οὐδ' ἔτι τῆλε φίλων καὶ πατρίδος αἴης
δηρὸν ἀπεσσεῖται· ἔμπης δέ τοι ὅρκια δώσω.
ἴστω νῦν Ζεὺς πρῶτα, θεῶν ὕπατος καὶ ἄριστος,
ἱστίη τ' Ὀδυσῆος ἀμύμονος, ἣν ἀφικάνω·
ἦ μέν τοι τάδε πάντα τελείεται ὡς ἀγορεύω.   305
τοῦδ' αὐτοῦ λυκάβαντος ἐλεύσεται ἐνθάδ' Ὀδυσσεύς,
τοῦ μὲν φθίνοντος μηνός, τοῦ δ' ἱσταμένοιο.''
   Τὸν δ' αὖτε προσέειπε περίφρων Πηνελόπεια·
''αἲ γὰρ τοῦτο, ξεῖνε, ἔπος τετελεσμένον εἴη·
τῶι κε τάχα γνοίης φιλότητά τε πολλά τε δῶρα   310
ἐξ ἐμεῦ, ὡς ἄν τίς σε συναντόμενος μακαρίζοι.
ἀλλά μοι ὧδ' ἀνὰ θυμὸν ὀΐεται, ὡς ἔσεταί περ·
οὔτ' Ὀδυσεὺς ἔτι οἶκον ἐλεύσεται, οὔτε σὺ πομπῆς
τεύξηι, ἐπεὶ οὐ τοῖοι σημάντορές εἰσ' ἐνὶ οἴκωι
οἷος Ὀδυσσεὺς ἔσκε μετ' ἀνδράσιν, εἴ ποτ' ἔην γε,   315
ξείνους αἰδοίους ἀποπεμπέμεν ἠδὲ δέχεσθαι.
ἀλλά μιν, ἀμφίπολοι, ἀπονίψατε, κάτθετε δ' εὐνήν,
δέμνια καὶ χλαίνας καὶ ῥήγεα σιγαλόεντα,

291–2 (= 14.334–5) omitted in some MSS

ὥς κ' εὖ θαλπιόων χρυσόθρονον Ἠῶ ἵκηται.
ἠῶθεν δὲ μάλ' ἦρι λοέσσαι τε χρῖσαί τε,   320
ὥς κ' ἔνδον παρὰ Τηλεμάχωι δείπνοιο μέδηται
ἥμενος ἐν μεγάρωι· τῶι δ' ἄλγιον ὅς κεν ἐκείνων
τοῦτον ἀνιάζηι θυμοφθόρος· οὐδέ τι ἔργον
ἐνθάδ' ἔτι πρήξει, μάλα περ κεχολωμένος αἰνῶς.
πῶς γὰρ ἐμεῦ σύ, ξεῖνε, δαήσεαι εἴ τι γυναικῶν   325
ἀλλάων περίειμι νόον καὶ ἐπίφρονα μῆτιν,
εἴ κεν ἀϋσταλέος κακὰ εἱμένος ἐν μεγάροισι
δαινύηι; ἄνθρωποι δὲ μινυνθάδιοι τελέθουσιν.
ὃς μὲν ἀπηνὴς αὐτὸς ἔηι καὶ ἀπηνέα εἰδῆι,
τῶι δὲ καταρῶνται πάντες βροτοὶ ἄλγε' ὀπίσσω   330
ζωῶι, ἀτὰρ τεθνεῶτί γ' ἐφεψιόωνται ἅπαντες·
ὃς δ' ἂν ἀμύμων αὐτὸς ἔηι καὶ ἀμύμονα εἰδῆι,
τοῦ μέν τε κλέος εὐρὺ διὰ ξεῖνοι φορέουσι
πάντας ἐπ' ἀνθρώπους, πολλοί τέ μιν ἐσθλὸν ἔειπον.''
    Τὴν δ' ἀπαμειβόμενος προσέφη πολύμητις Ὀδυσσεύς·   335
''ὦ γύναι αἰδοίη Λαερτιάδεω Ὀδυσῆος,
ἦ τοι ἐμοὶ χλαῖναι καὶ ῥήγεα σιγαλόεντα
ἤχθεθ', ὅτε πρῶτον Κρήτης ὄρεα νιφόεντα
νοσφισάμην ἐπὶ νηὸς ἰὼν δολιχηρέτμοιο,
κείω δ' ὡς τὸ πάρος περ ἀΰπνους νύκτας ἴαυον·   340
πολλὰς γὰρ δὴ νύκτας ἀεικελίωι ἐνὶ κοίτηι
ἄεσα καί τ' ἀνέμεινα ἐΰθρονον Ἠῶ δῖαν.
οὐδέ τί μοι ποδάνιπτρα ποδῶν ἐπιήρανα θυμῶι
γίγνεται· οὐδὲ γυνὴ ποδὸς ἅψεται ἡμετέροιο
τάων αἵ τοι δῶμα κάτα δρήστειραι ἔασιν,   345
εἰ μή τις γρῆϋς ἐστι παλαιή, κεδνὰ ἰδυῖα,
ἥ τις δὴ τέτληκε τόσα φρεσὶν ὅσσα τ' ἐγώ περ·
τῆι δ' οὐκ ἂν φθονέοιμι ποδῶν ἅψασθαι ἐμεῖο.''
    Τὸν δ' αὖτε προσέειπε περίφρων Πηνελόπεια·
''ξεῖνε φίλ'· οὐ γάρ πώ τις ἀνὴρ πεπνυμένος ὧδε   350

<hr>

319 κ' εὖ : κεν   326 ἐπίφρονα : ἐχέφρονα   341 κοίτηι : οἴκωι   346–8
deleted by many editors, following Aristarchus

ξείνων τηλεδαπῶν φιλίων ἐμὸν ἵκετο δῶμα,
ὡς σὺ μάλ' εὐφραδέως πεπνυμένα πάντ' ἀγορεύεις·
ἔστι δέ μοι γρηῢς πυκινὰ φρεσὶ μήδε' ἔχουσα,
ἣ κεῖνον δύστηνον ἐῢ τρέφεν ἠδ' ἀτίταλλε,
δεξαμένη χείρεσσ', ὅτε μιν πρῶτον τέκε μήτηρ,   355
ἥ σε πόδας νίψει, ὀλιγηπελέουσά περ ἔμπης.
ἀλλ' ἄγε νῦν ἀνστᾶσα, περίφρων Εὐρύκλεια,
νίψον σοῖο ἄνακτος ὁμήλικα. καί που Ὀδυσσεὺς
ἤδη τοιόσδ' ἐστὶ πόδας τοιόσδε τε χεῖρας·
αἶψα γὰρ ἐν κακότητι βροτοὶ καταγηράσκουσιν.''   360
    Ὣς ἄρ' ἔφη, γρηῢς δὲ κατέσχετο χερσὶ πρόσωπα,
δάκρυα δ' ἔκβαλε θερμά, ἔπος δ' ὀλοφυδνὸν ἔειπεν·
''ὤ μοι ἐγὼ σέο, τέκνον, ἀμήχανος· ἦ σε περὶ Ζεὺς
ἀνθρώπων ἔχθαιρε θεουδέα θυμὸν ἔχοντα.
οὐ γάρ πώ τις τόσσα βροτῶν Διὶ τερπικεραύνωι   365
πίονα μηρία κῆ' οὐδ' ἐξαίτους ἑκατόμβας,
ὅσσα σὺ τῶι ἐδίδους, ἀρώμενος ἧος ἵκοιο
γῆράς τε λιπαρὸν θρέψαιό τε φαίδιμον υἱόν·
νῦν δέ τοι οἴωι πάμπαν ἀφείλετο νόστιμον ἦμαρ.
οὕτω που καὶ κείνωι ἐφεψιόωντο γυναῖκες   370
ξείνων τηλεδαπῶν, ὅτε τευ κλυτὰ δώμαθ' ἵκοιτο,
ὡς σέθεν αἱ κύνες αἵδε καθεψιόωνται ἅπασαι,
τάων νῦν λώβην τε καὶ αἴσχεα πόλλ' ἀλεείνων
οὐκ ἐάαις νίζειν· ἐμὲ δ' οὐκ ἀέκουσαν ἀνώγει
κούρη Ἰκαρίοιο, περίφρων Πηνελόπεια.   375
τῶι σε πόδας νίψω ἅμα τ' αὐτῆς Πηνελοπείης
καὶ σέθεν εἵνεκ', ἐπεί μοι ὀρώρεται ἔνδοθι θυμὸς
κήδεσιν. ἀλλ' ἄγε νῦν ξυνίει ἔπος, ὅττι κεν εἴπω·
πολλοὶ δὴ ξεῖνοι ταλαπείριοι ἐνθάδ' ἵκοντο,
ἀλλ' οὔ πώ τινά φημι ἐοικότα ὧδε ἰδέσθαι   380
ὡς σὺ δέμας φωνήν τε πόδας τ' Ὀδυσῆϊ ἔοικας.''
    Τὴν δ' ἀπαμειβόμενος προσέφη πολύμητις Ὀδυσσεύς·
''ὦ γρηῦ, οὕτω φασὶν ὅσοι ἴδον ὀφθαλμοῖσιν

374 ἀνώγει : ἄνωγε

ἡμέας ἀμφοτέρους, μάλα εἰκέλω ἀλλήλοιϊν
ἔμμεναι, ὡς σύ περ αὐτὴ ἐπιφρονέουσ' ἀγορεύεις.''   385
    Ὣς ἄρ' ἔφη, γρηῢς δὲ λέβηθ' ἕλε παμφανόωντα,
τοῦ πόδας ἐξαπένιζεν, ὕδωρ δ' ἐνεχεύατο πουλὺ
ψυχρόν, ἔπειτα δὲ θερμὸν ἐπήφυσεν. αὐτὰρ Ὀδυσσεὺς
ἷζεν ἀπ' ἐσχαρόφιν, ποτὶ δὲ σκότον ἐτράπετ' αἶψα·
αὐτίκα γὰρ κατὰ θυμὸν ὀΐσατο, μή ἑ λαβοῦσα   390
οὐλὴν ἀμφράσσαιτο καὶ ἀμφαδὰ ἔργα γένοιτο.
νίζε δ' ἄρ' ἄσσον ἰοῦσα ἄναχθ' ἑόν· αὐτίκα δ' ἔγνω
οὐλήν, τήν ποτέ μιν σῦς ἤλασε λευκῶι ὀδόντι
Παρνησόνδ' ἐλθόντα μετ' Αὐτόλυκόν τε καὶ υἷας,
μητρὸς ἑῆς πατέρ' ἐσθλόν, ὃς ἀνθρώπους ἐκέκαστο   395
κλεπτοσύνηι θ' ὅρκωι τε· θεὸς δέ οἱ αὐτὸς ἔδωκεν
Ἑρμείας· τῶι γὰρ κεχαρισμένα μηρία καῖεν
ἀρνῶν ἠδ' ἐρίφων· ὁ δέ οἱ πρόφρων ἅμ' ὀπήδει.
Αὐτόλυκος δ' ἐλθὼν Ἰθάκης ἐς πίονα δῆμον
παῖδα νέον γεγαῶτα κιχήσατο θυγατέρος ἧς·   400
τόν ῥά οἱ Εὐρύκλεια φίλοις ἐπὶ γούνασι θῆκε
παυομένωι δόρποιο, ἔπος τ' ἔφατ' ἔκ τ' ὀνόμαζεν·
''Αὐτόλυκ', αὐτὸς νῦν ὄνομ' εὕρεο ὅττι κε θῆαι
παιδὸς παιδὶ φίλωι· πολυάρητος δέ τοί ἐστι.''
    Τὴν δ' αὖτ' Αὐτόλυκος ἀπαμείβετο φώνησέν τε·   405
''γαμβρὸς ἐμὸς θυγάτηρ τε, τίθεσθ' ὄνομ' ὅττι κεν εἴπω·
πολλοῖσιν γὰρ ἐγώ γε ὀδυσσάμενος τόδ' ἱκάνω,
ἀνδράσιν ἠδὲ γυναιξὶν ἀνὰ χθόνα πουλυβότειραν·
τῶι δ' Ὀδυσεὺς ὄνομ' ἔστω ἐπώνυμον. αὐτὰρ ἐγώ γε,
ὁππότ' ἂν ἡβήσας μητρώϊον ἐς μέγα δῶμα   410
ἔλθηι Παρνησόνδ', ὅθι πού μοι κτήματ' ἔασι,
τῶν οἱ ἐγὼ δώσω καί μιν χαίροντ' ἀποπέμψω.''
    Τῶν ἕνεκ' ἦλθ' Ὀδυσεύς, ἵνα οἱ πόροι ἀγλαὰ δῶρα.
τὸν μὲν ἄρ' Αὐτόλυκός τε καὶ υἷέες Αὐτολύκοιο
χερσίν τ' ἠσπάζοντο ἔπεσσί τε μειλιχίοισι·   415

389 ἀπ' : ἐπ'   401 Εὐρύκλεια : Ἀντίκλεια variant in scholia.   φίλοις MSS :
φέρουσ' p   408 πουλυβότειραν : βωτιάνειραν   after 412 additional line in
p, ending . . . ἵκετο μέτρον

μήτηρ δ᾽ Ἀμφιθέη μητρὸς περιφῦσ᾽ Ὀδυσῆϊ
κύσσ᾽ ἄρα μιν κεφαλήν τε καὶ ἄμφω φάεα καλά.
Αὐτόλυκος δ᾽ υἱοῖσιν ἐκέκλετο κυδαλίμοισι
δεῖπνον ἐφοπλίσσαι· τοὶ δ᾽ ὀτρύνοντος ἄκουσαν,
αὐτίκα δ᾽ εἰσάγαγον βοῦν ἄρσενα πενταέτηρον·   420
τὸν δέρον ἀμφί θ᾽ ἕπον, καί μιν διέχευαν ἅπαντα,
μίστυλλόν τ᾽ ἄρ᾽ ἐπισταμένως πεῖράν τ᾽ ὀβελοῖσιν,
ὤπτησάν τε περιφραδέως δάσσαντό τε μοίρας.
ὣς τότε μὲν πρόπαν ἦμαρ ἐς ἠέλιον καταδύντα
δαίνυντ᾽, οὐδέ τι θυμὸς ἐδεύετο δαιτὸς ἐΐσης·   425
ἦμος δ᾽ ἠέλιος κατέδυ καὶ ἐπὶ κνέφας ἦλθε,
δὴ τότε κοιμήσαντο καὶ ὕπνου δῶρον ἕλοντο.
  Ἦμος δ᾽ ἠριγένεια φάνη ῥοδοδάκτυλος Ἠώς,
βάν ῥ᾽ ἴμεν ἐς θήρην, ἠμὲν κύνες ἠδὲ καὶ αὐτοὶ
υἱέες Αὐτολύκου· μετὰ τοῖσι δὲ δῖος Ὀδυσσεὺς   430
ἤϊεν· αἰπὺ δ᾽ ὄρος προσέβαν καταειμένον ὕλῃ
Παρνησοῦ, τάχα δ᾽ ἵκανον πτύχας ἠνεμοέσσας.
  Ἥλιος μὲν ἔπειτα νέον προσέβαλλεν ἀρούρας
ἐξ ἀκαλαρρείταο βαθυρρόου Ὠκεανοῖο,
οἱ δ᾽ ἐς βῆσσαν ἵκανον ἐπακτῆρες· πρὸ δ᾽ ἄρ᾽ αὐτῶν   435
ἴχνι᾽ ἐρευνῶντες κύνες ἤϊσαν, αὐτὰρ ὄπισθεν
υἱέες Αὐτολύκου· μετὰ τοῖσι δὲ δῖος Ὀδυσσεὺς
ἤϊεν ἄγχι κυνῶν, κραδάων δολιχόσκιον ἔγχος.
ἔνθα δ᾽ ἄρ᾽ ἐν λόχμῃ πυκινῇ κατέκειτο μέγας σῦς·
τὴν μὲν ἄρ᾽ οὔτ᾽ ἀνέμων διάη μένος ὑγρὸν ἀέντων,   440
οὔτε μιν Ἠέλιος φαέθων ἀκτῖσιν ἔβαλλεν,
οὔτ᾽ ὄμβρος περάασκε διαμπερές· ὣς ἄρα πυκνὴ
ἦεν, ἀτὰρ φύλλων ἐνέην χύσις ἤλιθα πολλή.
τὸν δ᾽ ἀνδρῶν τε κυνῶν τε περὶ κτύπος ἦλθε ποδοῖϊν,
ὡς ἐπάγοντες ἐπῆισαν· ὁ δ᾽ ἀντίος ἐκ ξυλόχοιο,   445
φρίξας εὖ λοφιήν, πῦρ δ᾽ ὀφθαλμοῖσι δεδορκώς,
στῆ ῥ᾽ αὐτῶν σχεδόθεν· ὁ δ᾽ ἄρα πρώτιστος Ὀδυσσεὺς
ἔσσυτ᾽ ἀνασχόμενος δολιχὸν δόρυ χειρὶ παχείῃ,

434 = *Iliad* 7.422, deleted by Bothe

οὐτάμεναι μεμαώς· ὁ δέ μιν φθάμενος ἔλασεν σῦς
γουνὸς ὕπερ, πολλὸν δὲ διήφυσε σαρκὸς ὀδόντι   450
λικριφὶς ἀΐξας, οὐδ' ὀστέον ἵκετο φωτός.
τὸν δ' Ὀδυσεὺς οὔτησε τυχὼν κατὰ δεξιὸν ὦμον,
ἀντικρὺ δὲ διῆλθε φαεινοῦ δουρὸς ἀκωκή·
κὰδ δ' ἔπεσ' ἐν κονίῃσι μακών, ἀπὸ δ' ἔπτατο θυμός.
τὸν μὲν ἄρ' Αὐτολύκου παῖδες φίλοι ἀμφεπένοντο,   455
ὠτειλὴν δ' Ὀδυσῆος ἀμύμονος ἀντιθέοιο
δῆσαν ἐπισταμένως, ἐπαοιδῇ δ' αἷμα κελαινὸν
ἔσχεθον, αἶψα δ' ἵκοντο φίλου πρὸς δώματα πατρός.
τὸν μὲν ἄρ' Αὐτόλυκός τε καὶ υἱέες Αὐτολύκοιο
εὖ ἰησάμενοι ἠδ' ἀγλαὰ δῶρα πορόντες   460
καρπαλίμως χαίροντα φίλως χαίροντες ἔπεμπον
εἰς Ἰθάκην. τῶι μέν ῥα πατὴρ καὶ πότνια μήτηρ
χαῖρον νοστήσαντι καὶ ἐξερέεινον ἅπαντα,
οὐλὴν ὅττι πάθοι· ὁ δ' ἄρα σφίσιν εὖ κατέλεξεν
ὥς μιν θηρεύοντ' ἔλασεν σῦς λευκῶι ὀδόντι,   465
Παρνησόνδ' ἐλθόντα σὺν υἱάσιν Αὐτολύκοιο.
  Τὴν γρηῦς χείρεσσι καταπρηνέσσι λαβοῦσα
γνῶ ῥ' ἐπιμασσαμένη, πόδα δὲ προέηκε φέρεσθαι·
ἐν δὲ λέβητι πέσε κνήμη, κανάχησε δὲ χαλκός,
ἂψ δ' ἑτέρωσ' ἐκλίθη· τὸ δ' ἐπὶ χθονὸς ἐξέχυθ' ὕδωρ.   470
τὴν δ' ἅμα χάρμα καὶ ἄλγος ἕλε φρένα, τὼ δέ οἱ ὄσσε
δακρυόφι πλῆσθεν, θαλερὴ δέ οἱ ἔσχετο φωνή.
ἁψαμένη δὲ γενείου Ὀδυσσῆα προσέειπεν·
''ἦ μάλ' Ὀδυσσεύς ἐσσι, φίλον τέκος· οὐδέ σ' ἐγώ γε
πρὶν ἔγνων, πρὶν πάντα ἄνακτ' ἐμὸν ἀμφαφάασθαι.''   475
  Ἦ καὶ Πηνελόπειαν ἐσέδρακεν ὀφθαλμοῖσι,
πεφραδέειν ἐθέλουσα φίλον πόσιν ἔνδον ἐόντα.
ἡ δ' οὔτ' ἀθρῆσαι δύνατ' ἀντίη οὔτε νοῆσαι·
τῇ γὰρ Ἀθηναίη νόον ἔτραπεν· αὐτὰρ Ὀδυσσεὺς
χείρ' ἐπιμασσάμενος φάρυγος λάβε δεξιτερῆφι,   480

458 φίλου : φίλα, cf. H. Dem. 107, 180   461 φίλως χαίροντες : φίλην ἐς
πατρίδ', φίλως ἀπέπεμπον   474 μάλ' : σύ γ' (some MSS and p)

τῆι δ' ἑτέρηι ἕθεν ἆσσον ἐρύσσατο φώνησέν τε·
"μαῖα, τίη μ' ἐθέλεις ὀλέσαι; σὺ δέ μ' ἔτρεφες αὐτὴ
τῶι σῶι ἐπὶ μαζῶι· νῦν δ' ἄλγεα πολλὰ μογήσας
ἤλυθον εἰκοστῶι ἔτεϊ ἐς πατρίδα γαῖαν.
ἀλλ' ἐπεὶ ἐφράσθης καί τοι θεὸς ἔμβαλε θυμῶι,   485
σίγα, μή τίς τ' ἄλλος ἐνὶ μεγάροισι πύθηται.
ὧδε γὰρ ἐξερέω, καὶ μὴν τετελεσμένον ἔσται·
εἴ χ' ὑπ' ἐμοί γε θεὸς δαμάσηι μνηστῆρας ἀγαυούς,
οὐδὲ τροφοῦ οὔσης σεῦ ἀφέξομαι, ὁππότ' ἂν ἄλλας
δμωιὰς ἐν μεγάροισιν ἐμοῖς κτείνωμι γυναῖκας."   490
    Τὸν δ' αὖτε προσέειπε περίφρων Εὐρύκλεια·
"τέκνον ἐμόν, ποῖόν σε ἔπος φύγεν ἕρκος ὀδόντων.
οἶσθα μὲν οἶον ἐμὸν μένος ἔμπεδον οὐδ' ἐπιεικτόν,
ἔξω δ' ὡς ὅτε τις στερεὴ λίθος ἠὲ σίδηρος.
ἄλλο δέ τοι ἐρέω, σὺ δ' ἐνὶ φρεσὶ βάλλεο σῆισιν·   495
εἴ χ' ὑπὸ σοί γε θεὸς δαμάσηι μνηστῆρας ἀγαυούς,
δὴ τότε τοι καταλέξω ἐνὶ μεγάροισι γυναῖκας,
αἵ τέ σ' ἀτιμάζουσι καὶ αἳ νηλίτιδές εἰσι."
    Τὴν δ' ἀπαμειβόμενος προσέφη πολύμητις Ὀδυσσεύς·
"μαῖα, τίη δὲ σὺ τὰς μυθήσεαι; οὐδέ τί σε χρή.   500
εὖ νυ καὶ αὐτὸς ἐγὼ φράσομαι καὶ εἴσομ' ἑκάστην·
ἀλλ' ἔχε σιγῆι μῦθον, ἐπίτρεψον δὲ θεοῖσιν."
    Ὣς ἄρ' ἔφη, γρηῦς δὲ διὲκ μεγάροιο βεβήκει
οἰσομένη ποδάνιπτρα· τὰ γὰρ πρότερ' ἔκχυτο πάντα.
αὐτὰρ ἐπεὶ νίψεν τε καὶ ἤλειψεν λίπ' ἐλαίωι,   505
αὖτις ἄρ' ἀσσοτέρω πυρὸς ἕλκετο δίφρον Ὀδυσσεὺς
θερσόμενος, οὐλὴν δὲ κατὰ ῥακέεσσι κάλυψε.
τοῖσι δὲ μύθων ἄρχε περίφρων Πηνελόπεια·
"ξεῖνε, τὸ μέν σ' ἔτι τυτθὸν ἐγὼν εἰρήσομαι αὐτή·
καὶ γὰρ δὴ κοίτοιο τάχ' ἔσσεται ἡδέος ὥρη,   510
ὅν τινά γ' ὕπνος ἕλοι γλυκερός, καὶ κηδόμενόν περ.
αὐτὰρ ἐμοὶ καὶ πένθος ἀμέτρητον πόρε δαίμων·
ἤματα μὲν γὰρ τέρπομ' ὀδυρομένη, γοόωσα,

---

493 οὐδ' : οὐκ   494 ἔξω δ' ἠΰτε περ κρατερὴ δρῦς ἠὲ σίδηρος Plutarch

ἔς τ' ἐμὰ ἔργ' ὁρόωσα καὶ ἀμφιπόλων ἐνὶ οἴκωι·
αὐτὰρ ἐπεὶ νὺξ ἔλθηι, ἕληισι τε κοῖτος ἅπαντας,   515
κεῖμαι ἐνὶ λέκτρωι, πυκιναὶ δέ μοι ἀμφ' ἁδινὸν κῆρ
ὀξεῖαι μελεδῶναι ὀδυρομένην ἐρέθουσιν.
ὡς δ' ὅτε Πανδαρέου κούρη, χλωρηῒς ἀηδών,
καλὸν ἀείδηισιν ἔαρος νέον ἱσταμένοιο,
δενδρέων ἐν πετάλοισι καθεζομένη πυκινοῖσιν,   520
ἥ τε θαμὰ τρωπῶσα χέει πολυηχέα φωνήν,
παῖδ' ὀλοφυρομένη Ἴτυλον φίλον, ὅν ποτε χαλκῶι
κτεῖνε δι' ἀφραδίας, κοῦρον Ζήθοιο ἄνακτος,
ὡς καὶ ἐμοὶ δίχα θυμὸς ὀρώρεται ἔνθα καὶ ἔνθα,
ἠὲ μένω παρὰ παιδὶ καὶ ἔμπεδα πάντα φυλάσσω,   525
κτῆσιν ἐμήν, δμωιάς τε καὶ ὑψερεφὲς μέγα δῶμα,
εὐνήν τ' αἰδομένη πόσιος δήμοιό τε φῆμιν,
ἦ ἤδη ἅμ' ἕπωμαι Ἀχαιῶν ὅς τις ἄριστος
μνᾶται ἐνὶ μεγάροισι, πορὼν ἀπερείσια ἕδνα.
παῖς δ' ἐμὸς ἧος ἔην ἔτι νήπιος ἠδὲ χαλίφρων,   530
γήμασθ' οὔ μ' εἴα πόσιος κατὰ δῶμα λιποῦσαν·
νῦν δ' ὅτε δὴ μέγας ἐστὶ καὶ ἥβης μέτρον ἱκάνει,
καὶ δή μ' ἀρᾶται πάλιν ἐλθέμεν ἐκ μεγάροιο,
κτήσιος ἀσχαλόων, τήν οἱ κατέδουσιν Ἀχαιοί.
ἀλλ' ἄγε μοι τὸν ὄνειρον ὑπόκριναι καὶ ἄκουσον.   535
χῆνές μοι κατὰ οἶκον ἐείκοσι πυρὸν ἔδουσιν
ἐξ ὕδατος, καί τέ σφιν ἰαίνομαι εἰσορόωσα·
ἐλθὼν δ' ἐξ ὄρεος μέγας αἰετὸς ἀγκυλοχείλης
πᾶσι κατ' αὐχένας ἧξε καὶ ἔκτανεν· οἱ δ' ἐκέχυντο
ἀθρόοι ἐν μεγάροις, ὁ δ' ἐς αἰθέρα δῖαν ἀέρθη.   540
αὐτὰρ ἐγὼ κλαῖον καὶ ἐκώκυον ἔν περ ὀνείρωι,
ἀμφὶ δ' ἔμ' ἠγερέθοντο ἐϋπλοκαμῖδες Ἀχαιαί,
οἴκτρ' ὀλοφυρομένην ὅ μοι αἰετὸς ἔκτανε χῆνας.
ἂψ δ' ἐλθὼν κατ' ἄρ' ἕζετ' ἐπὶ προὔχοντι μελάθρωι,
φωνῆι δὲ βροτέηι κατερήτυε φώνησέν τε·   545

521 πολυηχέα MSS : πολυδευκέα testimonia   526 deleted by Kirchhoff, cf. Lacey, C.R. 16 (1966) 1–2

'θάρσει, Ἰκαρίου κούρη τηλεκλειτοῖο·
οὐκ ὄναρ, ἀλλ' ὕπαρ ἐσθλόν, ὅ τοι τετελεσμένον ἔσται.
χῆνες μὲν μνηστῆρες, ἐγὼ δέ τοι αἰετὸς ὄρνις
ἦα πάρος, νῦν αὖτε τεὸς πόσις εἰλήλουθα,
ὃς πᾶσι μνηστῆρσιν ἀεικέα πότμον ἐφήσω.'   550
ὣς ἔφατ', αὐτὰρ ἐμὲ μελιηδὴς ὕπνος ἀνῆκε·
παπτήνασα δὲ χῆνας ἐνὶ μεγάροισι νόησα
πυρὸν ἐρεπτομένους παρὰ πύελον, ἧχι πάρος περ.''
    Τὴν δ' ἀπαμειβόμενος προσέφη πολύμητις Ὀδυσσεύς·
''ὦ γύναι, οὔ πως ἔστιν ὑποκρίνασθαι ὄνειρον   555
ἄλληι ἀποκλίναντ', ἐπεὶ ἦ ῥά τοι αὐτὸς Ὀδυσσεὺς
πέφραδ' ὅπως τελέει· μνηστῆρσι δὲ φαίνετ' ὄλεθρος
πᾶσι μάλ', οὐδέ κέ τις θάνατον καὶ κῆρας ἀλύξει.''
    Τὸν δ' αὖτε προσέειπε περίφρων Πηνελόπεια·
''ξεῖν', ἦ τοι μὲν ὄνειροι ἀμήχανοι ἀκριτόμυθοι   560
γίγνοντ', οὐδέ τι πάντα τελείεται ἀνθρώποισι.
δοιαὶ γάρ τε πύλαι ἀμενηνῶν εἰσιν ὀνείρων·
αἱ μὲν γὰρ κεράεσσι τετεύχαται, αἱ δ' ἐλέφαντι·
τῶν οἳ μέν κ' ἔλθωσι διὰ πριστοῦ ἐλέφαντος,
οἵ ῥ' ἐλεφαίρονται, ἔπε' ἀκράαντα φέροντες·   565
οἳ δὲ διὰ ξεστῶν κεράων ἔλθωσι θύραζε,
οἵ ῥ' ἔτυμα κραίνουσι, βροτῶν ὅτε κέν τις ἴδηται.
ἀλλ' ἐμοὶ οὐκ ἐντεῦθεν ὀΐομαι αἰνὸν ὄνειρον
ἐλθέμεν· ἦ κ' ἀσπαστὸν ἐμοὶ καὶ παιδὶ γένοιτο.
ἄλλο δέ τοι ἐρέω, σὺ δ' ἐνὶ φρεσὶ βάλλεο σῇσιν·   570
ἥδε δὴ ἠὼς εἶσι δυσώνυμος, ἥ μ' Ὀδυσῆος
οἴκου ἀποσχήσει· νῦν γὰρ καταθήσω ἄεθλον,
τοὺς πελέκεας, τοὺς κεῖνος ἐνὶ μεγάροισιν ἑοῖσιν
ἵστασχ' ἑξείης, δρυόχους ὥς, δώδεκα πάντας·
στὰς δ' ὅ γε πολλὸν ἄνευθε διαρρίπτασκεν ὀϊστόν.   575
νῦν δὲ μνηστήρεσσιν ἄεθλον τοῦτον ἐφήσω·
ὃς δέ κε ῥηΐτατ' ἐντανύσῃ βιὸν ἐν παλάμῃσι

---

558 a–b (= 20.369–70) in some MSS added after 558, wrongly   562
ἀμενηνῶν MSS : ψευστάων testimonia

καὶ διοϊστεύσηι πελέκεων δυοκαίδεκα πάντων,
τῶι κεν ἅμ' ἑσποίμην, νοσφισσαμένη τόδε δῶμα
κουρίδιον, μάλα καλόν, ἐνίπλειον βιότοιο,   580
τοῦ ποτε μεμνήσεσθαι ὀίομαι ἔν περ ὀνείρωι.''
    Τὴν δ' ἀπαμειβόμενος προσέφη πολύμητις Ὀδυσσεύς·
''ὦ γύναι αἰδοίη Λαερτιάδεω Ὀδυσῆος,
μηκέτι νῦν ἀνάβαλλε δόμοις ἔνι τοῦτον ἄεθλον·
πρὶν γάρ τοι πολύμητις ἐλεύσεται ἐνθάδ' Ὀδυσσεύς,   585
πρὶν τούτους τόδε τόξον ἐΰξοον ἀμφαφόωντας
νευρήν τ' ἐντανύσαι διοϊστεῦσαί τε σιδήρου.''
    Τὸν δ' αὖτε προσέειπε περίφρων Πηνελόπεια·
''εἴ κ' ἐθέλοις μοι, ξεῖνε, παρήμενος ἐν μεγάροισι
τέρπειν, οὔ κέ μοι ὕπνος ἐπὶ βλεφάροισι χυθείη.   590
ἀλλ' οὐ γάρ πως ἔστιν ἀΰπνους ἔμμεναι αἰὲν
ἀνθρώπους· ἐπὶ γάρ τοι ἑκάστωι μοῖραν ἔθηκαν
ἀθάνατοι θνητοῖσιν ἐπὶ ζείδωρον ἄρουραν.
ἀλλ' ἦ τοι μὲν ἐγὼν ὑπερώιον εἰσαναβᾶσα
λέξομαι εἰς εὐνήν, ἥ μοι στονόεσσα τέτυκται,   595
αἰεὶ δάκρυσ' ἐμοῖσι πεφυρμένη, ἐξ οὗ Ὀδυσσεὺς
ὤιχετ' ἐποψόμενος Κακοΐλιον οὐκ ὀνομαστήν.
ἔνθα κε λεξαίμην· σὺ δὲ λέξεο τῶιδ' ἐνὶ οἴκωι,
ἢ χαμάδις στορέσας ἤ τοι κατὰ δέμνια θέντων.''
    ῝Ως εἰποῦσ' ἀνέβαιν' ὑπερώια σιγαλόεντα,   600
οὐκ οἴη, ἅμα τῆι γε καὶ ἀμφίπολοι κίον ἄλλαι.
ἐς δ' ὑπερῶι' ἀναβᾶσα σὺν ἀμφιπόλοισι γυναιξὶ
κλαῖεν ἔπειτ' Ὀδυσῆα, φίλον πόσιν, ὄφρα οἱ ὕπνον
ἡδὺν ἐπὶ βλεφάροισι βάλε γλαυκῶπις Ἀθήνη.

586 τόδε : ποτὲ, τό γε

Αὐτὰρ ὁ ἐν προδόμωι εὐνάζετο δῖος Ὀδυσσεύς·
κὰμ μὲν ἀδέψητον βοέην στόρεσ', αὐτὰρ ὕπερθε
κώεα πόλλ' ὀΐων, τοὺς ἱρεύεσκον Ἀχαιοί·
Εὐρυνόμη δ' ἄρ' ἐπὶ χλαῖναν βάλε κοιμηθέντι.
ἔνθ' Ὀδυσεὺς μνηστῆρσι κακὰ φρονέων ἐνὶ θυμῶι   5
κεῖτ' ἐγρηγορόων· ταὶ δ' ἐκ μεγάροιο γυναῖκες
ἤϊσαν, αἳ μνηστῆρσιν ἐμισγέσκοντο πάρος περ,
ἀλλήλῃσι γέλω τε καὶ εὐφροσύνην παρέχουσαι.
τοῦ δ' ὠρίνετο θυμὸς ἐνὶ στήθεσσι φίλοισι·
πολλὰ δὲ μερμήριζε κατὰ φρένα καὶ κατὰ θυμόν,   10
ἠὲ μεταΐξας θάνατον τεύξειεν ἑκάστῃ,
ἦ ἔτ' ἐῶι μνηστῆρσιν ὑπερφιάλοισι μιγῆναι
ὕστατα καὶ πύματα, κραδίη δέ οἱ ἔνδον ὑλάκτει.
ὡς δὲ κύων ἀμαλῇσι περὶ σκυλάκεσσι βεβῶσα
ἄνδρ' ἀγνοιήσασ' ὑλάει μέμονέν τε μάχεσθαι,   15
ὥς ῥα τοῦ ἔνδον ὑλάκτει ἀγαιομένου κακὰ ἔργα·
στῆθος δὲ πλήξας κραδίην ἠνίπαπε μύθωι·
''τέτλαθι δή, κραδίη· καὶ κύντερον ἄλλο ποτ' ἔτλης,
ἤματι τῶι ὅτε μοι μένος ἄσχετος ἤσθιε Κύκλωψ
ἰφθίμους ἑτάρους· σὺ δ' ἐτόλμας, ὄφρα σε μῆτις   20
ἐξάγαγ' ἐξ ἄντροιο ὀϊόμενον θανέεσθαι.''
   Ὣς ἔφατ', ἐν στήθεσσι καθαπτόμενος φίλον ἦτορ·
τῶι δὲ μάλ' ἐν πείσῃ κραδίη μένε τετληυῖα
νωλεμέως· ἀτὰρ αὐτὸς ἑλίσσετο ἔνθα καὶ ἔνθα.
ὡς δ' ὅτε γαστέρ' ἀνὴρ πολέος πυρὸς αἰθομένοιο,   25
ἐμπλείην κνίσης τε καὶ αἵματος, ἔνθα καὶ ἔνθα
αἰόλλῃ, μάλα δ' ὦκα λιλαίεται ὀπτηθῆναι,
ὣς ἄρ' ὅ γ' ἔνθα καὶ ἔνθα ἑλίσσετο μερμηρίζων
ὅππως δὴ μνηστῆρσιν ἀναιδέσι χεῖρας ἐφήσει
μοῦνος ἐὼν πολέσι. σχεδόθεν δέ οἱ ἦλθεν Ἀθήνη   30

14 ἀμαλῇσι : ἀπαλῇσι

οὐρανόθεν καταβᾶσα· δέμας δ' ἤϊκτο γυναικί·
στῆ δ' ἄρ' ὑπὲρ κεφαλῆς καί μιν πρὸς μῦθον ἔειπε·
"τίπτ' αὖτ' ἐγρήσσεις, πάντων περὶ κάμμορε φωτῶν;
οἶκος μέν τοι ὅδ' ἐστί, γυνὴ δέ τοι ἥδ' ἐνὶ οἴκωι
καὶ πάϊς, οἷόν πού τις ἐέλδεται ἔμμεναι υἷα."   35
    Τὴν δ' ἀπαμειβόμενος προσέφη πολύμητις Ὀδυσσεύς·
"ναὶ δὴ ταῦτά γε πάντα, θεά, κατὰ μοῖραν ἔειπες·
ἀλλ' ἔτι μοι τόδε θυμὸς ἐνὶ φρεσὶ μερμηρίζει,
ὅππως δὴ μνηστῆρσιν ἀναιδέσι χεῖρας ἐφήσω,
μοῦνος ἐών· οἱ δ' αἰὲν ἀολλέες ἔνδον ἔασι.   40
πρὸς δ' ἔτι καὶ τόδε μεῖζον ἐνὶ φρεσὶ μερμηρίζω·
εἴ περ γὰρ κτείναιμι Διός τε σέθεν τε ἕκητι,
πῆι κεν ὑπεκπροφύγοιμι; τά σε φράζεσθαι ἄνωγα."
    Τὸν δ' αὖτε προσέειπε θεὰ γλαυκῶπις Ἀθήνη·
"σχέτλιε, καὶ μέν τίς τε χερείονι πείθεθ' ἑταίρωι,   45
ὅς περ θνητός τ' ἐστὶ καὶ οὐ τόσα μήδεα οἶδεν·
αὐτὰρ ἐγὼ θεός εἰμι, διαμπερὲς ἥ σε φυλάσσω
ἐν πάντεσσι πόνοις. ἐρέω δέ τοι ἐξαναφανδόν·
εἴ περ πεντήκοντα λόχοι μερόπων ἀνθρώπων
νῶϊ περισταῖεν, κτεῖναι μεμαῶτες Ἄρηϊ,   50
καί κεν τῶν ἐλάσαιο βόας καὶ ἴφια μῆλα.
ἀλλ' ἐλέτω σε καὶ ὕπνος· ἀνίη καὶ τὸ φυλάσσειν
πάννυχον ἐγρήσσοντα, κακῶν δ' ὑποδύσεαι ἤδη."
    Ὣς φάτο, καί ῥά οἱ ὕπνον ἐπὶ βλεφάροισιν ἔχευεν,
αὐτὴ δ' ἂψ ἐς Ὄλυμπον ἀφίκετο δῖα θεάων.   55
εὖτε τὸν ὕπνος ἔμαρπτε, λύων μελεδήματα θυμοῦ,
λυσιμελής, ἄλοχος δ' ἄρ' ἐπέγρετο κεδνὰ ἰδυῖα,
κλαῖε δ' ἄρ' ἐν λέκτροισι καθεζομένη μαλακοῖσιν.
αὐτὰρ ἐπεὶ κλαίουσα κορέσσατο ὃν κατὰ θυμόν,

---

38 ἀλλ' ἔτι : ἀλλά τί   45 πείθεθ' MSS : θάρσει p   48 ἐν πάντεσσι πόνοις
MSS : ... (c. 13 letters)]πων ἐρέω δέ[p   51a additional line in p: ... (c. 13
letters)]ειασ ἀπ[52 different version in p: perhaps [ἀλλ' ἐλέτω σε καὶ
ὕ]πνοσ ε[..]μ[.]..κ[(West)   53 omitted by p   55a additional line in
p:]ιοσμε[58a additional line in p: c. 15 letters,]σθεν ἀκὴν ἔχον.[See
Commentary

Ἀρτέμιδι πρώτιστον ἐπεύξατο δῖα γυναικῶν·   60
" Ἄρτεμι, πότνα θεά, θύγατερ Διός, αἴθε μοι ἤδη
ἰὸν ἐνὶ στήθεσσι βαλοῦσ' ἐκ θυμὸν ἕλοιο
αὐτίκα νῦν, ἢ ἔπειτά μ' ἀναρπάξασα θύελλα
οἴχοιτο προφέρουσα κατ' ἠερόεντα κέλευθα,
ἐν προχοῇς δὲ βάλοι ἀψορρόου Ὠκεανοῖο.   65
ὡς δ' ὅτε Πανδαρέου κούρας ἀνέλοντο θύελλαι·
τῇσι τοκῆας μὲν φθῖσαν θεοί, αἱ δ' ἐλίποντο
ὀρφαναὶ ἐν μεγάροισι, κόμισσε δὲ δῖ' Ἀφροδίτη
τυρῶι καὶ μέλιτι γλυκερῶι καὶ ἡδέϊ οἴνωι·
Ἥρη δ' αὐτῇισιν περὶ πασέων δῶκε γυναικῶν   70
εἶδος καὶ πινυτήν, μῆκος δ' ἔπορ' Ἄρτεμις ἁγνή,
ἔργα δ' Ἀθηναίη δέδαε κλυτὰ ἐργάζεσθαι.
εὖτ' Ἀφροδίτη δῖα προσέστιχε μακρὸν Ὄλυμπον,
κούρηις αἰτήσουσα τέλος θαλεροῖο γάμοιο,
ἐς Δία τερπικέραυνον – ὁ γάρ τ' εὖ οἶδεν ἅπαντα,   75
μοῖράν τ' ἀμμορίην τε καταθνητῶν ἀνθρώπων –
τόφρα δὲ τὰς κούρας ἅρπυιαι ἀνηρείψαντο
καί ρ' ἔδοσαν στυγερῇισιν ἐρινύσιν ἀμφιπολεύειν·
ὡς ἔμ' ἀϊστώσειαν Ὀλύμπια δώματ' ἔχοντες,
ἠέ μ' ἐϋπλόκαμος βάλοι Ἄρτεμις, ὄφρ' Ὀδυσῆα   80
ὀσσομένη καὶ γαῖαν ὕπο στυγερὴν ἀφικοίμην,
μηδέ τι χείρονος ἀνδρὸς ἐϋφραίνοιμι νόημα.
ἀλλὰ τὸ μὲν καὶ ἀνεκτὸν ἔχει κακόν, ὁππότε κέν τις
ἤματα μὲν κλαίηι, πυκινῶς ἀκαχήμενος ἦτορ,
νύκτας δ' ὕπνος ἔχηισιν – ὁ γάρ τ' ἐπέλησεν ἁπάντων,   85
ἐσθλῶν ἠδὲ κακῶν, ἐπεὶ ἄρ βλέφαρ' ἀμφικαλύψηι –
αὐτὰρ ἐμοὶ καὶ ὀνείρατ' ἐπέσσευεν κακὰ δαίμων.
τῇδε γὰρ αὖ μοι νυκτὶ παρέδραθεν εἴκελος αὐτῶι,
τοῖος ἐὼν οἷος ἦιεν ἅμα στρατῶι· αὐτὰρ ἐμὸν κῆρ
χαῖρ', ἐπεὶ οὐκ ἐφάμην ὄναρ ἔμμεναι, ἀλλ' ὕπαρ ἤδη."   90
    Ὣς ἔφατ', αὐτίκα δὲ χρυσόθρονος ἤλυθεν Ἠώς.

83 omitted in some MSS   ἔχει : ἔχειν; ἔπι von der Mühll   83a ἤτοι μέν τε
βροτῶν ἄλλος ὧι πένθος ἱκάνει some MSS

τῆς δ' ἄρα κλαιούσης ὄπα σύνθετο δῖος Ὀδυσσεύς·
μερμήριζε δ' ἔπειτα, δόκησε δέ οἱ κατὰ θυμὸν
ἤδη γιγνώσκουσα παρεστάμεναι κεφαλῆφι.
χλαῖναν μὲν συνελὼν καὶ κώεα, τοῖσιν ἐνεῦδεν,   95
ἐς μέγαρον κατέθηκεν ἐπὶ θρόνου, ἐκ δὲ βοείην
θῆκε θύραζε φέρων, Διὶ δ' εὔξατο χεῖρας ἀνασχών·
"Ζεῦ πάτερ, εἴ μ' ἐθέλοντες ἐπὶ τραφερήν τε καὶ ὑγρὴν
ἤγετ' ἐμὴν ἐς γαῖαν, ἐπεί μ' ἐκακώσατε λίην,
φήμην τίς μοι φάσθω ἐγειρομένων ἀνθρώπων   100
ἔνδοθεν, ἔκτοσθεν δὲ Διὸς τέρας ἄλλο φανήτω."

   Ὣς ἔφατ' εὐχόμενος· τοῦ δ' ἔκλυε μητίετα Ζεύς,
αὐτίκα δ' ἐβρόντησεν ἀπ' αἰγλήεντος Ὀλύμπου
[ὑψόθεν ἐκ νεφέων· γήθησε δὲ δῖος Ὀδυσσεύς].
φήμην δ' ἐξ οἴκοιο γυνὴ προέηκεν ἀλετρὶς   105
πλησίον, ἔνθ' ἄρα οἱ μύλαι ἥατο ποιμένι λαῶν,
τῇσιν δώδεκα πᾶσαι ἐπερρώοντο γυναῖκες
ἄλφιτα τεύχουσαι καὶ ἀλείατα, μυελὸν ἀνδρῶν.
αἱ μὲν ἄρ' ἄλλαι εὗδον, ἐπεὶ κατὰ πυρὸν ἄλεσσαν,
ἡ δὲ μί' οὔ πω παύετ', ἀφαυροτάτη δ' ἐτέτυκτο·   110
ἥ ῥα μύλην στήσασα ἔπος φάτο, σῆμα ἄνακτι·
"Ζεῦ πάτερ, ὅς τε θεοῖσι καὶ ἀνθρώποισιν ἀνάσσεις,
ἦ μεγάλ' ἐβρόντησας ἀπ' οὐρανοῦ ἀστερόεντος,
οὐδέ ποθι νέφος ἐστί· τέρας νύ τεωι τόδε φαίνεις.
κρῆνον νῦν καὶ ἐμοὶ δειλῆι ἔπος, ὅττι κεν εἴπω·   115
μνηστῆρες πύματόν τε καὶ ὕστατον ἤματι τῶιδε
ἐν μεγάροις Ὀδυσῆος ἑλοίατο δαῖτ' ἐρατεινήν,
οἳ δή μοι καμάτωι θυμαλγέϊ γούνατ' ἔλυσαν
ἄλφιτα τευχούσηι· νῦν ὕστατα δειπνήσειαν."

   Ὣς ἄρ' ἔφη, χαῖρεν δὲ κλεηδόνι δῖος Ὀδυσσεὺς   120
Ζηνός τε βροντῆι· φάτο γὰρ τίσασθαι ἀλείτας.

   Αἱ δ' ἄλλαι δμωιαὶ κατὰ δώματα κάλ' Ὀδυσῆος
ἀγρόμεναι ἀνέκαιον ἐπ' ἐσχάρηι ἀκάματον πῦρ.
Τηλέμαχος δ' εὐνῆθεν ἀνίστατο, ἰσόθεος φώς,

---

104 deleted by Knight, rightly   121 τίσασθαι : τίσεσθαι (cf. *Il.* 3.28, 366)
123 ἀγρόμεναι : ἐγρόμεναι

εἵματα ἐσσάμενος· περὶ δὲ ξίφος ὀξὺ θέτ᾽ ὤμωι·   125
ποσσὶ δ᾽ ὑπὸ λιπαροῖσιν ἐδήσατο καλὰ πέδιλα,
εἵλετο δ᾽ ἄλκιμον ἔγχος, ἀκαχμένον ὀξέϊ χαλκῶι·
στῆ δ᾽ ἄρ᾽ ἐπ᾽ οὐδὸν ἰών, πρὸς δ᾽ Εὐρύκλειαν ἔειπε·
"μαῖα φίλη, πῶς ξεῖνον ἐτιμήσασθ᾽ ἐνὶ οἴκωι
εὐνῆι καὶ σίτωι, ἦ αὔτως κεῖται ἀκηδής;   130
τοιαύτη γὰρ ἐμὴ μήτηρ, πινυτή περ ἐοῦσα·
ἐμπλήγδην ἕτερόν γε τίει μερόπων ἀνθρώπων
χείρονα, τὸν δέ τ᾽ ἀρείον᾽ ἀτιμήσασ᾽ ἀποπέμπει."
    Τὸν δ᾽ αὖτε προσέειπε περίφρων Εὐρύκλεια·
"οὐκ ἄν μιν νῦν, τέκνον, ἀναίτιον αἰτιόωιο.   135
οἶνον μὲν γὰρ πῖνε καθήμενος, ὄφρ᾽ ἔθελ᾽ αὐτός,
σίτου δ᾽ οὐκέτ᾽ ἔφη πεινήμεναι· εἴρετο γάρ μιν.
ἀλλ᾽ ὅτε δὴ κοίτοιο καὶ ὕπνου μιμνήσκοντο,
ἡ μὲν δέμνι᾽ ἄνωγεν ὑποστορέσαι δμωιῆισιν,
αὐτὰρ ὅ γ᾽, ὥς τις πάμπαν ὀϊζυρὸς καὶ ἄποτμος,   140
οὐκ ἔθελ᾽ ἐν λέκτροισι καὶ ἐν ῥήγεσσι καθεύδειν,
ἀλλ᾽ ἐν ἀδεψήτωι βοέηι καὶ κώεσιν οἰῶν
ἔδραθ᾽ ἐνὶ προδόμωι· χλαῖναν δ᾽ ἐπιέσσαμεν ἡμεῖς."
    Ὣς φάτο, Τηλέμαχος δὲ διὲκ μεγάροιο βεβήκει
ἔγχος ἔχων· ἅμα τῶι γε δύω κύνες ἀργοὶ ἕποντο.   145
βῆ δ᾽ ἴμεν εἰς ἀγορὴν μετ᾽ ἐϋκνήμιδας Ἀχαιούς.
ἡ δ᾽ αὖτε δμωιῆισιν ἐκέκλετο δῖα γυναικῶν,
Εὐρύκλει᾽, Ὦπος θυγάτηρ Πεισηνορίδαο·
"ἀγρεῖθ᾽, αἱ μὲν δῶμα κορήσατε ποιπνύσασαι,
ῥάσσατέ τ᾽ ἔν τε θρόνοις εὐποιήτοισι τάπητας   150
βάλλετε πορφυρέους· αἱ δὲ σπόγγοισι τραπέζας
πάσας ἀμφιμάσασθε, καθήρατε δὲ κρητῆρας
καὶ δέπα ἀμφικύπελλα τετυγμένα· ταὶ δὲ μεθ᾽ ὕδωρ
ἔρχεσθε κρήνηνδε, καὶ οἴσετε θᾶσσον ἰοῦσαι.
οὐ γὰρ δὴν μνηστῆρες ἀπέσσονται μεγάροιο,   155
ἀλλὰ μάλ᾽ ἦρι νέονται, ἐπεὶ καὶ πᾶσιν ἑορτή."
    Ὣς ἔφαθ᾽, αἱ δ᾽ ἄρα τῆς μάλα μὲν κλύον ἠδ᾽ ἐπίθοντο.

---

125 omitted in one MS   134 περίφρων : φίλη τροφός some MSS, p
138 μιμνήσκοντο : μιμνήσκοιτο   145 omitted in some MSS, cf. 125

αἱ μὲν ἐείκοσι βῆσαν ἐπὶ κρήνην μελάνυδρον,
αἱ δ' αὐτοῦ κατὰ δώματ' ἐπισταμένως πονέοντο.
    Ἐς δ' ἦλθον δρηστῆρες ἀγήνορες· οἱ μὲν ἔπειτα   160
εὖ καὶ ἐπισταμένως κέασαν ξύλα, ταὶ δὲ γυναῖκες
ἦλθον ἀπὸ κρήνης· ἐπὶ δέ σφισιν ἦλθε συβώτης
τρεῖς σιάλους κατάγων, οἳ ἔσαν μετὰ πᾶσιν ἄριστοι.
καὶ τοὺς μέν ῥ' εἴασε καθ' ἕρκεα καλὰ νέμεσθαι,
αὐτὸς δ' αὖτ' Ὀδυσῆα προσηύδα μειλιχίοισι·   165
''ξεῖν', ἦ ἄρ τί σε μᾶλλον Ἀχαιοὶ εἰσορόωσιν,
ἦέ σ' ἀτιμάζουσι κατὰ μέγαρ', ὡς τὸ πάρος περ;''
    Τὸν δ' ἀπαμειβόμενος προσέφη πολύμητις Ὀδυσσεύς·
''αἲ γὰρ δή, Εὔμαιε, θεοὶ τισαίατο λώβην,
ἣν οἵδ' ὑβρίζοντες ἀτάσθαλα μηχανόωνται   170
οἴκωι ἐν ἀλλοτρίωι, οὐδ' αἰδοῦς μοῖραν ἔχουσιν.''
    Ὣς οἱ μὲν τοιαῦτα πρὸς ἀλλήλους ἀγόρευον,
ἀγχίμολον δέ σφ' ἦλθε Μελάνθιος, αἰπόλος αἰγῶν,
αἶγας ἄγων αἳ πᾶσι μετέπρεπον αἰπολίοισι,
δεῖπνον μνηστήρεσσι· δύω δ' ἅμ' ἕποντο νομῆες.   175
καὶ τὰς μὲν κατέδησαν ὑπ' αἰθούσηι ἐριδούπωι,
αὐτὸς δ' αὖτ' Ὀδυσῆα προσηύδα κερτομίοισι·
''ξεῖν', ἔτι καὶ νῦν ἐνθάδ' ἀνιήσεις κατὰ δῶμα
ἀνέρας αἰτίζων, ἀτὰρ οὐκ ἔξεισθα θύραζε;
πάντως οὐκέτι νῶϊ διακρινέεσθαι ὀΐω   180
πρὶν χειρῶν γεύσασθαι, ἐπεὶ σύ περ οὐ κατὰ κόσμον
αἰτίζεις· εἰσὶν δὲ καὶ ἄλλαι δαῖτες Ἀχαιῶν.''
    Ὣς φάτο, τὸν δ' οὔ τι προσέφη πολύμητις Ὀδυσσεύς,
ἀλλ' ἀκέων κίνησε κάρη, κακὰ βυσσοδομεύων.
    Τοῖσι δ' ἐπὶ τρίτος ἦλθε Φιλοίτιος, ὄρχαμος ἀνδρῶν,   185
βοῦν στεῖραν μνηστῆρσιν ἄγων καὶ πίονας αἶγας.
πορθμῆες δ' ἄρα τούς γε διήγαγον, οἵ τε καὶ ἄλλους
ἀνθρώπους πέμπουσιν, ὅτις σφέας εἰσαφίκηται.
καὶ τὰ μὲν εὖ κατέδησεν ὑπ' αἰθούσηι ἐριδούπωι,

159 δώματ' : δῶμα   160 ἐς : ἐκ   170 ἀτάσθαλα : ἀεικέα   176 κατέδησαν :
κατέδησεν   182 ἄλλαι : ἄλλοθι   185 Φιλοίτιος ἠπείρηθεν variant quoted
by Eustathius   188 ὅτις σφέας εἰσαφίκηται : ἐπ' εὐρέα νῶτα θαλάσσης

αὐτὸς δ᾽ αὖτ᾽ ἐρέεινε συβώτην ἄγχι παραστάς·   190
"τίς δὴ ὅδε ξεῖνος νέον εἰλήλουθε, συβῶτα,
ἡμέτερον πρὸς δῶμα; τέων δ᾽ ἐξ εὔχεται εἶναι
ἀνδρῶν; ποῦ δέ νύ οἱ γενεὴ καὶ πατρὶς ἄρουρα;
δύσμορος, ἦ τε ἔοικε δέμας βασιλῆϊ ἄνακτι·
ἀλλὰ θεοὶ δυόωσι πολυπλάγκτους ἀνθρώπους,   195
ὁππότε καὶ βασιλεῦσιν ἐπικλώσωνται ὀϊζύν."
    ῏Η καὶ δεξιτερῆι δειδίσκετο χειρὶ παραστάς,
καί μιν φωνήσας ἔπεα πτερόεντα προσηύδα·
"χαῖρε, πάτερ ὦ ξεῖνε· γένοιτό τοι ἔς περ ὀπίσσω
ὄλβος· ἀτὰρ μὲν νῦν γε κακοῖς ἔχεαι πολέεσσι.   200
Ζεῦ πάτερ, οὔ τις σεῖο θεῶν ὀλοώτερος ἄλλος·
οὐκ ἐλεαίρεις ἄνδρας, ἐπὴν δὴ γείνεαι αὐτός,
μισγέμεναι κακότητι καὶ ἄλγεσι λευγαλέοισιν.
ἴδιον, ὡς ἐνόησα, δεδάκρυνται δέ μοι ὄσσε
μνησαμένωι Ὀδυσῆος, ἐπεὶ καὶ κεῖνον ὀΐω   205
τοιάδε λαίφε᾽ ἔχοντα κατ᾽ ἀνθρώπους ἀλάλησθαι,
εἴ που ἔτι ζώει καὶ ὁρᾶι φάος ἠελίοιο.
εἰ δ᾽ ἤδη τέθνηκε καὶ εἰν Ἀΐδαο δόμοισιν,
ὤ μοι ἔπειτ᾽ Ὀδυσῆος ἀμύμονος, ὅς μ᾽ ἐπὶ βουσὶν
εἷσ᾽ ἔτι τυτθὸν ἐόντα Κεφαλλήνων ἐνὶ δήμωι.   210
νῦν δ᾽ αἱ μὲν γίγνονται ἀθέσφατοι, οὐδέ κεν ἄλλως
ἀνδρί γ᾽ ὑποσταχύοιτο βοῶν γένος εὐρυμετώπων·
τὰς δ᾽ ἄλλοι με κέλονται ἀγινέμεναί σφισιν αὐτοῖς
ἔδμεναι· οὐδέ τι παιδὸς ἐνὶ μεγάροις ἀλέγουσιν,
οὐδ᾽ ὄπιδα τρομέουσι θεῶν· μεμάασι γὰρ ἤδη   215
κτήματα δάσσασθαι δὴν οἰχομένοιο ἄνακτος.
αὐτὰρ ἐμοὶ τόδε θυμὸς ἐνὶ στήθεσσι φίλοισι
πόλλ᾽ ἐπιδινεῖται· μάλα μὲν κακὸν υἷος ἐόντος
ἄλλων δῆμον ἱκέσθαι ἰόντ᾽ αὐτῆισι βόεσσιν,
ἄνδρας ἐς ἀλλοδαπούς· τὸ δὲ ῥίγιον αὖθι μένοντα   220
βουσὶν ἐπ᾽ ἀλλοτρίηισι καθήμενον ἄλγεα πάσχειν.
καί κεν δὴ πάλαι ἄλλον ὑπερμενέων βασιλήων

204 ὡς σ᾽ Doederlein   215 τρομέουσι : φρονέουσι

ἐξικόμην φεύγων, ἐπεὶ οὐκέτ᾽ ἀνεκτὰ πέλονται·
ἀλλ᾽ ἔτι τὸν δύστηνον ὀΐομαι, εἴ ποθεν ἐλθὼν
ἀνδρῶν μνηστήρων σκέδασιν κατὰ δώματα θείη.''   225
    Τὸν δ᾽ ἀπαμειβόμενος προσέφη πολύμητις Ὀδυσσεύς·
''βουκόλ᾽, ἐπεὶ οὔτε κακῶι οὔτ᾽ ἄφρονι φωτὶ ἔοικας,
γιγνώσκω δὲ καὶ αὐτὸς ὅ τοι πινυτὴ φρένας ἵκει,
τοὔνεκά τοι ἐρέω καὶ ἐπὶ μέγαν ὅρκον ὀμοῦμαι·
ἴστω νῦν Ζεὺς πρῶτα θεῶν ξενίη τε τράπεζα,   230
ἱστίη τ᾽ Ὀδυσῆος ἀμύμονος, ἣν ἀφικάνω,
ἦ σέθεν ἐνθάδ᾽ ἐόντος ἐλεύσεται οἴκαδ᾽ Ὀδυσσεύς·
σοῖσιν δ᾽ ὀφθαλμοῖσιν ἐπόψεαι, αἴ κ᾽ ἐθέλησθα,
κτεινομένους μνηστῆρας, οἳ ἐνθάδε κοιρανέουσι.''
    Τὸν δ᾽ αὖτε προσέειπε βοῶν ἐπιβουκόλος ἀνήρ·   235
''αἲ γὰρ τοῦτο, ξεῖνε, ἔπος τελέσειε Κρονίων·
γνοίης χ᾽ οἵη ἐμὴ δύναμις καὶ χεῖρες ἕπονται.''
    Ὣς δ᾽ αὔτως Εὔμαιος ἐπεύξατο πᾶσι θεοῖσι
νοστῆσαι Ὀδυσῆα πολύφρονα ὅνδε δόμονδε.
    Ὣς οἱ μὲν τοιαῦτα πρὸς ἀλλήλους ἀγόρευον,   240
μνηστῆρες δ᾽ ἄρα Τηλεμάχωι θάνατόν τε μόρον τε
ἤρτυον· αὐτὰρ ὁ τοῖσιν ἀριστερὸς ἤλυθεν ὄρνις,
αἰετὸς ὑψιπέτης, ἔχε δὲ τρήρωνα πέλειαν.
τοῖσιν δ᾽ Ἀμφίνομος ἀγορήσατο καὶ μετέειπεν·
''ὦ φίλοι, οὐχ ἡμῖν συνθεύσεται ἥδε γε βουλή,   245
Τηλεμάχοιο φόνος· ἀλλὰ μνησώμεθα δαιτός.''
    Ὣς ἔφατ᾽ Ἀμφίνομος, τοῖσιν δ᾽ ἐπιήνδανε μῦθος.
ἐλθόντες δ᾽ ἐς δώματ᾽ Ὀδυσσῆος θείοιο
χλαίνας μὲν κατέθεντο κατὰ κλισμούς τε θρόνους τε,
οἱ δ᾽ ἱέρευον ὄϊς μεγάλους καὶ πίονας αἶγας,   250
ἵρευον δὲ σύας σιάλους καὶ βοῦν ἀγελαίην·
σπλάγχνα δ᾽ ἄρ᾽ ὀπτήσαντες ἐνώμων, ἐν δέ τε οἶνον
κρητῆρσιν κερόωντο· κύπελλα δὲ νεῖμε συβώτης.
σῖτον δέ σφ᾽ ἐπένειμε Φιλοίτιος, ὄρχαμος ἀνδρῶν,

227 ἐπεὶ deleted by van Leeuwen   230 ξενίη τε τράπεζα : ὕπατος καὶ ἄριστος
(19.303)   237 ἕπονται : ἄαπτοι   248 δώματ᾽ : δῶμα   Cf. 159

καλοῖς ἐν κανέοισιν, ἐωινοχόει δὲ Μελανθεύς.   255
οἱ δ’ ἐπ’ ὀνείαθ’ ἑτοῖμα προκείμενα χεῖρας ἴαλλον.
    Τηλέμαχος δ’ Ὀδυσῆα καθίδρυε, κέρδεα νωμῶν,
ἐντὸς ἐϋσταθέος μεγάρου, παρὰ λάϊνον οὐδόν,
δίφρον ἀεικέλιον καταθεὶς ὀλίγην τε τράπεζαν·
πὰρ δ’ ἐτίθει σπλάγχνων μοίρας, ἐν δ’ οἶνον ἔχευεν   260
ἐν δέπαϊ χρυσέωι, καί μιν πρὸς μῦθον ἔειπεν·
‘‘ἐνταυθοῖ νῦν ἧσο μετ’ ἀνδράσιν οἰνοποτάζων·
κερτομίας δέ τοι αὐτὸς ἐγὼ καὶ χεῖρας ἀφέξω
πάντων μνηστήρων, ἐπεὶ οὔ τοι δήμιός ἐστιν
οἶκος ὅδ’, ἀλλ’ Ὀδυσῆος, ἐμοὶ δ’ ἐκτήσατο κεῖνος.   265
ὑμεῖς δέ, μνηστῆρες, ἐπίσχετε θυμὸν ἐνιπῆς
καὶ χειρῶν, ἵνα μή τις ἔρις καὶ νεῖκος ὄρηται.’’
    Ὣς ἔφαθ’, οἱ δ’ ἄρα πάντες ὀδὰξ ἐν χείλεσι φύντες
Τηλέμαχον θαύμαζον, ὃ θαρσαλέως ἀγόρευε.
τοῖσιν δ’ Ἀντίνοος μετέφη, Εὐπείθεος υἱός·   270
‘‘καὶ χαλεπόν περ ἐόντα δεχώμεθα μῦθον, Ἀχαιοί,
Τηλεμάχου· μάλα δ’ ἧμιν ἀπειλήσας ἀγορεύει.
οὐ γὰρ Ζεὺς εἴασε Κρονίων· τῶι κέ μιν ἤδη
παύσαμεν ἐν μεγάροισι, λιγύν περ ἐόντ’ ἀγορητήν.’’
    Ὣς ἔφατ’ Ἀντίνοος· ὁ δ’ ἄρ’ οὐκ ἐμπάζετο μύθων.   275
κήρυκες δ’ ἀνὰ ἄστυ θεῶν ἱερὴν ἑκατόμβην
ἦγον· τοὶ δ’ ἀγέροντο κάρη κομόωντες Ἀχαιοὶ
ἄλσος ὕπο σκιερὸν ἑκατηβόλου Ἀπόλλωνος.
    Οἱ δ’ ἐπεὶ ὤπτησαν κρέ’ ὑπέρτερα καὶ ἐρύσαντο,
μοίρας δασσάμενοι δαίνυντ’ ἐρικυδέα δαῖτα·   280
πὰρ δ’ ἄρ’ Ὀδυσσῆϊ μοῖραν θέσαν οἳ πονέοντο
ἴσην, ὡς αὐτοί περ ἐλάγχανον· ὣς γὰρ ἀνώγει
Τηλέμαχος, φίλος υἱὸς Ὀδυσσῆος θείοιο.
    Μνηστῆρας δ’ οὐ πάμπαν ἀγήνορας εἴα Ἀθήνη
λώβης ἴσχεσθαι θυμαλγέος, ὄφρ’ ἔτι μᾶλλον   285
δύη ἄχος κραδίην Λαερτιάδεω Ὀδυσῆος.
ἦν δέ τις ἐν μνηστῆρσιν ἀνὴρ ἀθεμίστια εἰδώς,

256 deleted by Blass

Κτήσιππος δ᾽ ὄνομ᾽ ἔσκε, Σάμηι δ᾽ ἐνὶ οἰκία ναῖεν·
ὃς δή τοι κτεάτεσσι πεποιθὼς πατρὸς ἑοῖο
μνάσκετ᾽ Ὀδυσσῆος δὴν οἰχομένοιο δάμαρτα.   290
ὅς ῥα τότε μνηστῆρσιν ὑπερφιάλοισι μετηύδα·
"κέκλυτέ μευ, μνηστῆρες ἀγήνορες, ὄφρα τι εἴπω·
μοῖραν μὲν δὴ ξεῖνος ἔχει πάλαι, ὡς ἐπέοικεν,
ἴσην· οὐ γὰρ καλὸν ἀτέμβειν οὐδὲ δίκαιον
ξείνους Τηλεμάχου, ὅς κεν τάδε δώμαθ᾽ ἵκηται.   295
ἀλλ᾽ ἄγε οἱ καὶ ἐγὼ δῶ ξείνιον, ὄφρα καὶ αὐτὸς
ἠὲ λοετροχόωι δώηι γέρας ἠέ τωι ἄλλωι
δμώων, οἳ κατὰ δώματ᾽ Ὀδυσσῆος θείοιο."
    Ὣς εἰπὼν ἔρριψε βοὸς πόδα χειρὶ παχείηι,
κείμενον ἐκ κανέοιο λαβών· ὁ δ᾽ ἀλεύατ᾽ Ὀδυσσεὺς   300
ἦκα παρακλίνας κεφαλήν, μείδησε δὲ θυμῶι
σαρδάνιον μάλα τοῖον· ὁ δ᾽ εὔδμητον βάλε τοῖχον.
Κτήσιππον δ᾽ ἄρα Τηλέμαχος ἠνίπαπε μύθωι·
"Κτήσιππ᾽, ἦ μάλα τοι τόδε κέρδιον ἔπλετο θυμῶι·
οὐκ ἔβαλες τὸν ξεῖνον· ἀλεύατο γὰρ βέλος αὐτός.   305
ἦ γάρ κέν σε μέσον βάλον ἔγχεϊ ὀξυόεντι,
καί κέ τοι ἀντὶ γάμοιο πατὴρ τάφον ἀμφεπονεῖτο
ἐνθάδε. τῶι μή τίς μοι ἀεικείας ἐνὶ οἴκωι
φαινέτω· ἤδη γὰρ νοέω καὶ οἶδα ἕκαστα,
ἐσθλά τε καὶ τὰ χέρεια· πάρος δ᾽ ἔτι νήπιος ἦα.   310
ἀλλ᾽ ἔμπης τάδε μὲν καὶ τέτλαμεν εἰσορόωντες,
μήλων σφαζομένων οἴνοιό τε πινομένοιο
καὶ σίτου· χαλεπὸν γὰρ ἐρυκακέειν ἕνα πολλούς.
ἀλλ᾽ ἄγε μηκέτι μοι κακὰ ῥέζετε δυσμενέοντες·
εἰ δ᾽ ἤδη μ᾽ αὐτὸν κτεῖναι μενεαίνετε χαλκῶι,   315
καί κε τὸ βουλοίμην, καί κεν πολὺ κέρδιον εἴη
τεθνάμεν ἢ τάδε γ᾽ αἰὲν ἀεικέα ἔργ᾽ ὁράασθαι,
ξείνους τε στυφελιζομένους δμωιάς τε γυναῖκας
ῥυστάζοντας ἀεικελίως κατὰ δώματα καλά."

289 πατρὸς ἑοῖο : θεσπεσίοισι   298 omitted by Eustathius, deleted by some
edd. (cf. 325)   302 σαρδάνιον : σαρδόνιον

"Ὣς ἔφαθ᾽, οἱ δ᾽ ἄρα πάντες ἀκὴν ἐγένοντο σιωπῆι·   320
ὀψὲ δὲ δὴ μετέειπε Δαμαστορίδης Ἀγέλαος·
"ὦ φίλοι, οὐκ ἂν δή τις ἐπὶ ῥηθέντι δικαίωι
ἀντιβίοις ἐπέεσσι καθαπτόμενος χαλεπαίνοι·
μήτε τι τὸν ξεῖνον στυφελίζετε μήτε τιν᾽ ἄλλον
δμώων, οἳ κατὰ δώματ᾽ Ὀδυσσῆος θείοιο.   325
Τηλεμάχωι δέ κε μῦθον ἐγὼ καὶ μητέρι φαίην
ἤπιον, εἴ σφωϊν κραδίηι ἅδοι ἀμφοτέροιϊν.
ὄφρα μὲν ὑμῖν θυμὸς ἐνὶ στήθεσσιν ἐώλπει
νοστήσειν Ὀδυσῆα πολύφρονα ὅνδε δόμονδε,
τόφρ᾽ οὔ τις νέμεσις μενέμεν τ᾽ ἦν ἰσχέμεναί τε   330
μνηστῆρας κατὰ δώματ᾽, ἐπεὶ τόδε κέρδιον ἦεν,
εἰ νόστησ᾽ Ὀδυσεὺς καὶ ὑπότροπος ἵκετο δῶμα·
νῦν δ᾽ ἤδη τόδε δῆλον, ὅ τ᾽ οὐκέτι νόστιμός ἐστιν.
ἀλλ᾽ ἄγε, σῆι τάδε μητρὶ παρεζόμενος κατάλεξον,
γήμασθ᾽ ὅς τις ἄριστος ἀνὴρ καὶ πλεῖστα πόρηισιν,   335
ὄφρα σὺ μὲν χαίρων πατρώϊα πάντα νέμηαι,
ἔσθων καὶ πίνων, ἡ δ᾽ ἄλλου δῶμα κομίζηι."
    Τὸν δ᾽ αὖ Τηλέμαχος πεπνυμένος ἀντίον ηὔδα·
"οὐ μὰ Ζῆν᾽, Ἀγέλαε, καὶ ἄλγεα πατρὸς ἐμοῖο,
ὅς που τῆλ᾽ Ἰθάκης ἢ ἔφθιται ἢ ἀλάληται,   340
οὔ τι διατρίβω μητρὸς γάμον, ἀλλὰ κελεύω
γήμασθ᾽ ὧι κ᾽ ἐθέληι, ποτὶ δ᾽ ἄσπετα δῶρα δίδωμι.
αἰδέομαι δ᾽ ἀέκουσαν ἀπὸ μεγάροιο δίεσθαι
μύθωι ἀναγκαίωι· μὴ τοῦτο θεὸς τελέσειεν."
    Ὣς φάτο Τηλέμαχος· μνηστῆρσι δὲ Παλλὰς Ἀθήνη   345
ἄσβεστον γέλω ὦρσε, παρέπλαγξεν δὲ νόημα.
οἱ δ᾽ ἤδη γναθμοῖσι γελώων ἀλλοτρίοισιν,
αἱμοφόρυκτα δὲ δὴ κρέα ἤσθιον· ὄσσε δ᾽ ἄρα σφέων
δακρυόφιν πίμπλαντο, γόον δ᾽ ὠΐετο θυμός·
τοῖσι δὲ καὶ μετέειπε Θεοκλύμενος θεοειδής·   350
"ἆ δειλοί, τί κακὸν τόδε πάσχετε; νυκτὶ μὲν ὑμέων

325 (= 298) deleted by Schwartz   351–7 cited by Plato, who omits 354, and
by Plutarch, who omits 353–4   351 ἆ δειλοί MSS : δαιμόνιοι Plato

εἰλύαται κεφαλαί τε πρόσωπά τε νέρθε τε γοῦνα,
οἰμωγὴ δὲ δέδηε, δεδάκρυνται δὲ παρειαί,
αἵματι δ᾽ ἐρράδαται τοῖχοι καλαί τε μεσόδμαι·
εἰδώλων δὲ πλέον πρόθυρον, πλείη δὲ καὶ αὐλή,   355
ἱεμένων Ἔρεβόσδε ὑπὸ ζόφον· ἠέλιος δὲ
οὐρανοῦ ἐξαπόλωλε, κακὴ δ᾽ ἐπιδέδρομεν ἀχλύς.''
   Ὣς ἔφαθ᾽, οἱ δ᾽ ἄρα πάντες ἐπ᾽ αὐτῶι ἡδὺ γέλασσαν.
τοῖσιν δ᾽ Εὐρύμαχος, Πολύβου πάϊς, ἄρχ᾽ ἀγορεύειν·
''ἀφραίνει ξεῖνος νέον ἄλλοθεν εἰληλουθώς.   360
ἀλλά μιν αἶψα, νέοι, δόμου ἐκπέμψασθε θύραζε
εἰς ἀγορὴν ἔρχεσθαι, ἐπεὶ τάδε νυκτὶ ἔϊσκει.''
   Τὸν δ᾽ αὖτε προσέειπε Θεοκλύμενος θεοειδής·
''Εὐρύμαχ᾽, οὔ τί σ᾽ ἄνωγα ἐμοὶ πομπῆας ὀπάζειν·
εἰσί μοι ὀφθαλμοί τε καὶ οὔατα καὶ πόδες ἄμφω   365
καὶ νόος ἐν στήθεσσι τετυγμένος οὐδὲν ἀεικής.
τοῖς ἔξειμι θύραζε, ἐπεὶ νοέω κακὸν ὔμμιν
ἐρχόμενον, τό κεν οὔ τις ὑπεκφύγοι οὐδ᾽ ἀλέαιτο
μνηστήρων, οἳ δῶμα κατ᾽ ἀντιθέου Ὀδυσῆος
ἀνέρας ὑβρίζοντες ἀτάσθαλα μηχανάασθε.''   370
   Ὣς εἰπὼν ἐξῆλθε δόμων εὖ ναιεταόντων,
ἵκετο δ᾽ ἐς Πείραιον, ὅ μιν πρόφρων ὑπέδεκτο.
μνηστῆρες δ᾽ ἄρα πάντες ἐς ἀλλήλους ὁρόωντες
Τηλέμαχον ἐρέθιζον, ἐπὶ ξείνοις γελόωντες·
ὧδε δέ τις εἴπεσκε νέων ὑπερηνορεόντων·   375
''Τηλέμαχ᾽, οὔ τις σεῖο κακοξεινώτερος ἄλλος·
οἷον μέν τινα τοῦτον ἔχεις ἐπίμαστον ἀλήτην,
σίτου καὶ οἴνου κεχρημένον, οὐδέ τι ἔργων
ἔμπαιον οὐδὲ βίης, ἀλλ᾽ αὔτως ἄχθος ἀρούρης.
ἄλλος δ᾽ αὖτέ τις οὗτος ἀνέστη μαντεύεσθαι.   380
ἀλλ᾽ εἴ μοί τι πίθοιο, τό κεν πολὺ κέρδιον εἴη·
τοὺς ξείνους ἐν νηῒ πολυκληῗδι βαλόντες
ἐς Σικελοὺς πέμψωμεν, ὅθεν κέ τοι ἄξιον ἄλφοι.''

362 αὐγὴν Wecklein   369 ἀνδρῶν οἳ κατὰ δώματ᾽ Ὀδυσῆος θείοιο (cf. 298, 328) some MSS   374 ἐρέθιζον : θαύμαζον (1.382)

῍Ως ἔφασαν μνηστῆρες· ὁ δ' οὐκ ἐμπάζετο μύθων,
ἀλλ' ἀκέων πατέρα προσεδέρκετο, δέγμενος αἰεί,   385
ὁππότε δὴ μνηστῆρσιν ἀναιδέσι χεῖρας ἐφήσει.
῾Η δὲ κατ' ἄντηστιν θεμένη περικαλλέα δίφρον
κούρη Ἰκαρίοιο, περίφρων Πηνελόπεια,
ἀνδρῶν ἐν μεγάροισιν ἑκάστου μῦθον ἄκουε.
δεῖπνον μὲν γὰρ τοί γε γελώωντες τετύκοντο   390
ἡδύ τε καὶ μενοεικές, ἐπεὶ μάλα πόλλ' ἱέρευσαν·
δόρπου δ' οὐκ ἄν πως ἀχαρίστερον ἄλλο γένοιτο,
οἷον δὴ τάχ' ἔμελλε θεὰ καὶ καρτερὸς ἀνὴρ
θησέμεναι· πρότεροι γὰρ ἀεικέα μηχανόωντο.

386 ἐφήσει : ἐφείη   387 κατ' ἄντηστιν : καταντηστὶ   394 πρότεροι :
πρότερον

COMMENTARY

At the beginning of book 19 the situation in the household is as follows (for a general summary of the whole poem, knowledge of which is presupposed here, see Introd. 2 (*a*), pp. 7–8).

Odysseus returned to Ithaca in book 13, and after being disguised as a beggar by Athene, spent several nights in the hut of Eumaeus, his loyal swineherd, without revealing his identity. Telemachus visited Eumaeus on returning to Ithaca from his unsuccessful voyage in search of his father; in book 16, he has encountered the beggar and learnt who he is; he then left him in the swineherd's care, having privately agreed that Odysseus would subsequently follow him to the palace. Books 17 and 18 followed Odysseus' progress from relatively comfortable lodgings on Eumaeus' farm to mockery and humiliation in the palace which should be his. The suitors bullied, insulted and attacked him, but he endured their ill-treatment. In book 18 he won a wrestling contest with the real beggar Irus, an unsympathetic figure; this episode in some respects foreshadows his greater triumph over the suitors. But in that book he also witnessed his wife's admission of defeat, in the scene in which she declared to the suitors that she was ready to marry one of them at last, however reluctantly. Whatever its other functions, this scene makes clear that the hero has no time to lose.

Thus by the end of book 18 Telemachus knows who the beggar really is, but no-one else suspects the truth; Penelope has shown a kindly concern for his welfare and has expressed interest in questioning him, but she has not yet had an opportunity to speak with him face to face. The suitors, apart from occasional amiable moments (as when they applaud his victory over Irus) have been offensive and brutal. Book 19 begins late in the evening, after the suitors have finished their feasting and retired to their homes for the night.

For a more detailed account of Penelope's apparent surrender in book 18, see Introd. 3 (*b*).

Scene: the setting throughout is inside or just outside Odysseus' house on Ithaca, except for the brief episode 20.241–7, where the suitors are probably in the agora, as in earlier episodes (see n.), and the even briefer change of scene at 20.276–8 (see n.).

Books 19 and 20 may be sub-divided as follows:

Book 19

1–52   Odysseus and Telemachus in the hall of Odysseus' palace: they plan and execute the removal of the armour, with Athene's supernatural guidance.

53–102   Penelope descends: preliminaries to conversation with Odysseus. The slave-girl Melantho abuses Odysseus and is rebuked.

103–360   First part of conversation between Odysseus and Penelope, concluding with summons to Eurycleia.

361–507   In washing Odysseus' feet, Eurycleia recognises her master by his scar; retrospective narrative describing how the wound was inflicted (392–466). Odysseus restrains her and binds her to silence.

508–604   Second phase of conversation. Penelope narrates a dream and Odysseus interprets it. Planning of the test of the bow.

Book 20

1–55   Odysseus' uneasy night.

56–94   Penelope's prayer to Artemis.

95–121   Omens forecasting Odysseus' success.

122–240   Early events of the day. Arrival of Eumaeus, Melanthius and Philoetius.

241–56   Abortive plotting of the suitors.

257–386   Events in the hall. Antinous is silenced by Telemachus. Ctesippus attacks Odysseus. Tension in the hall; vision of the seer Theoclymenus, who prophesies the suitors' doom (345–86).

387–94   Penelope hears the noise below; narrator's comment.

Book 19

1–52 The suitors have retired to their homes for the night (18.428), leaving Telemachus and Odysseus alone in the hall. Odysseus here proposes a scheme to dispose of the armour and weapons displayed as spoils in the hall, to prevent the suitors from making use of them later (cf. 22.24–5). This largely repeats his plan as described to Telemachus at 16.284–98, but without the proviso that they reserve weapons for themselves. This oversight is not disastrous, but needs to be remedied by Telemachus at 22.99–125. The repetition has seemed suspect to some scholars (in antiquity Zenodotus and Aristarchus already deleted the passage in book 16), especially as Telemachus finds he has no need to use the excuses suggested twice by Odysseus. But the episode, though weak in its strictly logical connection with the narrative, serves to emphasise (a) the foresight and authority of Odysseus, (b) the ready obedience and incipient manhood of Telemachus (19), and (c) the ignorance and blindness of the suitors: even if they thought to question what had happened, Telemachus would have a plausible answer, but they do not. One other factor is that Odysseus has not yet conceived the idea of using the great bow as the instrument of destruction; this must wait until Penelope mentions it in connection with the contest (see 572–81). The poet, however, knows already that these other weapons will be of secondary importance.

The scene also gives an opportunity for supernatural intervention by Athene, indicating the favour with which she looks on the enterprise (33–43). Her magical lamp sheds a beautiful light throughout the chamber, a sign of radiant divinity; contrast the horrible vision of blood and death recounted by Theoclymenus (20.351–7; compare esp. 37–8 with 20.354).

Cf. further Erbse, *Beiträge* 3–41; Fenik, *Studies* 111–14; Hölscher, *Die Odyssee* 238–40.

2 The brooding, deep-thinking Odysseus, whose silent endurance masks terrible power and anger, is a regular motif of books 17–21: e.g. 20.183–4, 300–2.

σὺν Ἀθήνηι 'with Athene's aid', not implying that she has already appeared.

3 ἔπεα πτερόεντα: a standard phrase used of many different speakers in both Homeric poems. With phrases such as this the Parryist argument that the epithet is effectively 'dead', and carries no special significance in an individual use, is at its strongest. For the opposite, a much rarer phrase, see 29n.

4 κατθέμεν: aorist infinitive of κατατίθημι.

4–13 These lines are marked with an asterisk in two manuscripts: the scholia and Eustathius regard this as signifying that this passage, not the parallel in book 16, is 'authentic'.

7–13 A speech within a speech. Narration which includes direct speech is commonplace in Homer. e.g. 141–7 below, *Il.* 9.254–8, *Od.* 4.371–424, 18.259–70; I. de Jong, *Narrators and focalizers* 279 n. 45.

7 τοῖσιν 'those (which Odysseus left ...)': the demonstrative use of the definite article, a use which is regular in Homer.

9 The description reminds the audience of the decay and anarchy that have succeeded the prosperity which Ithaca enjoyed while Odysseus reigned (cf. 19.109–14). Similarly in 21.394–5 Odysseus turns and tests the bow, to see if worms have got at it in the 20 years that it has lain in store.

9 ὄσσον: adverbial: 'so much has the blast of the fire reached them [i.e. affected them]'.

10 δαίμων: it is normal in Homer for mortals not to be sure which of the gods has done something to them: hence they often describe divine intervention in vague terms: cf. 125 ἀθάνατοι, 129 δαίμων, 138 δαίμων, 12.448 θεοί, etc. See Erbse, *Funktion* 265–6. But see further de Jong, *Narrators and focalizers* 158, with 239–40, who argues for a distinction between δαίμων and θεός: the former is used only by human speakers, on occasions when a god has intervened briefly and directly in their lives; the latter is used by both divine and human speakers, and tends to be more general.

11 στήσαντες: this goes closely with ἔριν and is virtually equivalent to ἐρίσαντες, but with the added nuance of starting, stirring up conflict.

12 καταισχύνητέ τε δαῖτα: there are three levels of significance here. Telemachus' excuse is to be given courteously (5), as if meant sincerely: we don't want a nasty rumpus. But for him and all the loyal household the very presence of the suitors already spoils the feast, so that the lines are both ironic and deceptive. More broadly, the notion of 'spoiling the feast' is another motif of these books: anticipated at 2.246–7, it is usually found as a complaint by the suitors about Odysseus' or Theoclymenus' presence (17.219–20, 446, 18.401–4, 20.376–80). In the end Odysseus will disturb and spoil the feast in a far more drastic way (see esp. 22.8–14).

13 'For iron draws/leads a man on of its own accord.' Probably proverbial (though we cannot be quite certain, as Homer, like Hesiod and indeed Shakespeare, is an important source for proverbs). Cf. Tertullian, *De pallio* 4, and the parody at Juvenal 9.37, where κίναιδος ('a male whore') replaces 'iron'. For other proverbial expressions in Homer cf. 17.218, 246; van der Valk, *Textual criticism* 202–4; E. Ahrens, *Gnomen in griechischer Dichtung* (Halle 1937).

15 Telemachus deals directly with the old nurse Eurycleia; this delays Odysseus' own encounter with her. On Eurycleia see 357n.

16 μαῖ': an affectionate form of address also used by Penelope (23.11, etc.) and by Odysseus himself once recognised (482, 500, etc.).

μοι: 'ethic' dative: 'do this *for me, please*'. This comes under the head of 'dative of advantage' (Goodwin, *Greek grammar* §§1165–71; Weir Smyth, *Greek grammar* §1486).

17 ὄφρα κεν . . . καταθείομαι 'for as long as I am putting away', 'until I can put away', with the verb in the aorist subjunctive and κεν used because the action is still in the future and will require an uncertain length of time. Cf. Monro, *Grammar* §287.

θάλαμον: a private room which is kept locked. See G. E. Mylonas, in Wace and Stubbings, *Companion* 492–3. This room is not the same as that in which the bow is stored, to which Penelope has the key (21.8).

17–18 ἔντεα . . . | καλά . . . ἀκηδέα: the enjambment (see Introd. 5(*a*) on Metre) seems to stress the first adjective, describing the state the arms were in and should be in.

18 μοι: 'ethic' dative again (16n.), but here indicating Telemachus' interest in the house and arms of his father.

19 ἐγὼ δ' ἔτι νήπιος ἦα: for the theme of Telemachus' growth to manhood, see Introd. 3(*b*), and in these books esp. 88, 159–61, 530–4; 20.310. The phrase itself occurs also at 2.313, and similar phrases at 18.229 = 20.310, and at 21.95 (the only case not used of Telemachus). There is irony in this exchange with the nurse: she thinks that Telemachus is asserting himself in a small matter, but he is in fact taking on the heavier responsibilities which she complainingly suggests he is neglecting.

ἦα: 1 sing. impf. indicative of 'to be' (Attic ἦν).

23 κήδεσθαι . . . φυλάσσειν: infinitives of purpose, cf. 64.

24 μετοιχομένη 'go with you' or 'follow behind you'? If the latter, there may be a pointed discrepancy with 33 πάροιθε: Athene is a goddess, not a mere servant, and so she takes the lead. But the former may be more likely in view of 25 προβλωσκέμεν, if that means 'to go before you' rather than 'to come forth'.

25 δ' = γάρ here (cf. Denniston, *GP* 169).

εἴας: 2 sing. impf. of ἐάω. The force of the imperfect is probably to describe a continuing state: 'you weren't allowing (when you said that) and you still are not.'

27–8 For the dismissive tone which Telemachus adopts here concerning the beggar, in order to keep his identity secret, cf. 17.10–15, 347.

28 χοίνικος 'measure' or 'ration', a fixed quantity of dry goods. Used instead of e.g. 'table', it may add to the lordly tone Telemachus is adopting.

29 τῆι δ' ἄπτερος ἔπλετο μῦθος: literally 'and for her (the) word was wingless'; clearly the opposite of 'winged words' (3, etc.). The phrase is found in three other places in the *Odyssey* (always with reference to women), never in the *Iliad*. Either it means that the speech has sunk in, or that she has nothing to say in response.

ἔπλετο: 3 sing. aorist middle from πέλω, an epic verb for 'to be'. Cf. e.g. 192 πέλεν, 20.223, 304.

33–4 Why does Athene not appear openly to both Odysseus and Telemachus? Perhaps to avoid any prolonging or overdramatising of the scene such as an epiphany might promote (Athene has so far never appeared openly to Telemachus, except perhaps in his half-dreaming state in 15.4–9). The invisible presence of the goddess creates an eerie but auspicious atmosphere, and allows Odysseus to show off his greater experience to his son. It is also typical of the gods in the *Odyssey*, like the human characters, not to deal quite openly with others: e.g. 7.19–38, 10.571–4, 13.221–5 and what follows in that scene.

34 χρύσεον λύχνον: the gods' possessions are always of the finest quality, and therefore 'golden' (*Il.* 4.2–3 and *passim*). This is the only example of a lamp in Homer; elsewhere light is provided by torches (48, 18.354, *Il.* 18.492, etc.). R. Pfeiffer, *Ausgewählte Schriften* (Munich 1960) 1–7, argues that this golden lamp is a cult object associated with the goddess for centuries before Homer. For illustrations of Mycenean lamps see F. H. Stubbings in Wace and Stubbings, *Companion* 529.

35 ὃν πατέρ' 'his father'. ὅς ἥ ὅν (or ἑός ἑή ἑόν) is a possessive adjective, Latin *suus*. Cf. e.g. 209, 210.

37 ἔμπης 'really now', 'actually'; cf. the more humorous 18.354–5, where one of the suitors mocks Odysseus' bald head: 'the bright light of the torches seems to me to be positively shining from his head, as he hasn't even a few tufts of hair on it'.

μεσόδμαι: the meaning of this term, which is also found in passages describing the construction of ships, is not clear. It presumably means something 'in the middle', probably crossbeams supported by the pillars or columns.

38 ἔχοντες: intransitive. 'The pillars that extend on high' (Cunliffe s.v. (II) (6)).

39 On supernatural radiance, which regularly accompanies an epiphany, see Richardson on *Homeric hymn to Demeter* 189.

40 θεός: there is an ellipse of a common type: 'a god, (one of those) who dwell in broad heaven'. Cf. e.g. Hes. *Th.* 450. This is preferable to the more obvious reading θεῶν, found in some MSS.

42 The theme of restraint of emotion, important throughout the second half of the poem, is introduced rather casually here. Cf. further for Telemachus 16.274–7, 17.489–91, 21.128–9; for Odysseus 16.190–1, 17.238, 284, 18.90–4, 20.9–30. Similarly Odysseus restrains and checks the nurse's emotions in 19.481.

43 δίκη 'way', 'usage', as often in Homer. Only in a few contexts (esp. *Il.* 16.388, 19.180–1, *Od.* 14.84) does the word have its later meaning of 'justice'.

45 ἐρεθίζω 'provoke', 'disturb'; cf. 9.494 (the companions of Odysseus beg him not to provoke the savage Cyclops). The word seems better suited to Odysseus' dealings with the maids than with Penelope, though it is true that he tantalises and upsets her (as he anticipates here, 46 ὀδυρομένη). This is a part of the testing-process which he insists on applying to his household: cf. 215n.

48 κείων: nominative singular participle from κείω, a verb normally used with a future sense: 'I go to rest', 'I shall rest', 'I shall lie down' (related to κεῖμαι). As often, the future conveys a purpose: 'he went about-to-lie-down' = 'he went in order to lie down'.

48–50 These lines linger on Telemachus' retirement to sleep. The point of the comparison with past occasions (πάρος ... καὶ τότ') is unclear. Perhaps the poet wishes to remind us how much Telemachus has gone through, and how much he has matured, since we saw him retire to the same room at the end of book 1 (425–44), after Athene's first visit. We next see the young man at 20.124.

51–2 = 1–2. This use of similar or repeated words to begin and end an episode or a digression is generally known as ring composition (cf. Fenik, *Studies* 92–9, and F. Cairns, *Tibullus: a Hellenistic poet at Rome* (Cambridge 1979) 194–5 for a bibliography on the technique). The label is useful enough, but we should remember that the 'digressions' do contribute something; we are returned to the main narrative, but the intervening passage must have some effect or advance the work in narrative or thematic terms. In this case the repetition emphasises further the hero's determination on revenge; and he is now alone, without his son as companion. Telemachus' presence in the ensuing scene would wholly alter its atmosphere (as comparison with some of the scenes in which he speaks with his mother immediately shows: esp. 23.96–128). Nor could Telemachus, for all his growing maturity, be trusted to keep his father's secret in so emotional an encounter.

53–102 The prelude to Odysseus' conversation with Penelope involves a brief skirmish with the disloyal and insolent slave Melantho, sister of the equally unpleasant Melanthius; both have been introduced in book 17, and both will meet their execution in book 22 (135–200, 474–9 – the mutilation of Melanthius, a gruesome scene; 446–73, the hanging of the maids). Both characters are associated with the suitors and with evil; the 'black' element in their names is patently symbolic. As enemies and mockers of Odysseus, betrayers of the royal family, they represent the opposite pole to loyal retainers such as Eumaeus and Eurycleia (again these are *noms parlants*), who support Penelope and Telemachus and observe the laws of hospitality and good behaviour.

53 ἴεν: 3 sing. imperfect indicative of εἶμι 'go'.

54 Penelope is compared with both goddesses also at 17.37; Helen is compared with Artemis at 4.122, and Odysseus flatters Nausicaa by guessing that she must be a goddess – 'surely you must be Artemis' (6.151; cf. the simile describing Nausicaa at 102–9). The combination indicates both Penelope's chastity and her beauty. Penelope seems to feel a special devotion to Artemis: 18.202–5, 20.61–90. This is perhaps because she is seen as virginal, like a bride (N. Felson–Rubin, in *Homer: beyond oral poetry*, edd. Bremer, de Jong and Kalff, 76). The line may also be seen as Odysseus' 'focalisation': this is how *he* sees his wife (Introd. 4(c) vii).

55 κάτθεσαν: the subjects of the verb are Penelope's attendants, who are assumed to have descended with her, as is only proper for a woman of her modesty (cf. the explicit lines at 1.331 = 18.207, etc.). This becomes clear at 60.

56–8 A luxury item comparable with those listed in the Pylos tablets of Mycenaean times (G. M. Calhoun and F. H. Stubbings in Wace and Stubbings, *Companion* 460–1, 533, with plates 36a–b).The way in which the poet dwells on the object serves to enhance our sense of its value and beauty, and so of the splendour of Penelope and her possessions. The glamour of the queen is contrasted with the unwashed and ragged state of the beggar.

56–7 τέκτων . . . Ἰκμάλιος: the etymology of the name is obscure. L. Lacroix, *Hommages W. Deonna*, Coll. Latomus 28 (Brussels 1957) 309–21, surveys various theories and prefers a derivation from ἰκμάς, a juice or fluid which might provide glue for the carpenter's work. The fact that the craftsman's name is mentioned at all is noteworthy: it puts this item in the class of precious objects prized for their provenance as much as for their intrinsic value. The description of the sceptre of Agamemnon in *Il.* 2.100–8 is rather different, as there the maker is divine (Hephaestus), and much more emphasis is laid on the successive kings who have used it. On the craftsman in epic see further F. Eckstein, *Archaeologia Homerica* II L i (Göttingen 1974) 3–38.

62 ὑπερμενέοντες: 'powerful', 'mighty', without necessarily implying excessive use of power (the traditional English rendering 'overweening' exaggerates this).

64 The details here are not merely scene-setting for its own sake: the light will be important later, for the revelation of the scar. See esp. 389.

ἔμεν: one of several epic forms of the present infinitive of the verb 'to be'. Cf. Introd. 5 (b), p. 87.

65 δεύτερον αὖτις: the first occasion was at 18.321–36.

67 ὀπιπεύσεις 'eye', 'ogle', 'leer at'. This accusation of trying to seduce women is particularly inappropriate, coming from one of the women who sleep with the suitors (18.325, Melantho is mistress of the repulsive Eurymachus). It is also insulting in view of Odysseus' apparent old age.

68 ὄνησο: aorist middle imperative (2 sing.) of ὀνίνημι 'to profit or help', in middle 'to derive profit from', 'get good from'. Loosely, 'make the most of the feast you have had'.

69 For the threat of a beating cf. Melanthius at 17.230–2, 20.180–2, and Melantho herself at 18.334–6.

εἶσθα: 2 sing. present (with future force) of εἶμι 'to go'. 'You will soon be heading for the door.'

71–88 On the function of Odysseus' speech here see Fenik, *Studies* 177–9. It is one of a series of passages in which characters, especially Odysseus himself, give voice to stern moral pronouncements based on the frailty of the human condition: in view of the uncertainty of success and prosperity, men should not deal harshly and unjustly with others, assuming that they themselves will always have the upper hand. The moral principles of the poem are conveyed more through the characters than by explicit statements from the poet (though see 20.394n.). Nevertheless, this speech also has considerable force in its context: Odysseus' stern warning momentarily unveils his wrath and anticipates the maid's punishment; it moves Penelope to exert her own authority; and it shows her that the beggar is, as Eumaeus has told her, a man of virtuous character and intelligence (17.580–4). There is also an obvious irony in 75–9.

Cf. 328–34n.; Hes. *WD* 717–18 (don't taunt the poor).

71 δαιμονίη (masculine δαιμόνιε), a word used by Homer only in the vocative, surely does not mean 'divine' or 'daemonic', though some scholars translate it this way. It expresses surprise or bafflement, an inability on the speaker's part to understand the words or actions of the addressee. In origin it may perhaps have implied that the addressee was 'touched' or under the influence of a god, and that this explained his or her strange behaviour. But since it is also applied to gods by gods (e.g. *Iliad* 1.561, 4.31), that meaning has evidently faded. See further E. Brunius-Nilsson, ΔΑΙΜΟΝΙΕ (diss. Uppsala, 1955). Translate e.g. 'What has got into you, woman?'

72 ὅτι δή: the particle implies that this is an inadequate reason ('*just* because'). Cf. Denniston, *GP* 231.

ῥυπόω: the variant οὐ λιπόω ('I am not anointed') is probably an attempt by over-sensitive ancient editors to ameliorate the picture: surely Odysseus, even in disguise, could not be 'filthy'. The variant does not occur in texts of the parallel line 23.115.

73 ἀναγκαίη: on 'necessity' in early Greek literature see Richardson on *Homeric hymn to Demeter* 216–17; Onians, *Origins of European thought* 332–3. In the *Odyssey*, the word is very commonly associated with slavery; in *Il.* 6.458 κρατερὴ δ' ἐπικείσετ' ἀνάγκη (Hector anticipating Andromache's future) it is virtually a euphemism for it. See further *Od.* 24.210, 14.272 = 17.441, 14.298, 1.154. Odysseus' beggarly condition reduces him to near-slave status.

76–7 πολλάκι . . . ἔλθοι 'and many a time I would give to a beggar such (as I am now), whatever he might be like and whatever he might come in need of'.

δόσκον is a frequentative form, indicating repeated action; ἔοι is 3 sing. present optative of εἰμί.

ὅτευ = οὗτινος.

78 ἦσαν: understand ἐμοί (possessive dative).

79 The subject of the verbs is 'men (in general)', 'people'.

80 ἤθελε γάρ που 'for so he willed, I suppose'. A fatalistic conclusion (peasant-wisdom?) which suits the beggar's resigned role. On που in such contexts see Fraenkel on Aesch. *Ag.* 182–3 (p. 112).

81 μή ποτε: by a common Greek idiom, we are to understand a verb such as 'beware' / 'look out' / 'take care lest . . .': cf. Cunliffe s.v. μή (3) (a); Goodwin, *Greek Grammar* §1372. In other contexts a verb for fearing might be supplied ('I am afraid in case'), as at 121, but here that would have to be sarcastic, and seems less appropriate.

83–4 ἤν . . . ἤ 'if . . . or if'. The two possibilities are presented as alternatives, but in fact both will come true.

84 ἐλπίδος αἶσα '(there is) a portion of hope', i.e. there is still room for hope, even if small. Cf. 16.101.

85 ὥς 'in this way', that is 'in the way you suppose', 'as you think'.

86 Ἀπόλλωνός γε ἔκητι 'by the will / good grace of Apollo'. For the phrasing cf. 19.319, 20.42. Why Apollo? Perhaps because he is associated with puberty and coming of age, as a protector of young men and perpetually young himself: cf. West on Hes. *Th.* 347; Aesch. *Suppl.* 686–7; L. R. Farnell, *Cults of the Greek states* (Oxford 1896–1909) IV 370. See also 15.526, where it is Apollo who sends the omen which Theoclymenus interprets as assurance of Telemachus' succession to the kingship of Ithaca. There may also be some anticipation of the imminent feast-day of Apollo (20.156, 278, 21.258, 267, 22.7), on which the slaughter will take place, executed with Apollo's weapon, the bow. (See further 17.494, where Penelope wishes that Apollo κλυτότοξος would strike down Antinous.)

87 The reference to Telemachus, as in the parallel scene at 18.338–9, probably looks forward to the execution of the maids by the young man in book 22. Line 88 is a further reference to his 'becoming a man': see 19n.

88 τηλίκος 'of such an age' (as to tolerate this sort of thing).

91 κύον ἀδεές: 'dog' or 'bitch' is a violent insult in the Homeric poems, used by Achilles to Agamemnon (*Il* 1.225, 9.373), by Odysseus to the suitors at the time of revelation (22.35), and by Helen of herself, in bitter self-rebuke (*Il.* 6.344, cf. *Od.* 4.145). See further J. M. Redfield, *Nature and culture in the Iliad* (Chicago 1975) 194–5.

οὔ τί με λήθεις: Penelope picks up Odysseus' words in 87–8 ('Telemachus sees what you're all doing') and caps them more severely ('*I* see your wrongdoing . . .').

92 ὃ σῆι κεφαλῆι ἀναμάξεις 'which you will wipe off on your own head', an obscure but clearly sinister phrase, possibly connected with ritual cleansing of a knife after sacrifice. Cf. Hdt. 1.155.3.

100–3 Eurynome, the loyal and virtuous servant, replaces the treacherous Melantho. She has been thought a superfluous figure who merely duplicates the functions of the old nurse Eurycleia, who also acts as housekeeper (e.g. 2.345–7, and that whole scene). Fenik, *Studies* 172–207 defends this practice of duplication, which we find also in the case of the two herdsmen, Eumaeus and Philoetius. Here the technique has an obvious function, to delay the important confrontation between Odysseus and Eurycleia (361–85).

104 = 7.237 (only), where Arete questions Odysseus after a long silence in which she has been watching him and has observed the clothes given him by Nausicaa. Arete's role as clever and influential queen (7.66–77) prefigures Penelope's, one of several ways in which Scheria anticipates Ithaca (see Introd., p. 11). In both scenes Odysseus skilfully evades the questioning. The differences are also important: the earlier scene is less dangerous, less emotional (Arete never weeps); both participants are more detached.

105 This is a standard line used in questioning a newcomer, but more piquant when Odysseus *is* in his own πόλις and home.

106–22 Here as in his later speeches at 165 and 221 Odysseus avoids an immediate answer. Later in the book his replies become more direct, the bond between husband and wife stronger (555, 583). Here already we have ironic ambiguity in his opening ὦ γύναι.

The evasion takes the form of flattery, but it is expressed through a significant simile. Odysseus praises Penelope in terms which suit *himself* – her glory is like that of a prosperous king whose land is rich and fruitful. It is typical of Odysseus to extract praise of himself from his unsuspecting interlocutors: see 8.492–5, 14.115–20. Here he takes the device still further.

108 In 9.20 Odysseus declared to the Phaeacians in similar words that his own κλέος reached the heavens (cf. 8.74). His glory is matched by his wife's, and they are alike in this as in other ways—enduring, intelligent (cf. 2.116–22 on Penelope's wiles) and cautious (as the testing motif suggests: see 215n.). Penelope refers to her own κλέος in 128 = 18.255, but hers is a different kind of 'glory' from the male heroic norm: it is won through fidelity and virtue rather than by warfare and heroic deeds. See further A. Edwards, *Achilles in the Odyssey* 79–82.

109 τευ = τινος 'a/some' – deliberately and humorously imprecise. Odysseus has of course a quite specific case in mind: cf. 106–22n.

ἤ is peculiar; it seems to have no function in the sentence, and may be simply a metrical filler. Alternatively it might be written ἤ ('either . . .'), if we assume a further comparison has been lost after 114.

ἀμύμονος: ἀμύμων is a common adjective of praise and admiration in both epics, traditionally rendered 'blameless', as if derived from μῶμος 'blame'. But the etymology is questionable; see A. Amory Parry, *Blameless Aegisthus* (Leiden 1973) for an extended discussion. The newly accepted translation is 'fine', 'fair', 'excellent'.

θεουδής: an 'Odyssean' word, i.e. one which occurs frequently in the *Odyssey* (in this case six times, four of them using this formula) but not in the *Iliad*. It recurs in this book at 364, in Eurycleia's mouth: there too there is irony, as she bemoans the gods' neglect of Odysseus' piety.

110 This line is omitted in quotations of this passage by Plato, Plutarch, and others. The line is a little flat, but hardly suspect on other grounds, unless it is felt that its conventional detail interrupts the stress on the king's justice and piety, and their rewards.

111 εὐδικίας: unique in the *Odyssey*, as is εὐηγεσίη in 114. Neither occurs in the *Iliad*. In general, the whole passage, and esp. the stress on the rewards of justice, recalls a famous passage in Hesiod (*WD* 225–47), in which the latter presents a picture of the ideal city of justice, contrasted with the city of ὕβρις in which evil flourishes. See West's commentary; also I. DuQuesnay, in F. Cairns, ed., *Papers of the Liverpool Latin seminar* 1 (1977) 61–3, who discusses the influence of both passages on later panegyric of rulers, including Virgil, *Ecl.* 4 and Horace, *Odes* 4.15. The idea that human behaviour affects the natural order, with virtuous men favoured by fine weather and prosperous conditions, evil men punished by the opposite, is also found in a famous simile in the *Iliad*, in which Zeus sends storms because he is enraged at the unjust behaviour of men in their legal disputes (16.384–92). Cf. further Aesch. *Eum.* 938–1020, and see the discussion of related ideas by P. Hardie, *Virgil's Aeneid: cosmos and imperium* (Oxford 1986) 204–7.

It is possible, but not necessary, to see the similarity between Homer and Hesiod as a case of direct imitation; but such a theme may have been traditional in poetry dealing with kings and justice. In the *Odyssey* itself we may compare the repeated passages in which Penelope and others recall Odysseus' just rule in the past (2.230–4, cf. 47; 4.687–

95, 5.7–12, 19.314–16). Here alone Odysseus himself characterises his reign, with an eye to the future; it is appropriate that his treatment should be grander and more expansive. In Hesiod, whose work denounces unjust and bribe-swallowing rulers (*WD* 38–40, 202–11, etc.), the picture of the just state remains an ideal; in the *Odyssey*, there is a hint of genuine hope for renewed prosperity in the future. (For the gloomy condition of Ithaca at present, see book 2 (the suitors' domination of the assembly); also 16.361–2, 375, 380; 20.105–21, 209–25.)

In general on the question of Hesiod's relation to Homer see G. P. Edwards, *The language of Hesiod* (Oxford 1971) ch. 8. Heroic epic and Hesiodic didactic poetry are not self-contained, exclusive worlds. 'Hesiodic' elements can be detected in both Homeric epics (e.g. the catalogue of Nereids in *Iliad* 18, the personified Litai and Ate of *Iliad* 9, the 'Hesiodic' simile of *Il.* 16.384–93, the procession of heroines in *Odyssey* 11). So too epic tales, characters and speeches appear even in the *Works and Days*. Hence we should be slow to suspect interpolation or intrusion in passages such as this. (See also 203n.)

113 παρέχῃι: the first syllable must be scanned long, exceptionally. This may be explicable by a reminiscence of an older form in which the root verb began with s: *παρσέχῃι, or it may be an extreme example of Homeric metrical licence (cf. M. L. West, *Greek metre* (Oxford 1982) 38–9 on Homer's freedom in this area). -ῃι is short before ἰχθῦς, an example of correption (see Introd. 5(*a*) p. 80).

114 ἀρετῶσι: ἀρετάω means 'to thrive', 'prosper', but there must also be some connotation of virtue and goodness, as the oxymoron in 8.329 οὐκ ἀρετᾷ κακὰ ἔργα would suggest. In the absence of the king, the people of Ithaca are harshly treated, and also corrupted by the evil of the suitors.

115 There is some illogicality in Odysseus' argument, which the simile cunningly masks. He can hardly say straightforwardly 'You are famous for your virtue and goodness, *therefore* do not ask me about my background'! By broadening the concept of κλέος and including the notions of justice, morality, peace, etc., he tries to make Penelope feel that it would be impolite or unkind to press her guest. σῶι ἐνὶ οἴκωι stresses the contrast with Odysseus' own fortunes (cf. 119), but with added irony for the audience.

117–20 Odysseus' words remind us again of his situation in Scheria, where he also dilated on his sufferings (esp. 8.154–7, 9.12–15) and

delayed revealing himself, and where he wept uncontrollably because
he was reminded of his misfortunes (8.83–95, 521–34). Here, however,
his self-control is greater, his excuses disingenuous. In this scene it is
Penelope who will break down and weep (204n.).

118 πολύστονος: found only here in the *Odyssey* (twice in the *Iliad*).
Cf. πολύτλας δῖος Ὀδυσσεύς. By avoiding his conventional epithet
while employing a near-synonym, Odysseus adds a further layer to his
deceptive role.

119 οἴκωι ἐν ἀλλοτρίωι: a minor instance of the typical irony of
these books, exploited by the hero as much as by the poet in his own
voice, and often more daringly.

120 Close to the words of Eurynome in 18.174, when she urged
Penelope to wipe away her tears before descending to the hall (prior to
the celebrated scene in which she asks the suitors for gifts: see Introd.
3(b)). The echo seems to be part of a complex network of formulaic
similarities between these scenes: thus in her next speech Penelope re-
peats some of what she said there (19.124 resembles 18.251; 19.125 =
18.252, cf. 18.181; 126–9 = 18.253–6). The earlier scene was public,
this one is private; both involve deception, but there Penelope was
the unconscious agent of deception, prompted to action by Athene;
here, Penelope is the victim of conscious and premeditated deception
by Odysseus.

κάκιον: the comparative is used in a weak sense, little more than
'bad as opposed to the alternative'. This is quite common in Homer: see
Monro, *Grammar* §122.

121 τίς: he thinks of course of Melantho, who abused him in the
preceding scene and in 18.321–40. But she is not the only one among
the slave-girls to betray the household: see 154, 496–8, 20.6–8, 22.417–
73.

νεμεσήσεται: cf. 146 (Penelope), 264. The meaning is to feel, or
express, blame or censure, to find fault with another's word or act. Both
husband and wife are alive to these delicate social sanctions (cf. 108
νεικέοι). νέμεσις means righteous indignation or reproach; the sense of
divine retribution, common in later Greek and more or less universal in
modern usage, is not Homeric. Nor does Homer personify Nemesis,
though Hesiod does in *Th.* 223, *WD* 200; such passages, like Apollo's
expression of divine displeasure in *Il.* 24.53, perhaps show the germs of
the later meaning.

122 δακρυπλώειν: or δάκρυ πλώειν, from πλώω/πλέω 'to flow'. Perhaps slightly comical diction: it occurs only here in Homer, not later.

To accuse a hero of drunkenness is a terrible insult: cf. *Il.* 1.225 (Achilles to Agamemnon, at the height of the quarrel). No major hero in Homer suffers the undignified experiences of the boozy Cyclops. Cf. J. Griffin, *J.H.S.* 97 (1977) 47, though he omits the case of the minor hero Elpenor (*Od.* 10.552–60). The suitors hurled this accusation at Odysseus in 18.331 and 391.

124–63 Penelope's speech. The queen begins with a brief deprecation of Odysseus' compliments (124–9). She then describes her situation and the pressure she is under to remarry. This includes an account of the trick of the web and its recent exposure. She concludes by referring to her parents' and Telemachus' wishes, hinting at the latter's resentment and suspicion of her. Her final lines resume her questioning of Odysseus.

Much of this speech is closely paralleled in other books. In particular, the web-story is almost identical to the account given by Antinous at the Ithacan assembly (2.93–110) and by Amphimedon in the underworld (24.126–50). Thus 19.130–2 = 16.122–4 = 1.245–7 (Telemachus' description of the situation to his father and earlier to Athene–Mentes); 19.133 resembles 1.248 = 16.125. Though 19.158–62 are not verbally repeated anywhere else in the poem, they do include topics prominent throughout the scenes involving Telemachus: for Penelope's family, compare 15.16; for Telemachus' suspicion of his mother, 15.7–42 generally, where Athene plays on his fears; 16.68–77; *P.C.P.S.* 31 (1985) 147 n. 21. For Penelope's consciousness that Telemachus is now a man, cf. above all 18.257–71. On 19.134–5 see n. ad loc.

All this repetition and similarity should not be seen as authorial negligence or laziness. It was a fallacy of analytic criticism to assume, when lines or passages are repeated in Homer, that one must be the 'original' passage, the other an imperfect redeployment, less apt or appropriate. No sympathetic reader will feel Penelope's speech to be derivative or second-hand. It is notable here that it is Penelope who narrates the tale of the web, whereas in books 2 and 24 it is a suitor. The tone, therefore, is entirely different. Whereas Antinous and Amphimedon complain of and resent Penelope's clever tricks, she herself grieves at her betrayal by the maids and the failure of her last stratagem in a long campaign of resistance (153–8). In book 13 Athene had assured Odysseus of his wife's loyalty (336–8, 379–81, esp. 381 νόος δέ οἱ ἄλλα μενοινᾷ; cf. 2.92, 18.283). This assurance is important in explaining his confidence and pleasure in her apparent (though bitter and reluctant) surrender in book 18 (esp. 281–3; Introd. 3(*b*)). But in this scene he learns her true feelings and hears how much she has plotted and struggled to defer her hateful remarriage. Her ingenuity in the web-trick matches his own deceptive skills.

124–5 Penelope's modesty is becoming, but in reality Athene has enhanced her beauty (18.190–7), as she elsewhere makes Odysseus more attractive (6.230–5 = 23.157–62). The queen's pessimism and failure to understand the divine influence at work are essential to the sombre tone of her speeches here, and to the irony of the whole scene.

ἐμὴν ἀρετήν picks up ἀρετῶσι in 114, as κλέος in 128 answers the same word in 108.

125 Ἴλιον εἰσανέβαινον 'went aboard ship to go to Troy'. Cf. 2.172, 18.252.

126 ἤιεν 'went' (3 sing. imperfect of εἶμι 'to go').

127 ἀμφιπολεύοι 'tend', 'care for'. Cf. esp. 24.244, 257 (of Laertes tending his vineyard). βίον probably means 'livelihood', 'property' rather than 'life', but both meanings are possible, and perhaps the distinction should not be pressed too hard.

128 Cf. 108n.

129 νῦν δ' ἄχομαι: after an unfulfilled condition it is very common to find νῦν δὲ, meaning 'but as it is (since that has *not* happened)': cf. *Il.* 1.354, *Od.* 1.166, Dem. 18.15, and often.

ἐπέσσευεν 'set in motion', 'sent against'. The image may be that of a wave or flood, as in the literal sense at 5.314, 431 (where Odysseus is buffeted by Poseidon's storm); cf. also 5.421 ἠέ τί μοι καὶ κῆτος ἐπισσεύῃ μέγα δαίμων | ἐξ ἁλός.

130 ὅσσοι: the number of the suitors is given by Telemachus as 108 (16,245–53). [Apollodorus] in *Epit.* 7.26–30 gives a tedious and largely imaginary list of all their names.

130–3 ὅσσοι ... οἵ τ' ... οἵ 'all those who ... and those who ... they woo me ...' In line 132 οἵ is the relative pronoun, in 133 the demonstrative.

131 These islands adjacent to Ithaca are usually mentioned together. This line recurs as 1.246 = 16.123; cf. 9.24 (Odysseus' description of his origins) = *Homeric hymn to Apollo* 429. Telemachus mentions in 16.251 that twelve of the suitors came from Ithaca itself, presumably lesser lords previously under the sway of Odysseus' family (a similar situation seems to prevail in Scheria: 6.54–5). In the Catalogue of Ships in *Iliad* 2, Odysseus' domain consists of Ithaca, including Neritos (apparently a mountain: cf. *Od.* 9.22, 13.351), Krokyleia and Aigilips (probably also natural features of Ithaca), Zacynthos and Samos (*sic*), with some mainlanders as well (*Il.* 2.631–7). This amounts to only twelve ships, the same number with which he departs from Troy in the *Odyssey* (9.159).

On the passage in the Catalogue, and on the geographical problems attending efforts to identify the islands of Odysseus, see G. S. Kirk, *The Iliad: a commentary* 1 (Cambridge 1985) *ad loc.* (pp. 220–2, cf. 182–3); R. Hope Simpson and J. F. Lazenby, *The catalogue of ships in Homer's Iliad* (Oxford 1970) 101–6.

132 εὐδείελον: stock epithet of Ithaca, and used only of that island (hence the humorous irony of Odysseus' enquiry to the disguised Athene in 13.234 'is this place some εὐδείελος island, or a promontory …?') It seems to mean 'bright' or 'shining', i.e. visible across the sea from some distance.

133 ἀεκαζομένην = ἀέκουσαν, 'unwilling'. Here it is indeed an understatement, as when Hector grimly uses it of Andromache's future enslavement (*Il.* 6.458).

τρύχουσι δὲ οἶκον: cf. 1.248 (Telemachus' complaints to Athene–Mentes); 16.125 (Telemachus to his father, whom he does not yet recognise). The wasting of Odysseus' wealth and herds (and so of Telemachus' inheritance) is often referred to, not least by the disconsolate Eumaeus (14.80–108; cf. ibid. 17–19), though in fact there does not seem to be any immediate danger of supplies being exhausted. It is a natural feature of story-telling for Odysseus to return just in the nick of time, at the very last moment, to rescue his wife (139–56n.) and save his wealth from dissipation; but the poet, equally naturally, allows him to enjoy continued prosperity rather than financial stringency after he has re-established his authority. On the tension between these notions (a king's infinite wealth and what the suitors' depredations would mean in real terms) see H. L. Levy, *T.A.P.A.* 94 (1963) 145–53. Similar ideas are developed by J. Griffin, in *Chios*, edd. J. Boardman and C. E. Vaphopoulou-Richardson (Oxford 1986) 3–13, though not all his examples are convincing.

134–5 Penelope's statement here seems contradicted by her actual behaviour in receiving and talking with Odysseus, a guest and suppliant. The contradiction is akin to one implicit in Eumaeus' account of her in 14.121–32, a speech which prepares us for book 19. As Eumaeus says, no beggar or stranger could persuade Penelope of Odysseus' return now, after all her disappointments and the lies she has been told in the past. But this does not mean that she will drive him away or treat him ill: 'she receives visitors kindly, and cares for you and asks you everything and as she weeps tears fall from her eyes, as is the way with a woman, when a husband has perished in a foreign land' (14.128–30). All of this is fulfilled in book 19, and indeed Eumaeus' own scepticism and reluctance to believe Odysseus prefigure Penelope's (14.115–408, with Fenik, *Studies* 156–7). Disbelief and pessimism remain her fixed attributes in book 23, when she cannot believe Eurycleia's good news. The doubts and despondency of Telemachus and Odysseus at earlier stages of the narrative form a part of the same thematic structure (see Introd. pp. 21, 28).

δημιοεργοί: cf. 17.382–7 for Eumaeus' categories of 'public labourers' (prophet, doctor, craftsman, bard), with the discussion by Finley, *World of Odysseus* 37, 53–6 and his ch. 3; also G. M. Calhoun and F. H. Stubbings in Wace and Stubbings, *Companion* 459, 537. Apart from heralds, Penelope's categories seem much less suitable: perhaps the tag οἳ δημιοεργοὶ ἔασιν (= 17.383) applies chiefly to the κήρυκες.

136 κατατήκομαι anticipates the key-word of the simile at 204–9 (see 204n.). The flash of metaphor in this simple but touching, self-contained line adds to the emotional weight of her words.

137 The division of the line at the caesura indicates the division between the two opposed parties, a mighty band of male suitors against one isolated female.

τολυπεύω ('to carry out', 'to carry through') in all other cases in Homer is used with 'war' (πόλεμον) as its object. Would the combination with δόλους here be felt by the audience as an abnormal use of the word? If so, it stresses the necessity for guile in the *Odyssey*, and its special appropriateness to women in general, who must work indirectly against the stronger sex, and to the wife of the cunning Odysseus in particular.

139–56 The story of the web of Penelope, the shroud which she wove by day and unpicked by night. Few stories in Homer are so well-known, almost proverbial. For the use of such devices in folk-tale in order to postpone an unwelcome event (often, as here, marriage) see Stith Thompson, *Motif index* κ 1227. The most famous parallel is the endless story-telling of Scheherazade, where the aim is to escape death, not marriage. It is fitting that Penelope, the ideal wife, should have recourse to such a device, for in Homer weaving is the woman's task *par excellence* (e.g. *Il.* 6.490–2, Hector's instructions to Andromache; we see her still carrying them out at 22.440–1. Cf. further *Il.* 3.125–8, *Od.* 6.305–7, etc.). The duty she owes to Laertes exemplifies her piety and her devotion to Odysseus' own house and family. (She cannot prepare a shroud for Odysseus himself, as he is not there in person to be buried; nor would it suit Homer's characterisation of Penelope for her to admit so firmly and finally that she is convinced her husband is dead.) Further, the verb ὑφαίνω (139, 149) has a metaphorical sense of scheming and plotting: see *Il.* 3.212, 9.93 = 7.324, 6.187, *Od.* 5.356, 9.422 (Odysseus' broodings in the cave of the Cyclops); Ar. *Lysistrata* 630 (in that play weaving is again thematic, as in lines 565–73, leading up to the famous simile at 574–86, in which the women apply domestic imagery to the problems of politics). See also C. Moulton, *C.Ph.* 74 (1979) 289–90.

It is also possible that Penelope's own name alludes to her famous task, if the etymology from πήνη ('thread'; in plural 'web' in later poetry) is correct. (On Homeric name-etymologies see 19.406–9n.) In that case the web may be one of the oldest elements in the story. A number of other points also make this probable: (1) the folk-tale quality of the stratagem; (2) the way that the story is brought in and told at length (including a passage of direct speech) three times, even though it is not a part of the main narrative, suggests that it was too well known to be left out. (3) The web story in fact conflicts with the main story-line of the *Odyssey* in two respects, for Laertes, though frail, is not dead, and the natural outcome of the trick's exposure, that the suitors should press for an immediate decision by the queen, does not follow. The last point can only partially be explained by the argument that the

suitors are distracted by Telemachus' activities, for they are content-
edly continuing their occupation of Odysseus' household in book 1 (as
also in 4.625–9), before they become aware of any danger from that
quarter. A simpler version of the tale would involve Odysseus' return in
the nick of time, immediately after Penelope's delaying tactics had been
exhausted; this is the sequence apparently envisaged by Amphimedon
in his account in 24.125–50, esp. 149 καὶ τότε δή (Page, *Homeric Odyssey*
120–1). It seems reasonable to suppose that the *Odyssey*-poet has ex-
panded an older story, enhancing the role of Telemachus, prolonging
the period of disguise for Odysseus, perhaps even resuscitating Laertes
(see esp. S. West, *P.C.P.S.* 35 (1989) 115–18, and cf. 16.117–20,
24.514–15, and Introd., p. 4 for the poet's interest in the family and
especially the father–son theme). But such reconstructions can only be
hypothetical.

138 φᾶρος is any cloak or mantle, but the use of it as a shroud is also
found at *Il.* 18.353, 24.580, Soph. *Ajax* 916, etc. It is further defined in
144. (The word occurs in Linear B: see H. P. and A. J. B. Wace in Wace
and Stubbings, *Companion* 503.)

ἐνέπνευσε: like the English 'inspire', this is a metaphor of breath: an
idea is blown into the mind from an external source. This is a process
which seems supernatural because no-one has any idea how it happens,
or where the thought comes from. See further Onians, *Origins of Euro-
pean thought* ch. 2, esp. 44–56; E. R. Dodds, *The Greeks and the irrational*
8–13, 80–1.

Although neither Penelope nor the poet identifies the god involved,
it is natural to think of Athene, who protects and guides Penelope
earlier in the poem, and who is the patroness of weaving and other
skills.

139 In general on the techniques of ancient weaving and for illustra-
tions of the types of loom, etc., see *OCD* s.v. 'weaving', with bibliog.; see
H. P. and A. J. B. Wace in Wace and Stubbings, *Companion* 498–503,
and F. H. Stubbings, ibid. 531–2.

140 λεπτὸν . . . περίμετρον: the former emphasises the fineness of
the threads, the latter their length.

142 ἐπειγόμενοι: understand περ ('wait for my marriage, eager
though you are').

εἰς ὅ κε 'until the time when'; κε, as often, introduces a certain vague-
ness: *some* time in the future, not a specified date.

143 μεταμώνια 'vain', 'wasted' (often of idle words). Later poets connected it with ἄνεμος (interpreting it as 'blown away by the wind'), e.g. Simonides, *PMG* 516, Pindar, *Ol.* 12.6a. There is a strong concentration of words associated with death in this speech: 141 θάνε, 143 ὄληται, 144 ταφήϊον, 145 throughout. Penelope gives no flattering hint of any pleasure at the prospect of remarriage, even before her trick is exposed.

144 For Laertes as 'hero' cf. 22.185, a reference to the old man's shield. Here the title serves to mark Penelope's reverence for her father-in-law.

145 Stock phraseology for death, not necessarily in battle. Cf. *Il.* 16.849 (Patroclus) ἀλλά με Μοῖρ' ὀλοὴ καὶ Λητοῦς ἔκτανεν υἱός; 8.70 = 22.210; *Od.* 11.171 (Odysseus to his mother) = 398 (to Agamemnon). Used also at *Od.* 3.238.

On Μοῖρα, with or without an initial capital (a distinction of course undetectable in oral performance, and not made in manuscripts until the medieval period), see Onians, *Origins of European thought* index s.vv. 'Moirai' and 'fate'; B. C. Dietrich, *Death, fate and the gods* (London 1965), esp. ch. 3; Burkert, *GR* 129–30; Erbse, *Funktion* 273–8. The basic meaning seems to be a 'portion' allotted by the gods.

τανηλεγέος θανάτοιο is a defining genitive ('the fate which consists of death . . .') rather than subjective ('the fate which death has in his possession'). τανηλεγέος is used by Homer only of death, and always in this genitive phrase, 'bringing long woe' (*perhaps* related to ἄλγος, ἀλγεινός?). The adjective is almost unknown outside epic.

This is one of the group of words sometimes misleadingly called 'glosses', the meaning of which may not have been clear even to the original epic poets.

146 Penelope's modesty recalls, in a far more serious and sombre context, the bashfulness of Nausicaa in book 6, esp. 6.273–86 (286 καὶ δ' ἄλληι νεμεσῶ), one of a number of ways in which the encounter with Nausicaa, who is clearly attracted by Odysseus, acts as a foil to the more mature relationship and lasting bond with Penelope. Thus in book 23, Odysseus takes a bath and is beautified by Athene, while Penelope sits to one side, as had happened with Nausicaa on the beach in Phaeacia.

148 ἐπεπείθετο: cf. 151 ἔπειθον. In the first case, a willing acceptance; in the second, the deceptive element of *peitho* is in play, and we should render 'deluded', 'fooled'. See further R. G. A. Buxton, *Persuasion in Greek tragedy* (Cambridge 1982), esp. ch. 2. Persuasion is commonly associated with the seductive charms of clever and attractive females: e.g. Hera in the Deception of Zeus (*Il.* 14, esp. 216–17; Buxton 36), Aphrodite in the *Homeric hymn to Aphrodite* (88–90) or in Pindar, *Pythian* 4.216–19, Helen in the *Troades* (967–8, and the whole scene), the women in Aristophanes' *Lysistrata* (see 203–4, the oath scene). Contrast the steadfastness of Odysseus against Calypso (9.33, 23.337) with the naive readiness of the suitors to be beguiled, both here and in the scene in book 18 (Introd. 3(*b*)).

149–50 ὑφαίνεσκον . . . ἀλλύεσκον: frequentatives, used of repeated action (cf. *Il.* 24.12, 15–17).

151 'Thrice . . . and then the fourth time' or the like is a conventional pattern in much story-telling and common in Homer: e.g. *Il.* 5.436–9, 16.702–9, 20.445–8; B. Fenik, *Typical battle scenes in the Iliad* (Wiesbaden 1968) 46. Nevertheless, the time-scheme of the *Odyssey* is consistent on this point: besides the parallel passages in books 2 and 24, see above all 13.377 (Athene to Odysseus): 'the suitors who have been lording it in your halls for *three years*'. It is now ten years since the fall of Troy (see 2.175–6, 17.327), and Odysseus has been imprisoned on Ogygia for seven of these (7.259). In book 11, when Anticleia's ghost describes Ithaca as prospering (181–7), she describes what she herself knew and what was still the case at the time of Odysseus' encounter with her; at this stage, the suitors had not yet begun their pursuit of Penelope. Page, *Homeric Odyssey* 40–1 is too severe on poet and commentators on this point.

Ἀχαιούς: although this is a general title for 'Greeks' in both poems (cf. Thuc. 1.3.3–4), it is commonly used of the suitors in these books (e.g. 20.3, 166, 271, 21.418). But contrast 20.277 with 276–8n.

153 πόλλ': sc. ὄντα, predicative: 'and when the days, being many, were accomplished'.

154 For the maids see Melantho's scene above (65–95), and nn.; 121n. Melantho is addressed as 'bitch' in 18.338, 19.91 (see n. there). The line is a more powerful and emotional variant on the neutral account of the maid's betrayal given in the parallel speeches (2.108–9 = 24.144–5 καὶ τότε δή τις ἔειπε γυναικῶν, ἣ σάφα ᾔδη, | καὶ τήν γ' ἀλλύουσαν ἐφεύρομεν ἀγλαὸν ἱστόν). The other version would have made perfect sense here, but the poet varies his formula in order to convey Penelope's resentment and anger. This is a fine instance of the poet's conscious control of his set lines and phraseology: he is not an automaton, reusing material without thought or discrimination. For many more examples see Macleod, *Iliad XXIV* 40–2, 46–7.

155 ὁμόκλησαν: the substance of their complaints is expressed by Antinous in the Ithacan assembly (2.85–128).

156 καὶ οὐκ ἐθέλουσ᾽, ὑπ᾽ ἀνάγκης: the tautology emphasises her distressed reluctance. Cf. *Homeric hymn to Demeter* 124, with Richardson's n. on 53 and 72.

καί = καίπερ.

158 τοκῆες: Penelope's father was Icarius (1.329 and often); her mother is not named in Homer, and later versions differed: some made her a Naiad, Periboea ([Apollod.] *Bibl.* 3.10.6 with Frazer's n.), but in the *Odyssey* Periboea is ancestress of Alcinous (7.57). It is unlikely that Homer knew any particular story about her parents: their sole function in the poem is as a further pressure on Penelope to remarry.

159 ἀσχαλάαι: cf. 534, again Penelope on Telemachus. See further 160, 124–63 nn.

κατεδόντων: cf. 133n., and for the idea of 'eating up' property, a metaphor found also in English and Latin, cf. 13.396 = 428 = 15.32, 17.378, 19.534; Callim. *Hymn to Demeter* (6) esp. 102–17; Ov. *Met.* 8.843–4, 875–6; Petronius 141 (with J. C. Bramble, *Persius and the programmatic satire* (Cambridge 1974) 1).

160 γιγνώσκων: Telemachus' awareness of his position dates only from Athene's intervention in book 1: see esp. 2.303–5, where Antinous hypocritically urges Telemachus to join them in feasting and drinking 'as you did before' (305 ὡς τὸ πάρος περ). Previously he was content to dream of his father, passively hoping for his return (1.114–7). His growing resentment and increased maturity are important themes in books 1–4; see esp. 2.270–80, 3.122–5, and further 16.300, 21.113–17, 125–9, 24.508. An ancient critic described the Telemachy as the 'education' (παίδευσις) of Telemachus (Porph. *ap.* Schol. *Od.* 1.93 and 284).

161 τῶι τε Ζεὺς κῦδος ὀπάζει 'and Zeus is granting him glory'. Grammatically τῶι could refer either to Telemachus or to the house. As one expects Zeus to give something to a person, the former is preferable, though the run of the passage (with οἴκου in the preceding phrase) seems harsh. A variant reading is ὄλβον ὀπάζει. ὄλβον gains some support from 18.19, κῦδος from Athene's proposals regarding Telemachus at 1.93–5 (esp. 95 κλέος ἐσθλόν). In both readings, the association with Zeus suggests that Telemachus is the proper heir to the kingdom. (On Zeus as patron of kings see *Il.* 1.278–9 (where κῦδος occurs), 2.204–6; Hes. *Th.* 96.)

162 ἐσσί: 2 sing. present indicative of εἰμί 'I am'.

163 A peculiar expression, found in a number of different contexts in Homer (cf. and contrast *Il.* 22.126) and Hesiod: see *Th.* 35 with West's helpful note. Here it obviously means 'you must have *some* parents (despite your reluctance to speak)'; it may be compared with the more transparent and more common 'feed'-line, 'I don't suppose you got here (to Ithaca) on foot', i.e. overland (1.173 = 14.190, 16.59, 224).

παλαιφάτου 'spoken (of) long ago' (of prophecies in 9.507 and 13.172), and hence simply 'old'.

164–202 After a preliminary protestation of continuing reluctance (165–71), the whole speech is devoted to one of Odysseus' virtuoso lies about his background and experience. This portion may be further subdivided: 172–8, 'ethnography' of Crete; 178–84, the stranger's family; 185–202, how he entertained Odysseus and his men in Crete. As yet he holds back more recent 'news' of the hero (see 269–72, 296–302).

On the lies see further Introd. 4(*c*), pp. 69–73.

165–8 Odysseus' opening is as cool and fluent as ever. Only later, when Penelope breaks down and weeps, does the poet give us some hint of the emotion which underlies his deception: see 210 θυμῶι μὲν γοόωσαν ἑὴν ἐλέαιρε γυναῖκα and 212 δάκρυα κεῦθεν. For this technique compare 16.190–1.

166 οὐκέτ' here means 'still not' ('will you still not stop questioning me . . . ?'), rather than the usual 'no longer'.

168–9 ἡ γὰρ δίκη [sc. ἔστι], ὁππότε . . . 'That is what inevitably/ habitually happens, whenever . . .' Cf. 43, where 'this is the δίκη of the gods' meant 'this is their regular practice'.

170 Perhaps a reminiscence of 1.3–4 '*many* were the towns of men he saw and their minds, many the *woes* he underwent in his heart upon the sea . . .' (cf. also 9.128, 13.90–1, 15.492, 16.63). More than conventional phrasing, these words seem almost to sound a few notes of the hero's signature tune.

171 Cf. 7.243 (Odysseus begins his reply to Arete; cf. also 7.241 with 19.221, another opening of a speech) = 15.402 (Eumaeus begins to recount his life story to Odysseus). Compare also, in a different way, 23.98–9, where Telemachus reproaches his mother for *not* questioning his father now that the slaughter is ended and Odysseus is home. There Telemachus does not realise the full depth of his mother's despondency and longing: she can question strangers, as here, but in book 23 she cannot bear to hope that her questioning will reveal her beloved husband.

172–8 A brief account of Crete and its peoples. See in general J. Boardman, *CAH* (2nd edn) III 3 (1982) 222–33; also R F. Willetts, ibid. 234–48, and his *Ancient Crete: a social history* (London and Toronto 1965) 24–35 on this passage; E. Meyer, in *Der Kleine Pauly*, ed. K. Ziegler and W. Sontheimer (Munich 1975) III 338–41; J. T. Hooker, *J.H.S.* 89 (1969) 60–71.

Two distinct questions arise from this passage. (a) What did the Greeks of Homer's time really know about Crete, past and present? (b) What did Crete mean to their imaginations and for the imaginative world of the *Odyssey*?

The answers to both questions are inevitably limited by our sources, but we may be fairly sure that they had little conception of either the antiquity of Minoan civilisation or the scale and nature of Cretan society of that earlier age. The contraction of time involved in making Minos, the great king of Crete in its heyday, the grandfather of a hero of the war of Troy, indicates the inadequacy of their chronology. Further, contemporary awareness of Cretans as active traders and of Crete as a transition point, like Cyprus, to the East and South, has been blended with remoter memories of Minoan sea-power and legend (cf. nn. below).

172 Κρήτη τις γαῖ' ἔστι: a type of scene-setting which commonly introduces a life-history: cf. *Il.* 6.152, *Od.* 15.403, and the delightful piece of misdirection in *Od.* 7.244, where Odysseus exploits the convention (Fenik, *Studies* 16–17). No such elaborate account of Crete occurs in the other lying stories: that is doubtless because this lie, told to Penelope, is the most important and forms the climax. Similarly Odysseus' alleged status is highest here, as Idomeneus' brother and direct descendant of Zeus.

174 ἐννήκοντα: contrast the 100 cities of the Catalogue (*Il.* 2.649; see Kirk on 646–8). The discrepancy is unimportant; both figures are poetic hyperbole.

175 The language barrier is not usually a problem in Homer, though he is of course aware that his characters would not all speak the same tongue: see esp. *Il.* 2. 803–6, on the multiple nationalities of Priam's allies. *Il.* 3.1–7, particularly the comparison of Trojan shouting to the raucous cries of the cranes, may hint at barbarian babbling, in view of the unusually nationalistic context (Griffin, *Homer on life and death* 4), but in general Greeks converse without difficulty with Trojans and allies, even with Egyptians and Cyclopes, and only pedantry would protest at this convention. Fifth-century drama, influenced by the antagonism between Greece and the East during the Persian wars, has much more interest in presenting foreigners as barbarians, exotic, cruel and decadent: see E. Hall, *Inventing the barbarian* (Oxford 1989), who also discusses the Homeric and archaic background (pp. 13–17, 19–55). In high tragedy, such as Aeschylus' *Persians*, many foreign names and words are employed to show the cultural gulf which separates them from the West: in lighter scenes in melodrama and comedy, foreigners may speak gibberish or ungrammatical Greek (Ar. *Ach.* 100, Eur. *Or.* 1369–1502). In the sophistic παίγνιον by Gorgias in defence of Palamedes, there is an amusing reference to the linguistic problem: Palamedes argues that in order to betray his countrymen to the Trojans he would have needed an interpreter (82 в 11 a.7 D–K).

A. Morpurgo Davies, 'The Greek notion of dialect', *Actes de la pre-mière rencontre internat. de dialectologie grecque* (= *Verbum* 10, 1987) 26, remarks that different Greek dialects and non-Greek languages are mentioned together here, and that it is not clear how conscious the early Greeks were of the distinction.

175–7 These lines have been suspected as an interpolation, especially in view of the reference to the Dorians, mentioned nowhere else in Homer. For a brief introduction to the complex historical problems raised by the lines see Willetts, *Ancient Crete* (172–8n.) 24–35. The names are distinctive and resonant, adding status to the speaker's family and homeland.

The 'Eteocretes' (True Cretans) are not mentioned elsewhere. For the Kudones see 3.292 (where Menelaus is received by them in Crete). For the Pelasgoi see *Il.* 2.840 (Hippothous' contingent; here as in 17.289 he is the son of Pelasgus); 10.429 (Dolon describes his background). In *Il.* 16.233 Achilles invokes Zeus as Dodonaean and Pelasgian. There is also a Pelasgian Argos in the domain of Achilles in the Catalogue (*Il.*

2.681; see Kirk's n.). The last two passages are thus connected by their association with that hero. In later times 'Pelasgian' was used to describe one of the oldest indigenous races of Greece: see Hdt. 1.57, Thuc. 1.3.2. Modern research has had no difficulty in finding fault with Herodotus' garbled account, but has had less success in finding something to put in its place: see A. B. Lloyd, *Herodotus Book* II (Leiden 1976) II 232ff.

177 Δωριέες: the invaders from the North *c.* 1100 B.C., who overwhelmed the Mycenaean civilisation and according to the common reconstruction brought about the so-called Dark Age of Greece: see further *CAH* II 2 (3rd edn, 1975) ch. 26 (V. Desborough and N. Hammond); contrast A. M. Snodgrass, *The dark age of Greece* (Edinburgh 1971), who questions the significance of the Dorian invasion and the concept of a 'dark age'. The Dorian invasion of course postdates the War of Troy (traditionally *c.* 1203 B.C.; cf. *CAH* loc. cit. 350); but it is not so much the anachronism that is disturbing here, as the fact that Homer elsewhere shows no knowledge of the Dorians. But it is poor logic to argue that 'this occurs here and nowhere else in Homer; *therefore* this is unHomeric'. Wilamowitz mocked such arguments with the formulation *einmal heisst niemals und zweimal heisst immer* ('once means never, twice means always'): see W. B. Stanford, *Enemies of poetry* (London 1980) 129. Similar considerations arise in the case of Theoclymenus' 'second sight' in 20.351–7 (see 20.345–86n.).

τριχάϊκες (probably from θρίξ + ἀΐσσω) should mean 'of flashing hair', but seems to have been interpreted as a reference to the triple division of the Dorian peoples into tribes: cf. Hes. fr. 233 M–W.

178 τῆισι δ' ἐνί 'among them', i.e. the 90 cities of line 174.

Κνωσός: Cnossos was the greatest and longest-lived of the Minoan cities; it was finally destroyed *c.* 1375–1350 B.C. and in modern times first excavated by Sir Arthur Evans. Cnossos is not mentioned elsewhere in the *Odyssey*, but see *Il.* 2.646, 18.591 (the shield of Achilles shows a dancing-place 'like that which Daedalus fashioned once in broad Crete for Ariadne of the lovely tresses'; for Cretan dancers see also *Il.* 16.617); *Homeric hymn to Apollo* 394, 475.

The variation between single and double sigma is a common Homeric licence, found also in the name of Odysseus himself.

Μίνως: cf. *Il.* 13.449–54 (Idomeneus declares his genealogy, in lines which bear some resemblance to 180–1 here); 14.321–2 (adding the fact that Minos was not only the favourite but also the son of Zeus, and the brother of Rhadamanthus); *Od.* 11.568–71 (Minos as arbitrator among the dead; this passage may, however, be a late addition). *Od.* 11.321–5 gives further details of Ariadne's story, though in a somewhat unusual version. On Minos see further Hes. *Th.* 947–9, Bacchyl. 17, Pl. *Grg.* 523a–527a, with Dodds's commentary, p. 374; Virg. *Aen.* 6.432; Apollodorus, ed. J. G. Frazer, index s.v.; A. B. Cook, *Zeus: a study in ancient religion* (Cambridge 1914–40) 1 464–7. In Hes. fr. 144 he is 'most kingly of mortal kings'; in Plato, he becomes the judge of the dead for their sins in life; for the more prosaic historians he is the first thalassocrat, founder of a naval empire that foreshadows Athens' own (Hdt. 1.171, 3.122; Thuc. 1.4–8). It is impossible to say how much genuine tradition underlies this mythological extravagance. The association of Minos with the Minotaur and the Labyrinth ([Apollod]. *Bibl.* 3.1.3– 4, 15.7–9, *Epit.* 1.7–11, with Frazer) seemingly preserves in mythical form some knowledge of the Cretan bull-dancers (so e.g. Cook, *Zeus* 1 490–521; W. K. C. Guthrie, *CAH* II 2 (3rd edn, 1975) 874, 884), and Linear B documents seem to preserve mention of a Daidaleion and a Mistress of the Labyrinth (Burkert, *GR* 23), but the canonical story of Theseus' heroic expedition to relieve Athens' youth from the doom of the Minotaur is surely a later version of Attic origin (see Plutarch's *Theseus*); the earliest references to Minos lack this strongly Attic slant (*Od.* 11.322–3 mentions Theseus and Athens, but [Hes.] *Aspis* 182 and fr. 298 do not).

179 ἐννέωρος (ἐννέα + ὥρη) can hardly mean 'nine years old', as it does at 11.311 and perhaps at 10.19; and 'for nine years' would give Minos an unexpectedly short reign for so great and famous a king. Hence many render it 'in each ninth year', following Plato, *Minos* 319b, who takes it as going with ὀαριστής rather than with βασίλευε. The idea would then be that Minos communed with or sought advice from Zeus at periodic intervals: cf. Moses and Jehovah, Numa and Egeria (see further West on Hes. *Th.* 22–34). The offspring of the gods naturally have special access to their parents: compare Achilles and Thetis, Polyphemus and Poseidon, Aristaeus and Cyrene in Virg. *Georg.* 4. For Minos' intimacy with Zeus see Plato, loc. cit. and *Laws* 624a; Hor. *Odes* 1.28.9 *Iouis arcanis Minos admissus.* Beyond the stock notion of great men as divinely descended, there surely lies some more exotic religious ritual: later tradition presented Minos as conferring with his father in the Idaean cave in which, according to Cretan myth, the god was born (Burkert, *GR* 38–9, 127, esp. Callimachus, *Hymn to Zeus* 1–54, with McLennan's commentary).

ὀαριστής: ὀαρίζω is 'to hold converse with', but the implications are often more intimate: the words are used of love in *Il.* 14.216, of lovers at *Il.* 22.127–8 (linked with 6.516). *Il.* 13.291 and 17.228 are grim distortions of this idea, applying the language of love-making to battle. In this passage the implication is that Minos enjoyed privileged access to Zeus, something that no other mortal in Homer attains: in the narrative of the poems Zeus always works through intermediaries, though in other tales he clearly descended to earth like other gods, not least in the pursuit of love (*Il.* 14.315–27).

180 Deucalion is Idomeneus' father also in *Il.* 13.451–2. There seems to be no connection between him and the more famous Deucalion, son of Prometheus and husband of Pyrrha, the Greek equivalent of Noah, who is first mentioned in the Hesiodic *Catalogue* (frr. 2–7). For a third Deucalion, a Trojan nonentity slain by Achilles, see *Il.* 20.478.

183 ἅμ' Ἀτρεΐδησιν: for the recruiting-drive organised by the Atridae see the Cyclic *Cypria* (OCT Homer v, p. 103 = *Ep. Gr. fragm.*, ed. Davies, p. 31.40–4); also e.g. *Il.* 9.252–9, 11.19–23, 765–82. But the phrase does not necessarily mean that they visited Crete in person.

Αἴθων: it is exceptional for Odysseus to give himself a name in the lying stories: he does so elsewhere only to Laertes, where the names are clearly *noms parlants*, though the exact sense is uncertain: υἱὸς Ἀφείδαντος Πολυπημονίδαο ἄνακτος. | αὐτὰρ ἐμοί γ' ὄνομ' ἐστὶν Ἐπήριτος (24.305–6), perhaps 'son of Unsparing the son of Man-of-much-woe, and my own name is Man-of-strife' (see Stanford's notes; but also S. West, *P.C.P.S.* 35 (1989)140 n. 72). We should expect the name Aithon also to be significant: it means 'hot' and 'fiery', and is often used of flashing weapons and armour. Aithon is the name of one of Hector's horses (*Il.* 8.185, juxtaposed with Xanthus, Podargus and Lampus, all names which allude to their energy or appearance). Perhaps it is unnecessary to seek a further implication beyond that of a fiery and violent warrior (such as Odysseus will show himself in the slaughter); for other speculations see G. E. Dimock in *Essays on the Odyssey*, ed. C. H. Taylor (Indiana 1963) 71; but many of his suggestions are wild. (In [Hes.] fr. 43 (1).2–6 M–W (restored), and in Hellan. *FGrH* 4 F 7, the insatiable Erysichthon is called Aithon because of his raging/burning hunger; but despite Odysseus' hearty appetite this is scarcely relevant.)

185 We meet here the motif of 'guest-friendship', frequent in the lies and thematically important throughout the *Odyssey*: cf. 191, 194–5, 253–4; and elsewhere, e.g. 4.169–70, 8.546, 9.267–80, 477–9, 14.56–9, 402–6; *Il.* 6.212–31; Finley, *The world of Odysseus* 95–103; Introd., p. 23. Gifts given to visitors are a regular feature of guest-friendship, especially when the visitor is about to depart: e.g. 1.309–18, 11.336–52, 13.10–15, 15.113–30. Cf. Griffin, *Homer on life and death* 27; M. Mauss, *The gift* (originally Paris 1925; Eng. tr. 1954).

Odysseus has a more-than-average enthusiasm for picking up wealth along the way: see esp. 11.355–61, where his willingness to stay in Scheria 'for a whole year' if he can then return home πλειοτέρηι σὺν χειρί is a little surprising after his earlier impatience with delay. The phrase 'for a whole year' is, however, conventional (4.595; cf. 14.196; see Fenik, *Studies* 167); and Odysseus' longing to depart revives later, to be described in a powerful simile (13.28–35). In the end he returns home with wealth greater than the Trojan loot he has lost (13.137–8 = 5.39–40), and conceals this new wealth with Athene's aid before playing the beggar (13.361–71). The exchange and especially the acquisition of gifts continues to be a feature of his lies (e.g. 14.285–6, 323–6, etc.; Fenik, *Studies* 168). See also 18.281–3, his delight in Penelope's skill at cajoling gifts from the suitors; 19.413n.; Stanford, *The Ulysses theme* 255 n. 18.

186–7 Cape Malea is on the south-easternmost promontory of the Peloponnese opposite the island of Cythera; it is a notoriously difficult and dangerous spot for ships throughout antiquity, as shown particularly by the proverbial phrase quoted by Strabo (8.6.20, 378): Μαλεάς δὲ κάμψας ἐπιλάθου τῶν οἴκαδε ('once you've rounded Cape Malea, forget what you left at home'). This spot figures in the true story of Odysseus, at 9.80, but there he is driven off course in the early stages of his *return* from Troy, and he does not come to Crete. Menelaus suffers from storms at the same place (3.286–90; cf. 4.514 on Agamemnon), and is driven to Crete (3.291) before his better-known adventures in Egypt. Since Odysseus is unaware of Menelaus' route, this is a parallelism introduced by the poet: cf. Introd. 4(*c*)ix, p. 71.

ἱέμενον: acc. masc. sing. of the present participle of ἵημι (found only in middle form) 'to aim at', 'be eager for', 'desire'. Here instead of an

infinitive it is followed by the adverb Τροίηνδε: 'as he was eagerly mak-
ing for Troy'.

188 Amnisos is on the northern coast of Crete, not far from Cnossos.
The detail in the following line is accurate: it is barely a real harbour at
all, certainly not a safe anchorage.

The reference to 'the cave of Eileithyia' (who is mentioned only here
in the *Odyssey*; in the *Iliad* see 11.270, 16.187, 19.103, 119) is a clear case
of genuine religious tradition dating back to Minoan times. See Bur-
kert, *GR* 25–6; M. P. Nilsson, *Minoan–Mycenean Religion* (Lund 1950)
73, 521–3; R. F. Willetts, *C.Q.* 8 (1958) 221–3. Caves were important
in Cretan religion (Burkert, loc. cit.); they also appear several times in
the *Odyssey*, generally with some kind of supernatural or numinous as-
sociations: see the set-piece descriptions of Calypso's dwelling-place
(5.55–75) and of the secluded harbour of Ithaca with the cave of the
Nymphs (13.96–112, cf. 355–60). On the negative side, there is also the
bloody lair of the Cyclops (9.216–23, etc.). Again we see the poet creat-
ing analogies between the lies and the 'real' events of the poem.

192–3 τῶι ... | οἰχομένωι go together: 'for him on his journey to
Ilion with his beaked ships it was the tenth or eleventh day'; i.e. he was
ten or eleven days into his voyage.

192 δεκάτη ἢ ἑνδεκάτη: the vagueness seems purely conversational,
with no significance: cf. 2.374, 4.588 (eleventh or twelfth). Contrast
the grim precision of Priam in *Il.* 24.664–8, agreeing on the truce with
the Greeks and concluding 'on the twelfth day, we shall fight again, if
we must' – here there is no room for uncertainty.

194–5 The stress on the hospitality shown by 'Aithon' to Odysseus
emphasises not only his virtue but Penelope's obligation to befriend
and show equal generosity to her visitor.

τὸν μέν: answered by καί οἱ τοῖς ἄλλοις (196). Aithon drew on his
own resources to give hospitality to Odysseus (πρὸς δώματα ... κατὰ
οἶκον), but organised a levy for the entertainment of his men.

195 ἐνδυκέως 'kindly', 'devotedly'. The word is constantly used in
the context of hospitality, and often as here with φιλέειν. It is far more
common in the *Odyssey* than in the *Iliad*, where there are only four
instances, confined to the last two books.

196 οἱ: dative referring to Odysseus. 'I gave to him for the rest of his
companions'; it was left to Odysseus to do the distribution.

197 δημόθεν ... ἀγείρας: as Alcinous does to finance his magnificent gifts to Odysseus (13.14–15). Cf. also 14.285, in another false tale: Odysseus spent seven years in Egypt πολλὰ δ' ἄγειρα | χρήματ' – as a popular freeloader or in some kind of service to the king? So also 22.55; 23.356–8.

198 Festivity involves sacrifice, as splendidly described in the narrative of Telemachus' visit to Pylos, 3.404–63, the fullest account of the ritual in epic. See further Eur. *El.* 791–839, with commentaries by J. D. Denniston and M. Cropp; Burkert, *GR* 55–9; *Homo necans* (Eng. tr. Berkeley and Los Angeles 1983) 1–12.

ἱρεύσασθαι: infinitive of purpose, as in English 'oxen to sacrifice'.

πλησαίατο: 3 pl. aor. middle optative from πίμπλημι 'fill'.

199 δυώδεκα: like seven, nine or ten, a conventional figure. Thus Odysseus has 12 ships (9.159) and 12 amphorae of wine (9.204); Aeolus has 12 children (10.5, though here the number may be chosen to match the months of the year), Alcinous has 12 fellow βασιλῆες, and so forth. Odysseus' expedition must remain with Aithon long enough for him to be acquainted with the hero and to be able plausibly to answer Penelope's questions.

200–1 οὐδ' ἐπὶ γαίηι | εἴα ἵστασθαι 'did not allow us even to stand up on the land' (*sc.* far less to put out to sea). The vivid picture is reminiscent of Hesiod's complaints about harsh weather and the perils of sea-travel: cf. Hes. *WD* 504–35, esp. 518 τροχαλὸν δὲ γέροντα τίθησιν, apparently meaning that the force of the wind propels the old man along faster than he wishes to go.

203–12 After this long exchange we are shown Penelope's reaction not through speech (for at first she is overcome), but through a simile. The poet in fact employs a *pair* of contrasting similes, as sometimes in describing opposing warriors (*Il.* 3.21–37 on Menelaus and Paris; 4.422–7 and 433–6, the opposing forces; 15.679–94, Ajax vs Hector). Penelope and Odysseus are both distressed – Penelope by the memories which the false tale arouses, Odysseus by the grief he is unavoidably causing his wife to suffer; but they react in opposite ways. Penelope weeps openly and wholeheartedly, whereas Odysseus contains and suppresses his emotion, keeping his face firm and immobile. The wife's spontaneity and passion are contrasted with the husband's hard-won self-discipline. The subjects of the similes are also contrasted: melting snow versus hard iron and horn. Moreover, they differ in length: Penelope's simile is lush and elaborate, and the account of her condition extends over six lines; whereas the description of Odysseus is more taut and concise.

Penelope constantly weeps in the *Odyssey*, often crying herself to sleep upstairs (1.362–4, 19.602–4, etc.). By contrast, Odysseus' tears are rare, and come at dramatic and climactic moments in the narrative: see esp. 8.83–92 and 521–31; 16.190–1, 213–19; 17.304–5; 23.232–40. (Though 24.318–26 seem not to involve weeping, 318–19 clearly imply violent emotion, and Odysseus breaks into an agitated outburst of reassurance to his father, losing all his previous self-control.) The development of his powers of self-discipline, his capacity to mask his feelings, is an important aspect of his characterisation (Introd. 2(*b*)). Here we see these qualities subjected to their severest test.

203 Ἴσκε is from ἐΐσκω 'to make like/equal to', 'liken'. Cf. esp. 4.279 (Helen's imitation of the voices of the Greek wives); *Il.* 16.41 ἐμὲ σοὶ ἴσκοντες (Patroclus to Achilles: 'the Greeks will think I am you'); *Od.* 16.187 (Odysseus to his son: 'why do you liken me to / think me like a god?'). ἴσκεν in *Od.* 22.31 is less certain, but may mean 'imagined' (though some translate it as 'spoke', both there and in this passage: the ancient critics already found this hard to decide, and uses of the verb by Apollonius and Theocritus seem to take 'say', 'speak' as the correct sense). Translate: 'he uttered many a lie which he made seem like the truth'; that is, the lies are plausible, realistic. In part this plausibility derives from the use of so many true ingredients, as outlined in the notes above. In ancient criticism the art of Homer's (or Odysseus') lies was much admired: see Arist. *Poetics* 24 1460a18–26 (218n. below); Hor. *Ars poetica* 151 *atque ita mentitur, sic ueris falsa remiscet*, and ibid. 338.

The line is similar to the words of the Muses to Hesiod on Mt Helicon, where they initiate him in the pursuit of poetry: see *Theogony* 27–8 ἴδμεν ψεύδεα πολλὰ λέγειν ἐτύμοισιν ὁμοῖα, | ἴδμεν δ' εὖτ' ἐθέλωμεν ἀληθέα γηρύσασθαι. See West's commentary *ad loc.*; Thalmann, *Conventions of form and thought* 146–9. It is not necessary to assume a direct connection either way (though the possibility that Hesiod is polemicising against epic 'falsehoods' need not be ruled out). What matters for the *Odyssey* is that the hero's persuasive falsehoods associate him with the art of the poet: see further 11.364–9, 17.518–21, 21.406–11; C. Moulton, *Similes in the Homeric poems* (Göttingen 1977) 145–53; C. W. Macleod, *Collected essays* (Oxford 1983) ch. 1. But unlike Demodocus and Phemius, and unlike himself in the earlier lie-scenes, Odysseus himself is moved, as well as his audience, though for different reasons.

204 τήκετο ('melted', 'dissolved') is the key-word of the simile, repeated in various forms four times in the next four lines. Cf. 136; 263–4 (μηκέτι νῦν χρόα καλὸν ἐναίρεο μηδέ τι θυμὸν | τῆκε πόσιν γοόωσα). In 8.522 it is also used of *Odysseus'* grief when he hears Demodocus' account of the fall of Troy. There he unsuccessfully struggled to mask his pain, whereas here he succeeds. Compare also the simile of the sick father wasting away (5.396) and then recovering; that simile is applied to Odysseus, and is closely connected with a simile in 23.233–40, describing the reunion of Odysseus and Penelope. It can hardly be coincidence that all the instances of this verb or its compound κατατήκομαι are used of the hero or of his wife.

For such emphatic repetition and reduplication see Macleod, *Iliad XXIV* 50–1 (and his nn. on 258–9, 688, 771–2); J. D. Denniston, *Greek prose style* (Oxford 1952) 80; Fehling, *Wiederholungsfiguren* 126, 146.

205–7 The melting of the snow obviously corresponds to Penelope's flood of tears, but it also has a more symbolic significance. Penelope's resistance to flattery and scepticism in the face of good news are weakening in the face of Odysseus' tactful and sympathetic rhetoric. They will weaken further as this scene progresses. Furthermore, the return of Odysseus is chronologically and symbolically associated with the arrival of spring: see N. Austin, *Archery* ch. 5. Amongst much else, he cites 5.466–73, 483–5, 14.457–522, 529–33, 15.392–4, 19.63–4 on the wintry weather conditions; 5.171, where the scholia attribute Odysseus' reluctance to set sail to the stormy season; and 21.411, 22.340, complex but suggestive allusions to the swallow, the traditional harbinger of spring. See further E. K. Borthwick, *G.&R.* 35 (1988) 14–22.

206 The West wind is not usually gentle in Homer, except in Elysium (4.567) or in heaven (7.119). Contrast e.g. *Od.* 4.402, 5.295, 12.289, *Il.* 11.305.

209 παρήμενον: sc. περ: concessive, 'although he sat there beside her'. On the paradoxical language here see Macleod, *Iliad XXIV* 41: the poet avoids the standard phrasing Ὀδυσῆα φίλον πόσιν, which would be flatter, and would fail to highlight the irony. The contrast between Odysseus' situation and Penelope's is further brought out by the balancing possessive adjectives in 209 (ἑόν) and 210 (ἑήν).

210 ἐλέαιρε: the detail is important, as Homer is in danger of making Odysseus seem inhumanly callous. It may still be asked why he does not reveal himself to his wife in this scene, as may have happened in an earlier version of the tale (cf. esp. 24.127, 167–9; Introd. 3(c), pp. 34–5). The answer lies partly in caution, for Odysseus is following the advice of Agamemnon (11.441–3) and Athene (13.307–10, 402–3) not to reveal himself until the proper time. Could Penelope be trusted not to reveal her joy and relief to the suitors? Another factor is the growth in Odysseus' reserve and independence, his determination never to reveal more than is absolutely required, a theme to which the poet gives still greater prominence in the second half of the poem, when the hero has returned to his homeland. This self-discipline, born out of experience of the dangers involved in bragging and openness (shown above all in book 9), has become second nature to him, so much so that later, with Laertes in book 24, he cannot break free of it even after the danger is past. The poet of the *Odyssey* is fascinated by the themes of concealment and partial knowledge, trust and failure to believe, appearance and reality.

211 There seems to be no special significance in horn and ivory here, other than their hardness. For more imaginative speculations, concentrating especially on the Gates of Ivory and Horn in 562–7 below, see A. Amory, *Y.Cl.S.* 20 (1966) 3–57.

213 τάρφθη: 3 sing. aor. passive from τέρπω 'delight', 'satisfy'. For the paradoxical expression compare *Il.* 23.10 and 98, 24.513–14; *Od.* 11.212, 19.249, 23.231 ἵμερον ... γόοιο. This does not imply self-indulgence, still less any artificiality or insincerity in the lament. *Od.* 15.400 and Virg. *Aen.* 1.203, which speak of the pleasure in *remembering* suffering when it is past, express a more straightforward conception.

215–28 For a third-century B.C. papyrus of these lines see *P.S.I.* 979, re-edited by S. West, *The Ptolemaic papyri of Homer* 270–2.

215 πειρήσεσθαι: Penelope attempts to 'test' Odysseus, as he has tested others and is indeed testing her (though without any real doubts): see 19.45n. The theme is important throughout the second half of the poem: see Introd. pp. 12, 62. Odysseus has so far been tested himself by Athene, in the duel of wits in book 13; like Agamemnon (11.442–3, 454–6), she advises him to follow this course with his household (13.336), and we see him doing so with Eumaeus (14.459, 15.304). See also 16.304–5, 17.360–4. This testing of others is particularly linked with the hospitality theme. Stories in many cultures tell of gods

visiting men in disguise, seeking out and rewarding virtue, and punish-
ing the wicked. See Genesis 18:1–5; 19:2; Hebrews 13:1; Hollis on
Ovid, *Met.* 8.611–724; R. Lane Fox, *Pagans and Christians* (Harmonds-
worth 1986) ch. 4. The *Odyssey* alludes to such tales at 17.483–7, where
some of the suitors, alarmed by the menacing words of the disguised
hero, fear that Odysseus may in fact be a god. He is not, but several
passages play on his resemblance to a god in this role (see 7.199–206,
16.183–5, 23.62–4), and he is certainly an instrument of divine punish-
ment, as the increasing support of Athene and the moral authority of
his pronouncements (esp. 22.413–18) both stress. See further West on
Hes. *WD* 249ff.; E. Kearns, *C.Q.* 32 (1982) 2–8. Hellanicus, *FGrH* 4 F
26 seems to have interpreted Apollo's and Poseidon's period of service
to Laomedon as a divine test (*Il.* 21.441–56): see L. Pearson, *Early
Ionian historians* (Oxford 1939) 182.

Here Penelope tries her own hand at testing but is unequal to her
husband, who successfully side-steps. In book 23 she again devises a test
(this time without so explicit a warning as in 215 here), and is success-
ful, so vindicating her reputation for cleverness and proving herself a
worthy wife for Odysseus.

218 ἄσσα = τινά, acc. pl. neuter of τις. This adds a note of generality
to the enquiry: 'tell me, what sort of things were they, those clothes he
had on . . . ?'

ἕστο: 3 sing. pluperfect middle of ἕννυμι, which in the middle means
'to put clothes on oneself'; the perfect has the sense 'I have put on' = 'I
am wearing', and the pluperfect 'I was wearing'. Cf. 237.

Aristotle in *Poetics* 24 1460a18–26 explains the 'paralogismos' here
(the Aristotelian passage is discussed by N. J. Richardson, in F. Cairns,
ed., *Papers of the Liverpool Latin seminar* IV (1983) 219–35, esp. 221–2).
Penelope knows that if her guest had entertained Odysseus, he should
be able to answer this question; she therefore assumes, wrongly, that
since he is able to answer it, he must have entertained him as and when
he says. That is, she knows that A implies B, and wrongly thinks that
therefore B implies A.

Clothing, as a mark of wealth and status, is of considerable impor-
tance in Homer. For some of the uses, symbolic and emotional, to
which it is put, see Griffin, *Homer on life and death* 2–7, 28–9; W.
Schadewaldt, *Hermes* 87 (1959) 15–32 = *Hellas und Hesperien* (2nd edn,

Zürich–Stuttgart 1960) I 79–93. See also below, 19.317–22, (with n.), 336–44.

219 καὶ ἑταίρους: the construction changes at this point: after two clauses which contain indirect questions, Penelope adds as an afterthought a further question, making ἑταίρους the direct object of εἰπέ (218).

221 ἀργαλέον ... εἰπέμεν: a similar protestation opens Odysseus' response to Arete's awkward question in 7.241. As often, Homer anticipates rhetorical techniques and theory (cf. Introd. 4(c); Quintil. 10.1.46–51; L. Radermacher, *Artium scriptores* (Vienna 1951) I–10). It is commonplace for a speaker to emphasise the difficulty of the case confronting him: e.g. Ar. *Wasps* 650, 950, Thuc. 2.35.2, Isoc. 4.13, Arist. *Rhetoric* 1415a2. In fact, of course, it is very easy for Odysseus to answer the question, so that this is a mischievous touch.

ἀμφὶς ἑόντα 'being [i.e. having been] apart', 'being separated'. For this use of ἀμφίς cf. 24.218, Cunliffe s.v. I(2).

224 ἰνδάλλεται normally means 'seems' but here must mean 'thinks' or perhaps 'pictures to itself'. Cf. the double sense of δοκέω ('seem' and 'think'). ἦτορ is the subject.

226–31 'And on his cloak there was a brooch of gold with double sheaths [sc. for the pins]. On the face the brooch was richly wrought: there was a hound with a dappled fawn in the grip of its front paws, keeping tight hold of it as it gasped. Everybody marvelled at it, at the two beasts, and the way that, though they were made of gold, one had the fawn in his grip and was throttling it, while the other, desperate to escape, was jerking its feet, convulsed.'

This is a miniature *ekphrasis*, a digression describing a work of art: Achilles' shield is a much vaster example. For further parallels see C. J. Fordyce on Catullus, poem 64 (p. 273 of his commentary). Other short examples in Homer are the descriptions of Agamemnon's sceptre (*Iliad* 2.101–8) and shield (11.32–40). It is a regular feature of such descriptions to stress their lifelike quality and to refer to the wonder of an observer, almost deceived by the illusion: cf. *Il.* 18.549, Hes. *Th.* 584, Apoll. *Arg.* 1.763–7, Virg. *Aen.* 5.254 *anhelanti similis*, G. Zanker, *Realism in Alexandrian poetry* (London, Sydney and New Hampshire 1987) 43–50. Here, however, Penelope will feel wonder at the detailed *description* of the work of art, and what it seems to imply. Hers is a more complex response than the simple admiration of the women referred to in line 235.

Though detailed, the description is hardly plausible: a hound, however well-trained, cannot strangle its prey with its forefeet. The hound is 'humanised', by a process common in similes: cf. Macleod, *Iliad XXIV* 50 on *Il.* 13.200.

Later *ekphraseis* regularly bear some thematic relation to the narrative in which they appear; for Achilles' shield this has been argued in detail by O. Taplin, *G.&R.* 27 (1980) 1–21. Here we might see an analogy between Odysseus (as a hunter and warrior) and the dog, and between the suitors and the fawn. (Cf. the simile at 4.335–40 = 17.126–31.) The appearance of Odysseus as a hunter in the digression on the scar may also be related.

For archaeological comment on the description of the brooch, see H. L. Lorimer, *Homer and the monuments* (London 1950) 511–15; P. G. Guzzo, *Stud. Etr.* 36 (1968) 277–307.

229–30 λάων . . . λάε: the sense of this verb was already disputed in antiquity, as the references to Crates and Aristarchus in the scholia show; see also Hesychius s.v. In the *Homeric hymn to Hermes* 360 it seems to mean 'see'; but here the meaning 'grip', 'hold' is essential.

231 ἄσπαιρε πόδεσσι: for the meaning 'move convulsively' rather than the usual 'gasp', 'pant', cf. 22.473 ἄσπαιρον δέ πόδεσσι μίνυνθά περ, οὔ τι μάλα δήν; also *Iliad* 13.443, where the verb is used of a heart thumping or throbbing.

232–4 'superfine linen' (F. H. Stubbings, in Wace and Stubbings, *Companion* 532)? S. Zukor and J. D. Bishop, 'Homer's best-dressed man', *C.W.* 47 (1953–4) 118, identify it as material made from *pinna nobilis* (sea silk, sea wool), an expensive and rare fibre from fish found off the shores of Sicily and S. Italy.

233 'like the skin (λοπόν) upon a dried-up onion'. The accentuation and role of κατα in the phrase are very obscure, however: adverb or preposition, and if the latter, does it govern λοπόν or κρομύοιο? Best of a bad lot of explanations is to take κάτα as preposition + accusative governing λοπόν, and meaning something like 'on' or 'over' (LSJ в 2).

235 Odysseus' vanity shows through here in a very amusing way; cf. 239–40 'since Odysseus was a friend to many people; for there were few of the Achaeans like *him*'; 265–7. Also comparable are the touches of

conceit or self-praise which adorn his later narrative of his adventures
after Penelope has recognised him: see 23.328, 337, 339.

γ' after ἤ μέν is emphatic: 'there really were *lots* of women who ad-
mired him'. Cf. Denniston, *GP* 114.

237–40 It is crafty of Odysseus, after such a startling feat of 'mem-
ory', to feign uncertainty on another point.

240 ἔσκε: 3 sing. of an iterative past tense of the verb 'to be', indicat-
ing repeated or continuous action, 'used to be'. Cf. 247, 315.

244–7 The way in which the name itself is held up is typically Odys-
sean: cf. Eumaeus' delay in naming his master, until 14.144 (contrast
40, 42, 67, 70, 122, 133–8). See Fenik, *Studies* 24–5, 28–9.

244 καὶ μέν 'and furthermore', introducing a new point (Denniston,
GP 390).

246–7 'He was round in the shoulders, dark-skinned, curly/woolly-
headed, and Eurybates was his name.' All three adjectives are unique
in Homer: though for μελανόχροος cf. 16.175 μελαγχροιής (of Odysseus
restored to his normal appearance). Eurybates appears in the *Iliad* at
2.184 (where he is an Ithacan and attends on Odysseus), and also at
1.320, 9.170, in both of which he is a herald subordinate to Agamem-
non. Was this a regular name for a herald ('broadly-ranging')? There is
no suggestion in the *Iliad* that he is black-skinned.

248 ἤιδη: 3 sing. pluperfect of εἴδω 'know', but normally used, in
Homeric Greek as in Attic, as the imperfect of οἶδα. Hence the full force
of the pluperfect is not felt.

οἱ refers to Odysseus, not to Eurybates.

249–50 These lines closely resemble 23.205–6, where Penelope
reacts to Odysseus' angry speech about his marital bed, the sign which
finally proves his identity to her. This is a significant echo: here, Pene-
lope has tried to test the beggar's credentials but has been outwitted;
she believes a false tale is 'firm' and true. In book 23, it is Odysseus who
is outwitted, and Penelope's joyous certainty is justified. (The lines are
also adapted for the case of Laertes, 24.345–6; but this episode is more
of a 'pendant' to the major sequence of recognitions.)

250–1 These lines are omitted in some manuscripts, doubtless be-
cause a scribe's eye slipped from γόοιο at the end of 249 to the occur-
rence of the same word at the end of 251. This common source of
textual error is known as 'homoeoteleuton' ('similar ending'): see e.g.

M. L. West, *Textual criticism and editorial technique* (Stuttgart 1973) 24–5.
The same cause presumably lies behind the omission of 275–7 in a few
MSS: again, 274 and 277 end with the same word.

251 On the paradoxical notion of 'taking pleasure in grief' see 213n.

256 πτύξασ' ἐκ θαλάμου: a 'brachylogy' or abbreviated expression
for the fuller description, which would run 'after folding them I brought
them out of my chamber, and gave them to him (πόρον)'.

257–8 Cf. *Il.* 18.59–60 and 440–1 (Thetis of Achilles). Thetis' pa-
thetic prediction is correct, while Penelope's, though expressed with
equal anguish, is mistaken: hence there is irony here of the 'comic' kind,
where the audience knows that things are not as bad as the character
thinks, whereas in the *Iliad* we witness Thetis' grief-stricken acceptance
of destiny and know that her prediction is accurate. This contrast sums
up much of the difference between the *Iliad* and the *Odyssey*.

260 Κακοΐλιον οὐκ ὀνομαστήν 'Evil-Ilium, not to be named', i.e.
that place which we should avoid naming. For the expression see also
597, 23.19 (all spoken by Penelope). Similar expressions are found at
Iliad 3.39 = 13.769 Δύσπαρι ('Vile-Paris'), 16.31, *Od.* 18.73; Fehling,
Wiederholungsfiguren 287–93.

263 ἐναίρεο: normally 'kill', with the implication of taking armour
as spoil (ἔναρα). Here it must be used in a weakened sense, e.g. 'ruin',
'spoil'.

263–4 χρόα . . . | τῆχε: both words look back to the description and
simile at 204–9.

264 μέν is answered by 268 ἀλλά; the intervening sentence is paren-
thetic, explaining why Odysseus does not reproach her for her grief.
οὐδέν is adverbial: 'not at all'.

265–7 For the form of the argument (*a fortiori*) cf. e.g. *Il.* 2.292–7
('men grow weary of campaigning even after a month away from their
wives and families, whereas here we are, besieging Troy for nine *years*'),
18.362–7 (Hera speaking: 'even a mortal injured as I have been would
seek recompense; how much more am I, the sister and wife of Zeus,
entitled to it'). For the word-play (ὀδύρεται ... 'Ὀδυσῆ') cf. 1.55,
5.160, 14.142–4, 174; Rank, *Etymologiseerung* 51.

265 τίς is feminine here, as the sense shows.
ἀλλοῖον is linked with 267 ἤ ('different from', 'inferior to'). The sen-
tence structure is curious: 266 seems to hold up the argument. Either
266 or 267 might be deleted.

268 σύνθεο 'put together in your mind', 'mark my words'. Aorist imperative (2 sing.) middle of συντίθημι, which in Homer is normally used in the middle.

271 For the Thesprotians see Introd. 4(c), p. 72. In what follows Odysseus again mingles truth and falsehood: 270–3 (as far as δῆμον) are false, but from there on he gives a true but selective narrative of his own experiences down to 282 (omitting seven years with Calypso!), then lapses into fiction once more, until the end of his narrative at 299. After that the oath which follows expresses truth but in a misleadingly distanced way.

This is the first point in the conversation with Penelope at which Odysseus has given any hint that he has any *recent* news of her husband. The audience, who know that what he now says is a lie, are unlikely to notice the artificiality of this delay, but it provides a striking example of the way in which Homeric narrative, for all its psychological subtlety, admits improbable and unnatural sequences of events. In 'real life', it would be natural for Odysseus, even when lying, to produce the recent news first, and if he had indeed held it up until now, Penelope might reasonably be outraged and angry that he had not said what he knew before. But the poet, as always, prefers to delay revelations, even when they are untrue; and it suits the mood of the scene for Odysseus to win Penelope's confidence gradually, through narrative about the distant past, rather than coming directly to the present situation. For realism made subordinate to dramatic or thematic ends cf. also (amongst many examples) 19.337–42 (Odysseus' insistence on remaining in his rags makes no sense in realistic terms, but suits the poet's thematic structure: the hero cannot yet dress well because he is not yet master in his home); 20.227–37n.

271–2 ἀγχοῦ . . . | ζωοῦ: two successive lines beginning with unquestionably emphatic enjambment.

273 αἰτίζων: so too Menelaus had to go begging in his long wanderings: see 4.78–91. As discussed in the Introduction (p. 71), Menelaus' travels form a parallel, on a smaller and less momentous scale, for the wanderings of Odysseus. For the stress on collecting gifts cf. 281, 293–5, 413, etc.; see 185n.

273–5 These events are more fully described in Odysseus' narrative to the Phaeacians, at 12.260–446.

275 ὀδύσαντο: for the play on the hero's name see 265–7, 406–9 nn.

275–7 Cf. 250–1n.

278–82 This implies that as soon as his ships were wrecked and his companions lost, Odysseus' next landfall was in Scheria. In fact of course he was washed to Ogygia, the island of Calypso, and only continued his journey after seven years' imprisonment there (described in book 5). It was on his voyage from Ogygia that he was again wrecked and washed to Scheria (5.282–493). The omission of this amorous interlude avoids upsetting Penelope further (Telemachus had mentioned Calypso in his account of Menelaus' narrative at 17.142–4; but Odysseus does not know this). The gap in the story is filled, with appropriate tact, in the exchange between husband and wife in book 23 (333–7).

279 ἀγχίθεοι: in Homer this adjective is used only of the Phaeacians, here and at 5.35. It seems to signify their special status, as a people particularly favoured by the gods, with whom they deal directly and whom they have even entertained to dinner. See esp. 7.201–3; also 6.201–3, 7.321–8, 8.556–63 on their magical ships, 7.81–132 on the wondrous palace and gardens of Alcinous.

280 θεὸν ὥς: an inversion of the normal word order: 'they honoured him like a god'. Normally ὥς in the sense of 'like', 'as', is unaccented, but when it follows the word to which it relates, as here, an accent is added. Contrast 285, where ὥς is the adverb 'so', 'thus'.

282–3 καί κεν πάλαι . . . | ἤην 'and Odysseus would have been here long ago . . .' For κε (= Attic ἄν) + indicative in unfulfilled conditions see Monro, *Grammar* §324.

283 εἴσατο: 3 sing. aorist middle of εἴδω 'see' or 'discern'. 'But this seemed better to him in his heart', 'this' being defined in the next line. For the meaning 'seem' in the middle (cf. Latin *videor*) see Cunliffe s.v. II(1).

287–300 Largely repeated from 14.316–35, the parallel scene between Odysseus and Eumaeus. In Homer the name Pheidon occurs only in these two passages.

290 πέμψουσι: the future indicative is retained, although this line is in fact part of what King Pheidon said: see Goodwin, *Greek grammar* §1497 (alternatively this verb might have been changed into the future optative).

294 ἕτερον 'the next (owner)'.

296–9 Cf. 14.327–30, in the parallel lie told to Eumaeus. Dodona, the greatest oracle of the Greek world after Delphi, is already mentioned in the *Iliad* (16.233–5). Oracles there were received from a sacred oak. The idea seems here to be that Zeus will speak directly to the questioner, but later authors preferred a less direct means of communication: according to one tradition, the oak gave signs itself by rustling and creaking (Ov. *Met.* 7.629–31, Philostr. *Imag.* 2.33); according to another, birds in the tree, especially doves, gave oracular signs by their cries or movements (Philostr. loc. cit., Soph. *Trach.* 172 with Easterling's n.; Hdt. 2.51–7 rationalises this). See further H. W. Parke, *The oracles of Zeus* (Cambridge, Mass. 1967) chh. 1–3; H. Thomas and F. H. Stubbings, in Wace and Stubbings, *Companion* 294–5; Burkert, *GR* 114–15.

299 ἤ . . . ἦε: it is commonplace for enquirers to consult oracles by offering them alternatives ('shall I do X or Y?'), rather than asking open questions. See P. Amandry, *La Mantique apollinienne à Delphes* (Paris 1950) 149–59.

302–7 To end with an oath is a powerful and emotive climax. On casuistical oaths, which avoid actual lies but misdirect or mislead the hearer, see R. Parker, *Miasma* (Oxford 1983) 186–7, esp. *Iliad* 15.36–44.

303–7 = 14.158–62.

304 ἱστίη τ' Ὀδυσῆος: on the 'hearth' and Hestia, the goddess associated with it, see J.-P. Vernant, *Myth and thought among the Greeks* (Eng. tr. London 1983) ch. 5; S. Goldhill, *Reading Greek tragedy* (Cambridge 1986) 71–3. For the sanctity of the hearth cf. e.g. Hes. *Th.* 454, *WD* 734.

The line also appears at 14.159 (where it is less apt), 17.156, 20.231.

306 λυκάβαντος: a mysterious term which in Homer appears only in this line and in the parallel passage in book 14. It obviously means a span of time, but 'year' (normal in later usage) is intolerably flat as a prophecy, while 'day' seems too definite and would involve deleting the passage in book 14 as an intrusion from this book. Dio Chrys. 7.84 understood it as 'month'. Austin, *Archery* 244–6 persuasively argues that the word refers to the period of the 'dark of the moon', i.e. while the old moon is fading and before the new begins (see 307), a matter of a few days; and he links with this the suggestion of the scholia that the festival of Apollo (86n.) to be celebrated next day is the feast of Apollo Noumenios (of the New Moon). For earlier interpretations along these lines see Eisenberger, *Studien* 263 n. 21.

307 For such parallel but opposed expressions see Fehling, *Wiederholungsfiguren* 310–11: e.g. *Il.* 9.78, 13.513; less close, 1.95, 22.135, 23.363.

308–11 = 17.162–5 (Penelope to Theoclymenus) = 15.536–8, (Telemachus to Theoclymenus). There is a general parallel between the role of Theoclymenus in book 17, where he foretells Odysseus' return to the queen, and the role of Odysseus in this scene.

313 πομπῆς 'escort', or 'a sending-off', genitive after τεύξῃι (from τυγχάνω) in the next line.

315 εἴ ποτ' ἔην γε 'if it/he was ever truly so', a pathetic phrase also found in *Il.* 3.180, 24.426, *Od.* 24.289.

316 The infinitives follow ἔσκε in the preceding line: 'such as Odysseus *was* (if he was ever truly so) for sending off and welcoming honoured guests'. The two verbs are in the reverse of the logical order, as Odysseus must welcome the guests before he sends them off. This trick of style is known as ὕστερον πρότερον ('back to front'): cf. 535.

317–22 Odysseus has been told several times that Penelope or Telemachus will treat him generously and offer him a cloak and other garments (14.132, 515–17, 15.337–9, 16.79, 17.550–8; later see 21.339). It seems to be a leitmotiv; and indeed the gift of clothing is one aspect of hospitality and humanity in the *Odyssey*. Calypso clothed Odysseus before he left her island, but those clothes were lost in the sea (symbolically?). Nausicaa dresses him in book 6; clothes are among the gifts the Phaeacians send him off with (13.10). In book 13 Athene transforms his clothes along with his person, and even when the change in his form seems to be ignored, his clothes continue to be described as rags (13.434–8, 18.108–9). He is to remain the ragged, despicable old beggar until his triumph is complete. Hence he refuses the gifts here (337–8); he changes his clothes only later, in book 23, in hopes of overcoming Penelope's doubts. This is one means whereby the *Odyssey* explores the question of what makes a man himself, what constitutes his identity. See also 22.1, where Odysseus sheds his rags and reveals his identity in violent action against his enemies.

320 λοέσσαι . . . χρῖσαι 'wash and anoint him', aorist infinitives (from λούω and χρίω) used as imperatives.

326 νόον . . . μῆτιν: accusatives of respect. 'If I surpass to any degree (τι) other women *in* intelligence and thoughtful counsel.'

327 ἀϋσταλέος 'dry', 'squalid', 'dirty'. Only here in Homer.

328–34 This passage draws on the ethical ideas which are also pro-

minent in Odysseus' speeches at 18.130–42 and elsewhere: cf. 19.71–
88n. Rashness, cruelty and arrogance come to grief; generosity, mercy
and gentleness are advocated, on both moral and prudential grounds.
Man's mortality and insecure hold on the future (328 ἄνθρωποι …
μινυνθάδιοι τελέθουσιν) should make him refrain from callous or exces-
sive behaviour, which may recoil upon himself. Throughout, the poet
recognises, and makes us realise, that human beings have certain duties
towards one another which they neglect at their peril. Cf. Introd.
pp. 22–3.

328 μινυνθάδιοι: elsewhere in the *Odyssey* only at 11.307, in one of
the narratives about the legendary heroines of the past. The word is
more frequent in the tragic *Iliad*, where it is particularly associated with
Achilles (1.352 etc.).

329 ἀπηνὴς … ἀπηνέα 'hostile', 'unfriendly'. The quality charac-
terises the suitors: see 18.381 (Odysseus rebukes Eurymachus). But it is
also used of Penelope later in the poem, by Telemachus (23.97) and by
herself (23.230). There the 'unfriendliness' consists of her slowness to
accept that the slayer of the suitors is truly her husband.

330 δέ: here 'apodotic'; that is, it appears in what amounts to the
apodosis or main clause of a conditional sentence, as 329–31 could be
rephrased as 'if a man is unkind, then everyone curses him …' For this
use of δέ, which lays emphasis on the clause in which it appears, see
Goodwin, *Greek grammar* §1422; Denniston, *GP* 177–81.

332 This line mirrors 329 in structure: the two ways of life are pre-
sented antithetically.

333 κλέος: cf. 108n., 128.
διὰ … φορέουσι: tmesis.

334 πολλοί τέ … ἔειπον 'many people call him a noble man'. The
τε, like the 'gnomic' aorist, indicates a generalisation.

338 ἤχθεθ', ὅτε 'have been hated by / hateful to me, (from the time)
when', that is, 'ever since'. ἤχθετο is 3 sing. aorist of ἐχθάνομαι 'to incur
disfavour of', 'become distasteful to'.

340 This anticipates Odysseus' wakeful night of resentment and
anxiety described at the start of book 20.

κείω 'I shall lie', cf. 48n.

342 ἄεσα: 1 sing. aorist of ἰαύω 'to lie', 'rest', 'pass the night'.

344–8 Odysseus asks for an older woman to wash him rather than a
young one (a) because of the treacherous behaviour of the younger

servants (154, cf. Eurycleia at 372–4) and the ill-treatment he has al-
ready suffered from Melantho (65n.); (b) because he does not want to
be accused of seduction or low behaviour (cf. 67); (c) because old age
and experience bring greater understanding and sympathy for hard-
ship, as 346–7 imply and Eurycleia's behaviour shows. For this concep-
tion see K. J. Dover, *Greek popular morality in the time of Plato and Aristotle*
(Oxford 1974) 268–72. Odysseus' words certainly do not imply that he
expects or wants to be recognised by an old servant such as Eurycleia
(so Page, *Homeric Odyssey* 126–7.). The deletion of 346–8, ascribed to
Aristarchus, is therefore unnecessary.

346 κεδνὰ ἰδυῖα: cf. 1.428 (of Eurycleia); 20.57, 23.182, 232 (of
Penelope).

350 γάρ is apologetic; the sentence explains why she has used the
startlingly intimate ξεῖνε φίλε. Elsewhere in the *Odyssey* this phrase is
used only by Telemachus to the disguised Athene (1.158). The punc-
tuation of these lines is difficult: there is a parenthetic passage which
begins with οὐ γάρ here and goes on to 352 ἀγορεύεις, and perhaps this
section should be enclosed by dashes or brackets.

351 φιλίων is a comparative adjective in the nominative (=φίλτερος);
the alternative, to read it as genitive plural of the regular adjective, is
much less satisfactory, both here and in the parallel passage in 24.267–
8. Cf. Erbse, *Beiträge* 209. The sentence is difficult, however: φιλίων by
this argument is co-ordinate with πεπνυμένος (it would be easier if this
were shown in the Greek, with an added τ' after φιλίων), but the two
are not exactly balanced ('so intelligent . . . more dear'), and it is only
πεπνυμένος ὧδε which is taken up in 352 by ὡς . . . πεπνυμένα.

353 The name of Eurycleia is held up, to take Odysseus by surprise.
The stress on her role in nursing the hero prepares for the retrospect to
his childhood (392–466); it also makes us realise that here we have a
servant who knows him intimately, and may well recognise him.

354 κεῖνον of course means Odysseus, the one always uppermost in
Penelope's thoughts. For this technique see Macleod on *Il.* 24.702: add
Od. 4.832, 17.243.

357 περίφρων: a regular epithet of the old nurse (491, 20.134,
21.381). She was introduced at 1.428-35 at some length, clearly as the
chief female servant in the palace. Her special status was there estab-
lished, not least by the high price of 20 oxen which Laertes paid for her
(contrast *Il.* 23.705 (four seems to be a standard price)); this status

appears strikingly at 19.401–4, where it is she (rather than Odysseus'
mother Anticleia) who brings the infant to Autolycus and asks him to
name the child. Her role as Odysseus' and Telemachus' nurse binds her
more to the male side of the family; her loyalty is beyond question, and
her delight in the suitors' undoing (not to mention the young maids
getting their just deserts) is boldly realistic (495–8, 22.401–8, 420–34).

358 νίψον σοῖο ἄνακτος ὁμήλικα: the word order here is exploited
to shock or surprise the listener, who momentarily fears that the queen
has indeed recognised the hero: but instead of 'your master's feet' or the
like, ὁμήλικα reassures us. For the technique, cf. 363; 14.365–6.

360 This implies that the beggar is older than Odysseus would be
naturally (as opposed to being aged by suffering and travels). On the
extent to which the hero is disguised see 380–1n.

361–507 Odysseus and Eurycleia. This interlude, which also in-
cludes the further digression on the scar, separates two phases of Odys-
seus' conversation with his wife: in the first she is seeking information
and passively accepts news, while in the second she takes the initiative
and declares her intentions. When the scene began we may have antici-
pated a recognition by or revelation to Penelope; by now it is fairly
clear that this is not to occur on this occasion. Instead the poet surprises
us with an unpredicted and accidental recognition by Eurycleia, in
Penelope's presence (476–9). The queen's blindness is contrasted with
the nurse's sudden insight; Odysseus' cleverness and self-discipline are
upset by a sudden accident and oversight on his part (390–1). The hero
is thus shown to be cunning but not infallible. The motif of spontaneous
recognition, uninitiated by Odysseus, has already been used with the
dog Argus in 17.290–327, but there the dying animal's response went
unnoticed, and so no danger threatened. Here the poet enhances the
tension: will Penelope see Eurycleia's reaction? For other careless mis-
takes by Odysseus see Fenik, *Studies* 45.

Odysseus was recognised once before by a woman (Helen), while she
was washing his feet when he was in Troy disguised as a beggar; the
episode was recounted in book 4 to Telemachus (242–64, esp. 252–3).
See Introd. 4(c), p. 65.

For a discussion of the whole scene, see W. Büchner, *Rh.M.* 80 (1931)
129–36.

363 'O woe is me, my child, how helpless I am to aid you' (literally,
'helpless for / as regards you'; genitive of reference). The nurse's speech

begins with apparent recognition of Odysseus; only gradually does it become clear that she is in fact apostrophising the supposedly absent king. The speech continues to blur the gap between beggar and king: she addresses her master in the second person at 367, 369, refers to him in the third at 370–1, addresses the beggar at 372–4, 376, while σέθεν in 377 is ambiguous, poised between Odysseus and the beggar she sees before her. The speech reaches an apt climax with a comment on the resemblance between the two.

365–8 In Homer, and in Greek religion generally, sacrifices and worship are seen in terms of reciprocal favours: mortals do good to the gods by giving them pleasant offerings, and the gods are expected to show their appreciation: *do ut des*. This reduction of religion to 'a kind of commercial transaction' (Plato, *Euthyphro* 14e) was disparaged by later thinkers, but continued to be the central principle of sacrifice, and the formula 'if I have ever given you something which pleased you, help me now' (*Il.* 1.39–41) remains a regular element in prayers. See further *Iliad* 4.43–9, 20.298–9, 22.168–72, 24.33–4, 66–70; *Od.* 1.66–7, 19.396–8, 21.265–8, and Garvie on Aesch. *Cho.* 255, 483–5; H. Yunis, *A new creed: fundamental religious beliefs in the Athenian polis and Euripidean drama* (*Hypomn.* 91, Göttingen 1988) 50–6, 102–6.

366 κῆ': elided from κῆε, 3 sing. aorist of καίω 'burn'.

367 ἧος: here not temporal but final, 'in order that': cf. 4.800, 5.386, 6.80, 9.376.

369–72 Cf. Philoetius at 20.204–7; Fenik, *Studies* 22–3.

369 οἴωι is an exaggeration: she ignores the fates of Achilles, the Ajaxes, Antilochus, etc. The unreasonable overstatement adds rhetorical force as well as characterising the querulous old nurse.

371 τευ: 'somebody's', = τινός. Cf. 109.

380–1 The beggar's resemblance to Odysseus raises the question whether we are to suppose that he has been magically transformed or only changed by time and disguised. The poet is not entirely consistent; the two conceptions coexist over much of the poem. For the magical transformation by Athene see 13.397–403, 429–38; the process is reversed in 16.172–6 for the recognition by Telemachus, after which the disguise is restored (454–9). Passages such as 17.20–3, 195–6, 202 and 337 imply that he is an aged figure. Eurymachus' abusive reference to Odysseus' shiny bald head (18.354–5) also implies transformation. On the other hand, the scar and Eurycleia's swift reaction to it suggest that Odysseus is only disguised, not magically changed. More problematic are 18.67–70 (where Odysseus' mighty shoulders, chest and arms are mentioned as he strips for the fight with Irus, and Athene is said to fill out his limbs), and the present passage: is Odysseus recognisable or not? The story is clearly more exciting if there is at least the possibility of a friend or servant identifying the disguised king, as here, and we may suspect that the poet wanted to have it both ways: magical concealment is a common device in the *Odyssey* (e.g. Athene's use of mist in books 7 and 13), but in the more human and psychological drama of the later books supernatural metamorphosis would be out of place. It is in general noticeable, even in the wanderings of books 9–12, that the poet tends to play down or humanise the more fantastic elements: e.g. in book 10 the magical plant *moly* is forgotten after Odysseus has received it from Hermes, and it is Odysseus' own strength of will that frustrates Circe (10.327, 329). See further Page, *Folk-tales in Homer's Odyssey* 55, 69, etc.

A further example of the poet's 'wanting it both ways' may be seen in book 11, which uses two contradictory conceptions, νεκυομαντεία and κατάβασις. According to the former, Odysseus is standing at an entrance to the underworld and the shades flock up to meet him and drink the blood; according to the latter, he descends and (like Virgil's Aeneas) witnesses events in Hades itself. Analysts take the former to be the basic conception of the 'original' poet; but even in the scene with Achilles, which few would wish to excise as an interpolation, there is reference to the 'asphodel meadow' (539) which is part of the landscape of the underworld (573, cf. 24.13).

383–5 Shameless (and therefore humorous) prevarication by Odysseus.

384–5 These lines are preserved (with 17.357–68, 19.400–12a) in one of the earliest papyri of the *Odyssey*, P. Hibeh 194 (3rd cent. B.C.): see S. West, *The Ptolemaic papyri of Homer* 267–70. No significant new readings seem to emerge.

387 τοῦ πόδας ἐξαπένιζεν: τοῦ refers to the bowl in the previous line. 'She washed his feet from it.' The verb occurs only here, and is remarkable for its double prefix; presumably ἐξ- refers to the motion with which the nurse draws forth the water *from* the bowl, while ἀπο-

goes more with the washing movement (wiping away dirt, etc., from the feet). It might (as Prof. Kenney suggests) be better to read ἐξ ἀπένιζεν.

388 ἐπήφυσεν: 3 sing. aorist of ἐπαφύσσω 'draw (water) from a vessel and put (it) in another'. It occurs only here in Homer.

388–90 θερμὸν . . . ἐσχαρόφιν: the heat is needed to warm the water, the hearth (cf. 63–4) produces light, and so reveals the scar. Homer carefully paves the way for the revelation.

390 αὐτίκα . . . ὀΐσατο: 'for at once in his heart he felt forebodings . . .'

390–1 This is the first time the scar has been mentioned. It is to be used as proof of identity twice later, with Eumaeus and Philoetius at 21.217–20, and with Laertes at 24.331–5. It is also referred to by Eurycleia in her eager report to her mistress (23.73–6), but there this token is subordinated to a means of identification more appropriate to Penelope – the secret of the marital bed (as also with Laertes, to whom Odysseus goes on to mention the trees in the orchard which his father promised him).

Here the reference to the scar comes as a surprise to the modern reader: a key fact, it seems to us, has been delayed and revealed at the last moment, without preparation. For the technique cf. Fraenkel on Aesch. *Ag.*, Appendix A; *Iliad* 9.567 (the fact that Meleager had killed his uncles), 18.9–11; 24.574–5 (with Macleod's note); *Od.* 8.565–71; Aesch. *PV* 910–12, Hdt. 3.64.4, 4.80.4, Thuc. 3.23.1, Virg. *Aen.* 12.735–7, Apul. *Met.* 2.30 (the fact that the two men had the same name). As the range of these examples shows, this is not simply a primitive or archaic technique: it coexists with the devices of extensive preparation, foreshadowing, and anticipation.

The digression on the scar at such a moment of tension has provoked much discussion. The days in which the entire passage was simply excised as an interpolation are happily passed. A more thought-provoking account of the passage was given by E. Auerbach in the famous first chapter of his *Mimesis* (first publ. in German, Bern 1946; Eng. tr. Princeton 1953), a discussion which has often been reprinted (e.g. in *Twentieth-century literary criticism, a reader*, ed. D. Lodge (London 1972) 316–32). In essence, he argued that the Homeric narrative style typically dwells on what is present in the poet's imagination at the moment: the 'full foreground' is all-important. The seemingly disproportionate amount of space given to this story from Odysseus' youth is just an extreme version of this narrative tendency, which also gives us, for example, the genealogy of heroes, the history of their weapons, or the description of Agamemnon's or Achilles' shields.

Criticisms of Auerbach's general argument are summarised by de Jong, *Narrators and focalizers* 22–3 and expounded at length by M. Lynn-George, *Epos: word, narrative and the Iliad* (Basingstoke and London 1988) 2–27; A. Köhnken, *A.&A.* 22 (1976) 101–14 criticises his handling of this particular episode. Most importantly, his account exaggerates the uniformity of Homer's style and underestimates the degree of considered and deliberate digression or placement of interludes. Even those who see Homer's narrative episodes as paratactic or 'connected together without lacunae in a perpetual foreground' (Auerbach, *Mimesis* 9) must admit that the present passage is an extreme case; hence we need to explain why this technique is employed here and on such a scale. (a) It shows us the bond between Eurycleia, the old family servant, and the hero: she was present when he received the name which has proved so well-chosen; she recalls his return after the expedition which seems to mark his growth to manhood (410). (b) The expedition to Parnassus presents an analogy and a contrast to the war of Troy. Both are heroic exploits; in both Odysseus joins his peers and shows his prowess; in both he seeks and obtains gifts (413, 460; cf. 185n.). The contrast lies partly in the scale of the adventure, partly in the nature of Odysseus' homecoming: in his youth, straightforward and joyous (412, 461, 463); in the present, secret and circuitous. In recounting a memorable moment in Odysseus' coming of age, the story sheds light on the character and experiences of the older and wiser man. (c) The episode recounting the giving of his name forms a foil to the namelessness and suppression of identity which is a condition of Odysseus' success in the *Odyssey*.

I. de Jong, *C.Q.* 35 (1985) 517–18 argues that the scar story is 'embedded focalization': it presents indirectly Eurycleia's recollections and thoughts on seeing the scar, rather than straightforward exposition by the narrator. This is possible, but seems less likely for the later part of the episode (e.g. 439–45, the boar's lair; 462–6, where Eurycleia's presence is not mentioned).

For tokens of this kind used to reveal identity cf. Aesch. *Cho.* 164–211; Eur. *El.* 524–46; *Ion* 1320–54; Men. *Perikeiromene* 755–78; Longus,

Daphnis and Chloe 4.18–24, 30–4. There is a parodic version of the scar in Eur. *Electra* 573–4: there, the old man identifies Orestes by a scar which he got in childhood while chasing not a wild boar, but a pet fawn round the royal courtyard with his sister.

392 ἄναχθ' ἑόν: the narrator's viewpoint, not the nurse's as yet (cf. Introd. 4(*c*), p. 67).

αὐτίκα: cf. 390. The narrative is accelerated, then slowed unexpectedly in the 'flashback'.

394 Αὐτόλυκον: the name means 'the wolf himself', an appropriate name for so devious a character. He is mentioned also in *Iliad* 10.266–71, again in a disreputable context (he broke into a hero's house and stole a boar's-tusk helmet), but there his relationship with Odysseus is not specified. Already in early poetry he was a well-known figure, and there seem to have been stories connecting him with other legends. [Hesiod] in the *Catalogue* (frr. 64, 67 M–W) made him the son of Hermes, and like Homer associated him with trickery and fraud; Pherecydes seems to have given a more detailed account of his exploits, presumably drawing on [Hesiod] and others (*FGrH* 3 F 81, 120). According to one story he was a member of the *Argo*'s crew; somewhat inconsistently, he was said to be Jason's grandfather as well as Odysseus' (see [Apollod.] *Bibl.* 1.9.16). See further Stanford, *Ulysses theme* ch. 2; J. S. Clay, *The wrath of Athena* 56–60, 68–70, etc.

395 ἐκέκαστο: 3 sing. pluperfect of καίνυμαι 'excel'.

396 κλεπτοσύνηι θ' ὅρκωι τε 'in thieving and oaths'. The skill with oaths presumably means the ability to twist the terms of an oath so as to avoid perjury (cf. 302–7n.).

397 Ἑρμείας: on Hermes see W. Burkert, *GR* 156–9; L. Kahn, *Hermès passe* (Paris 1978). As god of trickery, trade and theft he is an ideal patron for Autolycus and indeed for Odysseus, whom he helps to avoid Circe's traps in book 10. Hermes is friendly towards men (*Il.* 24.334–5) and, a thief himself (*Il.* 24.24), indulgent to thieves: they may even invoke his aid when stealing (Hipponax, frr. 3a, 32 West). A god naturally favours those like himself, and they receive from the god what he himself excels in: cf. the relationship between Odysseus and Athene, Paris and Aphrodite, Pandarus and Apollo. See also Hes. *WD* 78, where Hermes gives to Pandora, the first woman, 'lies and wily words and a thieving character' (cf. 67).

Later authors such as Ovid, *Met.* 11.312 follow Hesiod (394n.) and make Hermes Autolycus' father.

397–8 On the principle of *do ut des* see 365–8n.

400–12 See 384–5n.

401 The scholia refer to an alternative version of this line, giving the name Anticleia in place of Eurycleia. The reading has no real authority, but does interestingly suggest that at least one ancient reader was struck by the prominence of the nurse in place of the mother in this scene (cf. 357n.).

404 πολυάρητος 'much prayed-for'; because the line of Odysseus was not favoured with many male offspring: Telemachus is an only son of an only son of an only son (16.117–20). Is Eurycleia actually hinting at a possible name for the boy? (The name is found in later inscriptions: see Richardson on *Homeric hymn to Demeter* 220, and cf. Polyeuktos, or Arete.)

406–9 The naming of Odysseus. Significant names are common in Homer and in Greek literature generally, e.g. Prometheus ('Foresighted'), Pandora (interpreted by Hesiod explicitly as 'she who has gifts from all the gods': but see West on Hes. *WD* 81), Calypso ('concealer'), Antinous ('contrary', 'hostile'), Noemon son of Phronios (4.630, 'Thoughtful son of Sensible'!), Scylla (cf. σκύλαξ 'puppy' or 'she-pup': the connection is made at 12.85–6), or the names of the seafaring Phaeacian youths listed at 8.111–17. Even names which are not transparently meaningful may be given an etymology or used in a punning way in a suitable context: thus Pentheus calls to mind πένθος ('sorrow') in Eur. *Ba.* 367, 508; for more examples see L. P. Rank, *Etymologiseerung*; H. von Kamptz, *Homerische Personennamen* (Göttingen 1982); M. Griffith, *H.S.C.Ph.* 82 (1978) 83–6.

Although bearing an unlucky or potentially sinister name does not, even in myth, predetermine one's future, it is obviously tempting fate to give a child such a name, and Autolycus' choice seems at best mischievous. The name is here derived from ὀδύσσομαι 'to be angry with or against', but the participle used in 407 could be middle ('since I have come here after cherishing anger against many') or passive ('after having been the object of many people's anger'). Both would suit different aspects of Odysseus' career. The poet plays on the etymology elsewhere in the *Odyssey*: see 1.62, 5.340, 423, 19.275. A different verbal link, with ὀδύρομαι ('grieve'), may be glanced at in 1.55; cf. 265–7n.. In all these cases, as in the present passage, the word-play is meant to draw attention to the many hardships and conflicts which Odysseus, the 'much-enduring' hero, must undergo. See also W. B. Stanford, *C.P.* 47 (1952) 209–13.

Cf. Sophocles, fr. 965 Radt (Odysseus speaking): ὀρθῶς δ᾽ Ὀδυσσεύς εἰμ᾽ ἐπώνυμος κακῶν · | πολλοὶ γὰρ ὠδύσαντο δυσμενεῖς ἐμοί.

406 Nominative is used for vocative where two people are simultaneously addressed (L. R. Palmer, in Wace and Stubbings, *Companion* 129).

409 ἐγώ: the verb of which this is the subject is delayed for a few lines (412 ἐγὼ δώσω).

410 ἡβήσας 'when he is a young man': the first hint that the hunting expedition which follows has something of the nature of a *rite de passage*, a transitional ritual between youth and manhood, literally a 'blooding'. Odysseus is to leave his homeland, to go on a journey, to enter the wilder and more dangerous world of his mother's relatives on Mt Parnassus, and to prove himself in combat in this environment. For this aspect of hunting in a number of Greek myths see P. Vidal-Naquet, *The black hunter* (Eng. tr., Johns Hopkins 1986), esp. 85–156; J.-L. Durand and A. Schnapp, in *A city of images*, ed. C. Bérard and others (Eng. tr., Princeton, N.J. 1989) 53–70, with illustrations. It fits this interpretation that a number of phrases in the description of the fight are drawn from standard (Iliadic) battle-diction; for the audience, this description serves as a reminder of martial epic; for Odysseus, as a preparation for life as a warrior. Cf. 390–1n. We should note, however, that in the text as it stands the initial purpose of Odysseus' journey to Parnassus is not to hunt (nor does Autolycus mention this aspect of the proposed visit), but to obtain gifts from his maternal relatives. It is possible that gift-exchange rather than hunting is the underlying institution.

Both the naming of the boy by his maternal grandfather, and the 'initiatory' period with his grandfather and uncles, seem to assume a special relationship with the mother's side of the family. This is discussed by J. Bremmer, *Z.P.E.* 50 (1983) 173–86, who hypothesises that a custom of 'fostering' children with the mother's father may underlie this and similar myths.

412 χαίροντ᾽: cf. 461, 463, and in general 390–1n. above.

The papyrus of this passage (cited in 384–5n.) has a fragment of an additional line after the conclusion of Autolycus' speech. The line concluded with the words ἵκετο μέτρον and presumably referred to Odysseus' reaching the age of youthful vigour (cf. 4.688, 11.317, 18.217 and 19.532). That is, it served to introduce the next episode rather than extending the scene in which the child receives his name.

413 δῶρα: the boy Odysseus, like the man, relishes the thought of accumulating gifts! Cf. 185n.

416 Ἀμφιθέη: named only here in the *Odyssey*. The same name is found elsewhere of other mythological figures. We might expect the wife of Autolycus and mother of Anticleia to have more of a personality, but there seem to be no other stories about her.

περιφῦσ': nominative feminine aorist participle from περιφύω, lit. 'grow around', hence 'to embrace or hold tightly'. The main verb of the sentence is κύσσε in the next line.

420–5 For the ritual of sacrifice see 198n. Festivity, and 'safe', ritualised killing in a social context, precede violent and perilous killing in the hunt.

The lines used to describe the sacrifice and its aftermath (421–7) are heavily formulaic. This is one of the most frequent and unvarying 'typical scenes' in Homeric epic: see W. Arend, *Die typischen Scenen bei Homer* (Berlin 1933) 64–78.

421 ἀμφί θ' ἔπον: tmesis; 'and they got busy with it'.

425 δαιτὸς ἐΐσης 'the feast in which all equally shared'. On the importance of equal shares in Homer see 20.282n.

428–66 The hunt. See further F. H. Stubbings, in Wace and Stubbings, *Companion* 526; D. B. Hull, *Hounds and hunting in ancient Greece* (Chicago 1964). For a simile describing boar-hunting, see *Il.* 13.470–5 (but lions and wolves are much more common).

429 βάν: 3 pl. aorist indicative of βαίνω 'go'.

433–4 = *Iliad* 7.421–2. Some editors delete the second line here, but there is no real objection to its presence.

435 ἐπακτῆρες 'hunters' or 'beaters', going in advance of the heroes themselves. They are referred to again in 444–5. Cf. *Il.* 17.135 (simile).

439–43 The description of the boar's lair is similar to 5.478–83, the passage in which Odysseus finds shelter amongst the olive-bushes on the shore of Scheria, just after he has escaped from the sea. Lines 440–2 = 5.478–80 with only tiny variations; 443 is similarly close to 5.483. It is difficult to see what, if any, significance this has. In book 5 Odys-

seus, who has narrowly escaped destruction at sea, is reduced to the
level of a beast seeking primitive shelter (though the reference to the
thicket combining wild and cultivated olives (5.477) *may* hint at a tran-
sition from the wildness of the ocean to a civilised community). But the
desperate condition of Odysseus in book 5 is clear without reference to
book 19, and when we come to read book 19 itself, it may be far-fetched
to compare the savage but doomed boar, here slain by the youthful
Odysseus, with the older Odysseus who finds a similar lair but emerges
to survival and eventual triumph. A casual reuse of formulae is the
simpler explanation.

440 τήν refers of course to the λόχμη, not to the boar, which is male
(439 μέγας).

δίάη: 3 sing. imperfect of διάημι, 'blow through'.

ἀέντων: agreeing with ἀνέμων; genitive plural of ἀείς, present parti-
ciple of the defective verb ἄημι 'blow'. 'Neither the strength of the
moist-blowing winds penetrated that grove, nor . . .' ὑγρόν is the ad-
verbial use of the neuter adjective.

442 περάασκε: 3 sing. past iterative of περάω 'make one's way': 'nor
did the rain ever penetrate right through'.

443 ἤλιθα strengthens πολλή: 'a very great scattering of leaves'.

450 διήφυσε: 3 sing. aorist of διαφύσσω, which normally means
'draw off', e.g. wine. Here it must mean 'ripped through', 'tore open'.
Cf. Latin *haurio* (*Oxford Latin Dictionary* s.v. 2–3).

451 λικριφίς 'crosswise', 'sideways'; cf. *Il.* 14.463, of a similar nar-
row escape in human combat. For other similarities to Iliadic combat-
scenes see next n.; also 452 ~ *Il.* 5.98; 453 ~ *Il.* 11.253.

οὐδ' is adversative: 'but it did not reach . . .'

454 = *Il.* 16.469 (the death of Patroclus' mortal horse Pedasos, slain
by Sarpedon).

456 ἀμύμονος ἀντιθέοιο: double adjectives of praise, because Odys-
seus has shown himself a man, and has been 'blooded'.

457 ἐπαοιδῆι 'incantation' or sung spell. The word occurs nowhere
else in Homer, but the term and the idea are common in magical con-
texts in later literature: e.g. Pindar, *Pythian* 3.51 (on the divine healer
Asclepius); Virg. *Aen.* 7.757; see further W. Burkert, *Rh.M.* 105 (1962)
36–55, esp. 40; R. Pfister, *RE* Suppl. IV 324–44. It may not be neces-
sary, however, to see this as *magical* incantation; in the more everyday
setting of the battlefield, soothing words are used as part of the regular

healing process when Patroclus is looking after the wounded Eurypylus
(*Il.* 15.393 ἧστό τε καὶ τὸν ἔτερπε λόγοις, ἐπὶ δ᾽ ἕλκεϊ λυγρῷ | φάρμακ᾽
ἀκέσματ᾽ ἔπασσε . . .).

461 χαίροντα φίλως χαίροντες: for the stress on mutual pleasure
(which the alternative readings would not emphasise), cf. 17.83. For
the significance of this detail see 390–1, 471 nn.

463–4 'they asked him everything, as to the wound, what had hap-
pened to him [lit. what he has suffered]'. The sense is complete by the
end of 464, and the next few words add more precision.

464 εὖ κατέλεξεν: another feature of Odysseus' adult character is
anticipated, his skill as a story-teller, almost a poet (cf. 203n.).

465–6 These lines are close to, but not identical to, 393–4, the lines
which initiated the digression. This device of ring-composition is an
obvious way to make clear the divisions and direction of the narrative.
Cf. 51–2n.

467 καταπρηνέσσι 'downturned', i.e. with the flat of her hand. The
added detail gives a clear picture of her hands working their way along
his leg, washing and rubbing until she suddenly feels the scar. The
whole passage from 467–73 is marvellously vivid, with fast movement,
sudden noise of metal and water (469, 470), and three clauses describ-
ing the nurse's overwhelming emotional response to her discovery. The
fast accumulation of clauses changes the pace completely after the lei-
sured conclusion to the digression: the nurse's instant reaction reminds
us that the whole scar-narrative has filled only a split second of 'real'
time.

468 προέηκε φέρεσθαι 'let go his foot to fall', that is, so that it fell to
the ground of its own weight. προέηκε is 3 sing. aorist from προΐημι
'send forth'. Cf. the use of the infinitive after verbs such as πέμπω.

471 χάρμα καὶ ἄλγος: the emotions of the nurse as she recognises the
scar are to be contrasted with the simpler narrative of the digression
(joy at 412, 461, 463). Her delight is mixed with pain: grief at Odys-
seus' ragged condition and fear for his safety. For such mixed emotions
in recognition-scenes cf. 22.500–1, 23.210–12, 231–40, Eur. *IT* 832,
Helen 625–97, esp. 644, 648–9.

472 πλῆσθεν: 3 pl. aorist passive from πίμπλημι 'to fill'.

473 ἀψαμένη δὲ γενείου: to clasp the beard or (as here) the chin is a
gesture of respect or supplication (on which see esp. J. Gould, *J.H.S.* 93
(1973) 74–103) – here rather the former. Paradoxically, it is the mas-

ter who is in the slave's power. This is a gesture of devotion and esteem, but Odysseus responds with a gesture of violent and threatening constraint (479–81).

474–5 φίλον τέκος ... ἄνακτ' ἐμὸν: the phrasing helps us grasp their relationship: Eurycleia's devotion to Odysseus combines quasi-maternal love and a servant's loyalty.

477 πεφραδέειν: 'reduplicated' (i.e. with extra augmentation at the start of the word) infinitive from φράζω 'to tell'.

478–9 Penelope's enforced inattention and Athene's decisive move to distract her are crucial to the question whether she recognises or suspects the identity of Odysseus in this book: see Introd. 3(c).

480 ἐπιμασσάμενος: aor. participle from ἐπιμαίομαι 'to handle', 'touch', 'grasp'. Cf. 468 of Eurycleia. Here the meaning is more forceful: in 468 'she recognised him as she handled him', here 'feeling for her throat he grasped it with his right hand'. χείρ' is elided from χειρί.

481 ἔθεν ἄσσον 'close to him'. ἄσσον is treated as if it were a preposition taking the genitive: cf. *Il.* 14.247, etc.

482 There is a contrast between ὀλέσαι and ἔτρεφες: you nurtured me, gave me life, so why are you trying to destroy me?

483 τῶι σῶι ἐπὶ μαζῶι: Eurycleia was Odysseus' wet-nurse; cf. Cilissa in Aesch. *Choephori* 749–50. This was not invariable practice for the heroic age: contrast Hecuba and Hector (*Il.* 22.83).

488–90 There is of course an ellipse here: 'I shall not hold back from slaying even you, my nurse (*if* you do not obey me and keep silent about my return).'

490 κτείνωμι: Odysseus has already determined that the wicked maids such as Melantho must be punished by death. See 22.417–73 for the execution (in a way, a sequel to this scene, as Odysseus there asks Eurycleia for the information which he declines here, 500–2). The eventual killing of the maids (and the mutilation of Melanthius which follows) is one of the scenes in Homer most repulsive to modern taste, but it is unlikely that the original audience, or the poet himself, felt any qualms about the treatment the disloyal slaves receive: they were openly siding with the suitors against their mistress and Telemachus; their behaviour is by any standards aggressive and callous; like the suitors, they receive a number of warnings; and much emphasis is laid on the affection with which Penelope had brought up Melantho and hence on her ingratitude (18.321–5). For condemnation of faithless servants in general see 17.320–3 (Eumaeus).

493–4 Again the themes of secrecy and self-restraint (see 42 and 210 nn.). Eurycleia's determination is as firm as her master's (the comparison with 'rock or iron' in 494 recalls the simile used of Odysseus at 211).

493 μένος: her strength of will contrasts with her physical weakness (356).

500–2 Odysseus' refusal to listen now to Eurycleia's talk of the women does not preclude his applying to her for the information in 22.417–18. In fact he has no further direct exchanges with the maids, though 501 might lead us to expect further testing (misdirection?); but at the opening of book 20 he watches them leave the halls to go and sleep with the suitors. Probably the main reason for his rejecting Eurycleia's help here is that Odysseus must remain the figure of authority, the one in charge.

501 εἴσομ': future with middle form from οἶδα 'to know' (see Cunliffe s.v. εἴδω (c)).

502 ἐπίτρεψον δὲ θεοῖσιν: Odysseus of course knows that he has divine support; and in the later scene with Eurycleia after the slaughter he attributes his victory to divine punishment of the wicked (22.411–16). Cf. also 22.288–9.

503–4 There is a curious interlude here, as Odysseus and Penelope are left alone together (perhaps with a few nameless maids, cf. 601) while the nurse fetches fresh water. Plainly, they do not converse: we must be intended to assume that Athene is still 'turning her thoughts away' (see 479). Such suspension of action is not uncommon in Homer: see Fenik, *Studies* 61–71 for this and other examples. In this case, however, the narrator minimises the oddity by making us think of Eurycleia's actions rather than anybody else's.

506–7 These lines reverse Odysseus' actions in 388–91, and so conclude the episode of the scar.

508–604 In the last phase of the book Penelope takes the initiative, first restating her determination to remarry and recalling the reasons already given, then describing a dream which Odysseus interprets favourably, and finally proposing the test of the bow, which Odysseus approves. On the psychology of Penelope's continued pessimism in the face of so much encouraging news and a favourable dream, see Introd. 3(c).

509 The 'question' is in fact deferred till 535, where Penelope asks her husband to interpret a dream she has had. But the digression on her unhappy nights, prompted by the remark in 510 that it will soon be

time to sleep, includes much that is relevant to her situation and to the
decisions which the dream may influence.

510 γάρ explains τυτθόν in the preceding line: it will be a short
question, because the time for sleep is near.

510–11 ἔσσεται . . . | ὅν τινά γ' ὕπνος ἕλοι 'there will be . . . [sc. for
anyone], at least (γε), whom sweet sleep may take hold of, for all his
cares' (but not for me). 'The choice of the Optative shows want of con-
fident expectation of the result intended' (Monro, *Grammar* §304(a)).

513 On 'delighting in grief' cf. 213n.

517 This is a very weighty line, four long words each with some
reference to her pain and grief.

518–24 The simile/myth of the nightingale, Pandareos' daughter.
Similes comparing human characters and their experiences to mythical
tales are rare in Homer; normally the similes move us into a more
everyday and unheroic world. *Iliad* 13.298–305 (Meriones and Ido-
meneus compared with Ares entering battle) is one exceptional in-
stance (see further Introd. 4(d)). It is especially unusual for a mythical
simile to be used by a character rather than the poet. Here the compar-
ison, though formally a simile, borders on the more extended form of
mythological paradigm, and the closely connected passage in 20.66–78
(Penelope's prayer to Artemis) crosses the boundary-line.

The myth of the nightingale is first referred to here; in later literature
it takes several forms. The one which became canonical (especially
through Ovid) is the Attic version which marries Procne, daughter of
Pandion, to Tereus of Thrace and makes her child-killing deliberate
and horrifying. According to the version used here (explained by the
ancient scholia), Aedon, daughter of Pandareos king of Crete, marries
Zethus, king of Thebes, tries to kill one of the offspring of her sister-in-
law, Niobe, out of jealousy, but instead accidentally (523 δι' ἀφραδίας)
kills their own son Itylus (usually called Itys). She is subsequently
transformed into a nightingale, who perpetually mourns her child: the
bird's cry is taken by the poets to be a constant calling of his name.

Cf. West on Hes. *WD* 568; Aesch. *Agam.* 1140–5; Thuc. 2.29.3;
[Apollod.] *Bibl.* 3.14.8; Ovid, *Met.* 6.424–674. On the nightingale see
D'Arcy W. Thompson, *Glossary of Greek birds* (Oxford 1895, 2nd edn
1936) 16–22.

The immediate point of comparison is between the shifting notes of
the nightingale's warbling song (521) and the turning of Penelope's

thoughts to and fro in search of a solution to her problem (524). Secondary points of contact between narrative and simile are (a) the grief and deprivation of both women: Aedon has lost her son, Penelope her husband; (b) the death of a son: Aedon slew her son unwittingly, whereas Penelope fears that inaction on her part may cause Telemachus' death (522 ∼ 525?).

518–19 ἀηδών | . . . ἀείδησιν: for the etymological pun cf. Eur. *Helen* 1109–10, Theoc. 12.6–7 (Rank, *Etymologiseerung* 35).

518 χλωρηῖς: meaning obscure, but possibly a colour-term. See E. Irwin, *Colour terms in Greek poetry* (Toronto 1974) 68–73. In her discussion of the commoner adjective χλωρός she shows that it is often associated with moisture, illness or fear: hence 'pale' seems apt for that word. χλωρηῖς is rarer and less easy to interpret: most commentators have accepted 'green', giving the bird the colour of its surroundings (as if 'amid green leaves'). Irwin proposes 'throbbing', with reference to the nightingale's throat as she sings. (Usage elsewhere is unhelpful: Adesp. *PMG* 964b simply repeats Homer's phrase; Simonides, *PMG* 586.2 looks like misunderstanding of Homer; Bacchyl. 5.172 surely means 'white-necked', *pace* Irwin.)

521 πολυηχέα ('far-echoing') or πολυδευκέα ('sweet'?)? Cf. van der Valk, *Textual criticism* 82–3, preferring the former. The latter is not mentioned by the scholia.

524 ὀρώρεται: 3 sing. perfect middle from ὄρνυμι. In the active this verb means 'to stir', 'rouse', 'raise'; in the middle, 'to be stirred up', 'rise'. 'Thus my heart is moved in different ways, this way and that . . .'

525 μένω . . . φυλάσσω: both subjunctives, indicating deliberation: 'am I to . . .?' (Goodwin, *Greek grammar* §1358).

ἔμπεδα πάντα: cf. 23.203, 206 (Introd. 1 (*b*) p. 13).

526 δμωιάς (female slaves), not δμῶας (male slaves or serfs), should be read, if the line is to be retained at all. But see the discussion by W. K. Lacey, *C.R.* 16 (1966) 1–2, who argues for its deletion as a gloss on πάντα in 525. He insists that by the conventions of Homeric marriage, any slaves brought by Penelope as part of her dowry would become the property of her husband's household; Penelope therefore could not take them with her when she left. On the problem of the Homeric 'dowry' see 20.341–2n.

527 = 16.75. The combination of reverence for her husband's bed (her sense of duty and obligation) and respect for what is said by the people (i.e. how her behaviour will *look*) shows that Homeric society combines elements of 'guilt-culture' and 'shame-culture': see further 2.130–7, 23.148–51, Macleod on *Il.* 24.435; K. J. Dover, *Greek popular morality* (Oxford 1974) 226–42, with further bibl.

δήμοιό τε φῆμιν: cf. 6.273–88, 14.239, 21.323, 24.201; West on Hes. *WD* 760–1.

528 ἄριστος 'best' in social rather than moral terms: i.e. 'most distinguished', almost 'most eligible'. Cf. 15.521, where Telemachus speaks of Eurymachus as by far the ἄριστος of the Ithacans, though he undoubtedly sees through his hypocritical façade; also 20.335. There are, however, some more decent or virtuous suitors, especially Amphinomus (20.240–7n.) and Leiodes (21.144–7, 22.310–29).

529 ἔδνα 'marriage-gifts'. The nature of dowries or marriage-gifts in Homer has been a prominent part of arguments as to the historical reality (or realistic presentation) of Homeric society. See 20.289, 335, and 341–2, with n.

530–4 Cf. 159–61, with notes.

535–58 The dream and its interpretation. This passage has been much discussed, not least because it is the only 'symbolic' dream in Homer; for the most part Homeric dreams are highly formalised, involving a single figure, usually divine, who advises or comforts the sleeper as a waking companion might do (cf. Dodds, *The Greeks and the irrational* 104–8). Symbolic dreams, often obscure to the sleeper, are more common in later poetry: e.g. Aesch. *Pers.* 181–200, Moschus, *Europa* 8–15, Virg. *Aen.* 4.465–73 (cf. Pease's commentary on 465 for more examples). This dream explains itself: the geese are the suitors, the eagle Odysseus. More puzzling is the attitude of Penelope: in 537 she 'rejoices' as she watches the geese eating, and in 541–3 she weeps at their slaughter. Why, if she so detests the suitors? Dodds, 123 n. 21, interpreted the conflict as 'inversion of affect', a Freudian concept according to which real-life response is the reverse of the dream-response, but this approach seems too dependent on modern theory. Others have tried to argue that Penelope secretly (subconsciously?) desires the suitors' presence and admiration (e.g. G. Devereux, *Psychological Quarterly* 26 (1957) 378–86; A. V. Rankin, *Helikon* 2 (1962) 617–24; N. Felson-Rubin in Bremer et al., *Homer: beyond oral poetry* 61–83). But is there quite so striking a discrepancy as scholars have maintained? Penelope grieves while she thinks the dead geese are themselves, but says nothing of any distress after the eagle explains what their death symbolises (Rankin 619 arbitrarily supposes that Penelope is aware of these identifications throughout her dream. This hardly suits the similarity to scenes in which bird omens are interpreted in waking life). Lines 541–3 present an image of her ignorance; as in the narrative, there is a gap between her perception of the situation and the reality. Felson-Rubin 82 n. 34 points to the unresolved ambiguity in 552–3: when Penelope looks round and sees the 'geese' still alive, does this mean the real geese or the suitors they represent? Felson-Rubin sees this as 'provocatively enigmatic' on Homer's part; but the important point is surely that nothing has changed for Penelope: she wakes to the same conditions, and finds 'it was only a dream'.

535 ὑπόκριναι καὶ ἄκουσον: the expression is an example of ὕστερον πρότερον ('back to front'; cf. 316), as Odysseus must listen to the dream before he can interpret it. For interpreters of dreams in Homer see *Iliad* 1.63, 5.148–51; see further E. R. Dodds, *The Greeks and the irrational* ch. 4 and *The ancient concept of progress* (Oxford 1973) ch. 10.

538 αἰετός: see D'Arcy W. Thompson, *Glossary of Greek birds* (Oxford 1895, 2nd edn 1936) 1–10. The eagle makes frequent appearances in similes and omens in both poems: in the *Odyssey* see esp. 15.160–81 (Helen interprets an omen), 20.240–47 (an eagle-omen dissuades the suitors from further plotting), 24.538 (Odysseus attacking the rebellious Ithacans is compared with an eagle, in the manner of the *Iliad*). As king of the birds it is the bird of Zeus (cf. *Il.* 24.315–16, Aesch. *Ag.* 114–15), and so connotes kingship and victory. On bird-similes in the poem see Moulton, *Similes* 135–9.

542 Ἀχαιαί: not merely servants, but Penelope's equals among the noblewomen of Greece.

545 φωνῆι δὲ βροτέηι: for animals with human powers of speech in the narrative proper cf. *Iliad* 19.404–18 (Achilles' horse is briefly granted speech by divine intervention). In dreams the rules are more relaxed.

κατερήτυε 'he restrained'.

547 ὄναρ . . . ὕπαρ '(this is) not a dream, but true vision'. Cf. 20.90.

549 ἦα: 1 sing. imperfect from εἰμί 'I am'. Cf. 19.19.

550 ἐφήσω: the shift into the future tense suits the real-life situation, in which the suitors still live.

556 ἄλληι ἀποκλίναντ' 'bending it (the dream) in a different direction'. ἀποκλίναντα is in the accusative and infinitive construction introduced by οὔ πως ἔστιν in the previous line: 'it is in no way possible (for anyone) to interpret the dream twisting it to mean anything else'.

558a–b In some MSS two additional lines follow 558: μνηστήρων, οἳ δῶμα κατ' ἀντιθέου Ὀδυσῆος | ἀνέρας ὑβρίζοντες ἀτάσθαλα μηχανόωνται. These lines reappear as 20.369–70 (reading μηχανάασθε in the second line). The lines are unduly wordy here, and the case for including them in the text is weak.

560–1 For deceptive dreams see *Iliad* 2.1–36, where Zeus sends a dream to Agamemnon promising imminent victory, a trick which results in the king's humiliation. In the *Odyssey* dreams are often misleading or partially true rather than simply false (e.g. 4.835–7, where the dream withholds information from Penelope; 15.10–42, where Athene's account of Penelope is unfair, but there is good reason for Telemachus to return home as swiftly as possible; 20.88–94 with nn.). The dream Penelope describes is of course both true and encouraging, but her pessimism does not allow her to accept this: cf. Eur. *Iph. Taur.* 42–58, where Iphigenia misinterprets an auspicious dream as meaning that Orestes is dead.

561 πάντα: neuter plural, accusative of respect, 'in all things', 'in every case'.

562–7 The Gates of Sleep are most famous through Virgil's mysterious imitation (*Aen.* 6.893–8), but they were already proverbial before his day: see Pl. *Charmides* 173a, anon. *A.P.* 7.42.1–2, Hor. *Odes* 3.27.39–42. See further E. L. Highbarger, *The gates of dreams* (Baltimore 1940), esp. ch. 4; Rank, *Etymologiseerung* 104–8.

564–5 ἐλέφαντος, | . . . ἐλεφαίρονται 'those which come through the polished ivory, they are the ones which deceive, bringing words that are unfulfilled'. There is an etymological pun connecting ἐλέφας ('ivory') and ἐλεφαίρομαι ('deceive' or 'do harm to': cf. *Il.* 23.388, Hes. *Th.* 330); similarly and even less plausibly κέρας ('horn') and κραίνω ('fulfil') are implicitly connected. For such word-play see W. B. Stanford, *Ambiguity in Greek literature* (Oxford 1939) 98–9; Fehling, *Wiederholungsfiguren* 260–3, who cites e.g. 12.104–6 (Charybdis connected with ῥοιβδέω 'to swallow down'). Cf. 406–9n. on significant names.

The detail with which the poet makes Penelope explain the two Gates suggests that the idea is an invention for this context. Certainly it appears nowhere else in Homer, not even in the episode describing the false dream Zeus sends to Agamemnon (560–1n.). On the other hand, at 4.808–9 Penelope is described as slumbering softly 'at/in the gates of dreams', lines which may employ a simpler and more traditional idea. See Highbarger (562–7n.).

A. Amory, *Y.C.S.* 20 (1966) 3–57 discusses the references to horn and ivory and relates this passage to others in the poem, especially 19.211. Many of the conclusions she draws seem over-subtle, and the paper received a hostile response from A. B. Lord, *H.S.C.P.* 72 (1968) 34–46: see Amory's reply in *C.Q.* 21 (1971) 1–15.

571 εἶσι: 3 sing. of εἶμι 'I shall go'; here 'come' is more idiomatic in English: 'this dawn/day that is coming will be the ill-omened dawn that will separate me from Odysseus' house.'

572–81 The contest. 'For now I shall set forth a contest, (namely) the axes, which he used to set out in a line in his halls, like ship-props, twelve in number altogether. Then standing a considerable distance back he would shoot an arrow through' (572–5). Through what? is the natural question, and on this the nature of the test depends. The view that Odysseus fires an arrow with such violence that it shatters 12 axe-heads and passes through all of them is generally rejected as being a patent physical impossibility, the stuff of fairy-tales rather than 'real-istic' epic. The other possibility seems to be that the axe-heads, or (more probably, in view of 21.421–2) the handles, have some kind of hole, an aperture large enough for an arrow to pass through each in turn. See Page's discussion cited below, with illustrations. Page (103) also briefly considers the idea that the poet has inherited the language concerning the exploit, without fully understanding what he is describ-ing, a view which perhaps deserves more consideration than it has re-ceived. See further 21.73–6, in which Penelope proposes the test to the suitors, 21.118–23 (Telemachus sets out the axes), 21.420–3 (Odysseus accomplishes the feat). In the event much more is made of the momen-tous task of stringing the bow itself; strength becomes more important than skill (as also in *Od.* 8.186–98).

See esp. D. L. Page, *Folk-Tales in Homer's Odyssey*, Appendix, 95–113. Also F. H. Stubbings, in Wace and Stubbings, *Companion* 534; P. Brain and D. D. Skinner, *G.&R.* 25 (1978) 55–8 (reporting a test and endors-ing Page's view); P. Jones, *Companion ad loc.* (pp. 183–5); Fernández-Galiano, in the Italian commentary on the *Odyssey*, VI (Rome 1986) xi–xxv. Page's discussion also quotes the impressive parallels to this

contest in the Sanskrit epics, the *Mahābhārata* and the *Rāmāyaṇa*: see
further Stith Thompson, *Motif index* H 331; V. Zhirmansky, *Proc. Brit.
Acad.* 52 (1966) 267–86.

For other contests to win a bride compare the wooing of Helen (first
in Hes. frr. 200–4 M–W); Pind. *Pythian* 9.111–18, and in historical
times the marriage of Cleisthenes of Sicyon's daughter Agariste (Hdt.
6.126–30). See further M. W. Edwards in Bremer et al., *Homer: beyond
oral poetry* 60 n. 13.

577 βιόν: the bow is fetched by Penelope at the opening of book 21,
and its history described by the poet in detail at 21.11–41. On the
ambiguity of the bow as a weapon (it is associated with deception and
ambush, because it can be used from a safe distance, rather than in
hand-to-hand combat), see *Iliad* 4.242, 11.385, Aesch. *Pers.* 239–40,
Soph. *Ajax* 1120–3, Eur. *Heracl.* 157–64, with Bond's notes; Lucan
8.385.

580 The line spent describing the house longingly is a way of pre-
senting the attachment Penelope feels for it, the lingering desire to
remain there. Its structure follows the so-called 'law of increasing mem-
bers', a climactic device whereby each phrase is longer and more em-
phatic than the one preceding. Cf. *Il.* 2.325 (of the omen portending
the Greeks' eventual triumph) ὄψιμον, ὀψιτέλεστον, ὅου κλέος οὔ ποτ'
ὀλεῖται; 20.232; 1.145 (where a further climax follows in the next line);
E. Fraenkel, *Horace* (Oxford 1957) 351n.; L. P. Wilkinson, *Golden Latin
artistry* (Cambridge 1963) 175–6; G. S. Kirk's commentary on *Iliad* 1–4
(Cambridge 1985), refs. in his index s.v. 'rising threefolder'.

581 (= 21.79) 'which one day I think I shall remember even in
my dreams'. The pathos of this conclusion is hard to parallel even in
Homer; at the very moment in which Penelope resolves that she must
leave her home, she foresees a future in which she will long for it and
still remember it with love and devotion. Cf. Sappho 16.15–20, 94.6–
29 L–P, for comparable treatment of the theme of memory.

585–7 The prophecy is two-sided: (a) Odysseus will return before
the contest can reach its conclusion; and (b) the suitors will *never* be
able to string and shoot the bow, however long his return is delayed.

The poet never tells us explicitly when the hero conceives his plan to
use the contest of the bow as the occasion and means for destroying his
enemies, but in view of this speech, it seems natural to suppose that he
forms this design at once. Some have found his subsequent despondency

and perplexity in the opening scene of book 20 surprising: why is he so worried there after being so confident here? There is, however, no inconsistency: it is natural (and dramatically effective) for Odysseus, once alone, to reflect on the remaining difficulties before him, and the emphasis in book 20 is laid more on the number of enemies involved, and on the consequences of his victory (20.30, 39–43).

585–6 πρὶν ... | πρίν 'Sooner will the cunning Odysseus return here, before these men ...' The first use of the word is adverbial ('sooner'), the second is as a conjunction introducing an accusative + infinitive clause (τούτους ... ἐντανύσαι διοϊστεῦσαί τε), which embraces a subordinate participial clause (τόδε ... ἀμφαφόωντας, with ἀμφαφόωντας agreeing with τούτους).

589–90 Penelope's delight in the stranger's company is like the pleasure felt by the Phaeacians (11.333–4, 373–6) and by Eumaeus (17.513–21).

590 τέρπειν: again Odysseus is associated with the pleasure poetry brings: cf. Phemius Terpiades, and 203n.

592 τοι: gnomic (Denniston, *GP* 543). Cf. 43.

ἑκάστωι: here neuter rather than masculine: 'the immortals have laid down a place (or proper portion, quantity) for everything for mortals upon the grain-bearing earth'.

596 πεφυρμένη: feminine nominative singular of the perfect participle passive from φύρω 'moisten', 'stain'.

597 = 260; see n. on that line.

599 Penelope here politely responds to the guest's refusal of luxury at 340–2.

There is a change of construction: στορέσας is aorist participle, nominative sing. masc. (agreeing with Odysseus), while θέντων is 3 pl. aor. imperative from τίθημι, the subject being the servants: 'or else let them lay you a bed'.

600–4 These lines are formulaic: 600–1 = 18.206–7, 602–4 = 1.362–4 = 21.356–8, 603–4 = 16.450–1. The repetition is part of the poet's structural technique. In a series of scenes (books 1, 16, 17, 18, 19 and 21) Penelope descends to the hall and tries to intervene or participate in the action; at the end of all but the scene in book 17 (which does not involve the suitors) she withdraws to her chamber, usually after some rebuff or setback (as when in book 1 she is rebuked by Telemachus). Here there is no obvious setback, but the episode has passed without recognition, and although Penelope thinks she has tested and assured herself of her guest's *bona fides*, she has not; although she has tried to take a firm step with the decision to hold the contest, that contest will in fact be stage-managed by Odysseus. In book 21 she is to be dismissed by Telemachus again, for her own safety, but she does not understand his motives. It is only in book 23 that she herself will at last successfully take the initiative and show herself her husband's equal in cunning.

604 ἡδύν: Penelope herself gives an account of her sleep in 20.83–90 which makes it seem far from 'pleasant'. The line is, as already mentioned, formulaic, but there is no real contradiction. The poet wishes to contrast Penelope's peaceful sleep with Odysseus' restless and angry night (see the following scene); similarly in 20.55–60 the position is reversed, and Odysseus' ὕπνος ... λυσιμελής is juxtaposed with Penelope's tearful wakefulness. For another functional contradiction of this kind compare the end of *Iliad* 1 (Zeus and the rest all asleep) with the opening of book 2 (everyone asleep except Zeus); and see further C. M. Bowra, *Tradition and design in the Iliad* (Oxford 1930) 101–2.

Book 20

Although the closing lines of book 19 clearly end an episode, it is some-what artificial to separate book 20 from what follows (on the artifici-ality of the book-divisions see Intr. 1 (*b*), p. 8). From this point on all events in books 20 and 21 form a part of the preparation for the slaugh-ter in book 22. Nevertheless, the reappearance of Penelope, and the announcement of the contest, at the start of book 21 do mark an accel-eration of pace, and book 20 can be viewed as setting the stage and establishing once more the moral emphases of the conflict. Book 20 falls roughly into three phases: the night, the early morning (including the arrival of the suitors and the various supporting characters, such as Melanthius, Eumaeus and Philoetius (see 122–256n.)), and the feast-ing (lines 1–91, 92–247, 248–394 respectively). The night is marked by Odysseus' anxiety and loss of confidence; the following day, which begins with good omens, advances with increasingly positive signs of Odysseus' impending success: he is treated courteously and respectfully by the servants, and the attempts of the suitors to bully or assail him are fruitless. The authority and status of both Odysseus and Telemachus are still further enhanced in the later part of the book. By contrast, the deliberations of the suitors, who might still mount (however belatedly and outrageously) a direct assault upon Telemachus, come to nothing, as they cheerfully ignore the ominous sign of the eagle of Zeus (240–7n.). In the closing part of the book we are shown once again the suitors' imperviousness to warnings, in the haunting scene of Theoclymenus' prophecy. Throughout, the keynote is the suitors' hybristic folly (cf. 170, 370), as they ignore the warnings of the gods and mock or abuse men. In earlier scenes in books 17 and 18, the hero has already witnessed the wickedness of the suitors; now, on the day of his retribution, they wade still further into sin. The exceptionally stern and explicit moral comment by the narrator at the end of the book (394n.) makes plainer than ever before that their doom is sealed.

On the book in general, see Eisenberger, *Studien* 273–92; brief but helpful comments also in van der Valk, *Textual criticism* 212–15.

1–55 Odysseus' uneasy night. After the encounter with Penelope, Odysseus and his wife sleep separately, and both have restless and unhappy nights. Lines 1–55 (Odysseus) and 56–91 (Penelope) complement one another; and the two episodes are united at the end of the passage, where Penelope's strange sense that Odysseus has been with her is answered by Odysseus' momentary intuition that his wife may have recognised him (87–90, 93–4). The two scenes are also contrasted: Odysseus is visited and comforted by a goddess, whereas Penelope, though she prays to Artemis, receives no reply and feels no relief.

The first part of the episode, in which Odysseus lies awake, first angry and then despondent, shows us the hero alone for the first time (apart from momentary intervals such as 19.51–2) since his arrival in Ithaca. It is natural, and appropriate, that in such a position he should be plagued by doubts and by the pessimism we have seen so often in the first half of the poem. For a somewhat similar episode on the eve of a crisis see Shakespeare, *Henry V* iv.i.

The scene with Athene is closely related to their last long encounter in book 13, and should also be compared with the scene between Odysseus and Telemachus in book 16 (esp. 240–69). In book 13 they matched wits and she assured him of her support, which he gladly acknowledged (13.383–91, esp. 389–91: 'If you would stand at my side

as readily as you did then, grey-eyed one, I would do battle with three
hundred men with you as my ally'). In book 16 he spoke with this kind
of confidence to the more pessimistic Telemachus, citing Athene as his
helper (233, 259–61): 108 suitors, depressingly listed by Telemachus,
cause him no dismay when he is assured of Zeus and Athene as allies.
Here we see Odysseus' own renewed doubts calmed by the goddess's
more light-hearted confidence (note esp. 49–50, which caps 13.389–90
quoted above).

For slackening confidence in a mortal despite having received divine
assurances, cf. 15.300 (contrast 15.31–2, if genuine); Macleod on *Il.*
24.181–7.

The opening scene, and in particular the presentation of Odysseus'
indecision, are discussed by J. Russo, *Arion* 7 (1968) 275–95 (repr. in
German in *Homer*, ed. J. Latacz, *Wege der Forschung* 463, Darmstadt
1979, 403–27), and by J. F. Morris, *T.A.P.A.* 113 (1983) 39–54.

1 προδόμωι 'vestibule' or 'entrance hall'. It is appropriate that
Odysseus, at home but not recognised or accepted as master of the
house, should occupy a 'liminal' position. On the nature and scale
of the Homeric house there is a clear and sensible account by T. D.
Seymour, *Life in the Homeric age* (London 1907) ch. 6, though inevitably
this is dated in approach and especially in archaeological terms. For a
more up-to-date treatment, concentrating on the archaeological re-
mains, see H. Drerup, *Archaeologia Homerica* o (Göttingen 1969); also
the comments by S. West (Oxford *Odyssey*) on 1.103–4, Hainsworth on
6.303–4. The beggar Odysseus' admiring words at 17.264–71 make
clear that it is to be thought of as a majestic structure, bigger than the
normal house familiar to Homer's audience, but it is not in quite the
same class as the palaces of Menelaus and Alcinous (see 4.43–4, 7.81–
111). It is unlikely that the poet could have drawn a map of the whole
building, though a reasonably consistent picture may be deduced. At
the front there is an open court, the αὐλή, surrounded by walls and a
gate normally open; then comes the πρόδομος, after that the central
hall or μέγαρον in which most of the daytime action (especially feast-
ing) takes place. In a rather vague geographical relation to this are the
various private chambers (some, including Penelope's, upstairs), store
rooms and servants' quarters. The marital chamber of Odysseus and
Penelope, the literal and symbolic heart of the house, is built around an
olive tree carved and trimmed by the hero himself: this must be locked

away deep in the building, or Odysseus could have seen for himself that his bed had not been tampered with (see 23.177–206). But some features of the building are plainly introduced as needed, and perhaps invented *ad hoc*: e.g. the θόλος (small outhouse? rotunda?) in the courtyard, the site of the execution of the maids (22.442, etc.), or the mysterious ῥῶγες, 'clefts' or 'passage-ways' (22.143 only), through which Melanthius makes his way into the weapons-store.

More important than the physical layout is the emotional and thematic use the poet makes of these features. The half-way status of the πρόδομος and the centrality of the marital chamber have already been cited. The threshold (οὐδός) is another significant spot: see e.g. 17.339–41, where Odysseus lingers there awaiting his first reception on his return, and 22.2, where he takes up position there with the great bow, barring the route of escape.

2 κάμ = κατά, here contrasted with ὕπερθεν.

3 This line, like 250–3, casts doubt on the thesis of Vidal-Naquet, *The black hunter* 25, that the suitors do not sacrifice to the gods. So does the presence among them of a seer, Leiodes (see esp. 22.321–5). See further 14.28. But it is true that they do not pray to or invoke them: their religious observances are purely mechanical and devoid of the kind of piety which we witness in Nestor's Pylos and at Eumaeus' hut.

ἱρεύεσκον: frequentative ('they were constantly sacrificing'), like ἐμισγέσκοντο in 7.

Ἀχαιοί: cf. 19.151n.

6 ἐγρηγορόων 'wakeful', 'in a state of waking'. This is the only instance in Homer of this present participle cognate with ἐγείρω (which has pf. middle infinitive ἐγρήγορθαι, etc.).

ἐκ μεγάροιο: the women rendezvous with the suitors elsewhere (cf. 123n.); the latter have already returned to their homes (18.428), as is their normal practice at night (1.424).

γυναῖκες: on the infidelity of the maids see (besides the unpleasant figure of Melantho, who represents this category) 19.496–501, 22.417–73. Odysseus' anger is at their treachery, and has nothing to do with 'sexual jealousy' (Dimock, *Unity* 264).

7 πάρος περ 'before this, certainly'; 'a grim hint that this intercourse will not continue much longer' (Denniston, *GP* 482).

8 γέλω: their laughter is ironically inappropriate, like the suitors' mirth in a series of scenes (esp. 345–7 below: see 345–86n.).

10 A formulaic situation frequent in both poems: pondering two alternatives is the customary way in which Homer emphasises the difficulties of making a decision (cf. 4.117, 6.141, 10.50, 16.73, 17.235, 18.90, 22.333, 24.235). It is normally, as here, the second alternative which is adopted. (But at 17.235–8 both alternatives are rejected; at 4.120–2 the appearance of Helen forestalls Menelaus' decision.) In several of the passages cited the choice facing Odysseus is between open expression of his emotions and restraint or self-concealment: in book 10 he endures despite despair, rather than cast himself overboard after his men have opened the bag of winds; in book 18 he forces himself to strike Irus gently rather than pulverising him and arousing the suitors' suspicions; and so forth. Here the indecision is prolonged by a simile and a soliloquy, enhancing our sense of the difficulty Odysseus feels in suppressing his anger. The uncertainty of Odysseus is then developed, as he turns from one dilemma (should he slay the women, or refrain?) to another (how can he win his victory? how will he then cope with the consequences?). Finally, a divine intervention resolves his doubts.

On this as a typical scene or situation, see W. Arend, *Die typischen Scenen bei Homer* (Berlin 1933) 106–15; C. Voigt, *Überlegung und Entscheidung* (Berlin 1933); on the expansion and development of its typical features, see Russo and Morris (1–55n.).

11–12 τεύξειεν ... ἐῶι: these optatives in indirect speech are equivalent to subjunctives in direct speech, expressing the hero's deliberation (in direct speech the sentence would run 'am I to dash forth and bring death upon ... or should I allow ...?'). See Monro, *Grammar* §302.

12 ἐῶι: 3 sing. present optative of ἐάω 'allow'. On the use of the optative see preceding n.

ὑπερφιάλοισι: cf.291,and Parry, *MHV* 159.

13 ὕστατα καὶ πύματα: the same phrase is used in 4.685; cf. 20.116 πύματόν τε καὶ ὕστατον, also found in *Il.* 22.203 and *Homeric hymn to Hermes* 289.

ὑλάκτει 'barked', anticipating the simile which follows. So also at 19.204 τήκετο provides a 'cue' for the simile. (Imitations of this passage in Aeschylus are discussed by P. Mazon, *R.E.G.* 63 (1950) 11–19.)

14–16, 25–30 Two similes in quick succession, both of them somewhat unusual, the second much more so (cf. 22–30n.). Similes often 'cluster' at moments of special importance: see e.g. *Il.* 2.455–83, 17.735–61.

There is a reversal in the first simile: Odysseus, not the women, is compared to a bitch, but in his case it is a loyal and protective one. Similes describing animals protecting their young are common, but here the application is unusual: Odysseus is not wanting to protect the maids, but feels angry and possessive towards them: they correspond more to the unknown man at whom the bitch snarls. For comparable 'restructuring' of the simple or obvious analogy a simile might be expected to provide, cf. esp. *Il.* 22.93–6; 24.480–4, with Macleod's n.

G. P. Rose, *T.A.P.A.* 109 (1979) 215–30 tries to link this simile with earlier references to dogs in the poem, seeing these as forming a significant sequence; this analysis does not seem very persuasive to me.

14 βεβῶσα: feminine nominative singular of the perfect participle from βαίνω. This tense often has the sense 'to stand' (cf. LSJ s.v. A2), and here the verb should be taken closely with περί: 'taking position over her pups', 'bestriding'. Cf. *Il.* 17.6, 137, and Cunliffe s.v. βαίνω (1) (6).

16 The subject of ὑλάκτει is κραδίη, supplied from 13 above.

18–22 Soliloquy of this kind is not common in Homer, though the passage is clearly an extension of the battlefield monologues in which a warrior contemplates retreat but rejects the idea with the formulaic line 'But why has my *thumos* said such a thing to me?' (*Il.* 21.562 etc.; B. Fenik in *Homer: tradition and innovation*, ed. Fenik (Leiden 1978) 68–90). In later literature cf. esp. Eur. *Medea* 1056–80, 1242–6, parodied by Ar. *Ach.* 450, 480–9; W. Schadewaldt, *Monolog und Selbstgespräch* (Berlin 1926). Odysseus draws strength from his past experiences and successes (cf. the anticipated future satisfaction in 12.208–12). On the psychological conceptions here see S. Halliwell, in *Characterization and individuality in Greek literature*, ed. C. B. R Pelling (Oxford 1990) 36–42, rightly arguing against over-primitive views of Homer. See also R. W. Sharples, *G.&R.* 30 (1983) 1–7.

18 τέτλαθι: the theme of 'endurance' is extremely important in the *Odyssey*; it is particularly associated with the 'much-enduring' hero, but Telemachus too has to endure taunts and humiliation from the suitors, and Penelope must suffer from her husband's long absence and their odious attentions. Compare also the sufferings of other heroes, notably Menelaus, in returning home, and the sorrow they still endure even at home, after the losses of the war (esp. 3.103–17; 4.90–112, 183–8). Odysseus' endurance often involves self-control and concealment of his true emotions: see 19.210 with n.

κύντερον: there seems to be a pun on κύων (14). Odysseus is like a bitch; he has endured more 'dog-like' (i.e. more outrageous and shameless) things than this.

19 μοι: we might have expected τοι (which was in fact a variant known to ancient editors).

20 μῆτις: in the Cyclops episode of book 9, the poet puns on and plays with the resemblance between the pseudonym Outis ('Nobody', 'No-man') and the equivalent Metis, and the intellectual concept μῆτις ('plan', 'clever counsel'). The crucial instance is 9.414 ὡς ὄνομ' ἐξεπάτησεν ἐμὸν καὶ μῆτις ἀμύμων ('thus my name and my excellent plan deceived him'), where the 'name' is of course 'No-man'. Cf. also 9.410 εἰ μὲν δὴ μή τίς σε βιάζεται …; 422; for another pun in this general area see 460 κακῶν, τά μοι οὐτιδανὸς πόρεν Οὖτις. Here, as Odysseus recalls that triumph, his language echoes the witty wording of these passages in book 9. See further A. J. Podlecki, *Phoenix* 15 (1961) 125–33, esp. 130; N. Austin, 'Name-magic in the *Odyssey*', *Calif. Studies in Class. Phil.* 5 (1972) 1–19; on the general topic of puns on names see 19.406–9n.

22–30 'Thus he spoke, reproaching his heart down in his breast. And in him his heart endured and remained firm, in submission (ἐν πείσηι), unflinchingly; but he himself kept on twisting this way and that. As when a man is cooking a stomach filled with fat and blood, while a well-stoked fire is blazing, and turns it this way and that, eager for it to be roasted very quickly – so he twisted and turned hither and thither as he pondered how he was to lay his hands upon the shameless suitors, being only one man against many.'

For the dish itself (a Greek precursor of haggis), cf. 18.44–5. For another cooking simile see *Il.* 21.361–5. On the 'vulgarity' of many similes see Introd. 4(*d*). What the passage here above all conveys is the sheer physical quality of both Odysseus' discomfort and his endurance. His emotions, his heart, are seen as physical objects which he can handle and thrust down (esp. 22 καθαπτόμενος). For this way of visualising the emotions in early Greek literature cf. Onians, *Origins of European thought* 13–43, 46–53, etc. But the simile also has an ambiguous relationship to the narrative. Ostensibly it is Odysseus who is the haggis twisting and turning – that is, he has a passive role; but he is also the man of line 25, who should be in control and preparing his food; his eagerness for revenge corresponds to the impatience and hunger of the man in the simile. This ambiguity matches the uncertain position of

Odysseus in the narrative at this point: is he agent or victim, avenger or helpless onlooker? As often in Homer, the simile describes a simple and everyday physical event, but is used to communicate or suggest more complex emotions and moods.

23 πείσηι occurs only here in Homer. For the meaning 'submission', 'obedience', cf. πείθω 'persuade' (which becomes πείσω, ἔπεισα, etc. in other tenses). Others see the word as a nautical metaphor, e.g. 'his heart remained at anchor' (cf. πεῖσμα 'stern-cable').

25 πολέος . . . αἰθομένοιο: genitive absolute.

31 δέμας δ' ἤϊκτο γυναικί: Athene assumes her usual form for open encounter with a mortal, and Odysseus at once recognises her (37). Contrast the scenes in which she takes the appearance of a specific human (e.g. 2.268, 6.22–3) or that of an anonymous young man (13.222). On divine disguises see further J. S. Clay, *Hermes* 102 (1974) 129–36.

ἤϊκτο is 3 sing. pluperfect middle of εἴκω 'to liken'; 'she had given herself / taken the likeness of a woman'.

32 στῆ δ' ἄρ' ὑπὲρ κεφαλῆς elsewhere is a phrase often associated with dream-visions (cf. 4.803, 6.21, *Iliad* 2.20, 59), but not exclusively: see 23.4, where it is used of Eurycleia hovering over Penelope's bedside. Cf. 94n. The present episode may be a deliberate variation on that type of scene: the whole point here is that Odysseus is discontentedly awake, as the next line emphasises.

33–5 Athene knows the answer to her question already (as her form of address in 33 shows): although what she says is literally true, Odysseus is not in the position of a man 'at home with his wife and son'. The goddess is teasing her favourite, mockingly inviting him to explain why he is so anxious. This teasing style of question or challenge is quite common in Homer: cf. 22.224–35 (Athene again, but angrier there); *Iliad* 5.800–13 (Athene and Diomedes); Fenik, *Studies* 38.

33 αὖτ': 'in impatient or remonstrative questions, again, now, this time' (Cunliffe s.v. (4)). Cf. esp. Sappho 1.15 and 18 δηῦτε.

40 μοῦνος ἐών . . . ἀολλέες: cf. the suitor Leiocritus' confidence in their numbers at 2.244–51.

41–68 These lines are preserved in a papyus dating from between 285 and 250 B.C. (P. Hibeh 23, S. West, *Ptolemaic papyri of Homer* 272–6). The papyrus includes several additional lines (51a, 55a, 58a, all only partially preserved); see also 52–3n.

41–3 These lines, like 23.118–53, clearly prepare for the events of book 24 (esp. 413–548), in which the kinsmen of the suitors angrily proclaim their grievances at the assembly and subsequently embark on a futile attack upon Odysseus. It would be easy to cut out the present passage, and those who believe that book 24 is post-Homeric will naturally do so. Excision of the longer section in book 23 requires more drastic surgery (though strictly only 118–22 and 138–40 actually refer to subsequent events).

45 σχέτλιε 'you stubborn man'; cf. 13.293 (again Athene to Odysseus) σχέτλιε, ποικιλομῆτα, δόλων ἆτ' . . .

καὶ μέν: introducing a general proposition from which a specific conclusion (here an *a fortiori* argument) will be drawn; cf. esp. *Il.* 18.362 (19.265–7n.); Denniston, *GP* 390.

τίς: here almost 'most people': 'there are many people who pay heed to an inferior comrade, one who is mortal . . .'

τε . . . πείθεθ': the verb = ἐπείθετο; the gnomic use of the past tense, and the use of τε, indicate a generalisation.

46 οὐ τόσα: that is, 'not so much wisdom as I have' (Athene). ὅς has ἑταίρωι, not τίς, as its antecedent.

49 Cf. 13.389–91, 'if you were to stand by me as readily as you did before, grey-eyed one, I would even do battle with three hundred men alongside you, goddess whom I revere . . .' (see 1–55n. above). Athene's words of encouragement echo Odysseus' earlier boldness.

50 νῶϊ: acc. of the first person dual, 'us two', emphasising their companionship and enhancing her reassurance.

51 This line is followed by an additional one in the papyrus (cf. 41–68n.), of which all that is certain is (after a space large enough for *c.* 13 letters):

]ειασ απ[.

For possible supplements see West, *Ptolemaic papyri* 274–5.

It may be significant that, although the hypothetical antagonists have been described as 'eager to kill us' (50), Athene promises not 'you would kill them all', but 'you would drive away their cattle and herds' – another appeal to Odysseus' acquisitive nature (cf. 19.185n.).

52–3 The infinitive with the article is rare in early poetry: τὸ φυλάσσειν in 52 seems to be the only instance in Homer (West on Hes. *WD* 314). In the papyrus this sole example is removed, but we cannot tell how. The text of 52 ran:

[ἀλλ' ἐλέτω σε καὶ ὕ]πνοσ ε[. .]μ[.] . . . κ[

Line 53 is then omitted in the papyrus. Clearly the sentence ran differently and more briefly, but we have no way of knowing whether this was a scholarly 'improvement' intended to remove the syntactical anomaly, or whether it preserves a genuinely earlier version.

53 ὑποδύσεαι 'you will rise out of your troubles'. Dimock, *Unity* 266 sees a pun on Odysseus' name.

55 After this line the papyrus offers an additional line of which only a few letters are legible; supplement is almost entirely conjectural.

56–94 Penelope's prayer to Artemis; Odysseus awakens.

56–7 For the phrasing, cf. and contrast 23.342–3, on the following night, with husband and wife reunited: ... ὅτε οἱ γλυκὺς ὕπνος | λυσιμελὴς ἐπόρουσε, λύων μελεδήματα θυμοῦ. The adjective λυσιμελής ('loosener of limbs') there seems to trigger a verbal association in the poet's mind with the phrase λύων μελεδήματα ('freeing from cares'). Here we have the reverse association. In neither case is there any good reason for assuming that the poet saw the phrases as synonymous, and thus attributing to him a tautology.

δ': another instance of 'apodotic' δέ: cf. 19.330n.: 'while sleep took hold of him . . . as for his wife, *she* . . .'

58 Contrast the rough bed laid for Odysseus at 2–4.

Line 58 is followed in the papyrus by an additional line, again only partly preserved, which after *c.* 15 letters lost reads

]σθεν ἀκὴν ἔχον . [

The line is unlikely to be authentic: ἀκὴν ἔχειν ('to keep silent') is not a Homeric phrase. The line may have conveyed a sense such as 'her attendant women kept silent', perhaps in order to explain how Odysseus could hear Penelope's private prayer (so West, *Ptolemaic papyri* 276).

60 For an earlier prayer by Penelope to Artemis see 18.202–5.

61–6 For comparable prayers in which the speaker longs to be removed from his or her present existence, see esp. *Iliad* 6.345–8 (Helen; similarly retrospective, and expressed in similar language); also, less closely resembling the present case, *Il.* 22.481 (Andromache); Aesch. *PV* 152–7, 582; Soph. *Trach.* 1086–8; parody in Ar. *Wasps* 323–33. Artemis is invoked as archer-goddess (62 ἰόν, 80 βάλοι): cf. *Il.* 24.605–9; *Od.* 15.411 with Hoekstra's n.; Burkert, *GR* 149–52.

61–82 These lines form a unified structure, chiastically arranged (A, B, myth, B, A): if only Artemis (A) would slay me, or a storm carry me away (B), as happened to the daughters of Pandareos ... so may the Olympians do away with me (B), or may Artemis (A) kill me. Within this framework 66–78 narrate a mythological paradigm (example), the obscure story of the daughters of Pandareos. Lines 66–82 are sometimes considered spurious, and may indeed be drawn from a separate mythological tradition or adapted from a different poem; but we still need to give some account of why any poet, interpolator or no, would have thought them appropriate here. The story is one of happiness cruelly shattered: the daughters were favoured by the gods and had every possible gift bestowed on them, but in a moment when they were left unguarded they were abducted by the Harpies and carried off to a grisly end (beneath the earth?). Similarly Odysseus and Penelope had enjoyed perfect happiness, but with her husband long vanished (77n.), Penelope's own desire for life has departed (80–2). The analogy between myth and narrative is elusive but not impenetrable: happiness lost, hopes gone, loved one(s) dead, and behind it all the work of jealous or malignant gods. More specifically, there is also a parallel in the prospect of marriage for the daughters and for Penelope, though this is both a parallel and a contrast. The daughters of Pandareos (Aedon, Cleothera and Merope, according to the scholia) were robbed of marriage and delivered to a terrible fate; but Penelope would prefer such a fate to the dreadful prospect of remarriage (82). In the myth it seems that the Harpies are responsible for the catastrophe, but 'the gods' in general have already struck down the parents (67), and Zeus is described as knowing all things (75), and so presumably must bear some responsibility for the abduction (for the ambiguous role of Zeus cf. *Homeric hymn to Demeter* 9, 30, etc.). Hence Penelope in line 79 calls for the 'Olympians', not the Harpies, to remove her from human sight.

61–4 αἴθε ... ἕλοιο | ... ἢ ... | οἴχοιτο: like εἴθε in Attic, αἴθε introduces a prayer ('if only ...'); the optative, as the name suggests, is the mood for expressing wishes or prayers of all types, but often, as here, the implication is that the wish is simply unattainable; cf. Nestor's frequent refrain εἴθ' ὡς ἡβώοιμι, 'if only I were young again ...' (*Il.* 7.157, etc.).

63 θύελλα: cf. 66 θύελλαι and contrast 77, where the storms are personified as the Harpies (see n.).

65 προχοῆις: normally the places where a river enters the sea, its mouth(s); oddly used of Ocean. But see West on Hes. *WD* 757.

ἀψορρόου 'Ωκεανοῖο 'backward-flowing Ocean' (cf. *Il.* 18.399). In Homer and other early Greek literature Ocean is not a sea but a vast river which surrounds the inhabited world (as Ocean forms the rim of the design of Achilles' shield, which is a microcosm of the world: *Il.* 18.607–8); because it has no greater sea into which to send its waters, it must 'flow back' into itself. Herodotus makes fun of the persistent place given to Ocean by early map-makers and geographers (Hdt. 2.21–3, 4.8 and 36). Cf. J. O. Thomson, *History of ancient geography* (Cambridge 1948) 34–5, 39–41, etc. On the personified river-god Oceanus see *Il.* 21.195–7, West on Hes. *Th.* 133, 337–70.

67 τοκῆας μὲν φθῖσαν θεοί: according to the scholia here and on 19.518, the parents of the girls were Pandareos, son of Merops, and Harmathoe, daughter of Amphidamas. Their crime was to steal 'the dog of Zeus', a golden animal made by Hephaestus (like the magical dogs of gold and silver which guard Alcinous' palace in 7.91–4?). Although Pandareos tried to hide it with his friend Tantalus, Hermes located the stolen article and Pandareos fled with his family, first to Athens and then to Sicily. They were observed by Zeus and their punishment followed swiftly. The source of the story is not named by the scholia. Here it is worth observing that the gods' motive for striking down the parents is omitted, perhaps in order to enhance the sense of divine unfairness and cruelty, which reflects Penelope's view of her own situation. Perhaps comparable is the omission in *Iliad* 4 of any explanation for the antagonism of Athene and Hera to Troy: the Judgement of Paris, which might have seemed too petty and trivial a cause for these tragic events, is not referred to until book 24, a passage which many scholars have excised as a later interpolation (24.25–30, with Macleod and Richardson *ad loc.*).

68 ὀρφαναί: instead of suffering the usual unhappy fate of orphans (*Il.* 22.490–9), the daughters are brought up by goddesses. The gods first justly punish the parents, then care for the daughters; this is contrasted with the cruelty of the Harpies. But see 61–82n. for the ambiguous role of the gods.

70–2 Cf. Hes. *WD* 70–82 (the various gods shower gifts on the first woman, Pandora).

71 μῆκος is an admirable female characteristic according to Greek and Roman views: cf. the description of Nausicaa (compared to Artemis in a simile) in 6.107; also 5.217 and e.g. Catull. 86.1 *mihi candida, longa, recta est*.

72 δέδαε: 3 sing. aorist from δάω; the root verb means 'to get to know', 'learn', but in this reduplicated aorist tense it means 'to teach': cf. 6.233 = 23.160.

77 ἅρπυιαι ἀνηρείψαντο: the storm-winds are personified as the monstrous Harpies ('Snatchers'), adding a far more sinister and malignant note to the girls' disappearance. The next line, with its reference to the even more terrifying Erinyes, reinforces this effect.

Cf. 1.241 (the Harpies, says Telemachus, have carried Odysseus far away, beyond all sight and knowledge, and so he has lost his glory), 4.727 (Penelope complains that the winds (θύελλαι) have carried away Telemachus without her knowing it). These parallels help us interpret the relevance of the myth and bind it more closely to the main tale of the *Odyssey*.

On the Harpies see further Hes. *Th.* 265–9, according to which they are two in number, Aello and Okypete, and are daughters of Thaumas and Electra (daughter of Ocean: cf. 65). They are treated more fully in Apollonius Rhodius (2.178–300) and in Virgil (*Aen.* 3.210–67). For these and other monstrous sea- or wind-creatures see E. Vermeule, *Aspects of death in early Greek art and poetry* (Berkeley 1979) chh. 5 and 6. For the iconographical theme of Harpies (?) carrying off presumably dead figures see B. S. Ridgway, *The severe style in Greek sculpture* (Princeton 1970) 95–6, with bibl. on p. 108.

ἀνηρείψαντο: 3 pl. aor. middle of ἀνερείπομαι, a defective verb used by Homer only in this part. It may be related to ἀναρπάζω 'snatch up/away'.

78 στυγερῇσιν ἐρινύσιν: the Erinyes are dark and chthonic deities associated with vengeance and curses, especially where family ties and broken obligations are concerned. They are very ancient deities (mentioned in the Linear B tablets) and invariably treated with respect and fear by mortals. In Homer they, like many of the more sinister powers of the underworld, appear only in passing allusions such as this one; they are not among the regular cast of divine characters. For other references see *Il.* 9.454, 565–72, 15.204, 19.87, 259, 418; *Od.* 2.135 (Telemachus fears that his mother may invoke the 'hateful Erinyes' against him, if he should drive her out); 11.280 (Epikaste (= Jocasta) and Oedipus); 15.234, 17.475; Burkert, *GR* 197–8; R. Parker, *Miasma* (Oxford 1983) ch. 4.

ἀμφιπολεύειν 'for them to be servants to (them, the Erinyes)', infinitive of purpose. It is probably easier to take the sentence thus, rather than treat the verb as referring to what the Erinyes themselves will do to the girls ('gave them to the hateful Erinyes for them to attend to': so e.g. Cunliffe s.v.: 'i.e. handed them over to their tender mercies'). On the latter reading the word is euphemistic. But this vaguer and less specific sense of ἀμφιπολεύειν is not clearly established in Homer. The closest analogy would be 18.254 = 19.127 εἰ κεῖνος γ' ἐλθὼν τὸν ἐμὸν βίον ἀμφιπολεύοι (Penelope, speaking of the kind of attention Odysseus would give her if he returned), where the verb seems to mean 'watch over', 'take care of'.

We are not told (because Penelope, a mere human, does not know) exactly what services the unfortunate girls had to perform for the Erinyes. This also suits the narrative situation, in which the terrible thing for Penelope, and for Telemachus before he learns the truth, is that they simply do not know what has happened to Odysseus: if he had died in battle or was buried in some known spot, they would not be so unhappy. See 1.234–43, 14.365–72; cf. Odysseus' own complaints at 5.306–11.

81 στυγερήν echoes 78 στυγερῇσιν ἐρινύσιν.

83 τὸ μέν is answered by αὐτάρ in 87, whereas 84 ἤματα μέν is answered by 85 νύκτας δέ.

The grammar of the rest of the line is peculiar. Most MSS have the infinitive ἔχειν, in which case the sentence changes its track after ὁππότε. Hence the word is usually emended to ἔχει (which is found in one MS). If this is right, τὸ μέν can be taken as the self-contained subject, and the translation runs: 'but this has in it an endurable ill, when one weeps by day, in dreadful agony at heart, but sleep takes hold of one by night – for then sleep makes a man forget everything, good and bad, when (sleep) engulfs both his eyes. But to me a god has sent evil dreams.' Less plausibly, with the same reading, τις ('someone') may be supplied from the next clause as the subject, in which case the translation might run: 'But one can at least bear misfortune, when . . .'

Line 83 is omitted in some MSS, and some include an additional line 83a, composed to alleviate the grammatical difficulty. It is not improbable that there is something more seriously wrong with the text here.

85 ὁ refers to 'sleep' (ὕπνος).

ἐπέλησεν: gnomic 3 sing. aorist of ἐπιλήθω 'to cause to forget'. Only in the middle does the verb have the meaning 'to forget'.

88–90 These lines must be taken closely with 92–4, which complement them. Penelope dreams of Odysseus in bed beside her; Odysseus half-dreams or fancies that Penelope is with him and standing by his bedside, recognising who he is. The coincidence has a hint of telepathy. Penelope's experience may be partly explained in rational terms: ancient writers acknowledged that dreams often include people and ideas that have preoccupied the mind during the day (Hdt. 7.16β.2; Cic. *Div.* 1.45). But 87 δαίμων shows that this is not Penelope's opinion, and in Homer dreams are always significant phenomena. Odysseus' situation is less clear: his brief impression of Penelope's awareness of him looks like the momentary disorientation of one who is not quite awake; but there seems more to it than that. These lines suggest again how close husband and wife have come to revelation, how intense are Penelope's longing for her husband and awareness of the affinity between herself and her guest. They convey with remarkable force the emotional tenseness of both the hero and his wife. At the same time, it is not unfair to the poet to suggest that there is some lack of clarity here owing to the limitations of his vocabulary for psychological states (esp. in the uncertainty about whether Odysseus is awake or not, and the abnormal use of δόκησε in 92).

See further J. Russo, *A.J.P.* 103 (1982) 1–21, an article full of interest, though his approach may be thought excessively psychoanalytical. For a survey of later examples of and ideas about telepathy in ancient times see E. R. Dodds, *The ancient concept of progress* (Oxford 1973) 159–76.

88 παρέδραθεν: 3 sing. aorist of παραδαρθάνω 'to sleep beside'. Cf. 143.

89 It is relevant that in conversation with Penelope Odysseus has himself *described* how Odysseus looked when he was on his way to Troy (19.224–35).

90 ὄναρ . . . ὕπαρ: for the antithesis, cf. 19.547. In both passages, awakening brings disillusionment for Penelope.

91 Ἠώς: dawn breaks, on the feast-day of Apollo (19.86n.), the day of Odysseus' vengeance, which will conclude with Odysseus and Penelope reunited. After the gloom and pessimism of the night, we pass at once to good omens and a more positive mood.

93–4 'then he pondered, and in his mind she seemed to him to be [i.e. he imagined that she was] standing by his head, already recognising him / aware of him.' On the unique use of δόκησε in 93 see J. Russo, *A.J.P.* 103 (1982) 15–16.

94 κεφαλῆφι 'by his head'. This hints at the regular pattern of a dream in Homer: see e.g. *Il.* 2.20, and Dodds, *Greeks and the irrational* 104–5. Cf. 32n.

98–101 For such prayers requesting divine confirmation or reassurance, cf. *Il.* 24.283–321, at 308–13. Odysseus with typical carefulness asks for a double omen, making assurance doubly sure (cf. Cic. *Div.* 1.106, Virg. *Aen.* 2.679–704, esp. 691 *atque haec omina firma*).

98–9 ἐθέλοντες . . . | ἤγετε . . . ἐκακώσατε: oddly, having invoked Zeus, Odysseus shifts into the plural, presumably addressing all the gods. This leads to a reference to Zeus in the third person at 101. The gods in book 1 were united in their endorsement of Zeus's decision to allow Odysseus to come home; the only absentee, Poseidon, has by now conceded defeat.

100 φήμην: a 'saying' or utterance which seems to carry more than its surface meaning, and hence functions like an omen. See further Pease on Cic. *Div.* 1.101.

104 This line should probably be deleted: the reference to clouds is contradicted by 114, and the omen is more effective if the thunder comes from a clear sky (cf. Archil. 122 West, Hor. *Odes* 1.34.7); moreover, the joy of Odysseus unnecessarily anticipates 120–1, where he rejoices at both the thunder and the lucky words of the slave.

105 προέηκεν: 3 sing. aorist of προΐημι 'let out', 'send forth'.

ἀλετρίς: cf. 7.103–4; *PMG* 869; L. A. Moritz, *Grain-mills and flour in classical antiquity* (Oxford 1968) ch. 1 (esp. 4–5). The suffering figure is given no name, perhaps because she is symbolic of the plight of all the people of Ithaca. She is also, however, a special case among the sufferers, being the weakest (110) and so most hard-worked of the women.

106 ἧατο: 3 pl. imperfect of ἧμαι 'sit', 'be in place'. In English 'where the millstones *stood*' is more natural.

οἱ . . . ποιμένι λαῶν: possessive dative, with the phrase 'shepherd of the people' apparently in apposition to οἱ: 'where stood the millstones that were his, the shepherd of the people's.'

107 ἐπερρώοντο: 3 pl. imperfect of ἐπιρρώομαι, here governing the dative τῆισιν: 'they were hard at work upon'.

108 μυελὸν ἀνδρῶν '(which makes) marrow in men'. The same phrase is used at 2.290.

114 τεωι = τινι 'to somebody'.

120 κλεηδόνι: cf. 100, to which this responds. This line is the same as 18.117, where Odysseus has been congratulated by the suitors on his victory over the beggar Irus, and they wish that Zeus and the other gods should grant him everything he wants – an ominous prayer for them (cf. 18.122–3). See also 2.35 φήμηι.

121 φάτο: a good example of the use of φημί to mean 'think' rather than 'say': cf. Cunliffe s.v. (7). Cf. 90.

τίσασθαι: a 'timeless' aorist. 'He thought he had his revenge on the sinners', he is sure of his revenge. Cf. *Iliad* 3.366, the same verb.

122–256 This passage presents a sequence of 'arrival-scenes', as the poet sets the stage for the final day of the suitors' lives. Telemachus, Eumaeus (162–72), Melanthius (173–84), Philoetius, a new character (185–240), and finally the suitors (248–56) appear in turn and each greets or deals with the beggar Odysseus in his own way. The one figure who is not specifically brought on the scene by the poet is the prophet Theoclymenus (mentioned suddenly at 350), who has not been referred to since 17.151–66, and whom the reader might by now have forgotten entirely. He breaks his silence to utter a solemn prophetic warning, and the absence of preparation for his appearance may reinforce the strange and shocking quality of the scene. See further 345–86n.

123 ἀγρόμεναι is the preferable reading, as some of the maids have to reassemble in the morning, returning from the suitors' houses.

ἀκάματον πῦρ: having no matches, the Greeks kept a brand of wood alive under the heaped wood-ash on the hearth: in this sense the fire is 'untiring'. Cf. 5.488–91, in which Odysseus, huddling beneath a heap of leaves and branches for the night to keep warm, is compared with a brand buried in ashes. See also *Homeric hymn to Demeter* 239 and *hymn to Hermes* 237–9.

124–7 Cf. 2.1–14 (125–6 = 2.3–4; 127 = *Il.* 10.135). But here there is greater emphasis on Telemachus' stature and weaponry, as is fitting when he has reached such a degree of maturity and is about to act alongside his father in battle.

124 ἰσόθεος φώς: elsewhere in the poem only at 1.324, also of Telemachus (after Athene's visit has aroused him).

125 εἵματα ἑσσάμενος 'having clad himself in clothes'; the verb is aorist middle participle from ἕννυμι 'clothe'. Cf. 143.

129–143 There is double irony here: Telemachus and Eurycleia now both know who the beggar is, but neither knows that the other knows. The royal tone Telemachus adopts shows his (sometimes uncertain) advance to manhood; the criticisms of his mother are surely more than an act, and merit the correcting rebuke of the nurse (135). On the tension between Telemachus and his mother see Introd. 3(b).

131 πινυτή: also used of Penelope at 11.445 (Agamemnon), 21.103 (Telemachus). See also 20.228 (Odysseus to Philoetius).

132 ἐμπλήγδην: only here in Homer, and perhaps unknown in later Greek; glossed in the scholia by ἀκρίτως, παραφρόνως, ('senselessly'). See van der Valk, *Textual criticism* 119 for references to ancient scholars who tried to interpret the word in terms less pejorative to Penelope.

135 οὐκ ἄν . . . αἰτιόωιο: 2 sing. present optative of αἰτιάομαι 'to blame'. 'You would not blame her …' i.e. 'I do not think you would find fault with her now, as she is guiltless.' The protasis or 'if'-clause (e.g. 'if you knew everything that happened') is suppressed. Cf. Monro, *Grammar* §300. An alternative interpretation is to take this as an early instance of the 'potential optative as imperative' (cf. *Il.* 2.250, Soph. *Antig.* 444–5, Chantraine, *Gramm. homérique* II 221), in which case the translation is 'you *should* not blame her'.

137 εἴρετο γάρ μιν 'for she asked him'.

138 μιμνήσκοντο is preferable to μιμνήσκοιτο, which would have to mean that Odysseus was repeatedly thinking of bed (i.e. 'whenever he thought …').

140–1 This accurately reports the exchange at 19.318–24, 335–60, cf. 599.

143 ἔδραθ': 3 sing. aor. of δαρθάνω 'sleep', 'take one's rest'. Cf. 88n.

ἐπιέσσαμεν: 1 pl. aorist of ἐπιέννυμι 'put (a garment or covering) upon'.

148 The full designation of Eurycleia, with her ancestry (elsewhere only 1.429, 2.347), suits a scene in which she is acting with authority.

149–56 The speech of Eurycleia, sending her subordinates about their household chores, is a good example of the kind of realistic detail which prompted [Longinus]' description of the *Odyssey*, and especially its second half, as a 'comedy of manners' (*On the sublime* 9.15). The scene already points the way to the 'below-stairs' bustle of comedy and mime, in which slaves and clever servants have important roles. (There are parallels in the *Homeric hymn to Demeter* 106, 285–91; see Richardson's commentary, pp. 32–3. It may be a 'typical scene', a stock element in the collective repertoire of the bards.)

But the short episode also has thematic importance: not only does it reinforce the picture of order and hard work which makes the household of Odysseus an ethical model (and which the suitors' invasion and the treachery of the maids threaten); also, the tasks of cleansing and washing the hall will be repeated in a grisly form at the end of book 22, when the guilty maids are forced to clean up the bodies and blood after the slaughter (22.437–53. In particular, compare 20.151–2 with 22.439 and 453; 150 with 22.438 and 452).

154 θᾶσσον: the comparative is emphatic ('quickly, now!') rather than a demand for more speed than has been shown so far. Cf. the similar use of comparatives in Latin (*ocius*, *citius* and so forth).

156 καί 'in fact', as often after conjunctions.

ἑορτή: this day is the festival of Apollo, as 277–8 make clear (cf. 19.86n.). As Apollo is himself an archer (*Il.* 1.37, 43–52, etc.; Burkert, *GR* 145–6), this makes the day especially appropriate both for the contest with the bow and for the slaughter that follows, in which the bow plays a deadlier part.

161 κέασαν: 3 pl. aorist from κεάζω 'chop' or 'split (wood)'.

162–84 Two encounters of similar length are deliberately juxtaposed: Eumaeus is everything that Melanthius is not. Consideration and politeness are contrasted with contempt and abuse (esp. 165 μειλιχίοισι ∼ 177 κερτομίοισι; otherwise the two lines are identical).

162 συβώτης: Eumaeus, the admirable servant who entertained Odysseus on his return to Ithaca (book 14) and escorted him to the palace on the previous day. He last appeared at 17.603–5, where after dinner he returned to his herds on the farm.

163 τρεῖς σιάλους: Eumaeus brings two extra for the festival; normally he provides only one (14.19, 27).

169–71 Odysseus' reply broadens the moral scope of the exchange. Eumaeus was anxious that the beggar (Odysseus) might have been ill-treated personally; Odysseus' prayer concerns the suitors' impious and immoral behaviour in general.

170 ὑβρίζοντες ἀτάσθαλα μηχανόωνται: strong moralising vocabulary of a kind much more prominent in the *Odyssey* than in the *Iliad*.

ὕβρις signifies violent and arrogant *action* rather than the conventional English translation 'pride'. For the word and its cognates (which altogether appear only four times in the *Iliad*, as opposed to 26 occurrences in the *Odyssey*) cf. 17.588 = 20.370, 1.368 = 4.321, and often elsewhere. Cf. N. Fisher, *G.&R.* 23 (1976) 177–93; 26 (1979) 32–47; D. Mac-Dowell, *Demosthenes: against Meidias* (Oxford 1990) 18–23. For ἀτάσθαλα ('deeds of rash wickedness'), another Odyssean word (26 examples of the adjective or its cognates, against 5 in the *Iliad*), cf. esp. 1.7 (the folly of Odysseus' comrades in eating the cattle of the sun), 1.34 (Zeus moralises), 22.47 (Eurymachus admits their guilt, too late), 317, 416, 23.67, 24.458.

173 For Melanthius see 17.212–60, where he meets Eumaeus and Odysseus *en route* for the palace, and abuses them both. He is the brother of Melantho, and meets a dreadful end in 22.474–7, after he has fought in support of the suitors. Cf. 19.490n. His speech, like many spoken by the suitors, flouts the Homeric standards of courtesy and hospitality.

178 This line closely resembles 19.66, the opening of Melantho's rude speech to Odysseus; similarly the latter part of 179 recalls Melantho's ἀλλ' ἔξελθε θύραζε (19.68, cf. 69).

182 εἰσὶν . . . δαῖτες Ἀχαιῶν: i.e. 'why don't you pester somebody else for a change?' It is ironic that Melanthius, a mere slave, should throw his weight around as though out of concern for his master's property. Moreover, the suggestion that 'there are other feasts to go to' recalls what is repeatedly said to the suitors (1.374, 2.139), who have outstayed their welcome in the same way as Melanthius sees Odysseus as doing, but on a vastly larger scale.

183–4 Again Odysseus' self-restraint is emphasised (cf. 300–2).

184 βυσσοδομεύων: a word found seven times in the *Odyssey*, not in the *Iliad*. It seems to mean 'devising deep down, i.e. secretly' (cf. *Il.* 24.80 βυσσόν = 'the deep'). The word is normally used of Odysseus (also of his 'double' Hephaestus in Demodocus' song, which tells how he laid a trap for Ares and Aphrodite, 8.273), but also of the suitors in two passages, 4.676, 17.66 (though never when Odysseus is present: once he arrives in the palace he takes over the role of schemer). This line itself is used elsewhere by the narrator at 17.465, 491.

185 ὄρχαμος ἀνδρῶν: again of Philoetius in 254. See Parry, *MHV* 152 on the rather casual use of such a title for a mere herdsman.

187 πορθμῆες 'ferry-men', who brought Philoetius over from the neighbouring island of Cephallenia (210). The word occurs only here in Homer, but is common in later Greek prose and poetry (e.g. Eur. *Alc.* 253 of Charon; Hdt. 1.24.3).

192 τέων: genitive plural of the interrogative τίς 'who?'

εὔχεται 'from whom does he *claim* descent' rather than 'boast', but the two come close together in Homeric usage. See A. W. H. Adkins, *C.Q.* 19 (1969) 20–33, on εὔχομαι and related words.

194 Deliberate ambiguity: 'truly he is like a royal king in his stature' or 'he is like our lord the king'. Philoetius senses immediately the power and authority to which Melanthius and the suitors are fatally blind. His pity for the stranger and his consciousness of the harsh and uncertain state of mankind in general also mark him as a sensible and virtuous man (cf. 227–8).

195–6 'but the gods (? do indeed) bring suffering upon men who travel far abroad, when they weave sorrow even into the lot of kings'. Philoetius' logic is a little opaque, blurred by his emotion and the ironies of the poet. He seems to be saying: poor fellow, he has the look of a king; but the gods really do give travellers a hard time, when even kings are destined to suffer (when they travel). The mention of the beggar's kingly looks reminds Philoetius of Odysseus and *his* ill-starred travels.

195 δυόωσι: unique in Homer, but cf. δύη ('suffering').

196 ἐπικλώσωνται 'weave for', 3 pl. aor. middle subjunctive of ἐπικλώθω 'spin the thread of destiny' (cf. the name Clotho, regularly one of the Three Fates). According to Homer and other early Greek poets, one's destiny is fixed at birth (*Il.* 20.127–8, 23.78–9, 24.209–10; *Od.* 7.198; Hes. *Th.* 82, 218–19). This does not, however, involve total predetermination; it is rather a looser sense that certain things are bound to happen; one cannot escape one's μοῖρα (cf. *Il.* 6.487–9; *Od.* 3.236–8). Cf. 19.145n.

197 δειδίσκετο 'he welcomed' (with a gesture): a defective verb found also in the participial forms δεδισκόμενος, δειδισκόμενος, and cognate with δείκνυμι.

199–225 Philoetius' long speech serves to characterise him and to show Odysseus that here he has another loyal ally. It also restates a number of important moral and religious themes of the poem. On another level, the poet introduces variation, so that the two herdsmen are not simply interchangeable. Philoetius' doubts and distress at Zeus's apparent indifference to good men help to distinguish him from the more steadfastly pious swineherd (see Eumaeus' speech at 14.83–8).

200 ἔχεαι: 2 sing. pres. indic. passive of ἔχω (normally ἔχει), 'you are in the hold of'.

201 = *Il.* 3.365, where Menelaus indignantly upbraids Zeus for allowing his sword to shatter, so frustrating his vengeful onslaught on Paris. In Greek religion, for a mortal to reproach or even abuse and accuse a god may be rash, but is not automatically wrong or inevitably punished. See further *Il.* 2.110–18, 12.164–5, 22.15–20; Theognis 373–82; Soph. *Trach.* 1264–74 (see next n.); M. Heath, *The poetics of Greek tragedy* (London 1987) 51. In the present case, Philoetius' pessimism and indignation are entirely understandable, but subsequent events will prove them wrong. Cf. Eurycleia's outburst at 19.363–9.

202–3 οὐκ ἐλεαίρεις ... λευγαλέοισιν: the construction is 'you do not feel any pity at mixing men [i.e. you do not refrain, through pity, from troubling men] ... with hardship and miserable sorrows'. For Zeus as a god who *does* feel pity see *Il.* 16.431–61, 17.198–209, 441–56, 20.20–3. But mankind is not privy to these moments of compassion and generous feeling.

ἐπὴν δὴ γείνεαι αὐτός: a curious phrase. Odysseus is not the son of Zeus or indeed related to him in any clear way, except that kings are conventionally 'descended from Zeus'. Nor, despite the title 'father of men and gods' (*Od.* 1.28, etc.), is Zeus usually thought of as creator or begetter of mankind: that role is often allotted to Prometheus (Burkert, *GR* 171). The phrase seems therefore to be a more general reference to Zeus's womanising, which is also familiar to the *Iliad* (see the famous catalogue of his conquests at 14.315–28). Divine lovemaking always seems to lead to pregnancy for the mortal woman involved (*Od.* 11.249–50 states this as a rule; cf. Richardson on *Homeric hymn to Demeter* 360–9). Hence Zeus has many children, many of whom live glorious but troubled lives, especially Heracles, Perseus. For a more developed, and sharper, reproach of divine callousness see Soph. *Trach.* 1264–74: 'lift him [the dying Heracles], my followers, and grant me full forgiveness of this, but mark the great cruelty of the gods in the deeds that are being done. They beget children, they are hailed as fathers, and yet they look upon such sufferings. No man can foresee the future, but the present is fraught with mourning for us, and with shame for the gods.' Also Eur. *Heracles* 339–47.

204 ἴδιον: 1 sing. impf. indicative of ἰδίω 'to sweat'. A sign of emotional upset: cf. Sappho 31.13 L–P, Theocr. 2.106–7.

205–6 Cf. 19.358–60, lines which employ very similar irony.

209 'then woe is me for [on behalf of, as regards] the excellent Odysseus . . .' The construction is the same as in 19.363 (Eurycleia's similar outburst).

209–10 Odysseus' kindness in setting up Philoetius parallels his generosity to Eumaeus, which the latter described in 14.137–47 (cf. 14.62–6 on what Odysseus *would* have done for him).

210 εἷσ': 3 sing. aorist of ἵζω 'I seat'; here, 'he settled', 'he installed me'.

'Cephallenians' appears to be a collective title for the subjects of Odysseus (see *Il.* 2.631, in the Catalogue of Ships; 4.330, the inspection of the troops; *Od.* 24.355, 378,429; Soph. *Phil.* 264). For ancient discussion of the point see Hellanicus, *FGrH* 4 F 144.

211–12 'and now they are beyond count, nor could a race of cattle with their broad foreheads yield (such) increase [i.e. increase so much] for a man in another way'. The last phrase can only make sense if ἄλλως is here taken to mean 'another and *better* way': no man has superior herds to these. For parallels see 8.176–7 οὐδέ κεν ἄλλως | οὐδὲ θεὸς τεύξειε ('nor could a god fashion you otherwise', i.e. improve on your appearance), 24.107 (somewhat easier); *Il.* 19.401. In view of these parallels, the alternative reading ἄλλωι (agreeing with ἀνδρί: 'for another man', 'for any other man') seems unnecessary.

211 αἱ μέν: cattle rather than bulls.

213 ἄλλοι 'other men' (with the implication that they do not belong to the household), i.e. the suitors.

214 παιδός 'the son of the house', i.e. Telemachus.

215 οὐδ' ὄπιδα τρομέουσι θεῶν: for the phrase, and the general idea that the gods are on the look-out for human wrongdoing, cf. 14.82, 88; 21.28, *Il.* 16.388; Hes. *WD* 251, 706. On the etymology of ὄπις θεῶν see W. Burkert, *M.H.* 38 (1981) 195–204.

217–23 That so worthy and hard-working a subordinate as Philoetius should be considering emigrating shows (like the bitter complaints of the slave at 112–19) how out of joint life in Ithaca is at present. (For other noteworthy passages on this theme see Eumaeus' complaints in 15.326–36, 352–79.) His reluctance to go away and leave Telemachus in the lurch, laudable in itself, marks him out as a potential ally.

218 υἱός is genitive singular. Like παιδός in 214, it refers to the master's son, not to Philoetius' own.

219 αὐτῇσι βόεσσιν 'cows and all'. This is odd, as it seems to suggest that Philoetius contemplates removing the herd with him, as though they were his own property: contrast 221. Perhaps he feels that it is better for them not to be eaten by the suitors?

221 βουσὶν ἐπ' ἀλλοτρίῃσι 'in charge of herds that belong to others', with the same implication of 'strangers' as in 213.

222–3 κεν . . ἄλλον . . . | ἐξικόμην 'I would long since have come to another mighty king in my flight'. For the accusative after ἐξικνέομαι cf. *Il.* 9.479 Φθίην, 24.481 ἄλλων . . . δῆμον.

222 ὑπερμενέων: see 19.62n.

224–5 'But still I think of the unhappy man, if he were to come back from somewhere . . .' An ellipse; more natural in English would be e.g. 'but still I long for the day when that unhappy man might return . . .'

225 σκέδασιν . . . θείη: lit. 'might make a scattering'. θείη is 3 sing. aor. optative of τίθημι.

227–37 Odysseus' solemn assurances to Philoetius skirt very close to self-exposure (esp. in 228 – *how* does Odysseus know this? – and in 233–4, where the prediction is startlingly specific). Some of what he says is repeated from his assurances to Eumaeus and to Penelope: 230–1 = 14.158–9 (to Eumaeus) = 19.303–4 (to Penelope) = 17.155–6 (Theoclymenus to Penelope), and 232 is a less emphatic and abbreviated version of 19.305–7. The natural response for Philoetius to make would be 'What makes you say that?', but the poet presupposes the explanations and 'evidence' given by the stranger in the earlier episodes; the narrative is accelerated, at some cost to realism.

227–8 ἐπεί governs both clauses (ἔοικας . . . γιγνώσκω).

228 'and since I am myself aware that your mind is an intelligent one' (lit. 'that for you intelligence arrives in your heart').

230–1 See 19.303–4 and n.

237 'then you would know how great is my strength and (how powerful) the hands that serve me'.

ἕπονται: the reading ἄαπτοι is also found, but seems less appropriate to the lowly Philoetius than to heroes and gods, for whom the phrase 'unapproachable hands' is otherwise reserved. (In the *Odyssey* the phrase occurs only of Achilles and Odysseus.) For this sense of ἕπω cf. Cunliffe s.v. (7–8).

240–7 The abortive conference of the suitors. This short and curious episode, which ends so inconclusively, provides the final example of a meeting of the suitors: these have formed a series in which the effective action of the suitors has steadily diminished (cf. 299n. on the series of throwing-scenes). In book 2, although it was Telemachus who summoned the assembly, the suitors have everything their way and Telemachus is humiliated. In book 4, after the suitors meet with their first setback (the discovery that Telemachus has set off in quest of his father without their knowledge), they cease their games to plan his assassination (658–74), but this plan eventually comes to nothing. In 16.342–408 they hold an assembly amongst themselves after their ambush has failed: there, after initial thoughts of further action, they are lulled into their usual torpor by the temporising advice of Amphinomus (400–5) – the same Amphinomus as here interprets the ominous sign as a reason for inactivity rather than a warning. This progression is matched by the increasing respect with which the beggar Odysseus, and Telemachus himself, are now treated in the palace: see 20.257–67 (Odysseus is set in a place of honour by Telemachus); 268–9 (the suitors fail to respond to Telemachus); 271–4 (Antinous submits, with a little blustering, before Telemachus); 320–37 (the suitors are silent at first when Telemachus rebukes Ctesippus, then Agelaus uneasily concedes that Telemachus must have his rights). All these passages indicate real or awkwardly feigned concessions to the authority of Telemachus and his family; all indicate that the suitors are losing control of the situation. See further Dimock, *Unity* 213–15, 223, 233, 272, 288.

241–2 On the suitors' plots against Telemachus see 4.658–74, 700–1, 842–7, 5.18–19, 13.425–8, 14.180–2, 15.28–35, 17.66.

242 ὁ . . . ὄρνις: we should say '*a* bird'; the article does not have its demonstrative force here. See Monro, *Grammar* §264, citing e.g. *Il.* 22.163 τό.

The omen obviously foreshadows the hero's victory over the suitors; for the eagle as king of the birds, and representative of Odysseus, cf. 19.538–50 (Penelope's dream), with 19.538n. The suitors might have taken the omen as favourable to themselves, with the helpless dove representing Telemachus, but for simplicity's sake (and to emphasise their inertia), the poet avoids this possible complication.

245 συνθεύσεται 'will (not) succeed', 'will (not) go right'. Apparently cognate with θέω.

247 ἐπιήνδανε: 3 sing. imperfect of ἐπιανδάνω, 'please', 'be acceptable'. Cf. 327.

250 Cf. 20.3n.

253 νεῖμε: 3 sing. aorist from νέμω 'give out', 'distribute'. Cf. the same part of the compound verb ἐπένειμε in the next line.

257 Telemachus has now returned from the agora (cf. 146).

κέρδεα νωμῶν: νωμάω 'handle', 'wield' is here used metaphorically of intellectual activity, planning: cf. 13.255 (of Odysseus) νόον πολυκερδέα νωμῶν, 18.216 (Penelope of Telemachus).

259 On Telemachus' 'focalisation' here see Introd. 4(c), p. 68. The line is also discussed by Aristotle, *Poetics* 22 58b29–30, who comments on the superiority of the poetic adjectives ἀεικέλιος and ὀλίγος to their more commonplace equivalents in ordinary speech, μοχθηρός and μικρός.

262 ἧσο: 2 sing. imperative from ἧμαι 'sit,' 'be seated'.

264–5 An emphatic statement that Telemachus intends to claim his inheritance (265 'it was for *me* that he acquired this').

268–9 These lines are repeated from 1.381–2 = 18.410–11; in each case the suitors are taken aback by Telemachus' tone of authority and rebuke.

268 ὀδὰξ ἐν χείλεσι φύντες 'biting in their lips with their teeth': ἐν belongs with φύντες (nom. plural aorist participle from φύω 'to fix one's hold on', 'attach to'). But 'in' is more naturally omitted in translation. ὀδάξ is an adverb cognate with δάκνω 'to bite', but perhaps felt by the poets to be connected rather with ὀδούς, ὀδόντος ('tooth').

269 ὅ 'that', 'at the fact that', so almost 'because'.

271 Ἀχαιοί: Antinous avoids addressing Telemachus direct, a sign of his unease or confusion: cf. Agamemnon apologising to Achilles (*Il.* 19.78–144); Clytemnestra deceiving Agamemnon (Aesch. *Ag.* 855–913).

273 γάρ refers back to 271 δεχώμεθα; for parallel 'long-range' uses of this particle see Denniston, *GP* 63.

εἴασε 'did (not) allow us'. The infinitive (e.g. 'to kill him') is suppressed, indicating the unease which tempers Antinous' antagonism. Telemachus knows about the suitors' plotting already, because of Athene's warnings in 15.28–35. On their assassination attempt see further 241–2n.

273–4 τῶι κέ μιν ἤδη | παύσαμεν 'then [i.e. if he had] we would soon have put a stop to him . . .' For the construction cf. 222–3.

274 λιγύν . . . ἀγορητήν: a sarcastic compliment, as in *Il.* 2.246 (Odysseus to Thersites).

275 ἐμπάζετο: 3 sing. imperfect from ἐμπάζομαι (+ genitive) 'care about', 'pay regard to'. Telemachus hears and understands the hostile words of Antinous, but restrains himself from replying in kind: on this theme see 19.42n.

276–8 These three lines seem to involve a change of scene, as the poet briefly gives us an account of the festival of Apollo in the town. The 'Achaeans' of 277 surely do not include the suitors, or the party in the palace in general. The normal life of the community, joining in public worship, is contrasted with the godless self-indulgence of the suitors. The changes of scene at 276 and again, back to the palace, at 279 are, however, peculiarly abrupt.

ἑκατόμβην: literally a sacrifice of a hundred beasts, scarcely a common occurrence in real life, but a regular event (often in the plural!) in epic. Probably the audience did not really think of a precise number of animals, but rather of an indefinitely large and splendid occasion.

282 ἴσην: 'equal shares for all' is an important part of the ritualised Homeric feasting: cf. the formulaic line δαίνυντ', οὐδέ τι θυμὸς ἐδεύετο δαιτὸς ἐΐσης (5 times in the *Iliad*, twice in the *Odyssey*). See further Griffin, *Homer on life and death* 14–17; M. Detienne and J.-P. Vernant, *La Cuisine du sacrifice en pays grec* (Paris 1979) 23–4. It is compatible with special privileges for the deserving (*Il.* 7.321, *Od.* 8.475–6; cf. the prizes at Patroclus' funeral games). What matters here is that Odysseus is given equal place with the aristocratic suitors, as opposed to being fobbed off with scraps, as on the preceding day.

284–6 (= 18.346–8); for Athene's provocation of the suitors see also 17.360–4, 18.155–6, and cf. Exodus 7–9, 10 : 1. This behaviour seems surprising to us, though it is less extreme than her 'temptation' of Pandarus to break the truce by shooting an arrow at Menelaus – an unprovoked attack which eventually costs the archer his life (*Il.* 4.86–126, 5.290–6 (where it is Athene who guides Diomedes' spear and so helps bring about Pandarus' doom)). Here the suitors are already clearly guilty, and Athene's intervention merely encourages them on the downward path: cf. Aesch. *Persae* 742 ἀλλ' ὅταν σπεύδηι τις αὐτός, χὠ θεὸς συνάπτεται. The actions of Athene are disturbing to those critics who think of the gods of the *Odyssey* as consistently virtuous and champions of morality, but this position can easily be exaggerated. Even Zeus's speech in book 1 allows that the gods may play *some* part in bringing misfortune upon men (33 οἱ δὲ <u>καὶ</u> αὐτοί ... 'they themselves *also* suffer hardships beyond what is their lot through their own folly': other renderings of καί are possible, but this seems to me the most convincing). See further the discussions cited in Introd. 1 (*a*), p. 5 n. 5.

286 δύη: 3 sing. aorist optative of δύω 'to go into', 'enter'; '... so that pain [or here, perhaps, resentment] might find its way still more into the heart of Odysseus'.

287 ἀνὴρ ἀθεμίστια εἰδώς 'a man who knew lawless things'; i.e. a man of lawless character. It is typical of Greek to express moral qualities in terms of knowledge: cf. *Il.* 24.40–1, Hes. *Th.* 236, or Socrates' saying 'virtue is knowledge'; Onians, *Origins of European thought* 15–20. The phrase resembles 9.189 and 428, both describing the Cyclops (cf. 296n.). We do not need to see this as a precise echo, but the two episodes, both involving lawless and barbaric treatment of an unrecognised guest, are obviously comparable ethically, and in their outcome.

288 Κτήσιππος: first mentioned here; killed by Philoetius at 22.285–92, where this episode is recalled.

289 The choice between πατρὸς ἑοῖο (printed here) and θεσπεσίοισι may seem somewhat arbitrary, as both give perfect sense and neither constitutes a regular formula with what precedes. See M. J. Apthorp, *The manuscript evidence for interpolation in Homer* (Heidelberg 1980) 59, who considers this a possible 'oral' variant. But 307 provides a strong argument for the former reading: Telemachus promises that Ctesippus' rich father would have had other uses for his wealth if his son had succeeded in his criminal assault. Cf. the more explicit taunting by Idomeneus of Othryoneus, suitor to Cassandra, at *Il.* 13.374–82.

292–5 Ctesippus begins his speech with deceptive politeness: only with the sneering tone of 297, and the aggressiveness of his action, does the falseness of his friendly pose become clear. Eurymachus at 18.351–3 begins a speech in similarly 'polite' manner, but there the poet fore-

warns us of the jeering intention in 350. For another false compliment
see 21.397–400 (dramatic irony).

296 ξεινίον 'a guest-gift'. On the importance of gifts in Homer see
19.185n. This abuse of the custom recalls the Cyclops' mocking offer of
a gift in return for Odysseus' wine – he will eat 'Nobody' last of all
(9.369–70; also the clumsy attempt at deception at 9.517).

297 λοετροχόωι 'one who pours out the water for baths'. The sneer
is intended to put Odysseus in his place; for Ctesippus, it is absurd to
think of him, a worthless beggar, doing the proper aristocratic thing
and exchanging gifts with his equals, who will themselves be inferior
slaves. There is a similar snobbish jibe from Melanthius at 17.222
('begging for scraps of meat, not swords or goblets' – the latter being
typical gifts from hosts to guests).

298 In the οἵ clause we must understand a verb like 'are' or 'live', as
at 325.

299 ἔρριψε: this is the last of three scenes in which one of the suitors
throws something at Odysseus (as predicted at 16.277, 17.230–2): cf.
17.458–88 (Antinous throws a footstool, which grazes Odysseus' shoul-
der without knocking him down; and Odysseus answers him back and
unnerves the other suitors); 18.387–411 (Eurymachus throws a similar
stool, but misses and hits a wine-steward; Telemachus warns him to
refrain). The present passage is climactic: Odysseus easily dodges the
cow's foot, Telemachus warns Ctesippus in the strongest terms (esp.
306–8), Agelaus calls for concessions; and a moment later Theocly-
menus intervenes and prophesies the suitors' doom. See further Fenik,
Studies 180–8. For a similar pattern indicating the diminishing power
and status of the suitors see 240–7n.

301 ἧκα 'gently', 'slightly'.

301–2 μείδησε δὲ θυμῶι | σαρδάνιον μάλα τοῖον 'he smiled with
real bitterness in his heart'. σαρδάνιον is a neuter acc. adjective used as
an adverb: 'bitterly', 'grimly'. It occurs only here in Homer, and later
uses such as Pl. *Rep.* 337a, often associated with smiling or laughing, are
obviously imitations of this passage. The folk-etymology canvassed in
antiquity was the name of a Sardinian plant which caused anyone
eating it to grimace at its bitter taste (see LSJ s.v; Virg. *Ecl.* 7.41
Sardoniis amarior herbis; even more far-fetched is the learned fantasy of
Timaeus, *FGrH* 566 F 64; Demon, *FGrH* 327 F 18: by an old Sardinian
custom, sons struck their fathers dead when they got too old, and the

fathers, recognising the propriety of their demise, died with a grin!). More plausible is the suggestion made by the scholia on Plato (loc. cit.) that the word is connected with σαίρειν 'to grin in a manner which shows the teeth', like a dog: this would suit Odysseus' anger and his dog-like fierceness (cf. 13–16 above). See further P. Kretschmer, *Glotta* 34 (1954–5) 1–9. On the role of laughter and mirth in this book see 345–86n., and cf. and contrast 22.371, the smile of the victor exercising his power to spare a victim; 23.111, where Odysseus smiles with admiration for his wife's cleverness and caution.

Our word 'sardonic' comes ultimately from this passage (omicron or omega replacing alpha in some authors, because the Greek name for Sardinia is Sardo).

μάλα τοῖον 'surely quite . . .' (Cunliffe), emphasising σαρδάνιον.

304 'Indeed, Ctesippus, this [i.e. this outcome, that you did not hit the stranger] was a far better thing for you in your heart.' The next line spells out what 'this' is. The line is straightforward apart from the odd use of θυμῶι, which may be a careless use of a routine line-ending (there are four other examples of lines ending ἔπλετο θυμῶι in the poem). Other translations have been suggested: 'as you thought' (intended sarcastically: Ctesippus *really* meant to miss, because he realised the possible consequences), 'if you consider it', etc., but none really convinces.

307 πατήρ: there is a clever ambiguity here: Ctesippus naturally takes Telemachus to mean his, Ctesippus', father; the audience relishes the potential allusion to Telemachus' own father.

310 Cf. 19.19n.

316–19 Cf. 16.106–11 (Odysseus to Telemachus).

318–19 στυφελιζομένους . . . | ῥυστάζοντας: the first participle is passive, agreeing with ξείνους, whereas the second is active, referring to the suitors, and has δμωιάς τε γυναῖκας as its object.

321 Ἀγέλαος: not previously mentioned; he reappears in book 22, where he takes a leading role after the slaying of Antinous and Eurymachus (131–41, 241, 247–56), abuses and threatens Athene–Mentor (213–23), and is finally killed by Odysseus (292–6).

322–44 Fenik, *Studies* 86–8 has an interesting discussion of the exchange between Agelaus and Telemachus, which, as he says, introduces a rather surprising change of tone: instead of abuse and derision, we now have a 'reasonable man's' tactful representations to Telema-

chus, and a courteous reply from the latter. The poet shows by this
exchange how perilous the suitors' situation has become: the wanton
misbehaviour of his fellows is briefly contrasted with the belated at-
tempt at diplomacy which Agelaus, however insincerely, produces. It is
far too late for any such overtures to save the suitors, and the immediate
transition to Theoclymenus' vision of doom underlines this in the most
emphatic way imaginable. But 328–32 (esp. 330) are illogical and self-
serving, as if the suitors were being detained at Penelope's pleasure; and
if there was still reasonable hope of Odysseus' return, why did the
suitors prematurely court his wife? In short, the poet allows Agelaus to
undermine his own credibility.

322–5 = 18.414–7 (Amphinomus, in a similar placatory speech to
which no-one replies).

325 Cf. 298n.

327 ἅδοι: 3 sing. aorist optative from ἀνδάνω 'to please'.

333 Agelaus puts his suggestion much more tactfully than Antinous
with his lordly demands in 2.111–14.

ὅ τ' = 'that': see Chantraine, *Grammaire homérique* II §435, citing this
passage and *Il.* 1.518, 16.433, 19.57.

335 ἄριστος: see 19.528n.

339 οὐ μὰ Ζῆν' . . . ἐμοῖο: μά goes with both Ζῆν' and ἄλγεα: 'by
Zeus and by the sorrows my father has suffered', perhaps with the
implication that Zeus caused these. Rather surprisingly, this is the only
occurrence of μά in the *Odyssey*; it occurs three times in the *Iliad*, each
time in the mouth of Achilles: see J. Griffin, *J.H.S.* 106 (1986) 52, who
suggests that the *Odyssey*-poet, here as in 2.80, is trying to give the
youthful Telemachus some of the heroic traits of Achilles.

Ἀγέλαε: Rank, *Etymologiseerung* 48, suggests a pun (Ἀγέλαε . . .
ἄλγεα); similarly Dr David Clark sees a play on ἀγέλαστος and cog-
nates. Both would be ominous for Agelaus.

341–2 These lines may reflect Telemachus' former attitude, but
here must be taken as insincere (oddly, after what amounts to an oath
in 339).

δῶρα: who gives the dowry (if that is the right word) in a Homeric
marriage has been much discussed, particularly in relation to the his-
torical reality which lies behind the poems, whether it be the real world
of the poet's own day or the tradition about earlier, heroic times. For
the bridegroom or suitor bringing gifts, see *Il.* 16.178, 190, *Od.* 15.16–

18, 18.275–9, 19.528–9, 20.335, etc.; for the father or family providing
them, e.g. *Il.* 6.191–5, 9.147–56, 22.51, *Od.* 4.735–6, 7.311–15, etc.
Here there is the further complication that remarriage is in question,
and the son of the 'bride' has a role to play as well. For discussion, see
W. K. Lacey, *J.H.S.* 86 (1966) 55–68; A. Snodgrass, *J.H.S.* 94 (1974)
116–17; I. Morris, *Cl. Antiq.* 5 (1986) at 105–10, supporting Lacey.
Generous exchange of gifts is so much a part of the Homeric world that
it is easy to suppose that the poet sees these customs as co-existing;
whether this actually reflects any historical practice is another matter.

343–4 Cf. Telemachus' similar statement at 2.132–7.

343 διεσθαι: infinitive from δίεμαι 'chase', 'drive', 'chase away'.

345–86 The vision of Theoclymenus and its aftermath. This is one of
the most remarkable and memorable scenes of the poem, involving a
macabre form of hysteria among the suitors and 'second sight' or in-
spired prophecy on the part of Theoclymenus. The scene, while unde-
niably effective, has often been thought 'unhomeric', in that it presents
a peculiarly eerie disruption of human existence by supernatural forces.
But for comparable passages see *Iliad* 11.53–5 and 16.459 (rain of blood
on the battlefield); 16.790–806 and 13.435 (divine intervention be-
wilders warriors and makes them helpless); and esp. *Od.* 12.394–6 (the
dead cattle of the sun low on the spit, and the hides move). On the
importance of the last passage, and of the parallel between Odysseus'
companions and the suitors, see 356–7n. For comparable scenes outside
Homer see Aesch. *Ag.* 1090–1129 (the prophetess Cassandra senses the
evil past of the house of Atreus, and even sees the dead children of
Thyestes); also *Njal's Saga* ch. 127, Daniel 5 (Belshazzar's feast); Hdt.
7.140, 9.120; Plut. *Pyrrhus* 31; Stith Thompson, *Motif index* D 474, E
761.1.

Here the following points need special emphasis: (a) the suitors lose
control of themselves and of the situation; they do not see what Theoc-
lymenus sees and do not grasp the significance of what he says. This
scene carries to extremes the motif of the 'wise adviser' or warner ig-
nored (1.37–43, 18.124–57, etc.; cf. Rutherford, *J.H.S.* 102 (1982)
149–50). (b) The bloodstained food develops the theme of the dis-
rupted feast. Feasting, like hospitality, is of moral and symbolic signifi-
cance in the poem. The suitors feast illegitimately, wasting another
man's possessions and depriving his son of his inheritance; it is fitting
that their selfish greed is punished at a feast, and by a guest whom they

have maltreated (see esp. 22.8–21). It is also appropriate that this
doom should be foreshadowed by an omen involving the defilement of
food (348 αἱμοφόρυκτα δὲ δὴ κρέα). (c) The laughter of the suitors, a
recurrent motif in this scene (346–7, 358, 374, 390), adds macabre em-
phasis to the irony of their ignorance and folly. They laugh when events
are most serious and ominous for them; yet their hysteria is combined
with weeping (349), unexplained and unappreciated by them. The
motif of inappropriate mirth and lightness of heart also reappears in the
prelude to the slaughter: 21.376–7. (d) Their loss of control here antici-
pates a later occasion, on which they experience panic in earnest at
22.297–99, when Athene holds up the aegis.

The figure of Theoclymenus was first introduced, with an elaborate
genealogy, at 15.223–95, where he supplicated Telemachus on the
coast of Pylos, being in flight after killing a man in Argos, and was
given safe passage to Ithaca. He also appears in two intervening scenes:
15.495–557 (in which on arrival in Ithaca he interprets a favourable
omen to Telemachus), and 17.151–66 (where he gives a somewhat
different interpretation to Penelope). The detail with which the poet
introduces him may suggest that he is an invented character, but his
family, which includes a number of mythical seers such as Melampus
and Amphiaraus, is well-known in legends normally separate from the
narrative of Odysseus. See further 15.225–55, with 11.281–97 (both
highly allusive and obscure passages about this family); [Apollod.]
Bibl. 1.9.11–13. It is peculiar that Theoclymenus makes such brief and
sporadic appearances in the *Odyssey* and that after this scene we see
and hear no more of him; but his inclusion seems more than justified by
this memorable scene, and we may guess that he is a late arrival in the
Odyssean saga, introduced by the master poet himself. See further
Page, *Hom. Odyssey* 83–8; Fenik, *Studies* 233–44; Erbse, *Beiträge* 42–54;
D. B. Levine, *C.J.* 79 (1983) 1–7. On the laughter of the suitors see the
interesting discussion by M. Colakis, *C.W.* 79 (1986) 137–41.

346 ἄσβεστον γέλω: the phrase also occurs at *Il.* 1.599 (the amuse-
ment of the gods at Hephaestus' playing the role of cup-bearer) and *Od.*
8.326 (again a divine scene: the gods laugh at the success of Hephaestus'
trap for Ares and Aphrodite). The scene in book 8 of the *Odyssey* seems
to echo or allude to the episode in the *Iliad* (see esp. W. Burkert, *Rh. M.*
103 (1960) 130–44). If this were not the case, and if ἄσβεστος γέλως
were a less striking phrase, it might be fanciful to look for any connec-

tion between this passage and its more famous parallels; some may still think it a wrong approach. If the recurrence of the phrase does, however, have any significance, it perhaps serves to draw attention to the gulf between men and gods: the divine laughter in both scenes is spontaneous and (in the *Iliad*) releases tension; the human laughter here is forced and false, and heightens our awareness of the suitors' deluded folly.

347 γναθμοῖσι . . . ἀλλοτρίοισιν 'with jaws not their own' – i.e. not under their control.

351–7 These lines are quoted by Plato, *Ion* 539a, who omits 354, and by Plutarch, who omits 353–4. These shorter versions do not indicate that the authors necessarily had a more abbreviated text of the scene, as ancient writers often quote from memory.

352 εἰλύαται: 3 pl. perfect passive of εἰλύω 'wrap', 'cover'. 'Your heads and faces and your limbs beneath have been engulfed in darkness.' In Tibullus (1.1.70) Death itself is described in similar terms: *iam ueniet tenebris Mors adoperta caput*. See K. F. Smith's n. on that line.

353 οἰμωγὴ δὲ δέδηε: lit. 'wailing is burning forth', a bizarre synaesthesia (a figure of speech wherein different senses are combined or blurred: here, sound and sight). An English example (from Keats's *Ode to a nightingale*) is the line '*tasting* of Flora and the country *green*'. On the figure generally see W. B. Stanford, *Greek metaphor* (Oxford 1936) 47–62; E. Irwin, *Colour terms in Greek poetry* (Toronto 1974) 205–13, citing e.g. Pind. *Ol.* 9.22, Aesch. *Pers.* 395; for a more detailed discussion of synaesthesia in Sophocles, see C. Segal, *I.C.S.* 11 (1977) 88–96. The unnatural use of language reflects the abnormality of what Theoclymenus sees or senses. δέδηε is 3 sing. perfect of δαίω 'light a fire', or in perfect and pluperfect tenses 'blaze', 'burn'.

354 This line anticipates passages such as 22.383–4, 407.

ἐρράδαται: 3 pl. perfect passive of ῥαίνω 'sprinkle'.

355–6 The image of ghosts descending to Hades foreshadows the episode which opens book 24, in which Hermes guides the suitors there. This is not necessarily an argument for the authenticity of that scene, as another poet could have been inspired by these memorable lines.

355 εἰδώλων: this word (lit. 'images') obviously means 'phantoms' or 'ghosts' here: cf. 11.83, 213, and the much more peculiar use at 602, which is probably by a later hand; *Il.* 23.72. In other passages in Homer it is used to refer to various supernatural phenomena: dreams, or illusory figures who take the place of mortal warriors in the *Iliad*.

356–7 The fatuous notion that these lines refer to a solar eclipse taking place at the time is mentioned in the scholia, and also by Plutarch (*On the face of the moon* 19, 931F); cf. M. W. Haslam on *P Oxy* 3710.36 (p. 107). Obviously the darkness is symbolic of the suitors' sins. Further, the idea that the sun should vanish and abandon its function is reminiscent of the threat made by the sun-god at 12.382–3, when Odysseus' men have killed his cattle: if he does not receive recompense, he will go down to Hades and shine among the corpses. The companions of Odysseus offend against the gods and are duly punished; but in their case there are, as has often been pointed out, extenuating circumstances (cf. Fenik, *Studies* 208–32): they are starving and can neither escape from the island nor support themselves otherwise, and they intend to honour and build a temple to the sun when they return home, 12.345–7. The suitors are far more straightforwardly guilty. For them, it is as if Helios has fulfilled his threat.

357 ἐπιδέδρομεν: 3 sing. perfect from ἐπιτρέχω 'to run towards', 'rush upon'. 'An evil mist has come swiftly overhead.'

361 ἐκπέμψασθε: this is a distorted version of the honourable offer of an escort to a guest-friend on his departure: thus Nestor sends his son Pisistratus as escort with Telemachus to Sparta (3.317–28, esp. 325), and the Phaeacians equip a whole ship to convey Odysseus home (13.38–52, etc.). Here we have a mocking version of such good manners, haughtily rejected by Theoclymenus. In his reply the prophet also refers to the custom (364 πομπῆας).

367 τοῖς strictly suits only πόδες in 365, but the general amplitude of the Homeric style, already illustrated in 365 itself, makes it unnecessary to consider excising 366.

370 For the language used, cf. 170 (Odysseus to Eumaeus), with n.

372 Peiraeus, a companion of Telemachus on his journey abroad, looked after Theoclymenus at his house in town while Telemachus visited Eumaeus' farm (see 15.539–49), and later escorted him to the palace (17.71–83). He is thus the natural person to entertain the prophet again, now that his welcome at the palace (and his function in the poem) is exhausted. True hospitality supersedes the mocking and inadequate hospitality of the suitors.

374 ἐρέθιζον is clearly the superior variant here, and confirmed by γελόωντες; θαυμάζον was appropriate in 1.382, but the suitors are by now accustomed to Telemachus' outspokenness. The imperfect is probably conative ('they tried to provoke ...'), especially in view of 384–6, where the poet makes clear that Telemachus resists the temptation to react to their jibes.

376 κακοξεινώτερος: as often, the suitors' scoffing comments only serve to condemn them. They assume that they are the only 'guests' whose comfort Telemachus should be looking after, while they mock and abuse his other guests and the young man himself.

378–9 These ill-considered criticisms were already repudiated by Odysseus at 18.366–86, in a spirited challenge to Eurymachus.

379 ἔμπαιον: the diphthong αι, naturally long, is short here, an instance of internal correption – a licence much rarer than correption between words (see Introd. 5(b), p. 80). On internal correption see M. L. West, *Greek metre* (Oxford 1982) 11; Monro, *Grammar* §384.

383 Σικελούς: 'Sicels' are never mentioned in the *Iliad*; in the *Odyssey* otherwise only at 24.211, 366, 389 (Laertes' attendant female slave is said to be a Sicel). In the lie he tells to Laertes Odysseus claims to have been driven to Ithaca from Sicania. In later Greek both names are firmly associated with Sicily, Sicania and Sicanoi being recognised as older terms (e.g. Hdt. 7.170, Thuc. 6.2). It is not clear how much, if anything, the poet knew about the real Sicily, which was already being colonised by the mainland Greek states in the late eighth century (traditionally Naxos and Syracuse were the first, founded *c.* 735 B.C.): see Dover in A. W. Gomme, A. Andrewes, K. J. Dover, *Historical comm. on Thuc.* IV (Oxford 1970) 198–210. Sicily would be a long way to send an unwelcome slave, and perhaps 'Sicels' is only a vague name for barbarian bogey-men over the seas. Rather similar are the references to a savage king Echetus (18.85, 116, 21.308) who specialises in mutilating his victims, and to whom the suitors angrily threaten to despatch Irus, and in the later passage Odysseus himself.

The scholia here correctly remark (on the assumption that the real Sicily is intended) that it is not likely that any of Odysseus' wanderings are to be placed in Sicilian waters. Many later readers of Homer, in ancient as in modern times, have tried to plot the hero's travels on the map: Thucydides comments with characteristic reserve on the stories of Cyclopes in Sicily (6.2.1), and the Straits of Messina were thought a plausible location for Scylla and Charybdis (Hecataeus, *FGrH* 1 F 82, Thuc. 4.24). On these fruitless debates see esp. Strabo, *Geography* bk 1; F. W. Walbank, *Historical comm. on Polybius* III (Oxford 1979) 577–87, commenting on Polybius 34.2–4 (known to us through Strabo's quotations). See further Heubeck, comm. on books 9–12 (English version) 4–5; H. H. and A. Wold, *Der Weg des Odysseus* (Tübingen 1968); Luce in Stanford and Luce, *The quest for Ulysses* 118–38.

ὅθεν … ἄξιον ἄλφοι 'whence it [the sale] would bring you a worthwhile price'. One would expect the verb to be plural, with 'the strangers' as subject, but a single idea (the sale, the deal) seems to be extracted from the preceding clauses as subject for ἄλφοι.

384 Cf. 275 with n.

385 Telemachus, in resisting this provocation, shows his maturity and follows his father's instructions at 16.274–7; cf. 17.489–91, 21.128–9.

387 κατ' ἄντηστιν: only here; the meaning, reading and even the proper word division (κατάντηστιν?) are all mysterious. Perhaps it refers to an aperture or break in the partition between Penelope's present position and the main hall. Others take the phrase to mean 'opposite', leaving the exact location vague. What matters is that Penelope hears what is happening without being seen: on this new day she does not appear to the suitors until 21.64, when she initiates the contest. The division between books 20 and 21, an editor's creation, obscures the probability that it is the suitors' lawless behaviour in book 20 which prompts her to fetch the bow and end their aimless rowdiness.

392–4 'There could not be another [sc. evening meal] more unpleasing than the kind of meal that a goddess and a man of might would soon be preparing to bring about. For they [the suitors] were the first to devise plans that were not fitting.'

392 δόρπου: the δεῖπνον is the principal meal of the day, the δόρπον is the evening meal, after work or (in the suitors' case) after the contest. At 21.428–30 Odysseus, with the bow in his possession and on the verge of self-revelation, declares that 'the time is come for the δόρπον to be made ready for the Achaeans, while it is day, and after that to amuse ourselves also with lyre and song; for these are the proper ornaments of a feast'. He then proceeds to shoot Antinous down. The image of the 'bitter supper' or disrupted feast is central to the *Odyssey's* presentation of Odysseus' revenge (cf. 19.12 and 20.345–86 nn.). For such images, which describe something horrific or abnormal in terms of something pleasant and familiar, cf. *Il.* 7.241 (Hector) 'I know well how to tread the measure on the dance-floor of Ares'; 13.291 'the weapon would

meet your chest or your belly as you came forward to the love-talk of
the front ranks'; 17.228; Aesch. *Ag.* 1186, 1189; E. Vermeule, *Aspects of
death in early Greek art and poetry* (Berkeley 1979) 99–107. For similar
techniques see *Od.* 9.230, 22.444 (grim understatement); F. P. Don-
nelly, 'Homeric litotes', *C.W.* 23 (1929–30) 137–40, 145–6.

394 πρότεροι γὰρ ἀεικέα μηχανόωντο 'for they were the first to
devise unfitting deeds'. The verb is 3 pl. impf. of μηχανάομαι 'devise',
'contrive'. The poet marks the end of an episode, and the prelude to the
contest, with a reminder of the guilt of the suitors. This guilt is ex-
pressed in terms of 'who started it', as is customary in Greek forensic
and diplomatic argument: cf. 16.72 = 21.133, *Il.* 4.67, 236, Hes. *Th.*
166, *WD* 708, Hdt. 1.1–4, J. Gould, *Herodotus* (London 1989) 83–5.

Such intervention by the poet to pass judgement on the characters of
his poem is extremely rare in Homer (though rather more common in
the *Odyssey* than in the *Iliad*). Some apparent cases (e.g. *Iliad* 18.310–
13, on the Trojans' foolish acceptance of Hector's rash plan) involve
comment on the folly of the character concerned, rather than moral
condemnation. On the whole question of the poet's 'objectivity' of
style, see J. Griffin, *J.H.S.* 86 (1986) 36–57; de Jong, *Narrators and
focalizers* (more concerned with the *Iliad*, but highly relevant to other
works).

On the moral position of the suitors see H. L. Levy, *T.A.P.A* 94
(1963) 145–53; Erbse, *Beiträge* 113–42.

ἀεικέα: there is a considerable body of scholarly literature discussing
whether such words carry a note of moral condemnation for the doer of
the deeds, or mean only that they are 'shaming, hard, bad, humiliat-
ing' for the victim: see C. Segal, *The theme of the mutilation of the corpse in
the Iliad* (Leiden 1971) 13 (favouring the former approach); Griffin,
Homer on life and death 85n. (taking the latter view, in a discussion of *Iliad*
22.395, 404, 23.176), *J.H.S.* 86 (1986) 44. As Griffin admits in the
article, the *Odyssey*-poet sometimes 'swerves from objectivity' (citing
20.287), and this seems to be another such case, where it is hard to
suppose that the adjective 'shameful' does not reflect on the agents, the
suitors.

BIBLIOGRAPHY

1. TEXTS

T. W. Allen (2nd edn, Oxford 1917–19); P. von der Mühll (Basel 1946); S. West et al. (see section 2 below)

2. COMMENTARIES

D. B. Monro, books 13–24 (Oxford 1901)

W. B. Stanford, 2 vols. (Macmillan, London 1947–8; 2nd edn, 1958–9)

S. West, J. B. Hainsworth, A. Heubeck, A. Hoekstra, J. Russo, M. Fernández-Galiano, *Omero: Odissea* (6 volumes, Fondazione Lorenzo Valla, Rome 1981–6). In this edition books 19 and 20 are dealt with by Russo (vol. v). An English version is being produced by Oxford in three volumes, of which two have so far appeared (vol. I, covering books 1–8, 1988; vol. II, books 9–16, 1989). Volume 3 will include some new introductory material by Russo.

See also Jones (cited in section 5 below)

3. TRANSLATIONS

A. Pope (1725–6; best read in the Twickenham edition, ed. M. Mack and others, volumes IX and X, London and New Haven 1967, with outstanding introduction to the Homeric translations in vol. VII). For the *Odyssey*, however, Pope had several collaborators, and books 19 and 20 are primarily the work of William Broome

S. H. Butcher and A. Lang (Oxford 1879). Mock-biblical prose: more successful in the majestic passages than in conveying the delicacy and humour of the poem

T. E. Shaw (Lawrence of Arabia) (Oxford 1932). Prose, with provocative preface

E. V. Rieu (Penguin Classics, London 1945, revised with new introd. by P. Jones, 1991). Prose. Very popular, but excessively colloquial

R. Lattimore (New York and London 1965). Long verse lines: highly acclaimed, but sometimes prosaic

R. Fitzgerald (New York 1961). Verse

W. Shewring (Oxford 1980). Dignified prose; the best translation for the beginner

4. WORKS OF REFERENCE

G. Autenrieth, *An Homeric dictionary*, tr. R. P. Keep (London 1877)

P. Chantraine, *Grammaire homérique* I–II (Paris 1948–53)

R. J. Cunliffe, *A lexicon of the Homeric dialect* (London 1924)

H. Dunbar, *Concordance to the Odyssey and hymns* (revised edn by B. Marzullo, Hildesheim 1962)

D. B. Monro, *A grammar of the Homeric dialect* (Oxford 1882; 2nd edn 1891)

G. L. Prendergast, *Concordance to the Iliad* (revised edn by B. Marzullo, Hildesheim 1960)

C. E. Schmidt, *Parallel-Homer* (repr. Göttingen 1965)

M. L. West, *Greek metre* (Oxford 1982)

5. CRITICAL AND OTHER SECONDARY WORKS

The following list does not include all items cited in Introduction or Commentary: it is simply a list of works which have proved regularly useful, combined with a list of some writings (usually articles) which have special relevance to books 19 and 20. Particularly valuable items are asterisked.

Amory, A., 'The gates of horn and ivory', *Y.C.S.* 20 (1966) 3 57
  'The reunion of Odysseus and Penelope', in *Essays on the Odyssey*, ed. C. H. Taylor, Jr (Indiana 1963) 100–21

*Austin, N., *Archery at the dark of the moon* (Berkeley, Los Angeles and London 1975)

Bremer, J. M., I. J. F. de Jong, and J. Kalff (edd.), *Homer: beyond oral poetry: recent trends in Homeric interpretation* (Amsterdam 1987)

*Burkert, W., *Greek religion* (Eng. tr., Blackwell, Oxford 1985)

Büchner, W., 'Die Niptra in der Odyssee', *Rh. M.* 80 (1931) 129–36
  'Die Penelopeszenen in der Odyssee', *Hermes* 75 (1940) 126–67

Cave, T., *Recognitions* (Oxford 1988)

Clarke, H. W., *Homer's readers* (London and Toronto 1981)

Clay, Jenny Strauss, *The wrath of Athena* (Princeton 1984)

Colakis, M., 'The laughter of the suitors in *Odyssey* 20', *C.W.* 76 (1986) 137–41

Davies, M. (ed.), *Epicorum Graecorum fragmenta* I (Göttingen 1988)

Dekker, Annie F., *Ironie in de Odyssee* (Leiden 1956)

Dimock G. E., *The unity of the Odyssey* (Amherst, Massachusetts 1989)

Dodds, E. R, *The Greeks and the irrational* (Berkeley and Los Angeles 1951)

Duckworth, G. E., *Foreshadowing and suspense in the epics of Homer, Apollonius and Virgil* (Princeton 1933, repr. New York 1966)

Edwards, A., *Achilles in the Odyssey*, Beiträge zur Klassischen Philologie 171 (Meisenheim am Glan 1985)

Eisenberger, H., *Studien zur Odyssee*, Palingenesia 7 (Wiesbaden 1973)

*Emlyn-Jones, C. M., 'The reunion of Penelope and Odysseus', *G.&R.* 31 (1984) 1–18

'True and lying tales in the *Odyssey*', *G.&R.* 33 (1986) 1–10

Erbse, H., *Beiträge zum Verständnis der Odyssee* (Berlin 1972)

Untersuchungen zur Funktion der Götter im Homerischen Epos (Berlin 1986)

Fehling, D., *Die Wiederholungsfiguren und ihr Gebrauch bei den Griechen vor Gorgias* (Berlin 1969)

*Fenik, B., *Studies in the Odyssey*, *Hermes* Einzelschrift 30 (Wiesbaden 1974)

Finley, M. I., *The world of Odysseus* (1956; 2nd edn, London 1978)

Griffin, J., *Homer on life and death* (Oxford 1980)

Homer, the Odyssey (Landmarks in World Literature, Cambridge 1987)

Hölscher, U., *Untersuchungen zur Form der Odyssee* (Leipzig 1939)

'The transformation from folk-tale to epic', in *Homer: tradition and invention*, ed. B. Fenik (Leiden 1978) 51–67.

Die Odyssee: Epos zwischen Märchen und Roman (Munich 1988)

*Jones, P., *Homer's Odyssey: a companion* (Bristol 1989).

Jong, I. J. F. de, *Narrators and focalizers* (Amsterdam 1987)

Kirk, G. S., *The songs of Homer* (Cambridge 1962)

Köhnken, A., 'Die Narbe des Odysseus', *A.u.A.* 22 (1976) 101–14

*Macleod, C. W., *Homer. Iliad XXIV* (Cambridge 1982)

Morris, J. F., '"Dream-scenes" in Homer: a study in variation', *T.A.P.A.* 113 (1983) 39–54

Moulton, C., *Similes in the Homeric poems*, *Hypomnemata* 49 (Göttingen 1977)

Murnaghan, S., *Disguise and recognition in the Odyssey* (Princeton 1987)

Onians, R. B., *The origins of European thought* (2nd edn, Cambridge 1954)

Page, D. L., *The Homeric Odyssey* (Oxford 1955)
  Folk-tales in Homer's Odyssey (Harvard 1973)
Parry, Milman, *The making of Homeric verse* (ed. Adam Parry, Oxford 1971)
Rank, L. P., *Etymologiseerung en verwante Verschijnselen bij Homerus* (diss. Utrecht 1951)
Richardson, N. J., 'Recognition scenes in the *Odyssey* and ancient literary criticism', in F. Cairns, ed., *Papers of the Liverpool Latin seminar* IV (1983) 219–35
Russo, J., 'Interview and aftermath; dream, fantasy and intuition in *Odyssey* 19 and 20', *A.J.P.* 103 (1982) 1–21
Rutherford, R. B., 'At home and abroad: aspects of the structure of the *Odyssey*', *P.C.Ph.S.* N.S. 31 (1985) 135–50
  'The philosophy of the *Odyssey*', *J.H.S.* 106 (1986) 145–62
Schadewaldt, W., *Neue Kriterien zur Odyssee-Analyse. Die Wiedererkennung des Odysseus und der Penelope* (Heidelberg 1959), repr. in his *Hellas und Hesperien* (2nd edn Zurich–Stuttgart 1960) I 58–78
*Stanford, W. B., *The Ulysses theme* (Blackwell, Oxford 1954)
Stanford, W. B., and J. V. Luce, *The quest for Ulysses* (London 1974)
Thalmann, W. G., *Conventions of form and thought in early Greek epic poetry* (Johns Hopkins University, Baltimore, 1984)
Thompson, Stith, *Motif index of folk literature* (6 vols., Copenhagen 1955)
Thornton, A., *People and themes in Homer's Odyssey* (London 1970)
Van der Valk, M. H. A. L. H., *Textual criticism of the Odyssey* (Leiden 1949)
Vester, H., 'Das 19 Buch der Odyssee', *Gymnasium* 75 (1968) 417–34
Vidal-Naquet, P., 'Land and sacrifice in the *Odyssey*', most recently reprinted in his *The black hunter* (Eng. tr. Baltimore 1986)
Wace, A. J. B., and F. H. Stubbings (eds.), *A Companion to Homer* (London 1967)
West, S. R., *The Ptolemaic papyri of Homer* (Cologne 1967)
Woodhouse, W. J., *The composition of Homer's Odyssey* (Oxford 1930)

For further bibliography the following survey-articles in the journal *Classical World* may be consulted:

F. M. Combellack, 'Contemporary Homeric scholarship, sound or fury?', *C.W.* 49 (1955–6) 17–26, 29–44, 45–55

J. P. Holoka, 'Homeric originality: a survey', *C.W.* 66 (1972–3) 257–93

M. E. Clark, 'Neoanalyis: a bibliographical review', *C.W.* 79 (1986) 379–94

J. P. Holoka, 'Homer studies 1978–1983', *C.W.* 83 (1990) 393–461 and 84 (1990) 89–156

INDEXES

1 Subjects

References are to pages of the Introduction (distinguished by the use of italic) and to book and line-numbers in the Commentary. The index is selective, particularly as regards proper names.

Greek words

References are to book and line numbers in the Commentary.